Writing, Publishing, and Reading Local Gazetteers in Imperial China, 1100–1700

HARVARD EAST ASIAN MONOGRAPHS 379

Writing, Publishing, and Reading Local Gazetteers in Imperial China, 1100–1700

Joseph Dennis

Published by the Harvard University Asia Center
Distributed by Harvard University Press
Cambridge (Massachusetts) and London 2015

The Harvard University Asia Center publishes a monograph series and, in coordination with the Fairbank Center for Chinese Studies, the Korea Institute, the Reischauer Institute of Japanese Studies, and other facilities and institutes, administers research projects designed to further scholarly understanding of China, Japan, Vietnam, Korea, and other Asian countries. The Center also sponsors projects addressing multidisciplinary and regional issues in Asia.

The Harvard University Asia Center gratefully acknowledges generous grants in support of the publication of this work from the Association for Asian Studies First Book Subvention Program and the James P. Geiss Foundation of Princeton, NJ, established in honor of the late James P. Geiss (1950–2000) and sponsoring research on the Ming dynasty.

Library of Congress Cataloging-in-Publication Data

Dennis, Joseph.
    Writing, publishing, and reading local gazetteers in imperial China, 1100–1700 / Joseph Dennis.
        pages cm. — (Harvard East Asian monographs ; 379)
    Includes bibliographical references and index.
    ISBN 978-0-674-50429-5 (hardcover : alk. paper)   1. Gazetteers—China—History.
    2. China—History, Local—Early works to 1800.   I. Title.
    Z186.5.C5D47 2015
    910.30951—dc23

                                                                                2014032677

Index by Anne Holmes

Last figure below indicates year of this printing
25 24 23 22 21 20 19 18 17 16 15

For Laurie, Christina, and Kerry Dennis

Contents

List of Maps and Figures   ix

List of Tables   xi

Acknowledgments   xiii

List of Abbreviations   xiv

Introduction   1

Part I: Impetus to Compile

1   Government Initiatives to Compile Gazetteers   17

2   Local Initiatives to Compile Gazetteers   64

Part II: Production Process

3   Editorial Process   117

4   Publishing Gazetteers   165

5   Financing Gazetteers   213

PART III: READING AND USING GAZETTEERS

6   Target Audiences and Distribution   251

7   Reading and Using Gazetteers   286

    Epilogue   341

    Bibliography   343

    Index   367

Maps and Figures

Maps

0.1 China's provinces, rivers, and major cities during the Ming dynasty xvi

1.1 The northwestern borderlands during the Ming dynasty 53

1.2 The southwestern borderlands during the Ming dynasty 55

2.1 Shaoxing Prefecture 71

4.1 Jiangxi block cutter business zones 198

4.2 Beijing and Handan block cutter business zones 202

4.3 Jiangnan block cutter business zones 205

7.1 Du Mu's trip to Ningxia 305

Figures

1.1. Gazetteer map, 1555 *Mahu fu zhi* 26

1.2. Star chart, 1566 *Huaiqing fu zhi* 26

1.3. Sacrificial animals and implements, 1477 *Xinchang xian zhi* 27

1.4. Local worthies, 1477 *Xinchang xian zhi* 27

1.5. Locals seeing off their departing magistrate, 1477 *Xinchang xian zhi* 28

1.6. Principles of compilation for the 1477 *Xinchang xian zhi* 39

2.1. Graves section, 1579 *Xinchang xian zhi* 84

2.2.	Birthday celebration at the Mo family temple	95
2.3.	Confucian school, 1477 *Xinchang xian zhi*	103
3.1.	Proclamation soliciting source materials for the 1779 *Ganzhou fu zhi*	146
3.2.	List of works consulted in compiling the 1512 *Songjiang fu zhi*	148
4.1.	Frontispiece of the 1485 *Neixiang xian zhi*	184
4.2.	1786 *Yanting xian zhi* title page	185
4.3.	Order from the Guangdong provincial education intendant granting permission to print the 1552 gazetteer of Xingning, Guangdong	188
4.4.	Li Dongyang's 1493 preface to the *Xuzhou zhi*	192
4.5.	Calligraphy for the 1554 *Anqing fu zhi* by farmer Xiang Bian	194
4.6.	Calligraphy for the 1554 *Anqing fu zhi* by farmer Zhu Gao	195
4.7.	Unbalanced, poorly composed calligraphy	196
4.8.	Craftsmen for the 1541 *Weinan xian zhi*	208
5.1.	Donor list for the 1477 *Xinchang xian zhi*	228
6.1.	Ningbo school library book list	278
7.1.	Gazetteer map of Lake Zaoli and Shangyu County	311
7.2.	Gazetteer map of Lake Xiagai	321

Tables

3.1   Number of gazetteers by Ming reign period and per year   120

3.2   Number of Ming gazetteers by modern province
or municipality   137

3.3   Gazetteers arranged by Ming province   138

3.4   Number of identified Song dynasty gazetteers by province   139

4.1   Jiangxi block cutters who worked on gazetteers   200

4.2   Beijing block cutters who worked on gazetteers   204

4.3   Handan block cutters who worked on gazetteers   211

5.1   Local gazetteer production costs   230

5.2   Size of printed area per half-folio   235

5.3   Paper costs of three local gazetteers   238

Acknowledgments

Researching and writing this book was a long process, and many people helped along the way. At the University of Minnesota, Ann Waltner, Ted Farmer, Mary Jo Maynes, and Christopher Isett gave insightful comments on my doctoral dissertation, and members of Ann's reading group, especially Ann, He Qiliang, Hsiao Li-ling, Hsieh Mei-yu, Fang Qin, Tony Jiang, Jiang Yonglin, Liu Lisong, Katie Ryor, Romeyn Taylor, Wang Liping, and Yuan Zujie, spent numerous hours reading sources with me. Bob Anholt tolerated our weekly meetings in his living room. The book benefited greatly from careful comments on drafts by Cynthia Brokaw, Laurie Dennis, Mark Dennis, Rui Magone, Sarah Schneewind, and two anonymous reviewers for the Harvard University Asia Center. I am grateful to Peter Bol, Katy Carlitz, Lucille Chia, Desmond Cheung, Kai-wing Chow, Roger Des Forges, Hilde De Weerdt, Du Yongtao, Asaf Goldschmidt, Martin Heijdra, Anne Gerritsen, Robert Hegel, Ihara Hiroshi, T. J. Hinrichs, Martin Hoffman, Wilt Idema, Joachim Kurtz, Fuji Lozada, Steve Miles, Nathalie Monet, Rebecca Nedostup, Tim Sedo, Sue Takashi, Mel Thatcher, Nancy Norton-Tomasko, and others, for their thoughts and assistance at various points along the way. I would also like to thank Morgan Jarocki of the University of Wisconsin Cartography Lab for making the maps, and Robert Graham and Wendy Nelson for their careful editing.

Financial support was provided by the Fairbank Center for Chinese Studies at Harvard University, the National Endowment for the Humanities, the University of Minnesota, Davidson College, the University of Wisconsin, Bibliothèque national de France, Mellon Foundation, and Union Pacific Foundation.

Abbreviations

BTGJ	*Beijing tushuguan guji zhenben congkan*
BNF	Bibliothèque nationale de France
DMB	*Dictionary of Ming Biography*
HSZP	*He Shi zongpu*
HY	Harvard-Yenching Library
HYM	Harvard-Yenching Library microfilm
LCM	Library of Congress microfilm
LSZP-YM	*Lü Shi zongpu, You Mu*
MDGB	*Mingdai guben fangzhi xuan*
MDHS	*Meidu Huang shi zongpu*
MDSM	*Mingdai shumu tiba congkan*
MGHY	*Meiguo Hafo daxue Hafo Yanjing tushuguan cang Zhongwen shanben huikan*
NLCD	National Library of China digital gazetteers (www.nlc.gov.cn)
NTGB	*Nanjing tushuguan guben shanben congkan: Mingdai guben fangzhi zhuanji*
RBC	*Riben cang zhongguo hanjian difangzhi congkan*
SKCM	*Sikuquanshu cunmu congshu*
SKQS	*Yingyin Wenyuange Siku quanshu*

SYFZ	*Song Yuan fangzhi congkan*
TYG	*Tianyige cang Mingdai fangzhi xuankan*
XCXZ	*Xinchang xian zhi*
XXSK	*Xuxiu siku quanshu*
YSJA	*Yu Shi Jing'an Fang Dong Zhai Cuihe Ci zongpu*
ZDJ	*Zhongguo difangzhi jicheng*
ZFC	*Zhongguo fangzhi congshu*
ZSX	*Zhongguo shixue congshu*

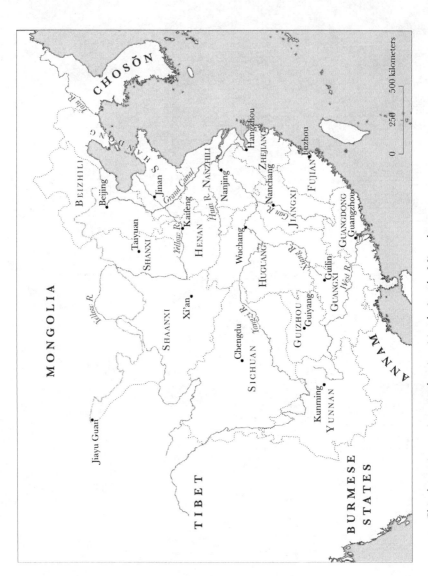

MAP 0.1 China's provinces, rivers, and major cities during the Ming dynasty

INTRODUCTION

This book is a study of a genre of Chinese writing called *difangzhi* 地方志, which is typically translated as "local gazetteer" or "local history." Neither translation fully reflects the contents of *difangzhi*, but I will use "local gazetteer," the most common term, throughout this book. A gazetteer is a cumulative record of a territorial unit published in book format, generally by a local government, and arranged by topics such as topography, institutions, population, taxes, biographies, and literature. Imperial China had nested hierarchies of territorial units and gazetteers. By the Ming dynasty (1368–1644), the base level was the county gazetteer. Above that were subprefectural and prefectural gazetteers, provincial gazetteers, and at the top of the pyramid, empire-wide gazetteers. Some smaller or specialized administrative units, such as villages, guard units, and border passes, and institutions, such as schools and temples, also published gazetteers.[1]

Compilers traced the genre's origin to requirements in the Zhou dynasty (ca. 1045–256 BCE) that each locale submit maps and geographical information to the central government. By the thirteenth century, gazetteers had attained the scope and form in which they were typically found down to the present, a mix of geography, history, literature, and government records. Gazetteers differ from "histories" 史 in that their records transcend dynasties, whereas histories cover single dynasties. In

1. Brook, *Geographical Sources*.

other words, gazetteers were tied to the land while histories were tied to the rulers.

The questions explored in this book required broad reading of numerous gazetteers. Although gazetteers emerged as a distinct genre in the Song dynasty (960–1279), only twenty-seven Song and thirty Yuan (1279–1368) gazetteers are extant.[2] The Ming is the first period from which a large number, approximately 1,014 titles, survive, and thus, it is the focus.[3] There are another seven thousand extant titles from the end of the Ming to the founding of the People's Republic in 1949, and gazetteers continue to be produced throughout China today. The significance of gazetteers, as well as their format and compilers' underlying agendas, have changed over time, and some findings about gazetteers from earlier periods may not apply to those published in later periods.

Although much research has been done on gazetteers, the range of questions addressed has been narrow. A large literature on local gazetteers was produced in the 1980s and 1990s in mainland China, Taiwan, and Japan, but that scholarship differs from this study. Intellectual historians explored categories of materials found in local gazetteers but did not analyze them from the perspective of social, legal, or economic history. In North America and Europe, Peter Bol, Timothy Brook, and Pierre-Etienne Will have written important articles on gazetteers.[4] This book is, however, the first monograph in English on local gazetteers, and the first in any language to examine the social contexts of their production, circulation, reading, and use.

This gap in scholarship is in part due to disciplinary boundaries: most scholars of Chinese literature have not considered gazetteers to be important literary works, and scholars of Chinese history have spent relatively little time on book genre questions. Scholars typically use

---

2.   Counts vary slightly, based on criteria for inclusion. The cited figures do not include numerous fragments held in other works. Bol, "The Rise of Local History," 44; Jun Fang, "A Bibliography," 123–38; Brook, "Native Identity," 236; Liu Weiyi, "Song dai fangzhi," 129–30.

3.   Ba Zhaoxiang, "Lun Mingdai fangzhi," 47–49. Ba does not include the six empire-wide gazetteers in his total. Li Yanqiu, "Ming dai Wenyuange."

4.   Bol, "Rise of Local History," 37–76; Brook, "Native Identity," 236–47; Will, *Chinese Local Gazetteers,* 1992.

gazetteers by examining individual entries or sections rather than the works in their entirety. By not taking gazetteers as objects of study, scholars have missed the potential such an approach has for studying Chinese local society, family life, local government, taxation, printing, literacy, and book culture, among other topics.

This study starts with a simple question: "What were Chinese local gazetteers?" It is an important question for scholars of late imperial China because gazetteers are one of the richest and most abundant types of historical source, and often the best source for local information, especially for locales outside of core regions. At first glance the question's answer seems straightforward: Gazetteers were simple collections of materials about particular places accompanied by short introductions to each topic. However, on closer examination it becomes clear that gazetteers were complex texts: They were sites where the central state interacted with local elites, fields for battles over social status and property interests, forums to shape public opinion and advocate policy, and much more. Studying their production, distribution, reading, and use can lead to insights into important historical questions. The key questions in this study relate to three topics: the production and dissemination of knowledge in late imperial China, the relationships between local societies and the central state in both core and peripheral regions, and the operations of the publishing industry.

I argue that local gazetteers were important points of intersection between the central government and local societies and one of the main vehicles for transmitting local information to central government officials, both those who were sent by the center to govern in the provinces and those who remained in the capitals. Gazetteers circulated local information to local and nonlocal readers and authors, helped bind locales to the centralizing state and dominant culture, and were important venues of local cultural production. They were used to collect a variety of textual information that was available only locally, such as stone inscriptions, unpublished local writings, and genealogies. Compilers could gather additional information through oral interviews and sketches, and make it available to local, national, and even international audiences. Beginning in the sixteenth century, Chinese local gazetteers informed Jesuit histories, geographies, and maps of China published in Europe, and Japanese monks and merchants collected them.

Gazetteers became foundational blocks in building the imagined empire.[5] As Peter Bol argued, the rise of local history reflected a fundamental change in the way that China's cultural elite thought about themselves and the country, and "ought to be seen as a sign that Song literati had begun to reconceptualize the nation as something less imperial, less derivative of court culture, and less centralized."[6] Gazetteers put forth a particular view of locality and what makes a civilized place. Officials, scholars, literati, and travelers who moved about China read and collected gazetteers as they traveled, and some of them used these collections as the basis for other kinds of works, such as books on famous mountains, literary anthologies, biographical collections, and more. Places that were part of the late imperial states were expected to have gazetteers demonstrating their participation in the civilized world. The importance of a gazetteer in creating a local identity as an integral part of a greater civilization was most salient in border regions and was reflected in the contents and manner of writing borderland gazetteers. Gazetteers of remote counties populated largely by non-Chinese-speakers provided examples of locals who accepted Chinese culture, strove to be virtuous, studied for the civil service examinations, paid taxes, and participated in the dominant society.

Examining gazetteers as points of contact between the center and the local can shed light on questions such as these: How did local elites connect to and influence central government officials and policy? How, in a vast empire, was local information produced, collected, and disseminated, both locally and translocally? How did the centralizing imperial state incorporate peripheral areas into the empire? Who had access to books, and what types of people were literate?

Because this is an interdisciplinary study and the range of questions is broad, I necessarily draw upon concepts derived from multiple scholarly fields, especially book history and social history. Robert Darnton's idea of the "communication circuit," which has been used to examine publishers, printers, shippers, booksellers, and readers and connect them to broader issues in society and culture, is useful in its outlines, even if it is not a perfect fit for noncommercial books of late imperial China.[7] The

5. Anderson, *Imagined Communities*.
6. Bol, "Rise of Local History," 76.
7. Darnton, "What Is the History of Books?," 67.

following chapters will apply social history analysis to the life cycles of gazetteers, from a project's conception to its compilation, physical production, distribution, and reception. But I will also draw upon scholars such as Thomas R. Adams and Nicolas Barker, who "reverse the historian's point of view and consider, not the impact of the book on society, but that of society on the book."[8] By taking gazetteers as objects of study, we can look in both directions.

This study is also part of a growing literature that seeks to place book history in a comparative perspective. Historians of Europe have produced a large literature on the role of printing and publishing in European social, political, and cultural transformations. Their work has been based on rich sources such as account books and other business records.[9] Historians of China, however, have been hampered by a scarcity of sources on production costs, book prices, financing methods, and other economic data.[10] Many types of sources available for studying early European publishers simply do not exist for Chinese publishers.[11] Nonetheless, the following analysis of gazetteers presents substantial new information on the economics of book publishing in imperial China.

Historians of Chinese print culture were long perplexed by Elizabeth Eisenstein's 1979 book, *The Printing Press as an Agent of Change*, in which she advocated the idea of a "printing revolution" in fifteenth- and sixteenth-century Europe and portrayed Gutenberg's printing press as a technological innovation of tremendous world historical significance. In her view, the press was a catalyst for the transformation from the medieval to the modern world, and a condition precedent to the Protestant Reformation and the Scientific Revolution. Movable type, the argument went, radically increased the flow of information, leading to a critical mass that enabled both intellectual and religious revolutions.

However, large-scale printing began in China more than five hundred years before Gutenberg, yet there was no evidence that it caused such radical transformations. By the 1990s a small number of historians

8. Adams and Barker, "A New Model," 49.

9. A few of the important works include: Eisenstein, *The Printing Press*; Johns, *Nature of the Book*; Febvre and Martin, *Coming of the Book*.

10. A few of the important works include: Chia, *Printing for Profit*; Chow, *Publishing, Culture, and Power*; and multiple works by Cynthia Brokaw.

11. Chia, *Printing for Profit*, 10.

were working on the history of Chinese print culture, not only because of the importance of the topic itself, but also because the rich literature on European and American print culture raised interesting comparative issues. For example, China and Korea had movable type centuries before Europe, yet the technology did not become popular in East Asia. Instead woodblock printing remained the dominant print technology until the coming of lithography in the nineteenth century because it was cheap, ubiquitous, and effective and did not require the capital outlay needed to buy mechanical presses and cast thousands of pieces of type for a Chinese-character font. Once woodblocks were cut, a publisher could make additional copies on demand from stored blocks, whereas movable type had to be reset for subsequent printings. By portraying Gutenberg's press as a "technological breakthrough," Eisenstein represented movable type and block printing as fundamentally distinct technologies. The difference, however, is overstated. Thousands of copies could be made from a set of woodblocks, and printed materials permeated Chinese society from an early date. Thinking comparatively about print culture can enhance understanding of the intersections of technology, politics, and culture. Some scholars of European print culture, such as Roger Chartier and Ann Blair, have been in dialogue with scholars of Chinese print culture, to the benefit of both fields.[12]

In addition to addressing substantive issues in Chinese history, this book also models new ways of reading gazetteers and is a reference for scholars who use gazetteers in their research. Throughout these pages I have included translations and explanations of key terms and materials.

The most important sources for this study were paratextual elements of gazetteers.[13] These include prefaces, postfaces, administrative petitions and orders related to compilation, lists of contributors to production and editing, and compilers' notes. Over the past decade I have examined more than five hundred gazetteers that were first published in the Song, Yuan, and Ming. Although my analysis included gazetteers from every Ming province and the regions directly administered by the two capitals, most were from eastern China, especially Henan, Huguang, Jiangxi, Jiangsu, Zhejiang, the Southern Metropolitan Region,

12. Blair, "Afterword," 349–60. Chartier, "Gutenberg Revisited," 1–9.
13. Genette, *Paratexts*.

the Northern Metropolitan Region, Fujian, and Guangdong because relatively few from the western provinces survive. Because there are few extant pre-1400 gazetteers, most gazetteers used herein were published in the fifteenth through seventeenth centuries. Later gazetteers, however, often reproduced prefaces and additional materials from earlier gazetteers, and these were used in studying the earlier centuries. Other important sources include genealogies (used in chapter 2), and travel diaries (used in chapter 7). Also used in chapter 7 are records of individual readings of gazetteers found in a wide range of sources. Many were found by searching databases for gazetteer titles, and others were found by skimming potential sources. The analysis is based on both intensive examination of particular gazetteers and extensive use of many gazetteers.

The seven chapters of this book are organized by the stages in the life of a gazetteer. With regard to gazetteer production, I examine why people compiled local gazetteers; who compiled them; the social networks involved; the editorial process, including the politics of gazetteer compilation; and the physical production, including costs, financing, labor, and the movements of materials, manuscripts, and craftsmen. On the consumption side, I examine how gazetteers were distributed, circulated, read, and used. I reconstruct communities of gazetteer readers both inside and outside of the local communities in which the gazetteers were produced, and analyze the ways in which those readers used gazetteers. Of course, the ways in which gazetteers were read affected how they were produced, and how they were produced affected how they were read. Explaining these mutual interactions is an important part of this study.

Chapter 1 examines why different levels of government compiled gazetteers. The chapter begins with stories about particular Ming emperors' compilation orders, then steps back for a broad overview of the genre's origins and development and how their compilation was universalized down to the county level in the Ming. Imperial gazetteer projects were critical to the spread of gazetteers in the Yuan and Ming, and I translate and discuss the two oldest extant sets of editorial rules, which were issued by the court in 1412 and 1418 to serve as the organizing principles for local gazetteers submitted to the court for use in the national gazetteer. The chapter then analyzes government initiatives from outside the court, mostly by local magistrates and prefects who had various motivations. The chapter concludes with an examination of compilation in borderlands, arguing that gazetteers were viewed by Chinese officials as tools for assimilating native peoples into the dominant Chinese culture and political order. Gazetteers were often the first Chinese-language literary project in a given locale and helped plant the seeds of written Chinese culture in non-Chinese, oral societies. At the same time, native chieftains used local gazetteers to enhance their positions in the Chinese state and promote their legitimacy to provincial and central government officials. They did this by publicly documenting their hereditary right to rule and demonstrating their conformance to Chinese elite norms.

Chapter 2 is a case study of the purposes and politics behind the compilation of the 1477 and 1579 editions of the *Xinchang xian zhi* 新昌 縣志 (Xinchang County gazetteer) and subsequent readings of the two editions. I approach gazetteers from a social history perspective and use a microhistory methodology. I start with the proposition that although gazetteers at first glance seem like compilations of miscellaneous information, they often were produced with specific agendas in mind. These underlying agendas varied from gazetteer to gazetteer, so by examining a gazetteer in its entirety one can learn about the society that produced it and gain insight into the meanings of the information found therein. These meanings would not necessarily be obvious to someone who was simply extracting data from individual sections for use in a topical study. By paying attention to the compilation process and reading a gazetteer as a whole, one can open new windows on a variety of questions.

To analyze the Xinchang gazetteers, I read them in conjunction with thirty genealogies of Xinchang lineages that I collected from the Utah Genealogical Society, the Xinchang County Archives, Shanghai Library, and Columbia University. Aggregating and analyzing the biographical information contained in the gazetteers and comparing it to information in the genealogies reveals that the individual compilers of the 1579 edition were close paternal, maternal, and marital relatives, and that they selected gazetteer entries to highlight their kinship ties, publicly establish their ancestral lines, and illustrate their leadership in local society. By writing the gazetteer as a public genealogy of their extended family, the gazetteer compilers mapped out a level of extended-family organization that lay between the lineages and the county government and legitimated their rights in local society. Through this microhistory of the gazetteer compilation and examination of the gazetteer as a strategic text, I extend to county gazetteers the logic of David Faure's argument that genealogies legitimated rights in local societies.[14]

Chapter 2 continues the analysis of Xinchang gazetteers through the lens of readers' responses, which show that contemporary readers viewed gazetteers as texts about lineage status in local society. I focus on a case in which members of the Huang lineage in Xinchang County argued that the local Confucian school instructor omitted their famous members from the 1477 gazetteer in retaliation for the Huangs' having sued him after he destroyed their first ancestor's grave to expand the school gardens. Public genealogy was but one agenda for writing a gazetteer. It is important to understand the range of potential agendas for writing gazetteers, because knowing why a gazetteer was compiled can affect how we interpret its contents and use it in our studies. For example, knowing that public genealogy was a potential agenda might lead to the discovery that the biographies of virtuous women contained in a given gazetteer were in fact biographies of the compilers' female relatives. In such a case one would have to be careful using those biographies in a study of virtuous women that aggregates and analyzes biographies from multiple gazetteers. One would have to consider the extent to which the set of biographies represented the ideal types of female virtue in a given time and place, and to what extent it was simply a collection of the best stories the compilers could come up with about their grandmothers, mothers, daughters, sisters, and wives.

Chapter 3 steps back from detailed case studies to look more broadly at editorial issues and how they affect our periodization of gazetteers. In the previous literature scholars disputed when the gazetteer genre flourished. Ba Zhaoxiang, based on his extensive count of Ming gazetteers, argued that it was only in the sixteenth century, whereas Zhang Sheng argued that it was earlier and that Ba excluded many early-Ming gazetteers from his count. I argue that their disagreement stems from their failure to define what they meant by "gazetteer," and that we can reconcile

14. Faure, "Lineage as Cultural Invention," 4–36.

their positions by carefully examining the editorial process. Thus, the chapter begins with an exploration of the meaning of "gazetteer." I argue that gazetteers should be thought of as living documents that were regularly updated, supplemented, revised, and recompiled, not as ad hoc isolated publications that quickly became out-of-date and remained so until recompilation decades later. Once we understand this fact, we can solve the periodization problem. Ba counted mainly the mature gazetteers while excluding their early incarnations. By including the early editions, and not confining our periodization to the Ming (as did both Ba and Zhang), we can see a long-term rise in local gazetteer production from Song to Qing, punctuated by periods of increased compilation during the founding and consolidation of dynasties, and from particular imperial projects; and periods of decline due to war.

Chapter 3 also explores details of the editorial process: the spaces in which editorial work was done, the types of people who worked on gazetteers, and payments to editorial personnel. I show that the "commodification of writing," which Kai-wing Chow postulated as a sixteenth- and seventeenth-century phenomenon, has antecedents in gazetteer writing by the early fourteenth century. The chapter concludes with a case study of the editing and printing of the 1537 *Hengzhou fu zhi* 衡州府志 (Hengzhou Prefecture gazetteer). It contains the notes of Liu Fu 劉黻, a retired official hired by the Hengzhou prefect to edit and publish the prefectural gazetteer. Liu provided a detailed account of his research methods, his difficulties in obtaining needed information from the prefecture's various county and departmental officials, his reasons for printing the gazetteer in his home rather than in the prefectural yamen, and problems he encountered in the printing process. Because his notes predate Matteo Ricci's observations on Chinese printing by a half century, cover different ground, and are written from an insider's perspective, they are a valuable source for the history of printing. In them Liu Fu explains the complex interactions between central government officials and members of local societies involved in compiling and publishing a gazetteer.

Liu Fu's notes serve as a bridge to chapter 4, which explores the publication of local gazetteers in both manuscript and print form. Thousands of gazetteers were compiled only as manuscripts, but printing was normative even in the Song and Yuan. Although gazetteer printing had much in common with that of other book genres, significant differences make a separate study worthwhile. Most importantly, bureaucratic involvement created a paper trail that reveals aspects of printing and publishing not readily apparent from the study of other book genres. Gazetteers were compiled throughout the empire, their place of production is generally known, and movements of craftsmen and manuscripts can be tracked by connecting craftsmen hometowns, subject locales, and production sites. Thus, studying them can enrich our understanding of geographic variations in book publishing and create a more dynamic picture of the printing labor market. Aggregating production information makes it possible to identify regional printing centers and map the zones in which craftsmen operated.

Chapter 5 is a study of how much gazetteers cost to produce and how their publication was financed. Understanding the economics of book production and consumption in different times and regions is important to a host of questions regarding the social, cultural, and political significance of books. In his 1974 book, *Chinese Vernacular Fiction*, Wilt Idema notes that the amount known about publishing economics in the Ming is limited, and as Lucille Chia wrote in her 2002 book, *Printing for Profit*, a study of publishing in Jianyang 建陽, Fujian, from the eleventh to seventeenth centuries, "There is a frustrating lack of data on book prices."[15] Gazetteers, however, are an untapped resource on economic aspects of book production. Chapter 5 presents an analysis of pieces of information retrieved from hundreds of gazetteers and brings to light new evidence of the per-page cost of producing a book in Ming China, labor and materials costs, and financing methods. My study of financing contributes to our understanding of gazetteers as a genre by showing that funds for publication came from both nongovernmental and governmental sources. It also adds to our knowledge of Ming local administration and taxation by examining allocation of government funds and community fundraising for local projects.

Chapter 6 analyzes intended and actual gazetteer audiences, along with distribution methods. Although the primary readers of local gazetteers were officials and literati, gazetteer compilers expected that at least some people other than elite males would read their gazetteers. After analyzing intended audience, I reconstruct actual audiences based on

15. Chia, *Printing for Profit*, 190.

records of gazetteer ownership by institutions and individuals. I also show that after small initial print runs, gazetteers were printed on demand, often for decades after the blocks were first cut. Blocks were usually stored in the local yamen or school, but sometimes they were kept in private homes to make it more convenient for commoners to print copies. Gazetteers produced in response to imperial edicts were generally sent to the court in the form of a manuscript copy; the original was kept in the yamen, and a copy was made for the Confucian school. These manuscripts often served as the foundation for gazetteers printed later.

Chapter 7 turns to how people read and used gazetteers. I apply Roger Chartier and Stanley Fish's idea of "interpretive communities," examining local audiences through "individual confessions" of readings found in records of lawsuits, travel diaries, collected works of people who were interested in local history, and comments recorded in book prefaces and colophons. I first look at how officials sent to govern in the provinces used gazetteers to familiarize themselves with the areas in which they were posted, to transmit policy ideas to their successors in office, as casual reading, and as texts through which to bond with members of the local elite. Because of the law of avoidance, officials were not natives of the territory they governed and needed a broad overview of the locales they would be governing. The chapter then tracks travelers' use of gazetteers on the road and shows that gazetteers were used as travel guides and that traveling officials and local officials used them in socializing at scenic sites. Local gazetteers were more detailed than merchant route books, which guided travelers on interprovincial travel but contained less information on particular locales.[16] Next, I examine gazetteer connections to lawsuits. Gazetteers were written documents with official status and were used as evidence in cases that had historical aspects, such as those over water rights. Because of this, people whose interests could be affected by the portrayal of local history in the gazetteer tried to influence content, and some even forged materials and bribed compilers. The chapter concludes with a study of gazetteer collectors and how gazetteers were used by authors on various topics.

I conclude the book by bringing together the various chapters' findings to argue that by the late fifteenth century gazetteers had become

16.   Brook, "Guides for Vexed Travelers," 32–76.

key nodes for collecting and disseminating local information. Local gazetteers were one of the basic sources for various types of writing that
were empire-wide in scope. In addition to travel writing, gazetteers were
a key source for biographical works, histories, encyclopedias, and works
of many other genres. Thus, when you think of local gazetteers and their
relation to cultural production in Ming China, you might imagine them
as cells in a honeycomb that covered the empire. Gazetteers were the
vessel in which materials gathered by dozens of contributors were distilled and deposited, like honey from bees. Gazetteer contents then became available for consumption and transformation into new cultural
products by locals, travelers, and those residing in other places. In the
Ming, gazetteers were an important genre, and they deserve our careful
attention. As Xie Zhaozhe 謝肇淛 (1567–1624) wrote in his postface to the
1612 gazetteer of Yongfu 永福, Fujian, "From now on locals will know
recent and past affairs. The [contents of the gazetteer] are like bright
pearls suspended in a deep room; arrayed therein, you can point to them.
They are like the hanging vines turning green in the marketplaces of the
five districts; passersby will happily look at them."[17]

---

17. *Yongfu xian zhi*, 379–80.

PART I

Impetus to Compile

CHAPTER I

Government Initiatives to
Compile Gazetteers

The Zhengde Emperor had a passion for travel. On September 15, 1519, he headed south along the Grand Canal, traveling from the northern capital, Beijing, to the southern capital, Nanjing, where he lingered among urban pleasures.[1] He demanded the prefectural gazetteer and dispatched four officials to collect other local gazetteers.[2] To the officials' dismay there was no gazetteer of Nanjing's prefecture, Yingtian 應天, or of Nanjing's two urban counties, Jiangning 江寧 and Shangyuan 上元.[3] Over the course of history such "southern tours" by Chinese heads of state were primarily political in motivation and effect—the Kangxi Emperor's 1684 southern tour promoted Qing legitimacy, and Deng Xiaoping's 1992 tour rallied support for China's economic reforms. The Zhengde Emperor's southern tour, however, was for personal pleasure, and an important effect was the frenzied production of local gazetteers.[4]

It is surprising that Nanjing lacked key gazetteers. After all, it is the city from which the Ming dynasty was founded in 1368. It was a major center of literati culture, full of historians, and beginning in 1370 the Ming court had repeatedly ordered local territorial administrations to

1. For more on the Zhengde Emperor's trip, see Goodrich and Fang, *DMB*, 312.
2. *Jiangning xian zhi*, 690.
3. Ibid., 689; *Shangyuan xian zhi*, 12.61b–65a.
4. On the history of imperial touring, see Chang, *Court on Horseback*.

compile them.[5] There was a 1344 gazetteer of Jinling 金陵, the older and smaller Yuan dynasty city in the same locale, and Nanjing's counties and prefecture had submitted materials for the 1461 imperial gazetteer, the *Da Ming yitong zhi* 大明一统志. A contributor to one local gazetteer compiled in response to the Zhengde Emperor's order also was surprised, so he made inquiries of former Nanjing officials and learned that many local gazetteers had been started—but none had been finished and published because those involved "dared not lightly narrate the history of a prefecture that contained an imperial court, palace, ancestral temple, and altars."[6] In fact, a major effort had been undertaken just a few years before the emperor's tour during the tenure of Yingtian prefect Bai Qi 白圻.[7] Fifty-seven scholars, led by Xu Lin 徐霖 (1462–1538), a wealthy Nanjing literati artist who had a large collection of local gazetteers from around the empire, set up a compilation bureau in the prefectural school.[8] Compilations, however, often did not outlast their official sponsor's tenure in office, and when Bai was transferred, the project stopped. But after the emperor arrived in Nanjing and asked for the gazetteer, the new prefect brought back Xu and the others to complete their work.

When they finished, the emperor summoned Xu for an audience. As it happened, Xu and the emperor shared interests that went well beyond local gazetteers. Both were libertines, and the emperor twice visited Xu at Satisfaction Garden, Xu's estate near Nanjing's entertainment quarter, and reportedly enjoyed Xu's company so much that they "slept and arose together."[9]

The rush to produce local gazetteers for the emperor was not confined to the Yingtian yamen, but also spread to county seats in the Nanjing region. After the magistrate of Yixing 宜興 received the emperor's order, he was "terrified day and night" and threw himself into the project. He quickly replaced damaged printing blocks from a 1449 edition,

    5.   Xie, *Guichao gao*, 9.39b; *Yongzhou fu zhi* (1383), preface, 1a. For more on the early-Ming imperial gazetteer compilation edicts, see Zhang Yingpin, *Mingdai Nanzhili*, 17–18.

    6.   *Shangyuan xian zhi*, 12.61–64b.

    7.   Bai served as Yingtian prefect from 1513 to 1515.

    8.   *Shangyuan xian zhi*, 12.61a.

    9.   Gu Qiyuan, *Kezuo zhui yu*, 199; *DMB* 591–93.

added some new materials, and printed a copy for the emperor.[10] In Jiangning, Magistrate Wang Gao 王誥 gave government student Liu Yu 劉雨 forty-five days to compile a gazetteer.[11] Liu, fortunately, had already been working on one for the entire capital region and was able to meet the deadline. Magistrate Wang quickly hired craftsmen to cut the woodblocks and in the winter of 1520–21 sent an imprint up the chain of command. The magistrate of Jixi 績溪 was less fortunate; he had to start from scratch by searching for old editions "among the people." He found two, ordered Confucian school students to do minor rearranging and rewriting, and quickly published a short gazetteer in the spring of 1521.[12] In Huating 華亭, compilers found an easy solution: they merely culled materials about Huating from the 1512 gazetteer of Songjiang 松江, Huating's superior prefecture, and published them as a county gazetteer.[13]

All this hustle was wasted. The emperor never had the chance to read the new gazetteers. He left Nanjing on September 23, 1520, taking his new friend Xu Lin with him, became seriously ill after falling into a river on the way back to Beijing, and died in the Forbidden City on April 20, 1521.[14]

The Zhengde Emperor's death started a chain of events that led to the compilation of yet another local gazetteer. Having left no heir, the late emperor's twelve-year-old cousin, Zhu Houcong 朱厚熜, was chosen to succeed him.[15] Ascending the throne as the Jiajing Emperor, Zhu was immediately embroiled in what became known as the Great Ritual Controversy. He insisted upon granting his recently deceased biological father the posthumous title "emperor" rather than maintain the line of imperial succession by becoming the adopted son of the Zhengde Emperor's deceased father, the Hongzhi Emperor (1470–1505). Court officials split over the appropriate course of action, and in 1524 more than one hundred protested the emperor's refusal to be adopted. All were punished, and eighteen were beaten to death.[16]

---

10. Shen Chi, *Jingxi wai ji*, 15.25.
11. *Jiangning xian zhi*, 690.
12. *Jixi xian zhi*, prefaces, 9.
13. Sun Cheng'en, *Wenjian ji*, 30.11b–12a.
14. *DMB*, 313.
15. Ibid., 1544–45.
16. Fisher, "The Great Ritual Controversy," 71–87; Fisher, *The Chosen One*.

In the aftermath, the emperor took steps to bolster his parents' prestige. In 1531 he raised the status of his hometown from department to prefecture and changed its name from the pedestrian "Anlu" 安陸 (peaceful land) to the regal "Chengtian" 承天 (succeed to Heaven), putting it on par with the Beijing and Nanjing capital prefectures, Shuntian 順天 (accord with Heaven), and Yingtian 應天 (respond to Heaven). In 1539, shortly after his mother's death, the Jiajing Emperor made his own southern journey to temporarily bury her with his father in Chengtian while Minister of Works Gu Lin 顧璘 (1476–1545) supervised construction of an appropriately grand imperial tomb.[17]

The emperor decided that Chengtian also needed a gazetteer to expound on his father's worthy deeds and added its compilation to Gu Lin's duties. Gu in turn hired Wang Tingchen 王廷陳 (1517 *jinshi*), a former Hanlin academician who was one of seven officials flogged and demoted for criticizing the Zhengde Emperor's southern tour. After brief service as a magistrate, Wang had retired, but the new emperor restored most of Wang's fellow critics to office, and Gu Lin turned the gazetteer project into a chance for Wang to "come out from the wilderness."[18] When the manuscript was finished, Gu presented it to the emperor and recommended that Wang be granted an office.[19] The emperor, however, was dissatisfied and canceled the project.[20] Ming-period commentators explained the cancellation as being the result of either the emperor's decision that the appropriate place to document his parents was in the dynastic history and veritable records (daily records of major events compiled by reign period), or "errors" in the text concerning the emperor and his father's "sagely administrations."[21] The manuscript, however, survived, and shortly before the emperor's death the gazetteer

17.   The tomb was not finished until 1566. Fisher, "Center and Periphery," 15–34.

18.   Wang Tingchen, *Mengze ji, juan* 21, appendix 3, 2b–3a; *DMB*, 1442–43; Shen Defu, *Wanli yehuobian*, 799–800.

19.   The manuscript title was *Xingdu zhishu* 興都志書 (Gazetteer of the flourishing capital).

20.   *Ming shilu* (Shizong), 5182.

21.   Gui Youguang, "Ti Xingdu zhi hou" 題興都志後, in *Zhenchuan ji*, 5.4a. A veritable record was in fact compiled for the lifetime of the father of the Jiajing Emperor, even though the father never served as emperor. Shen Defu, *Shilu nan ju* 實錄難據, in *Wanli yehuobian*, 61; *Chengtian fu zhi* (1602), 8.

was recompiled under the direction of an imperial grand secretary, but again the emperor was unhappy and eliminated the middle volume upon reading it.[22]

Members of the imperial family not only sponsored gazetteer projects and tried to insert records, they also sought to keep out records that could reflect badly on them. One prominent example is the ninth Prince of Chu 楚王, Zhu Huakui 朱華奎 (1572–1643), who destroyed the woodblocks of the 1591 gazetteer of Jiangxia 江夏, Huguang (modern Hubei Province), because it recorded the 1545 murder of his grandfather, Zhu Xianrong 朱顯榕, by his uncle, Zhu Yingyao 朱英耀, something that the prince "could not bear to hear."[23]

Later the prince, along with the chief grand secretary, Shen Yiguan 沈一貫, impeached the gazetteer's compiler, Guo Zhengyu 郭正域 (1554–1612), in connection with an investigation of Zhu Huakui's legitimacy. Zhu Huakui's father, the previous Prince of Chu, Zhu Yingxian 朱英㷭, who inherited the murdered Zhu Xianrong's principality, had long lacked an heir and Zhu Huakui was born a half year after his father's death in 1571. Upon Zhu Huakui's birth, rumors immediately arose that he had been secretly adopted from outside of the imperial family. Guo Zhengyu grew up in the prince's compound because his father was an officer in the guard unit, and presumably he had many contacts therein with strong opinions on Huakui's legitimacy. Prior to Zhu's investiture in 1580, an investigation was done and the prince was found to be a proper heir. But rumors persisted. In 1603, twenty-nine of the prince's cousins petitioned to reopen the investigation, and Guo, by that time the acting minister of rites, supported them.[24]

In response, the prince, with Shen Yiguan's support, attacked Guo, filing a memorial claiming that Guo had four grievances against him, one of which was destruction of the gazetteer blocks. The Wanli Emperor investigated the prince's claims, and Guo argued that he was being falsely accused by a prince trying to protect his title. The emperor rejected Guo's position, causing Guo to resign. Regarding the Jiangxia gazetteer's parricide record,

---

22.　Shen Defu, *Wanli yehuobian*, 800. The remainder is extant and titled *Chengtian da zhi* 承天大志 (Great gazetteer of Chengtian).

23.　Guo Zhengyu, *Wanli sanshiyi nian*, 153.

24.　*DMB*, 768–70.

the investigation revealed that the murder had already been recorded in the *Chu ji* 楚紀 (Record of Chu), the *Huguang tong zhi* 湖廣通志 (Huguang provincial gazetteer), and other books, and thus, it had not been "privately authored" (*si chuang* 私創) by Guo.[25]

These stories of gazetteer compilation and suppression, although interesting, are atypical. Few gazetteers were produced to satisfy an emperor's individual interest in a particular locale or enhance his parents' prestige, and few were destroyed because of a prince's dislike of the content. Yet these unusual cases do suggest themes that will emerge when we turn to the more routine production of these key historical sources: the centrality of particular interests and points of view in the designing of a gazetteer, the often contested and political nature of compilation, the multiplicity of ways gazetteers were initiated, and the variety of reasons people had for collecting and reading local gazetteers. This chapter and chapter 2 will explore motivations for compiling local gazetteers, show that both local literati and officials at all levels of government initiated gazetteer projects, and argue that despite the superficial similarity of many gazetteers, we need to read them as individual works shaped by various social, cultural, and political forces. By reading gazetteers holistically we can gain insight into various historical questions.

Emergence of the Gazetteer Genre

The precursors to gazetteers were closely tied to central government administrative practices. Compilers in late imperial China routinely attributed the genre's origin to "overseers of feudatories" (*zhi fang shi* 職方氏) in the Zhou dynasty (ca. 1045–256 BCE), who collected maps and geographical information. The founding text was considered to be the *Yugong* 禹貢 (Tribute of Yu) chapter of the *Shangshu* 尚書 (Book of Documents), a historical geography written in the Warring States period (475–221 BCE). Central government officials during the Qin (221–206 BCE) and Han (206 BCE–220 CE) dynasties continued to collect information on locales,

---

25. *Ming shilu* (Shenzong): 8146–47; Shen Defu, *Wanli yehuobian*, 124–25. The story also appears in the *Huguang zong zhi*, 472.

and Han scholars wrote geographies that covered the entire empire, such as Ban Gu's *Dili zhi* 地理志 (Geographical treatise) in the *Han shu* 漢書 (History of the Han).[26] As James Hargett and Hilde De Weerdt have discussed, the immediate precursor to the gazetteer genre was the "map guide" (*tujing* 圖經, *tuji* 圖記, or *tuzhi* 圖志).[27] Map guides were "collections of maps or illustrations with accompanying explanations or treatises" on topics such as local infrastructure and products.[28] By the Sui dynasty (581–618) the textual portion became the focus, and during the next few centuries local administrators were required to submit map guides to the central government. In the Northern Song (960–1127), local governments investigated changes in their area's towns, administrations, and populations every intercalary year and compiled their findings for the court.[29]

Local map guides became sources for geographies of the entire realm, such as the *Yuanhe junxian tuzhi* 元和郡縣圖志 (Commandery and county map guides of the Yuanhe reign), which was completed in 813. De Weerdt argues that emperors and court officials were the primary readers of such compilations in the Tang (618–907).[30] In the Northern Song, such comprehensive geographies were printed and distributed more widely. In 1007 the court ordered all locales to submit map guides for use in the *Xiangfu zhouxian tujing* 祥符州縣圖經 (Prefecture and county map guides of the Xiangfu era), which was printed by the central government in 1010 and distributed to lower-level government offices.[31] Similarly, in 1107 the court compiled a comprehensive geography, the *Jiuyu tuzhi* 九域圖志 (Map guides of the nine regions), and again ordered each locale to submit materials.[32] Peter Bol argues that map guides in this period were records for administrators and fit well with the New Policies' attempt to unify morality and customs and better regulate local society.[33]

26. Yee, "Chinese Maps," 71.

27. Hargett, "Song Dynasty Local Gazetteers"; De Weerdt, "Regional Descriptions," 123–29.

28. Hargett, "Song Dynasty Local Gazetteers," 409.

29. *Wujun tujing xu ji*, Zhu Changwen preface; Hargett, "Historiography in Southern Sung," 294.

30. De Weerdt, "Regional Descriptions," 125.

31. Chen Zhensun, *Zhizhai shulu jieti*, 237.

32. *Siming tu jing*, Huang Ding preface.

33. Bol, "Rise of Local History," 46.

By the Southern Song (1127–1279), a new genre, gazetteers 地方志, had emerged. Hargett argues that "by the tenth and eleventh centuries, *tujing* had assumed the form and thematic breadth of the genre known in late imperial China as *difangzhi*," and that by at least the late twelfth century gazetteers were increasingly thought of as being more historical than geographical texts. This switch can be seen in Zheng Xingyi's 鄭興裔 preface to the 1190 *Guangling zhi* 廣陵志, which he began by drawing a parallel between national and local historiography: "A locale having a gazetteer is like a state having a history" (*jun zhi you zhi you guo zhi you shi* 郡之有志猶國之有史). He explained that the gazetteer was "for examining the peoples' manners and investigating local customs. It creates a reference for the past and a mirror for the future."[34]

By the early 1200s the replacement of map guides by gazetteers was reflected in titles.[35] When revisions to the 1169 *Siming tujing* 四明圖經 (Siming map guide) were completed in 1227, *tujing* was dropped from the title and replaced with *zhi* because "the maps were few and the treatises numerous."[36] As the gazetteer genre emerged, the scope of included *tu* expanded beyond maps to include illustrations of government buildings, famous local sites, ritual objects and practices, star charts, famous local people, and historic scenes, such as those in figures 1.1–1.5. Thus, for earlier works the term *tuzhi* is best translated as "map guide" or "map treatise," but for later works "gazetteer with illustrations" is more accurate.

In the twelfth and thirteenth centuries, an expectation grew that significant towns would turn earlier map guides into full-fledged gazetteers. By the late twelfth century local officials considered it their duty to compile a gazetteer for the benefit of subsequent officials and started to criticize locales that lacked a gazetteer. Around 1175 the prefect of Jizhou 吉州 (modern Jiangxi Province), told a subordinate that Jizhou needed a gazetteer because "each of the realm's territories has a gazetteer; only Luling 盧陵 (Jizhou) lacks one."[37] Around 1199 a guest of the prefect of Chengdu 成都 (modern Sichuan Province) said to him, "These days each of the realm's territories has a gazetteer; how is it that only the great

34. Zheng Xingyi, *Zheng Zhongsu zou yi, juan xia*, 11a.
35. Hargett, "Historiography in Southern Sung"; Bol, "Rise of Local History," 44; Hargett, "Song Dynasty Local Gazetteers," 419.
36. *Siming zhi*, 4989.
37. Zhang Guogan, 578.

capital of Shu [Sichuan] does not?"[38] Although at this early date the claim that every place had a gazetteer was an exaggeration, the repeated appearance of this stock phrase does suggest that a norm was taking hold, at least for prominent locales.

A century later, officials were beginning to claim that they read gazetteers regularly. In 1300 the prefect of Nanfeng 南豐, Jiangxi, wrote, "No famous department or great county lacks a gazetteer, everywhere I have gone on my official travels I have always gotten the gazetteer and read it." But a half century earlier there were already hints that gazetteer production had spread beyond famous locales. A preface to the gazetteer of Deqing 德清, Jiangnan (modern Zhejiang Province), circa 1237–40, argued that because even distant and remote places have gazetteers, it was especially important for a county like theirs in the capital region to have one.[39]

Compilers routinely described a missing or inadequate gazetteer as a "gap in essential documentation" (*que dian* 闕典), arguing that gazetteers were to locales what histories were to states, and invoking Confucius's statement that he was unable to comment on the states of Qi 杞 and Song 宋 because they were "insufficiently documented" (*bu zu zheng* 不足徵 or *wenxian bu zu* 文獻不足).[40] As Xiong Wenhan 熊文韓 explained in the 1548 gazetteer of Ninghai 寧海, Shandong, "The duty for a state to have a dynastic history, a locale to have a local gazetteer, and a family to have a genealogy is the same. In the past, people had a saying that descendants' not compiling a genealogy was unfilial. That being so, can an official who fails to compile a local gazetteer be considered loyal?"[41] The author of a preface to the 1549 gazetteer of Weishi 尉氏, Henan, framed the duty as one of the present generation to future generations: "In my view, a locale having a gazetteer is like a family having a genealogy and a state having a history. How can records of their origins, the succession of their generations, their governance, and current affairs be discarded by those of one time period, never to be seen again?"[42]

38. Yuan Shuoyou, *Dongtang ji*, 18.16a.
39. Zhang Guogan, *Zhongguo gu fangzhi kao*, 352.
40. *Analects* 3.9, in Legge, *The Chinese Classics*, vol. 1, 158; Wang Zhi, *Yi'an wen ji*, 22.38a.
41. *Ninghai zhou zhi*, postface, 3.
42. *Weishi xian zhi*, Li Deguang postface, 1b.

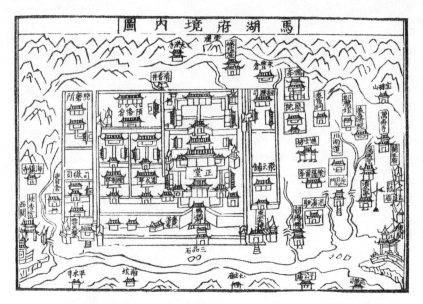

FIGURE I.I. Map of the prefectural seat of Mahu, Sichuan, from the 1555 *Mahu fu zhi* (Tianyige Library).

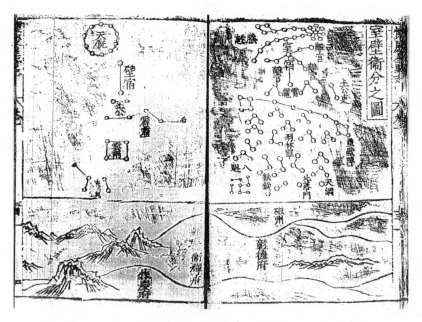

FIGURE I.2. Chart from the 1566 *Huaiqing fu zhi* showing the correspondence between four Henan administrative centers and lunar mansions and constellations (Harvard-Yenching Library).

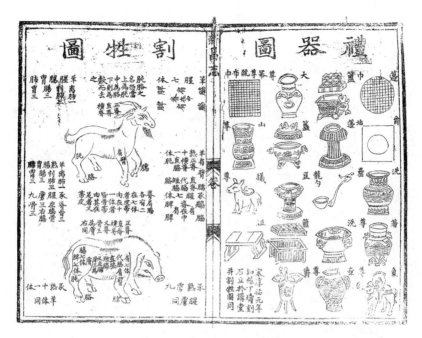

FIGURE I.3. Copies of stelae erected in the Xinchang Confucian school lecture hall in 1241, depicting ritual implements owned by the school and a chart for the butchering of sacrificial animals. 1477 *Xinchang xian zhi* (Xinchang County Archives).

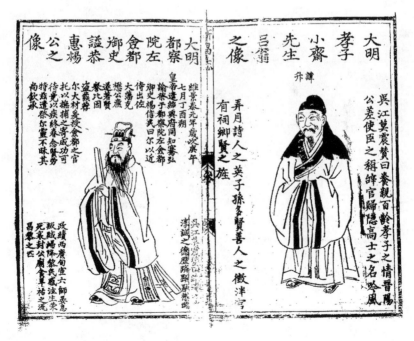

FIGURE I.4. Portraits and panegyrics of local worthies Lü Sheng and Yang Xinmin in the 1477 *Xinchang xian zhi* (Xinchang County Archives).

本朝知新昌縣
賈公去任罷
德厚而才器洪謙識
高而才亥領民
社於南淵而始
孝子甚寒澤之
紫也其清劲松也
挺雪水其一方
聲因澤洽乎
九重是以攀轅
卧轍乎洒萬民
之涵戾立祠當
像芳葉有世之
為鳳意斯人也
而弘德强立偏也
榮告草旦贊

FIGURE 1.5. Illustration and panegyric of local people seeing off magistrate Jia Ji as he departed Xinchang in 1380. 1477 *Xinchang xian zhi* (Xinchang County Archives).

Compilers buttressed their insistence on the importance of gazetteers by linking them to Zhu Xi (1130–1200), whose ideas became the core of Confucian learning and subject matter for the civil service examination. As Confucian school instructor Song Ji 宋驥 explained in 1438, "When Master Zhu governed Nankang Military Prefecture, the first thing he did upon arrival was consult the local gazetteer. Commentators say he understood administrative duties, and local gazetteers relate to the administrative system (*zhengti* 政體). They are not insignificant."[43]

Scholars of the Song have provided different explanations for the rise of local gazetteers. Hargett argued that while map guides were aimed at administrators, gazetteers also served "scholarly purposes and local interests" and included more biographical and literary materials. His study emphasized an intellectual reason for the change: Song literati were exploring the systematization of knowledge, and gazetteers were a vehicle for their efforts.[44]

Bol, in his study of local historiography in Wuzhou 婺州 Prefecture (Jinhua 金華), acknowledged the connection to intellectual change but argued that the changing social context was more important. Gazetteers were indeed products of expanding literati intellectual scenes far from the capital, but those local scenes arose from the Southern Song shift in elite families' focus from the capital to their native places. "The localist turn" identified by Robert Hymes, Robert Hartwell, and Beverly Bossler, Bol argued, is the key to understanding the rise of local history.[45] As the number of literati expanded, they compiled and printed more works on their native places. Gazetteers covered topics that local literati cared most about: schools, examinations, biographies, and local literature.[46] They paid "closer attention to their own local figures, events, institutions, and landscapes than ever before" and created continuous natural, cultural, and administrative histories of particular places. Literati who compiled a gazetteer created a past that made literati of the present heirs to that past and thereby laid a foundation for literati participation in running local society and the national government. Gazetteers described

43. *Pengcheng zhi*, 3rd preface; *Linying xian zhi*, old preface, 1.
44. Hargett, "Song Dynasty Local Gazetteers," 421; Bol, "Rise of Local History," 48.
45. Bol, "Rise of Local History," 73.
46. Ibid., 37–76.

local manifestations of intellectual and cultural traditions that were national in scope and "placed them as participants in a national culture
that transcended both local and dynastic boundaries."[47] The rise of local
history in Wuzhou, Bol argued, reflected a fundamental change in the
way that China's cultural elite thought about themselves and the country,
and "the rise of local history ought to be seen as a sign that Song literati
had begun to reconceptualize the nation as something less imperial, less
derivative of court culture, and less centralized."[48] Gazetteers put forth a
particular view of locality and what makes a civilized place.

The nature of this view on locality and civilization was expressed in
the categories gazetteers covered and excluded and how they changed
over time. Aoyama Sadao identified the following categories as common
to most Song gazetteers:[49]

> *yange* 沿革 changes in administrative units
> *sizhi* 四至 distances to the surrounding administrative capitals
> *jiangyu* 疆域 the borders
> *chengguo* 城郭 the walls of administrative seats
> *xiangcun* 鄉村 cantons and villages in the county
> *shanchuan* 山川 mountains and rivers
> *hukou* 戶口 population
> *fangshi* 坊市 urban quarters
> *qiaoliang* 橋梁 bridges
> *jindu* 津渡 fords
> *yanzha* 堰閘 the water conservancy system
> *puyi* 鋪驛 postal stations
> *tuchan* 土產 local products
> *xuexiao* 學校 schools
> *fengsu* 風俗 customs

Some Song gazetteers also included chapters on government offices,
storehouses, taxes, revenues, military installations, local officials, degree
holders, religious and cultural matters, historical figures, Buddhist clerics,

---

47. Ibid., 74–75.
48. Ibid., 76.
49. Aoyama, *Tō Sō chihōshi*. The translations follow those of Bol, "Rise of Local
History," 45.

Daoist immortals, monuments, shrines, temples, steles, and miscellaneous information.[50] As local literati culture strengthened, most gazetteers paid more attention to "worthy *shidafu*" and less to clerics and tales of the marvelous and strange that appeared in earlier works. Literati "life writings" appearing in gazetteers included not only formal biographies presented in defined categories, but also tables and lists of officials and examination graduates, eulogies, imperial grants of titles, prefaces to local lineage genealogies, poems written upon parting, and other genres.

The increasing importance of biographical and literary writings can be seen by comparing earlier and later editions from the same locale. One of the most extensive series of extant gazetteers comes from Ningbo 寧波 Prefecture, Zhejiang (known as Siming 四明 in the Song and Yuan). The 1227 *Siming zhi* had twenty-one chapters, only three of which were biographies (*xuren* 敘人 "narrating people"). The scope of biographies in the 1320 edition increased: Although it too had three formal biography chapters (*renwu kao* 人物考 "studies of prominent figures") out of twenty total chapters, it also had biographies of Buddhist monks and Daoist immortals in three chapters on religious institutions, and two chapters listing officials' names. The main category in the biography chapters was "worthies of the past" (*xianxian* 先賢). There also was one "virtuous woman" (*jiefu* 節婦) biography, five biographies under the heading "filial acts" (*xiaoxing* 孝行), and two under "recluses" (*yishi* 逸士). The third biographical chapter consisted of eulogies (*zan* 贊) and lists of examination graduates.

The coverage of religion was more extensive than typically found in later Ming gazetteers. The 1320 edition had an entire chapter on shrines, temples, and biographies of clerics in the prefectural gazetteer, plus additional materials in each of the six attached county gazetteers. In contrast, the county gazetteers did not have separate biography sections for worthies, virtuous women, the filial, or recluses. Over the next two centuries, biographies became even more important. In the 1560 edition, eighteen of forty-two chapters were formal biographies, subdivided into numerous categories, including famous officials, scholars of the Way, literary scholars, men who exhibited various types of Confucian moral

50. Bol, "Rise of Local History," 45.

behavior, the uncommonly talented, recluses, worthy visitors, those with special skills, Daoist immortals, and Buddhist monks.

Although the biographical categories in the 1560 edition were more finely differentiated, they still focused on the literati and ignored numerous categories of people. Most gazetteers before the twentieth century contain little on those who succeeded in business, industry, or entertainment. Literati calligraphers were often noted, but artisans working in ceramics, wood, and other media were left out. Women and minorities received only modest attention: women appeared primarily as paragons of virtue, and compilers of borderland gazetteers occasionally took an interest in describing the customs of non-Chinese locals and their interactions with the state. To the extent that doctors were covered, it reflected an increasing literati participation in medical practice as the size of the literati class increased, beginning in the Southern Song. Military officers were covered inconsistently, appearing in many gazetteers but in far fewer numbers than civil officials. Coverage varied somewhat by time and place. Gazetteers of northern and western border towns include more on military personnel and defense than those published in literati centers of Jiangnan. Even though there are exceptions, this was the general pattern.

Compilers' views on the purpose of a gazetteer also shaped content. Huang Wei 黃葦 identified three main approaches to gazetteer writing: historical, geographical, and functional, all of which could be found in the Song through Qing.[51] Historically oriented compilers often imposed on their gazetteers the traditional categories and order of dynastic histories: annals (*ji* 紀), tables (*biao* 表), treatises (*zhi* 志), and biographies (*zhuan* 傳), and emphasized officials and biographies. Some, such as Tong Chengxu 童承敘 (1521 *jinshi*), a member of the Hanlin Academy and a junior compiler in the Historiography Institute, even imitated Sima Qian's style in the *Shiji* 史記 (*Grand Scribe's Records*). In his 1531 *Mianyang zhi* 沔陽志 he commented at the end of each section, using "The Grand Scribe says . . ." (*shi yue* 史曰) or similar phrases.[52]

Compilers with a geographical orientation emphasized gazetteers as heirs to the tradition of the *Tribute of Yu*, the early geographic work.

51. Huang Wei, *Fang zhi xue*, 357–68.
52. *Mianyang zhi*, 5.1b.

They began their gazetteers with physical geography and addressed it in more detail. Wang Shunmin's 汪舜民 1502 *Huizhou fu zhi* 徽州府志 begins with two chapters on physical geography followed by two chapters on economic resources, because, according to the principles of compilation, "the prefecture having been created, it then has its constituent mountains, rivers, walled towns, townships, markets, and the like, which have their attached lands, people, taxes and the like, from which governance is established, from which spirits are honored and people cherished, from which talents are cultivated and scholars selected."[53] In Wang's view, the land ultimately generated the literati and thus had to come first.

The functional approach to gazetteer writing stressed its usefulness as a mirror for governance and cultural transformation. Huang argued that the functionalists' basic orientation was expressed by Guan Daxun 管大勳, who in 1572 wrote that "a gazetteer is a record. [The purpose] of recording a locale's affairs is not just to assemble documents, but to make them all aids to governance."[54] Tang Shunzhi 唐順之, the famous sixteenth-century literatus, argued that the root of locales having gazetteers lies in statecraft (*guoyi zhi you zhi ben yi jingshi* 國邑之有志本以經世).[55] The statecraft orientation can be clearly seen in the 1503 *Xinghua fu zhi* 興化府志. In his preface, compiler Zhou Ying 周瑛 argued that the gazetteer's primary purpose is cultivating good administration, material well-being, and proper customs.[56] Zhou and his co-compiler, Huang Zhongshao 黃仲昭, organized the gazetteer under the headings of the six ministries: personnel, revenue, ritual, war, punishments, and works, and included many materials that would have been directly useful in administration. The "treatise on law and punishment" (*xingfa zhi* 刑法志) began with a discussion of the role of law in governance.[57] Drawing on classical thinkers, the compilers argued that the goal of law is to eliminate punishments and therefore people must be made to understand the law. The treatise then presented selections from key legal texts of the Song, Yuan, and Ming, provided their tables of contents, and clarified terminology. For example, it explained that the Song used the Tang Code

53. *Huizhou fu zhi* (1502), *fanli*, 1b.
54. *Linjiang fu zhi* (1572), preface, 1b.
55. *Jiangyin xian zhi* (1640), Tang preface, 3a.
56. *Xinghua fu zhi*, Zhou Ying preface, 1b.
57. Ibid., *juan* 51.

but relied more on edicts (*chi* 勅), which, the treatise explained, were equivalent to Ming substatutes (*li* 例).[58] For the Ming, the treatise listed contents of the *Da Ming ling* 大明令 (Great Ming Commandment), the *Da Ming lü* 大明律 (Ming Code), the three editions of the *Da Gao* 大誥 (Grand Pronouncement), imperially issued regulations and substatutes, and the text of the imperially issued regulations attached to the *jiaomin bangwen* 教民榜文 (Placard of People's Instructions).[59] This last item was useful in understanding the jurisdiction of, and rules applicable to, community elders and administrative community heads (*laoren lijia* 老人里甲). Next the gazetteer listed punishments, the sizes and weights of "jail tools" (*yu ju* 獄具), such as shackles, and "new and old regulations on the redemption of crimes" (*xin jiu shu xing zeli* 新舊贖刑則例). This last section clarified conflicting rules from the various legal texts. It explained that to redeem a punishment of ten strokes of the light stick, the Ming Code rate was 600 *wen* 文 of copper coins, the Great Ming Commandment rate was one-half *jin* 斤 of copper, but that by then-current regulations the rate was either 50 *dou* 斗 of rice or 200 *guan* 貫 of copper coins (*sha* 鈔). The treatise concluded by arguing that the regulations were in accord with the times and reached things not addressed in the *Da Ming lü*, *Da Ming ling*, *Da gao*, or *Jiaomin bangwen*.

In addition to the legal treatise, other parts of the 1503 *Xinghua fu zhi* would have been useful to consult in day-to-day administration. Chapter 20 provided detailed instructions on performance of official rituals and commentary on their histories. The section on the "ritual upon taking office" (*shang guan li* 上官禮) filled one and a half folios of text and left little doubt about what an official should do. The chapter on ritual music discussed important pieces, such as the "music accompanying the sacrifices for former teachers" (*si xianshi yue* 祀先師樂), detailing instruments and even finger placement.[60] The two chapters on the civil service examination began with a four-folio explanation and detailed regulations regarding the exam.[61]

58. Ibid., 51.4b.
59. Ibid., 51.7a–51.22b.
60. *Xinghua fu zhi, juan* 23.
61. Ibid., 18.1a–4b.

Although many compilers took a position arguing for one of these three approaches to gazetteers, in fact most compilers mixed historical, geographical, and functional elements. In the *Mianyang zhi*, discussed above, even though Tong focused on biographies and officials, he nevertheless had chapters on Mianyang's physical geography, and even though Zhou stressed the practical in the *Xinghua fu zhi*, he still included numerous biographies. Thus, although documenting local literati culture was paramount in most gazetteers, compilers recognized that their local cultures were embedded in particular landscapes, and making the gazetteer useful to good government was integral to their collective identity.

The genre's maturation can be seen in the first empire-wide gazetteer, the *Huang Yuan da yitongzhi* 皇元大一統志 (Comprehensive gazetteer of the august Yuan), compiled soon after the Mongol conquest of the Southern Song and Khubilai Khan's founding of the Yuan dynasty in 1279. The project began with an edict in 1285 ordering the collection of "maps/illustrations and treatises from the 10,000 places."[62] In 1296, eleven years into the project, the compilation office circulated guidelines for compiling gazetteers at the circuit (*lu* 路) level, which Timothy Brook calls "significant as the first attempt by the central government to regulate the style and contents of local gazetteers." The project universalized gazetteer compilation at least down to the circuit level, if not as far down as the prefecture (*zhou* 州) or county (*xian* 縣) level.[63] Only thirty-five of the original one thousand *juan* are extant. Another major round of local gazetteer compilation followed the Yuan government's decision in 1343 to compile the official histories of the Liao, Jin, and Song dynasties.[64] During the Yuan, the types of materials in gazetteers continued to expand along with local interest in reading gazetteers and more intensive efforts by officials and local scholars to produce them. These officials included Mongols and Central Asians as well as ethnic Chinese.[65]

---

62. Shang Qiweng, *Mishu jian zhi*, 72.

63. Brook, "Native Identity," 241. Yuan circuits were similar in size to Ming prefectures (*fu* 府) and often shared the same territories. The term *zhou* is translated as "prefecture" for Yuan, but "subprefecture" for Ming.

64. Ibid., 243.

65. For more on Mongol and Central Asians' participation in gazetteer projects, see Dennis, "Early Printing," 128–33.

The Ming central government continued and expanded the Yuan practice of mandating gazetteer compilation. In the aftermath of the Mongol collapse and the defeat of rivals, the Ming needed to reconstitute local records to create a foundation for administration. It conducted a census, registered households for taxation, and began collecting and compiling gazetteers. In 1370, two years after the Ming founding, a national gazetteer, the *Da Ming zhi shu* 大明志書 (Gazetteer of the Great Ming), was printed and distributed by the palace library.[66] It covered the realm's "twelve provinces, 120 prefectures, 108 subprefectures, 887 counties, three pacification commissions, and one chief's office, from the sea in the east, to Qiongya 瓊崖 in the south, Lintao 臨洮 in the west, and Beiping 北平 in the north." In the spring of 1376 the court once again collected local gazetteers, this time through provincial administration commissions. In Huguang Province the commission opened a gazetteer office and ordered each prefecture to compile gazetteers based on old editions, supplemented with new information on the locale's population, land tax, topography, geography, local products, customs, famous people, famous officials, and stelae inscriptions.[67]

In 1395 the *Hongwu zhi shu* 洪武志書 (Gazetteer of the Hongwu reign) was published. The topics covered were "the capital, mountains and rivers, lands, changes in territorial administration, the system of palaces, towers, and gates, and the establishment of, and changes to, altars, temples, streets, markets, and bridges."[68] Additional empire-wide collection and compilation edicts followed in 1412, 1418, 1454, 1524, 1672, and later in the Qing and Republican eras.[69] Gazetteers produced in response to these later orders had more biographical and literary categories than the 1395 *Hongwu zhi shu*, which focused on physical geography and institutions.

Imperial compilation edicts stressed the need for better information as the underlying motivation. Like emperors before him, the Jiajing Emperor wanted to know more about his empire. His 1524 edict was the culmination of a process begun soon after he ascended the throne in 1522. In that year the court dispatched *jinshi* degree holders around the empire

---

66. *Ming shilu, Taizu*, 1149. The *Da Ming zhi shu* is no longer extant.
67. *Yongzhou fu zhi*, 3a–4a.
68. *Ming shilu, Taizu*, 3243. The *Hongwu zhi shu* is not extant.
69. Xue Xuan, "Yanling xian zhi xu" 鄢陵縣志序, in *Jingxuan wenji*, 13.8a; *Ming shilu, Taizong*, 2089; Huang Wei, *Fang zhi xue*, 858–910; *Chun'an xian zhi*, preface, 2b.

to collect materials to update the *Da Ming yitongzhi*, which by that time was over sixty years old. The 1524 edict required locales to compile and submit gazetteers to the Historiography Institute.[70] Similarly, the 1672 edict was issued as the Kangxi Emperor was consolidating Qing control.

For imperially initiated gazetteer projects, central government officials determined categories of required content by issuing "rules of compilation" (*fanli* 凡例). Compilers of locally initiated gazetteers also wrote *fanli*, but these applied only to their own gazetteers. Because *fanli* phrasing varied, scholars have translated *fanli* in a variety of ways: "reading directions," "general principles," "editorial principles," and "general rules."[71] *Fanli* first appeared as a discrete gazetteer section in the Southern Song. The oldest known example is found in the 1252 *Yufeng zhi* 玉峰志, a gazetteer of Kunshan 崑山 (modern Jiangsu Province).[72] It lists five principles:

> In all cases of things connected to areas that once were in Kunshan but now are in Jiading, do not record any of them because the locations are no longer under this county's jurisdiction.
>
> In all cases in which commemorative stelae are still extant, record the titles, but not the texts. For those that are no longer extant, also record the texts.
>
> In all cases in which newly compiled materials differ from what is recorded in the *Gazetteer of Wu Commandery*, include those items for which there is no discrepancy with what is heard and seen today.
>
> In all cases of writing biographies, record now both natives who have moved away, and non-natives who have moved here.
>
> In all cases in which matters appear repeatedly, record them in only one place.
>
> Related texts appearing in other sections also must not be repeatedly recorded.

The *Yufeng zhi* principles of compilation present a straightforward explanation to the compilers and readers about editorial choices. They do not address the underlying meaning of the gazetteer or establish the

---

70.   Huang Wei, *Fang zhi xue*, 863.

71.   Chow, "Writing for Success," 132; Li Xiaorong, "Gender and Textual Politics," 82; Meyer-Fong, "Packaging the Men," 10; Wilkinson, *Chinese History*, 155.

72.   *Yufeng zhi, fanli* (XXSK, 696:564).

content categories. Over the course of the Yuan, Ming, and Qing, many *fanli* came to include detailed explanations of a gazetteer's reasons for being and the compilers' approach to theoretical issues of gazetteer compilation. Single sets of principles also came to be used for multiple compilations. In contrast, the *Yufeng zhi* principles applied only to the *Yufeng zhi*. There are no extant Song dynasty examples of *fanli* drawn up for multiple local gazetteers.

Compilers often used *fanli* to enhance a gazetteer's authority. They portrayed the compilation as rigorous, fair, thoughtful, and sanctioned by officials, and as embodying high scholarly standards. Criteria were established and judgments explained. For example, many gazetteer compilers rejected the inclusion of biographies of living people because this could cause people to doubt their impartiality. The *fanli* section was the best place to clearly set forth rules that promoted the gazetteer's thoroughness and fairness (fig. 1.6).

In the Yuan, the government issued *fanli* for circuit gazetteers that were the foundation for the national gazetteer, a practice that continued in the Ming and Qing.[73] The earliest extant *fanli* for a national gazetteer project were issued in 1412. The seventeen official categories and their corresponding instructions are translated below:

> Principles of Compilation Promulgated in the
> 10th Year of the Great Ming Yongle Era

- Changes in Administrative Units (*jianzhi yange* 建置沿革). Celestial and terrestrial correspondence (*fenye* 分野).
  Record in detail from beginning to end every provincial administration commission, and every prefecture, subprefecture, and county yamen, starting with the territories to which they belonged according to the *Tribute of Yu* and Zhou dynasty history offices, continuing with their establishment and abolition in successive dynasties, changes in their names from past to present, as well as rebel territories at the beginning of our esteemed dynasty and the order in which false claimants to the throne submitted. Also record the constellations under which territories appear.
- Territory (*jiangyu* 疆域). Walls and Moats (*chengchi* 城池). Distances (*lizhi* 里至).

---

73. Han Zhangxun, "Fanli zong lun," 23–26.

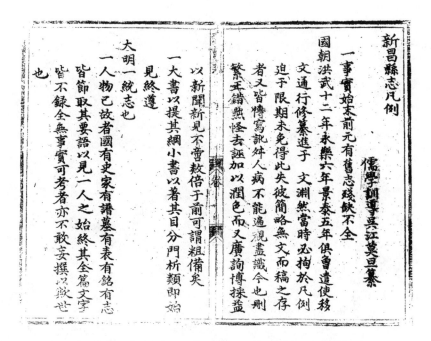

FIGURE 1.6. Principles of compilation for the 1477 *Xinchang xian zhi* (Xinchang County Archives).

Record in detail the widths and lengths of each prefecture, subprefecture, and county's lands, the distances to all neighboring territories' boundaries, the sizes, heights, and depths of their walls and moats, along with records of their renovations in successive dynasties. The "distances" sections of most old gazetteers stopped at the furthest edge of the prefecture, subprefecture, or county. Now, collectively record the locale's geography, the distances to Nanjing and Beijing, and each prefecture's and county's distances to neighboring jurisdictions' boundaries and yamens, and roads that can be taken to them. Also prepare maps of each prefecture and county's walls, moats, mountains, and rivers.

- Mountains and Rivers (*shanchuan* 山川).
For the mountains and rivers of the various places recorded in ancient records, if their names therein are different from how they are listed in current maps and registers, or if the names of small mountains and rivers were not fully recorded in former dynasties, then these should be collected under their present names. If famous

people of the past or present wrote commemorative poems, they
should be appended.

- Urban Neighborhoods (*fangguo* 坊郭). Townships and Villages
  (*xiangzhen* 鄉鎮).
  Collect and record by current name all neighborhoods, alleys, streets,
  markets, townships, wards, villages, hamlets, mutual protection
  organizations, and communities. For ancient names that are no longer
  in use, record them in the "antiquities" section and describe their
  current locations.

- Local Products (*tuchan* 土產). Tribute Taxes (*gongfu* 貢賦).
  Fully record the products produced by every locale, arranged by
  subprefecture and county. Also record all of the tax items from the
  Tribute of Yu. For tribute items, record the quotas. Accurately record
  all products found in former dynasties that no longer exist, and tribute
  items that exist now but did not in ancient times. For the land tax, use
  the acreage and tax figures from the Yellow Registers from the twenty-
  fourth year of the Hongwu reign (1391) and the tenth year of the
  Yongle reign (1412) as the standard. Also record former dynasties' tax
  quotas to show the increase or decrease from the past to the present.

- Customs (*fengsu* 風俗). Topography (*xingshi* 形執).
  Because the territories of the realm's subprefectures and counties are
  separated by mountains and rivers, their people's practices, preferences,
  dispositions, and customs cannot fail to have differences, and it is
  appropriate to investigate and document that which was taught by the
  ancients and the good practices and customs that are visible today. For
  topography, make characterizations like that Zhuge Liang (181–234)
  made of Jinling: "Bell Mountain is like a dragon jade, Stone Wall is like
  a tiger lair."[74]

- Population (*hukou* 户口).
  Collect and record all local population figures from former dynasties,
  and figures reported in the Yellow Registers from the twenty-fourth
  year of our esteemed dynasty's Hongwu reign (1391), to the tenth year
  of the Yongle reign (1412).

- Schools (*xuexiao* 學校).
  The flourishing and decline of schools built in former dynasties varies.
  You must examine what is documented in old gazetteers, and record

---

74.   Zhuge Liang's phrase described Jianye, the capital of the Wu kingdom established by Sun Quan in 229 CE. Wang Yinglin, *Yu Hai*, 173.34a. It later was renamed
Jinling, and in the Ming became Nanjing.

who founded them, why they went to ruin, and for those still standing, where they are located. If there is an extant commemorative stele for a famous person or worthy scholar, transcribe it. If a well-known person came from a particular school, then record the person along with the school's size, regulations, abstinence hall, and archery ground.

- Military Units (*junwei* 軍衛).
Collect and record all unit headquarters by prefecture, county, and place; the year, month, and day of each unit's establishment; whether or not there have been changes in the interim; and the distinguished commanders who had great accomplishments in battle, for both former dynasties and our esteemed dynasty. If there is a place for military drill, it should be recorded in detail.

- Offices (*xieshe* 廨舍).
Record in detail everything from provincial administration commission, provincial surveillance commission, regional military commission, salt transport offices; prefecture, subprefecture, county, and market shipping offices; post stations, inspection offices, granaries, storehouses, fishing household tax stations, and other yamens, to the altars grounds and neighborhood patrol stations, including offices' establishment in their present locations by year, month, day, and founder, locations within the territory, and changes to the institutional system. For those from former dynasties that have already been abolished and are no longer extant, record them all in the antiquities section. If commemorative stelae are still extant, transcribe them, leaving nothing out.

- Temples, Abbeys, Shrines, and Monasteries (*siguancimiao* 寺觀祠廟). Bridges (*qiaoliang* 橋梁).
The flourishing and decline of the realms' temples, abbeys, shrines, monasteries, and bridges varies. Those found in historical records or as ruins, and those currently existing, should be examined in detail and recorded. For those having commemorative stelae, transcribe the texts. For those that are newly built, record who founded them and when. Also record in detail the origins of those that were extant in the Hongwu reign (1368–98), and those that had returned to the forest but were later rebuilt.

- Antiquities (*guji* 古蹟). Ruins of Walls and Moats (*chengguo guzhi* 城郭故址). Buildings (*gongshitaixie* 宮室臺榭). Graves (*lingmu* 陵墓). Passes (*guansai* 関塞). Cliffs and Caves (*yandong* 巖洞). Gardens (*yuanchi* 園池). Wells and Springs (*jingquan* 井泉). Dams and Levees (*poyan* 陂堰). Scenic Sites (*jingwu* 景物).

Collect and record all that was not fully documented in old gazetteers' maps and registers. If only the name was recorded, but not the facts and not the place, you must investigate the details, collect them, and record them.

- Accomplishments of Officials (*huanji* 官蹟).

  Collect and record those officials, high and low, from the establishment of the locale as a territorial unit to our esteemed dynasty, who served in the locale and are famous for their administrative accomplishments, along with those who were promoted to important posts and are praised locally. Also collect and record the good administration of officials from the provincial administration commission, provincial surveillance commission, regional military commission, salt transport, and other yamens.

- Biographies (*renwu* 人物).

  Record the lives, past and present, of all local famous people, worthy scholars, loyal ministers, filial sons, righteous husbands, virtuous wives, literati, talents, degree holders, officials, hermit scholars, those who upheld righteousness to protect the community, and those who have taken meritorious action on behalf of the people. For people who are not natives of this place, but later moved here, still record them.

- Transcendent Beings and Monks (*xianshi* 仙釋).

  Fully record all known transcendent beings, extraordinary people, famous Buddhist monks, and lofty Daoists since antiquity, both those transmitted in local tradition who have clearly visible traces of remarkable skills or extraordinary actions, and those who were not locals but who once came and stayed in this place, and for whom there is clear proof of when they came.

- Miscellaneous Records (*za zhi* 雜志).

  Collect and record things about mountain forests, cliff caves, products, auspicious portents, flowers and trees, birds and animals, human affairs, the mysterious and supernatural, and the like, that have been passed down by local people, recited by them, and for which there is evidence.

- Literature (*shiwen* 詩文).

  Collect and record commemorative verses by poets from former dynasties to our esteemed dynasty, about mountains and rivers, scenic sites, customs, and human affairs.[75]

75. The text is taken from the *Shouchang xian zhi*, 23–30, except for the four paragraphs on population, schools, military units, and government offices, and two characters from the temples section that are now missing in the National Library of China's

It is not clear how many gazetteers used the 1412 *fanli*, and no national gazetteer using them was completed. Nevertheless, they are important as a baseline for studying how *fanli* changed over time and the priorities of the Yongle Emperor's court. Just six years later, in Yongle 16 (1418) the court ordered the compilation of the *Tianxia junxian zhishu* 天下郡縣志書 (Gazetteer of the realm's localities) and appointed Minister of Revenue Xia Yuanji 夏原吉 and two members of the Hanlin Academy to direct the project. They issued a revised set of *fanli* and the Ministry of Rites dispatched officials to "visit locales everywhere to widely collect traces of events and old gazetteers."[76] The revised rules overlapped substantially with the 1412 rules, but made some changes. They removed category headings and began each section with the character "一" (*yi*), followed by terms for categories that merged into the section's text. The new *fanli* combined some categories of the 1412 *fanli*, separated others, created new topics, removed a few items, and added details. Noteworthy changes were made to the categories and placement of biographies. Because this second set of *fanli* continued to affect gazetteer compilation into the late Qing dynasty, the categories and instructions (now in twenty-one sections) are translated in full:

Gazetteer Compilation Principles, Promulgated
in the 16th Year of the Yongle Era

- For changes in administrative units (*jianzhi yange* 建置沿革), narrate the historical establishment of prefectures and counties, starting with the region to which they belonged according to the *Tribute of Yu* and Zhou dynasty history offices, and including their division, combination, abolition, and establishment in successive dynasties, seizure by false claimants to the throne, and the prefecture that administered them upon pacification by our esteemed dynasty.
- For celestial and terrestrial correspondence (*fenye* 分野), record which of the [twelve] regions a territory belongs to, and the constellation under which it appears.
- For territory (*jiangyu* 疆域), list what is above, below, left, and right of the territory, how many *li* it is to the borders in the four directions, how wide it is, how long it is. For the four distances, list the place

---

imprint. Those sections and characters are taken from an earlier transcription. Fu, "You yi jian," 144–45.

76. *Ming shilu*, *Taizong*, 2089; *Shenxian zhi*, fanli, 1a–3b.

name and number of *li* to the neighboring counties' border offices, and
for the eight destinations, list how many *li* it is to the neighboring
prefecture, subprefecture, and county yamens. List the distance to the
prefectural seat, the provincial administration commission, Nanjing,
and Beijing, by land and water routes. For land routes, say how many *li*
it is. For water routes, say how many stations it is.

- For walls and moats (*chengchi* 城池), record what was built at what
  time, and who expanded it. If there are stelae texts, transcribe them.
  Record everything in the category of gate towers, battlements, and
  drawbridges.

- For mountains and rivers (*shanchuan* 山川), describe where the territory's ridges, rivers, streams, and the like originate. Transcribe all
  historical traces and stelae inscriptions at famous mountains and great
  rivers. For others, even if it is a small mountain or small river, if it has a
  name, record it too.

- For urban neighborhoods, villages, and markets (*fangguo zhenshi* 坊
  郭鎮市), record current neighborhoods, main streets, wards, and
  communities, and the dispersed villages and markets. If in former
  times there was a name that is no longer used, record it in the antiquities section.

- Record all local products (*tuchan* 土産), tribute taxes, cultivated and
  uncultivated land taxes, grain taxes, labor taxes, and monetary taxes,
  from former dynasties down to this dynasty's twenty-fourth year of the
  Hongwu era (1391), and the figures for the tenth year of the Yongle era
  (1412).

- For customs (*fengsu* 風俗), narrate the differences and similarities in
  practices and customs from former dynasties to the present. For
  topography (*xingshi* 形勢), characterize the mountains' and rivers'
  grandness and steepness in the manner of Zhuge Liang: "Bell
  Mountain is like a dragon jade, Stone Wall is like a tiger lair."

- For population (*hukou* 戸口), record in detail figures from former
  dynasties and the population registers from the twenty-fourth year of
  the Hongwu era (1391), and the tenth year of the Yongle era (1412) of
  this dynasty.

- For schools (*xuexiao* 學校), narrate their establishment and those who
  reconstructed them. Also record the buildings, offices, books, and stelae
  commemorative records. Also record in detail the school officials and
  the talents who passed the examinations or became tribute students.
  If there are stelae commemorative records, also transcribe them.

- For military units (*junwei* 軍衛), narrate when the units were established and record their yamens, offices, training grounds, military farm field locations, field acreage, and annual grain submission quota. Record all traces of military officers' meritorious service. Also record things such as stelae commemorative records.
- For prefectural and county offices (*junxian xieshe* 郡縣廨舍), describe in detail those built in former dynasties that still exist in this dynasty. Record in the antiquities section those built in the distant past but no longer extant, and those that have fallen into disuse. Also record in detail subordinate yamens such as post stations, village offices, granaries, storehouses, pavilions for announcements and commemorating goodness, altars, and neighborhood patrol stations. For those having stelae texts, transcribe them too.
- For temples and abbeys (*siguan* 寺觀), narrate when they were built and their subsequent renovations. For those having stelae texts, also transcribe them. If they have fallen into disuse, record them in the antiquities section.
- For shrines and monasteries (*cimiao* 祠廟), record in detail the Confucian temple's construction, all of its ritual implements, musical instruments, and stelae commemorative records, leaving out nothing. For other shrines and monasteries, also narrate their construction and how they were established, and record things such as imperial grants, edicts, and stelae commemorative records.
- For bridges (*qiaoliang* 橋梁), narrate the origins of their construction, their locations, and who subsequently renovated them. For those having commemorative stelae records, also transcribe them.
- For antiquities (*guji* 古蹟), collect and record the ruins of all city walls, offices, postal stations, mountain forts, granaries, and storehouses from former dynasties that once existed but no longer do, or that moved to another location. Collect records of the graves of emperors and kings of former dynasties, famous officials, and worthy scholars. For pavilions, platforms, towers, academies, and the like, whether they are maintained or abandoned, if they have commemorative stelae records, then fully transcribe them following the entry. Also record the current locations of fords, where roads pass, and famous cliffs and caves, wells and springs. Record the location of waterfalls and whether they have any verifiable efficacious or unusual properties. Record how gardens and ponds of former dynasties came to be constructed. For the mulberries and jujubes of this dynasty, fully record their locations in

each ward. For things like dikes and embankments, record the dynasty in which they were built. If there is no record of it, just record the present location. For those that have been abandoned, record the reasons why. Record temples and abbeys, shrines and monasteries, even if they are abandoned. Record all of the ruined streets and alleys and such.

- For accomplishments of officials (*huanji* 官蹟), beginning from a locale's establishment in a former dynasty, fully record those who have had administrative accomplishments that have been transmitted, or whose names are inscribed. For this esteemed dynasty, record every person who had an administrative accomplishment. For currently serving officials, only document the deeds, do not use flattering praise.
- For biographies (*renwu* 人物), record all worthies, martyrs, loyal ministers, famous generals, officials, filial children, compliant grandchildren, righteous husbands, virtuous wives, hermits, Confucian scholars, experts in methods and techniques, and those who were able to protect the community, from former dynasties to this esteemed dynasty.
- For transcendent beings and monks (*xianshi* 仙釋), collect and record those from former dynasties to today who are famous or who have traces of their numinosity.
- For miscellaneous records (*zaji* 雜志), record things about the locale, past and present, that are difficult to fit into the above categories. For example, in order to make it fully available for reference, record what can be collected on topics such as people's affairs and customs that can serve as warnings, the demonic and auspicious as signaled by grasses, trees, insects, and wild animals; floods, fires, devastation, drought, the mysterious and supernatural.
- For literature (*shiwen* 詩文), first compile one chapter of imperial edicts from the Sagely Dynasty for veneration. Next, collect and record texts such as poems, essays, commemorative records, and prefaces of famous gentlemen past and present that are relevant to administration and cultural transformation, and commemorative verses about mountains and rivers. Do not record superficial or impure texts.[77]

Although there was much overlap with the 1412 *fanli*, the 1418 *fanli* made significant revisions. Most noticeable was the biographical

77. *Shenxian zhi, fanli,* 1a–3b.

coverage. The following categories in the 1412 *fanli* were dropped in 1418: "famous people" (*mingren* 名人), "literati" (*wenren* 文人), "talents" (*caizi* 才子), and "degree holders" (*kedi* 科第). The following were added: "martyrs" (*lieshi* 烈士), "famous generals" (*mingjiang* 名將), and "compliant grandchildren" (*shunsun* 順孫). "Worthy scholars" (*xianshi* 賢士) was changed to "worthy people" (*xianren* 賢人), and "remarkable skills" (*qishu* 奇術) which often covered martial artists and doctors, was changed to "experts in methods and techniques" (*fangji* 方技) and moved out of the separate "transcendent beings and monks" section and into the main biography section. These changes reflect a reduction in categories for civilian scholars and an increase in categories for military personnel, perhaps reflecting internal tension between civilian and military officials in the Yongle reign period. Over the next centuries, most gazetteers had far fewer biographies of military officers than of civil officials. The second set of *fanli* also suggests that the directors were more concerned about inappropriate content than the issuers of the first. They added warnings against superficial or impure texts and prohibited flattery of currently serving officials.

As Zhang Yingpin's study of Southern Metropolitan Region gazetteers of the Ming dynasty shows, even though the imperial gazetteer project was suspended after the Yongle Emperor's death in 1424, these categories were influential, and later compilers looked to the Yongle-era *fanli* in organizing their texts.[78] Some, however, rejected the Yongle format. They created new categories, and made subsets of the 1412 and 1418 categories into their own sections. For example, most late-Ming and Qing (1644–1911) gazetteers turned subsets of the biographies section, such as virtuous women biographies, into their own chapters, or even multiple chapters broken down by subcategories. Terminology also changed slightly over time. Many late imperial gazetteers had sections similar in content to those of the 1418 *fanli*, but arranged under different headings; for example, the 1418 literature section, "*shiwen* 詩文," was more commonly called "*yiwen* 藝文."

For three decades the national gazetteer project languished, until in 1454 the Ministry of Rites was ordered to compile the *Huanyu tong zhi* 寰宇通志 (Comprehensive gazetteer of the realm). The Ministry of Rites

---

78. Zhang Yingpin, *Mingdai Nanzhili*, 163–75.

sent officials to each provincial administration commission as well as to the two capital region governments to oversee the collection and updating of old gazetteers, which were then submitted to the court. In one province, Yunnan, they completed the work in four months.[79] The national gazetteer was completed in 1456. However, after the Tianshun Emperor came to power in 1457, he found fault with the *Huanyu tong zhi* and the next year ordered its recompilation.[80] It was ultimately published as the *Da Ming yitongzhi* 大明一統志 (Comprehensive gazetteer of the Great Ming) in 1461. In the Qing, three comprehensive gazetteers were compiled and published. The first began in 1672, was completed in 1743, and printed in 1746. The second was completed in 1784 and printed in 1790. The third was completed in 1820 and printed in 1842.[81]

Government Initiatives from Outside the Court

Although periodic court orders were important stimuli to gazetteer compilation, most government-initiated projects began farther down the administrative hierarchy. Officials from territorial administrations—grand coordinators, provincial administration and surveillance commissioners, prefects, and local magistrates—were especially active. Thus, initiative could come from any one of the empire's numerous administrative units. The total number of lower-level units varied, but in the mature Ming structure there were thirteen provinces and two directly administered capital regions around Beijing and Nanjing. Each of these fifteen provinces and regions had between 5 and 19 prefectures (*fu* 府), for an approximate total of 150. The prefectures in turn each had an average of one subprefecture (*zhou* 州), and eight subordinate counties (*xian* 縣)—so

---

79. "Yunnan tujing zhishu" 雲南圖經志書, preface, 1, in *Yunnan zhi*, 283; *Huizhou fu zhi* (1556), 1457 preface, 1b. For further information, see Zhang Yingpin, *Mingdai Nanzhili*, 25–26.

80. *Ming shilu, Yingzong*, 6281.

81. Wilkinson, *Chinese History*, 944–45.

in total there were about 240 subprefectures and 1,140 counties.[82] Specialized administrative units, such as garrisons (*zhen* 鎮) and circuits (*tai* 臺), also produced gazetteers.[83]

Officials from superior territorial units spurred local gazetteer production by demanding them from administrators of subordinate locales, either for use in compiling their own gazetteers or simply to have in their offices.[84] Generally, locales that had recently published gazetteers could submit copies, whereas those without were required to compile new editions. In the fall of 1494, the Jiangxi provincial administration and surveillance commissions decided to compile a provincial gazetteer and ordered each subordinate territorial administration to compile a local gazetteer to serve as its foundation.[85] The 1542 gazetteer of Gushi 固始, Henan, was compiled pursuant to Henan Province Grand Coordinator Wei Jun's 魏鈞 order requiring all subordinate territorial units to submit gazetteers for his reference. The order allowed those with existing gazetteers to print and submit copies, while those without were to request assistance from the provincial education intendant's office or have local officials or Confucian school instructors compile new gazetteers.[86] In the above cases, jurisdictions were required to submit finished works, but in many others, subordinate units only had to collect, sort, and submit materials to the superior unit, which then combined and edited materials from all of its subordinate jurisdictions.

Such provincial orders could be accompanied by principles of compilation applicable to all subordinate-unit gazetteers. The 1547 gazetteer of Qishui County 蘄水縣, Huguang, was compiled pursuant to *fanli* issued by Huguang Provincial Administration Commissioner Ding Ming 丁明.[87] Many other Jiajing- and Wanli-era Huguang gazetteers also followed Ding's principles.[88] In the early Qing, Jia Hanfu 賈漢復 initiated provincial

82. Twitchett and Mote, *Cambridge History of China,* 8:10–15. Some subprefectures were directly under provinces rather than prefectures.

83. See, e.g., the 1514 *Xuanfu zhen zhi,* 1590 *Yuntai zhi,* and 1608 *Ganzhen zhi.*

84. *Hengzhou fu zhi* (1537), 1.14b–15b.

85. He Qiaoxin, "Nanfeng xian zhi xu" 南豐縣志序, in *Jiaoqiu wenji,* 9.17a.

86. *Gushi xian zhi* (1542), prefaces, 8a–b.

87. *Qishui xian zhi, fanli.*

88. Ba Zhaoxiang, "Lun Mingdai fangzhi," 50.

compilations while serving as governor of Henan in 1660 and Shaanxi in 1662. He issued rules of compilation and required each subordinate territory to open a compilation office and submit a completed gazetteer to the provincial capital. Jia's reasons for compiling gazetteers included helping to reestablish government and unity after the Qing founding, supplementing the historical record that had been neglected and damaged during the dynastic change, and making it possible to know the empire.[89] These compilations became the models for the nationwide compilation principles issued in 1672.[90]

In between empire-wide and provincial compilations, numerous projects were initiated by local magistrates and prefects acting independently of higher-level officials. Their motivations varied. Some wanted to better understand the locales in which they were serving. As one wrote, "If a county lacks a gazetteer, how can one investigate the glories of its landscape and people, the beauty of its governance, education, and customs, and the expansion or contraction in the tribute, taxes, and produce?"[91] Some were driven by a sense of duty to document the locale for subsequent administrators. Although, as discussed earlier, there was widespread agreement that such a duty existed, officials disagreed on the relative importance of gazetteer compilation. Some gave it great weight: Magistrate Dang Zhao 党炤, the compiler of the 1601 gazetteer of Huairen 懷仁, Shanxi, told a visiting inspector that compiling a gazetteer "is a primary duty in administration," and in 1544 a Jiangxi surveillance official wrote that "compiling a local gazetteer is a first duty in local administration."[92] But more commonly, compilation was discussed as something to be done once local administration was running smoothly, litigation had been reduced, reserve granaries were full, and schools and other government buildings had been renovated. Of course, many administrators never found time to update their gazetteers, demonstrating that it was not their priority.

Self-promotion was an important motivator. Other officials who read a magistrate's gazetteer would see records of his successful policy

89.   *Shaanxi tong zhi*, Jia preface, 3b–4b; *Henan tong zhi,* Jia preface, 1a–5b; Huang Wei, *Fang zhi xue,* 863.

90.   Huang Wei, *Fang zhi xue,* 863.

91.   *Dengfeng xian zhi*, preface, 1a.

92.   *Huairen xian zhi*, postface; *Yongfeng xian zhi*, *xiu zhi shi you* 修志事由 (Origins of the gazetteer compilation), 2a–b.

initiatives, construction of schools and city walls, poems written by or to the official, and a host of other documents that could enhance his reputation. For example, the prefect of Linting 臨汀, Fujian, made a large donation to build a new school, and in 1259, soon after it was built, set up an office inside the school to compile the gazetteer that recorded his good deed.[93] When other officials passed through town, magistrates often gave them copies of their gazetteers, thereby spreading knowledge of their successes. Gazetteer circulation will be addressed in detail in later chapters.

Initiatives in Borderlands: Knowing the Empire and Cultural Transformation

In borderlands, gazetteer compilation was an important part of central government attempts to incorporate unassimilated regions into the state. When the Ming conquered Yunnan Province in 1382, officials immediately compiled a sixty-one-*juan* gazetteer based on maps, records, and old gazetteers compiled under former rulers. The *Veritable Records* linked the Yunnan gazetteer project to the establishment of territorial administrations to "pacify the people."[94] The waves of gazetteer compilation that followed the founding of the Yuan, Ming, and Qing dynasties can be seen as a reflection of both the need for accurate information to serve as a foundation for control, and gazetteer compilers' axiom that when a territory's boundaries or place in the administrative hierarchy changes, a new gazetteer should be produced.[95]

The first part of this section will examine local gazetteers produced in Ming borderlands and compare them to those from the core, noting some of the particular motivations for their compilation. For borderlands, local gazetteers both signified incorporation into the state and acted as agents of cultural transformation in areas populated by non-Chinese

93. Wang Duanlai and Liu Xian, *Yongle dadian fangzhi jiyi*, 1468.
94. *Ming shilu, Taizu*, 2288.
95. Zhang Guogan, *Zhongguo gu fangzhi kao*, 366; Xu Mingshan, "Ningzhou zhi xu" 寧州志序, in *Fangu ji, juan shang*, 31b.

peoples. In southwestern China, they were important vehicles in state attempts to transform oral cultures into written cultures. The second part of this section will examine two gazetteer editions from Mahu Prefecture, Sichuan. The earlier edition was compiled under the auspices of the local hereditary native prefect, while the latter was compiled by non-native, nonlocal Chinese officials after the central government stripped the hereditary native prefects of their right to rule. Comparing the two editions, which span the transition from patrimonial rule to regular territorial administration, sheds light on underlying agendas for compiling gazetteers in the borderlands.

DISTINGUISHING CHINESE FROM BARBARIAN

Local gazetteers were important texts in Chinese discourse about civilized versus uncivilized peoples. An important goal of Chinese government in the late imperial period was "transformation through teaching" (*jiaohua* 教化), which meant encouraging the acceptance and practice of the dominant Confucian literati values, rituals, and customs. In the Ming, a borderland gazetteer served to mark a locale's membership in the civilized Chinese world. This function was explained by Magistrate Ren Guan 任官 in a postface he wrote for the 1546 gazetteer of Hezhou 河州, located in what is now the Linxia Hui Muslim Autonomous District (*Linxia Huizu Zizhi Qu* 臨夏回族自治區) in Gansu Province (map 1.1). He wrote:

> In my view, what distinguishes China from the outer barbarians is that we have literature. Gazetteers are a prominent and important form of literature. To be within China yet be without a gazetteer is to be unlettered. If [a locale] is unlettered, how is it valuing its place in China?! For this reason, from the imperial capital on down to each province, each prefecture, and each county, none lack a gazetteer. These serve to nurture culture and learning and distinguish Chinese from barbarian.[96]

Ren Guan's comment suggests that he was thinking of local gazetteers as products of preexisting local Chinese literary scenes, however

96. *Hezhou zhi* (1546), 250.

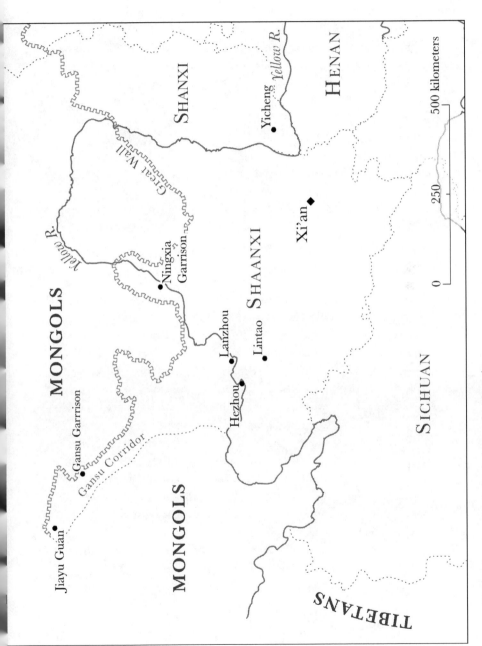

MAP 1.1 The northwestern borderlands during the Ming dynasty

limited they might be. But local gazetteers in the southwestern Ming borderlands not only reflected existing scenes, they also could be important vehicles for transforming oral and marginally literate non-Chinese cultures into literate and literary Chinese culture. A local gazetteer was often the first substantial piece of literature produced in a particular borderland locale. To compile a gazetteer, Chinese officials collected miscellaneous writings left by earlier officials, searched geographies and histories that covered larger geographic units, and added whatever they could gather locally from oral interviews and privately held documents. Such first-time gazetteers brought the locale into the literary Chinese empire— into the stream of its history and into its imagined geography.

An example of this is the 1550 gazetteer of Xundian 尋甸, Yunnan, which is now the Xundian Hui Muslim and Yi Autonomous District 尋甸回族彝族自治區 (map 1.2). Xundian was an isolated region that had long been governed by hereditary native officials. But after a violent succession dispute in 1476 the Ming central government established a prefecture and sent non-native, circulating officials to begin asserting central authority. At first, however, as the local gazetteer explains, "although Xundian was called a prefecture, in fact it was just an empty name placed above the subprefectures and counties. Furthermore, it was in the midst of Wuding 武定, Dongchuan 東川, Zhanyi 霑益, and other prefectures and departments that only knew barbarian customs and did not know Chinese ways."[97] The new officials were unable to control the area and in 1527 the chieftain An Quan 安銓 rebelled and sacked the prefectural town.[98] After the rebellion was suppressed, the central government stepped up efforts at direct control and assimilation of the native people.

Part of making Xundian Chinese was making it literate and literary. In 1542 the prefect bought sets of Chinese canonical books for the prefectural school and endowed it with educational trust lands.[99] Six years later a new prefect, Wang Shangyong 王尚用, arrived, and when he learned that Xundian had no local gazetteer, he asked his subordinates whether they could tolerate this "gap in essential documentation." In response to Prefect Wang's question, his subordinates said, "Xundian

97. *Xundian fu zhi, juan xia,* 48a.
98. Ibid., *juan shang,* 1b; *juan xia,* 10b.
99. Ibid., *juan shang,* 49–50.

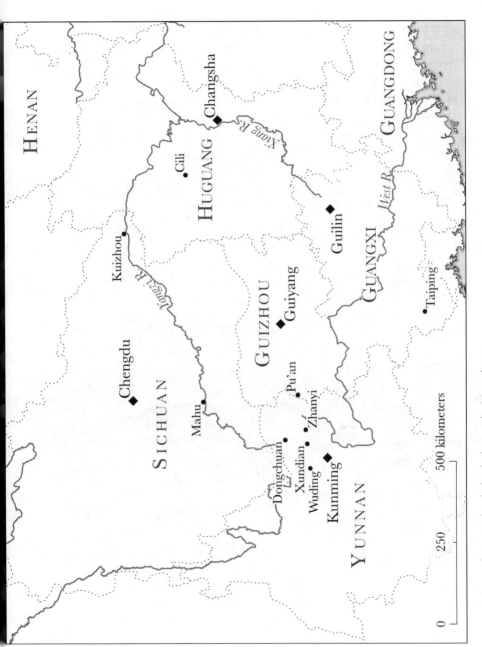

MAP 1.2 The southwestern borderlands during the Ming dynasty

has no old books, no virtuous elders, no documents, no famous officials or great ministers; how could we compile a local gazetteer?" The subordinates assumed that local gazetteers were for documenting a place's participation in Chinese civilization and government, and that if the place had not long been such a participant, there was nothing to record. Prefect Wang was exasperated by their response, and replied, "If that's the way it is, then would it not be better for us to just relax here among the barbarians because the day when we'll be able to compile a gazetteer will never come?"[100] Chastened by this, the subordinates and a visiting student from Kunming, the provincial capital, compiled a local gazetteer by drawing on the provincial gazetteer and interviewing local elders. In the prefect's view, even in a place where Chinese cultural resources were almost nonexistent, someone had to take the first step and produce a book that could serve as a foundation for future local scholars. It is worth noting here that the prefect's subordinates did not consider collecting information on physical geography to be sufficient reason to compile a gazetteer. Such information may have been part of putting a place on the Chinese map, but it was not the essence of gazetteers.

The preface to the "collected writings" section of the resulting gazetteer explicitly connects the written language embodied in the local gazetteer to what Prefect Wang calls the "civilizing" of Xundian: He wrote, "In the past, Xundian was a native territory and had no written culture. But after the circulating office was established, human written culture gradually took hold in this place. To gather these [newly produced] writings and publish them [here] is not without significance."[101] For the prefect, that significance was to nudge Xundian into the civilized, literature-producing world, the Chinese world that was distinct from that of people he considered "barbarians."

The power of local gazetteers to kick-start written, literary culture is often noted in borderland gazetteers. The 1565 gazetteer of Pu'an 普安 (Guizhou Province) states: "In the past, Pu'an was barbarian territory and previous generations were undocumented (*wu wenxian* 無文獻). When the local gazetteer was first compiled in the Yongle era (1403–25), it was still crude, but with the passing of generations and a succession of sagely

---

100.   Ibid., preface, 1b.
101.   Ibid., *juan xia*, 9b–10a.

emperors, culture transformed this distant land, and talents and literature gradually flourished."[102]

Substantial reliance on oral sources was not uncommon in early southwestern borderland gazetteers. For example, the 1575 gazetteer of Taiping 太平, Guangxi, says that although the prefecture was created from barbarian lands in 1368, there had been no office to document the past and the gazetteer compilers had to rely solely on privately held documents and the "facts as told by local elders" (*xianglao zhi koushi* 鄉老之口實).[103] Borderland gazetteers promoted literary culture not only by turning local oral history into written history, but also by giving students at local schools the chance to work on a literary project.

Of course, as gazetteers helped create local literature they did not necessarily record the histories of native peoples or even seek to describe them. Magistrate Chen Guangqian 陳光前, compiler of the 1573 gazetteer of Cili 慈利, Huguang, explained that the compilers of two earlier county gazetteers said that they did not record the "barbarians" 蠻夷 because "they are not the concern of county gazetteers."[104] Magistrate Chen however, included a chapter on "local barbarians" 土夷, which describes their rebellion and submission to "act as a warning." Although most Ming southwestern borderland gazetteers focused on the ways in which locales were Chinese, as Leo Shin points out, some gazetteers, especially ones from later in the Ming, reveal a keen interest in describing and demarcating native populations. According to Shin, the interest in demarcation reflects an evolution from an assimilationist policy to one of alliance as the Ming progressed.[105] The changing content of the Cili gazetteers may reflect this evolution in policy. As John Herman's work on Guizhou shows, in the sixteenth century non-native Ming officials textually incorporated subprefectural native domains into prefectural gazetteers, even when in fact such areas were controlled by indigenous rulers.[106] Emma Teng argues that in the Qing, such "entering the map" denoted incorporation into the empire.[107] Laura Hostetler shows that

102. *Pu'an zhou zhi*, 13a–b.
103. *Taiping fu zhi*, 161.
104. *Cili xian zhi*, 17.7a.
105. Shin, *Chinese State*, 1–3, 74.
106. Herman, "The Cant of Conquest," 148–49.
107. Teng, *Taiwan's Imagined Geography*, 3–46.

from the early to middle Qing, Guizhou gazetteers included increasingly detailed ethnographic descriptions of native peoples and documented more locales than did works compiled in the late Ming. This, she argues, reflects Qing officials' greater access as their colonization of Guizhou advanced.[108]

Because a gazetteer signified a place's membership in the Chinese world order, the lack thereof was an embarrassment to borderland residents who aspired to full participation in mainstream literati culture. In Liu Duan's preface to the 1513 gazetteer of Kuizhou 夔州, Sichuan, he explained that "Kuizhou should be famous, but in the past when people passed through and asked me whether there was a gazetteer and I responded, 'no,' they looked down on Kuizhou as a backward place." As the compiler of a 1550 gazetteer explained, "The gazetteer documents the prefecture and ties it to the state and realm."[109] From these cases we can see gazetteers as vehicles to promote Chinese culture and governance in zones of contact between Chinese and non-Chinese peoples.

MAHU, SICHUAN CASE STUDY

The previous examples concerned gazetteers initiated by nonlocal Chinese officials. But gazetteers also were compiled in native domains under the direction of native officials. This section analyzes the 1555 *Mahu fu zhi* 馬湖府志 and its previous edition, which was produced by Mahu's hereditary native ruling family. Mahu's prefectural town, now called Pingshan 屏山, is located on the border between Sichuan and Yunnan. Many of the area's people are now classified as members of the Yi minority 彝族. At the end of the Yuan dynasty (1368), Mahu was a route command governed by An Ji 安濟. The An family had controlled the Mahu area for a long time, although sources do not agree on how long. According to the *Ming shilu,* the Ans had ruled Mahu since the Tang (618–907), while a fifteenth-century stele stated that the Ans had ruled Mahu since the Han (206 BCE–220 CE).[110] In 1371 An Ji submitted to Ming rule

108.   Hostetler, *Qing Colonial Enterprise,* 127–57.
109.   *Guangping fu zhi,* prefaces, 4a–b.
110.   *Ming shilu, Xiaozong,* 1898; *Mahu fu zhi,* 3.2b–3b.

and a native prefecture was established. In return for formal submission, the Ans were granted hereditary rule as native prefects 土官知府.[111]

In 1495, however, the Ming central government rescinded the Ans' grant. The sixth An native prefect, An Ao 安鰲, was convicted of eight crimes punishable by death by slicing, twelve crimes punishable by decapitation, and three crimes punishable by strangulation. These included dismembering his father-in-law, dismembering another person to assist a sorcerer monk in calling forth a "nightmare demon" to kill his father-in-law's brother, raping his political opponents, digging up their family graves, burning down their houses, and so on. Following An Ao's execution, the central government used his violence as justification to convert the largely independent native prefecture into a regular unit of the Ming administrative structure headed by Chinese officials.[112]

During the An family's reign the prefecture produced at least one local gazetteer. Although no edition from the An period is extant, the first new local gazetteer after the change in governance, the 1555 *Mahu fu zhi*, comments on an earlier An family edition and includes records from the An gazetteer. This makes it possible to examine how the local gazetteer changed as the mode of government changed. As C. Patterson Giersch noted in his study of Qing Yunnan, in such "middle grounds" cultural practices were in flux.[113]

The preface to the 1555 gazetteer begins, "Mahu's old gazetteer records the An family's affairs in detail and with exaggeration; it is almost a genealogy. Thus, it is not worth reading." Assuming this characterization to be accurate, it raises the question: Why would the An family compile the prefectural gazetteer as if it were a genealogy? To answer this question, we should first look to Ming law governing succession in native domains.

Ming law required hereditary native officials to submit genealogical information to the central government to establish successors. After the Ming founding, succession for all native officials was handled by the Bureau of Honors 驗封司 in the Ministry of Personnel.[114] Late in the

---

111. *Mahu fu zhi*, 7.16.
112. *Ming shilu, Xiaozong*, 1895–98.
113. Giersch, *Asian Borderlands*, 7.
114. Li Dongyang and Shen Shixing, *Da Ming Huidian*, 31.

Hongwu period (1368–98), however, jurisdiction was split based on rank. Higher positions were placed under the Ministry of War, while lesser positions, such as the native prefects of Mahu, remained under the Bureau of Honors. In 1393 the court decreed that prior to succession of native officials in Huguang, Sichuan, Yunnan, and Guangxi, the Bureau of Honors had to verify that there was no competing successor, and ordered native officials to submit to the Ministry of Personnel "genealogical charts and texts" with reports.

Over time, more detail was required. A 1436 edict required native officials to report the names of sons and nephews who could succeed them. A 1441 edict required native officials to prepare four copies of a report listing their successors. The copies went to the three provincial offices (administration commission, surveillance commission and the regional military commission) and to the Ministry of Personnel for inspection. Thereafter the reports had to be revised every three years. Beginning in 1530 the reports also had to list all sons, grandsons, successors' ages, and birth mothers' names. Sonless native officials could wait until a son was born to submit a report, or list information on their younger brothers, nephews, and daughters.

As Leo Shin has pointed out, "One impact such rules and regulations had on native chieftains was the increased importance of genealogies."[115] He further notes that the above rules were not consistently enforced because "many chieftain families were too splintered to agree on a single genealogical chart." As a result, after a death contenders scrambled to present their own versions of the family tree.[116] The fact that genealogies established the right to rule in native domains provided a powerful incentive for native officials to disseminate their family histories, and gazetteers were an excellent place to do so. Gazetteers were public texts that became part of the stream of imperial history. Once compiled, they existed outside of the family and took on an air of authority. A gazetteer could not only list the family lines but also enhance descendants' legitimacy by describing ancestors' virtues. Chapter 2 will argue that some gazetteers from the Chinese core can be read as public genealogies of the local elite. What is different in the Mahu case is that legal requirements

<hr />

115.   Shin, *Chinese State*, 69–70.
116.   Ibid., citing Shen Defu, *Wanli yehuobian, bu yi*, 4.934.

regarding succession of native officials created an even stronger incentive to write the gazetteer as a genealogy.

The An family's documentation of their family history can be seen in records included in the new gazetteer. These records not only narrate the An lineage but also reveal how the Ans sought to shape the textual record to reflect their adherence to Chinese norms of good government. One such text is a 1474 record of the Eternal Life Abbey 萬壽觀. The document records An Ao's installation at the abbey of a statue of the Jade Emperor, the supreme ruler of Heaven in Chinese popular religion. The record begins by stating that Mahu had been governed by fifty-eight generations of the An family, beginning during the reign of Han Wudi (140–87 BCE). Regarding the installation it says, "Valuing this matter is valuing the god. Valuing the god is valuing the commoners 民. How could there be anything that unsettles them? This is why the prefect's descendants shall forever enjoy the fruits of this fief and not be despised or discarded." By using the term *min*, which contrasted registered taxpayers with unregistered natives who did not pay taxes, the author emphasized that An Ao was furthering the goals of the state. The record also described An Ao as "using Chinese forms to civilize barbarians and establish good governance."[117]

The desire of native officials to demonstrate Chinese-style good government in Chinese terms, as well as document their genealogies, can be understood in light of changing political organization in the southwestern borderlands over the course of the Ming. Shin argues that as the Ming progressed, native chieftains participated more in central government institutions and activities and that this "reflects an evolution of the organization of the borderlands peoples, from one based primarily on kinship ties to one based increasingly on political and military power."[118] While documenting kinship was clearly an important aspect of the An gazetteer, the Ans also used the gazetteer as a vehicle to reach out to Chinese elites. By playing to Chinese norms, the Ans sought to enhance their reputation with the Chinese officials who would have read the gazetteer, such as those in the provincial and central governments.

The 1555 *Mahu fu zhi* reflects the next phase of political organization, formal incorporation into the Chinese state as a regular territorial

117. *Mahu fu zhi*, 3.2b–3a.
118. Shin, *Chinese State*, 74.

unit. After An Ao's execution and the end of hereditary rule there was a gradual buildup of Chinese rule. However, the full arrival of Chinese-style government occurred only in the 1550s with Prefect Li Xingjian 李行簡, who constructed a yamen and compiled a "proper" gazetteer to replace the An edition.[119] Prefect Li spent the early years of his tenure constructing the prefectural town and making it "Chinese," and he used the later years to document his success. Prefect Li's gazetteer served to proclaim the arrival of Mahu as a Chinese place in the imaginations of the literati, and recounts the various ways in which he cleansed Mahu of the "An clan's vulgar practices."[120] For example, the An family lacked an appropriate yamen and conducted business at the native prefect's private residence. Chinese prefect Li constructed a fortified, 140-span government complex to proclaim the physical arrival of Chinese government. According to the preface, the native An regime lacked a city wall, but under the new Chinese regime there was a wall with a moat and locked gates to protect the people in times of crisis. The author concludes by saying the "gazetteer is like a gate tower on the wall; it is used to proclaim good governance."[121]

In so doing, the new gazetteer also minimized the An family's significance and denied the historicity of their ancient rule. The new gazetteer's table of administrators omitted everyone surnamed An prior to the Yuan dynasty and instead listed the various grand protectors 太守 of the Zangke 牂柯 Commandery, even though Zangke was well to the southeast of Mahu.

Conclusion

Gazetteers developed out of the earlier genre of map guides and over time became important vehicles for central government officials to learn about the empire. At various times in the Yuan, Ming, and Qing, the court initiated large-scale gazetteer compilation projects and issued rules

119. *Mahu fu zhi*, 2.4a.
120. Ibid., 2.2b–3b, 4.3b.
121. Ibid., Yu preface, 5a.

of compilation to shape the contents of the local gazetteers that served as the foundation for the comprehensive gazetteers. But as the number of educated people and locales in which they lived increased over the course of the Ming and Qing, initiative for compiling local gazetteers increasingly came from local people. Officials interested in statecraft promoted gazetteer production, not primarily for the value of the collected information to military campaigns or day-to-day administration, but rather because the projects themselves helped invigorate local literati culture, which was viewed as a key to strengthening the state after the "localist turn."

Gazetteers also spread the dominant Chinese written culture to non-Chinese or mixed regions that had not yet been "civilized." They served to bring lands at the margins of the Chinese cultural world into the imagined geography of the empire. Often they were the first substantial piece of Chinese literature produced in a formerly native domain, and their compilation could spur the growth of Chinese literary culture in a locale. The case of Mahu Prefecture shows that hereditary chieftains also compiled gazetteers and that such gazetteers related to the legitimacy of their rule. Such agendas can also be seen in gazetteers from Ming China's core, which will be discussed in chapter 2.

CHAPTER 2

Local Initiatives to Compile Gazetteers

In 1579 people in Xinchang 新昌, Zhejiang Province, were lobbying to get their ancestors' biographies included in Magistrate Tian Guan's 田琯 forthcoming county gazetteer. The project had become bogged down in bickering, so Tian turned for help to a retired minister of war, Xinchang native Lü Guangxun 呂光洵, and a group of prominent locals. Lü and the others quickly resolved the problems, and soon thereafter the gazetteer was published. The gazetteer's prefaces are unusually detailed and provide a list of editorial contributors. By examining the contributors' mutual relationships, the compilation process, the final product, and how it was received by readers, we can open windows not only on why locals compiled gazetteers but also on the meaning of kinship and the roles played by extended families in local society.

For social and economic historians of China, gazetteers are a familiar resource. We routinely glean facts from them, combine findings with related data from other sources, and analyze the sets in topical studies. But individual gazetteers as unified works receive less attention. This chapter examines editions of the *Xinchang xian zhi* 新昌縣志 (Xinchang County gazetteer) from 1477 and 1579 and argues that gazetteer sections often cannot be properly understood apart from their whole. Aggregating the genealogical information in gazetteer biographies and reading it together with genealogies from Xinchang reveals that the editors were members of a few densely intermarried lineage branches. The prefaces document this extended family's domination of the compilation process.

Viewing the gazetteer's construction and internal logic in conjunction with the editors' writings on genealogy further shows that the editorial committee's primary goal was to produce a "public genealogy" of their extended family. This genealogy was presented as a county gazetteer and superimposed on the materials typically found in the gazetteer genre.

The compilers' extended family consisted of the four Xinchang lineages that had been most successful in terms of official rank since the previous gazetteer's compilation in 1477, and of their maternal and affinal relatives. The 1579 edition records their mutual ties of marriage, discipleship, and community cooperation, and Magistrate Tian's successful administration. By monopolizing the biographical entries inserted into almost every gazetteer section and appending genealogical information to them, the compilers could publicly establish family lines and mark them as prestigious.

Lü patrilines, including those of gazetteer editor-in-chief Lü Guangxun, not only were described but also were textually combined into a higher-order descent group. Viewed through the genealogical lens, writing the gazetteer was a method for Xinchang's most successful men to enhance their legacies and build social cohesion among intermarried lineages. By recording their own and their relatives' virtues and publicly linking themselves to one another, the compilers defined a local elite and created a basis for continued cooperation and intermarriage among their descendants. As a unified work, the gazetteer tells us much more about the production of social status and the operation of family and local government in sixteenth-century Jiangnan than any individual section reveals about its subject matter.

Social status in late imperial China was gained in many ways. Scholars have long recognized examination success, literary cultivation, and lineage. Recent scholarship has added to this list. For example, Katherine Carlitz has shown how widow fidelity and ritual reform leadership brought prestige, and Craig Clunas notes that dwellings, graves, and gardens were parts of the "public landscape," entwined with social status, and were often described in genealogies and gazetteers.[1] This chapter will show how, in the case of one gazetteer, the compilers gathered numerous prestige markers into a single location, organized them around a

1. Carlitz, "Shrines"; Clunas, *Fruitful Sites*.

genealogical frame, and created a work that blurs the line between gazetteers and genealogies.

By understanding the gazetteer as the project of a cross-surname extended family and noting other projects undertaken by the same family members, we can hypothesize that elite extended family groups were key political actors at the county level, mediating between county officials and lineages that exercised authority at the village level. By comparing the 1477 *Xinchang xian zhi* to the 1579 edition, we also can postulate that the cross-surname extended family coalesced as fewer Xinchang lineages were producing exam graduates in the sixteenth century than in the fourteenth and fifteenth centuries. Examining the 1579 *Xinchang xian zhi* as an extended-family history demonstrates that documenting status in local society was an important motivation for compiling gazetteers. It also illustrates a research method for further studies in social and cultural history.

About Gazetteers and Genealogies

Sampling the same sections of multiple gazetteers is a valuable historical research method, but it does not exhaust gazetteers' potential value. Paying attention to the agendas that lay behind the compilations can lead to further insights. Such agendas likely varied by time and region. For example, as discussed in chapter 1, James Hargett argued that gazetteers were written as "scholarly monographs" beginning in the Southern Song. These not only collected administratively useful information but also served scholarly and community interests such as promoting the locale. Hargett further argued that beginning in the eleventh century, gazetteers served an educational purpose by presenting ideal models of behavior.[2] As also discussed in chapter 1, Peter Bol's study of local historiography in Jinhua explains that there was a resurgence of interest in Daoxue Neo-Confucianism among local officials and literati in late-fifteenth-century Jinhua and that the 1480 gazetteer "foregrounded their view of culture and government."[3] Timothy Brook, in his study of Yuan

---

2. Hargett, "Song Dynasty Local Gazetteers," 420–25, 431.
3. Bol, "Rise of Local History," 50.

dynasty local gazetteers, argued that the "impetus for writing a local gazetteer was to enhance the reputation of the place or institution being chronicled."[4] This chapter will explore another agenda for writing a gazetteer: creating a public genealogy of the compilers' extended family. By "genealogy" I mean both textual expression of a construct of kinship through recording the relationships between selected family members, and family history in a broader sense including descriptions of ancestors' lives, residences, graves, accomplishments, and status.

Scholars have documented several motivations for compiling genealogies, some internal to the descent group and some oriented toward a public. For example, Robert Hymes related Southern Song and Yuan genealogy writing to the building of local power bases, and Johanna Meskill argued that late-nineteenth- and early-twentieth-century first-edition genealogies could be used to create an organized kinship group rather than reflect a preexisting group.[5] Harriet Zurndorfer and Keith Hazelton have both noted that Huizhou genealogies had a public audience: Zurndorfer argued that late-Yuan and Ming dynasty Huizhou composite genealogies evidenced a conscious procedure to ensure the included descent groups' continued survival and status.[6] In fourteenth-century Huizhou, status derived from lineage as much as officeholding or wealth and the "records of great lineages" (*dazuzhi* 大族志) and "records of famous lineages" (*mingzuzhi* 名族志) publicly documented the leading lineages. Hazelton, studying sixteenth-century Huizhou, noted that because genealogy writing had an increasingly public nature and was strongly associated with officeholders, it should be understood as a way to consolidate gains won through the prestige of an official career.[7]

Other scholars have pointed to practical uses of genealogy that stem from acceptance of a common history. Ueda Makoto's study of local society in Zhuji 諸暨, Zhejiang, from the fourteenth to nineteenth centuries argued that family history in late imperial China was constructed and recognized as being needed to advance specific family goals and

4. Brook, "Native Identity," 237.
5. Hymes, "Marriage, Descent Groups," 122–23; Meskill, "The Chinese Genealogy," 141.
6. Zurndorfer, "The *Hsin-an ta-tsu chih*," 156, 212–13.
7. Hazelton, "Patrilines," 151, 163.

interests.[8] Ueda described two lineages that were related through the fourteenth-century uxorilocal marriage of one lineage's first-migrant ancestor, and reciprocal adoptions in the first generations. This ancestral connection was largely ignored until the nineteenth century when one lineage needed an ally in a struggle over water rights. The common ancestry again became "acknowledged history" (*ninshikisareta rekishi* 認識された歴史) by including the story in a genealogy.[9]

David Faure looks upon lineage as a flexible cultural form that served economic and political ends, and genealogies as constructions of agreed-upon lineage history.[10] Sometimes these histories were based upon fictions of common ancestry and were used to confer important rights within a village, such as the right to build a house, exploit natural resources, or enter into cooperative projects with people having the same surname.[11]

Although one can imagine that agendas for genealogy writing might be relevant to gazetteer writing, gazetteers are treated as a genre distinct from genealogies and have not been examined either as tools of family or social organization or as documents that legitimate rights in local society. The most obvious such right would be a hereditary right to lead, as seen in the case of Mahu Prefecture in chapter 1. A few scholars have noted areas where the genres intersect. For example, Melvin Thatcher observed that since the time of Zhang Xuecheng 張學誠 (1738–1801), late imperial China's best-known theorist of local gazetteers, some gazetteers have included genealogical sections.[12] Zhang argued for a four-tiered nested hierarchy of historical works: individual collected works, family histories, local histories, and dynastic histories. But the deep connection between genealogies and gazetteers predates Zhang Xuecheng by centuries.

In the late fifteenth century, it became increasingly common to begin a gazetteer preface by drawing an analogy between local gazetteers, genealogies, and state histories. This trend coincided in time with an

8. Ueda, "Chūgoku no chiiki," 58–65.
9. Ibid., 65.
10. Faure, "Lineage as Cultural Invention," 6–8, 28.
11. Ibid., 24.
12. Thatcher, "Local Historical Sources," 421. Also see Nivison, *Chang Hsüeh-ch'eng*.

intensification of lineage organization and genealogy compilation. What the authors meant by their analogies varied. Some argued that they were all histories, but on different scales, while others linked all three to identity formation.[13] The magistrate of Lueyang 略陽, Shaanxi, began his postface to the 1552 gazetteer by writing, "A gazetteer is to a locale what a history is to a state, and a genealogy is to a family. Without a history, how can we consider it to be a state? Without a genealogy, how can we consider it a family? Without a gazetteer, how can we consider it a locale?"[14] In other words, the texts helped define the subject.

Donald Leslie and Otto Berkelbach van der Sprenkel suggested that gazetteer biographies be used in conjunction with genealogies to construct family histories and study interlineage relations, and Pan Guangdan conducted such a study.[15] Liang Hongsheng has reported on village gazetteers published since the 1980s that are thinly disguised lineage genealogies published in gazetteer format as a way to avoid government concerns about genealogies and their role in promoting cohesion among extended families that could challenge state power.[16] These scholars have shown genealogy to be a distinct section of some gazetteers, gazetteers to be a supplemental tool for studying family history, and the gazetteer format being used as cover for publishing genealogies in villages dominated by a single lineage. What the 1579 *Xinchang xian zhi* adds to the picture is that extended-family genealogy could be the central organizing principle of a county gazetteer.

In thinking about genealogies and gazetteers as genres, we should be alert to the adaptable natures of both and pay attention to how a close reading of a work can give clues about the milieu in which it was produced. The 1579 *Xinchang xian zhi*, read as a whole, gives many such clues

---

13. *Lingshi xian zhi*, preface, 1a; *Yingshan xian zhi* (1576), preface, 1a; *Yongping fu zhi*, preface, 3b.

14. *Lüeyang xian zhi*, Li Yuchun preface, 1a.

15. Leslie, Mackerras, and Wang, *Essays on the Sources*, 73; van der Sprenkel, *Legal Institutions*, 97; van der Sprenkel, "Genealogical Registers"; Pan Guangdan, *Ming-Qing liangdai*.

16. Liang, "Pudie yu xinzhi," 339–48. One example of a genealogy compiled as a village gazetteer is the 1995 *Fushi zhi*. It covers many of the topics found in typical local gazetteers, but it is largely a history of the Zhao lineage.

about the nature and operation of kinship, the structure of power in local society, and the role of family in the Chinese imperial state, as well as
agendas for writing gazetteers.

The Politics of Compilation

In 1571 Zhang Yuanbian 張元忭 and Tian Guan passed the *jinshi* exam,
Zhang as optimus and Tian in the third tier.[17] While Zhang's early career
was in the capital, Tian went to Zhang's native place, Shaoxing Prefecture
紹興府, becoming magistrate of Xinchang County in 1574 (map 2.1).[18]

After arriving in Xinchang, Tian became friends with Lü Guangxun,
a colleague of Zhang Yuanbian's father, Zhang Tianfu 張天復. Lü and
the elder Zhang had fought insurgents together in Yunnan and both had
suffered for it.[19] In 1568 Zhang Tianfu was deprived of rank after the
government's defeat at Wuding, and Zhang Yuanbian spent the rest of
his life trying to restore his father's name.[20] Lü, meanwhile, was criticized and transferred from his post as minister of war in Beijing to minister of works in Nanjing.[21] Soon thereafter he retired to Xinchang,
where he wrote extensively and enjoyed his garden until his death in
1580.[22] Zhang Tianfu lived until 1578 and with Yuanbian was involved in
compiling gazetteers for Shaoxing's urban counties, Shanyin 山陰 and
Guiji 會稽.[23] Yuanbian also edited the 1587 *Shaoxing fu zhi* 紹興府志
(Shaoxing Prefecture gazetteer).[24]

In addition to Lü Guangxun, Magistrate Tian befriended other officials from Xinchang, including Lü Ruoyu 呂若愚, Guangxun's lineage
branch grandnephew, who served as Equipment and Communications

17.   Tian placed 123rd out of 396. Zhu Baojiong and Xie Peilin, *Ming-Qing jinshi*,
vol. 3, 2554–55.
18.   *XCXZ* (1919), 955.
19.   *Shaoxing fu zhi* (1587), 2886.
20.   *DMB*, 110.
21.   Lin Zhisheng, *Huang Ming ying shi*, 57, 266.
22.   *DMB*, 501–2; *XCXZ* (1579), 3.21b–22b.
23.   *DMB*, 110; *XCXZ* (1579), postfaces, 5a; *Guiji xian zhi*.
24.   *DMB*, 110.

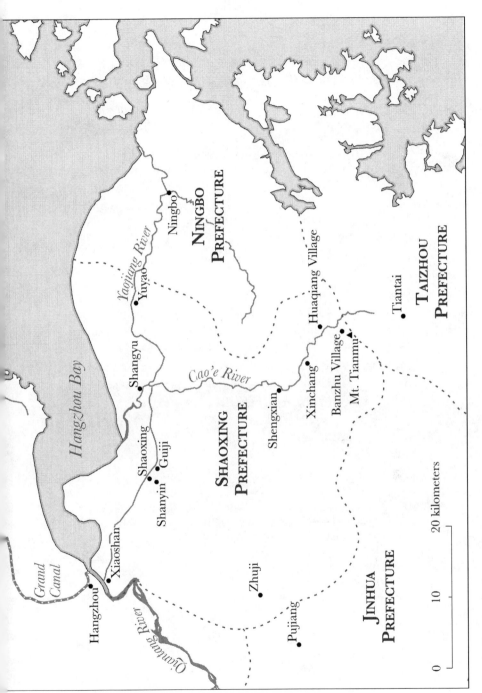

MAP 2.1 Shaoxing Prefecture

Bureau director in the Nanjing Ministry of War, and Pan Sheng 潘晟, who was temporarily out of office.[25] Pan had served as minister of rites in 1570–72 and would return to his position in 1578, shortly before the *Xinchang xian zhi* was published. Together, Magistrate Tian and the three officials traveled to local scenic spots and had "numerous and wide-ranging discussions."[26]

One year into his term Magistrate Tian decided to compile a new edition of the county gazetteer and to that end began reviewing and editing documents collected by former officials. In the spring of 1578 he presented his plan to the Zhejiang supreme commander and education intendant and was ordered to proceed. The local Confucian school instructor and two assistant instructors helped Magistrate Tian choose a six-person editorial committee, including Lü Guangxun as editor-in-chief and thirty-six researchers from among the county's government students.[27]

Magistrate Tian hired Zhang Yuanyi 張元益, a native of nearby Shanyin and disciple of Lü Guangxun's friend Tang Shunzhi 唐順之, to draft and polish the manuscript.[28] Pan Sheng and Lü Ruoyu critiqued and verified biographies.[29] Altogether, forty-six named individuals would be involved in the collecting, drafting, and editing process. Seven officials and subofficials played purely administrative roles, and Shaoxing prefect Jia Yingbi 賈應璧 wrote a preface.[30]

---

25. *XCXZ* (1579), 10.15b.

26. Ibid., prefaces, 16b.

27. Ibid., prefaces, 12b–13a, 16b, 17a–b; postfaces, 2a–b.

28. Ibid., prefaces, 17b. *Shanyin Baiyutan Zhang Shi*, ed. Zhang Yuanshu, genealogy descent chart biography of Zhang Yuanyi (unpaginated). Tang Shunzhi, *Jingchuan Xiansheng wen ji*, vol. 4, 6.6; vol. 6, 9.18–21, 9.27–29; vol. 10, 16.34–37. Zhang Yuanyi's relationship to Zhang Yuanbian is unclear. Both are from Shanyin, and they have the same surname and first character of their given names, but Yuanbian is not listed in Yuanyi's 1628 lineage branch genealogy.

29. *XCXZ* (1579), prefaces, 18a.

30. The seven men were: The supreme commander and the education intendant who ordered the compilation, the Confucian school instructor and two assistant instructors involved in selecting the editorial committee and materials collectors, and the vice magistrate and clerk who supervised the block cutting and printing. Ibid., prefaces, 18a–b.

The editorial committee and Zhang Yuanyi set up an office to examine the collected materials.[31] Pan Sheng established the gazetteer's categories, and the compilers began working on sections about Xinchang's geography, products, officials, and civil service examination.[32] The magistrate organized and wrote introductions to the various sections, and Zhang Yuanyi produced a partial first draft. All that remained were the biographical chapters, and at that point the process became difficult. Magistrate Tian described the scene: "How is one to deal with the county's literati and commoners who clamor to boast of their grandfathers and seek the inclusion of encomia, or who obtain false praise from literary figures, or who apply pressure with the help of powerful officials or family connections, or who jostle to come before me and give flattering responses to my questions, but then tell a different story after my back is turned?"[33] Magistrate Tian explained that the editing process stalled "because it was still the custom to falsify and exaggerate, true and false clashed and it was difficult for the appointed gentry to reconcile [their claims]."[34] Arguments ensued. As editor-in-chief Lü Guangxun explained to Zhang Yuanyi:

> Why is it that although our county's taxes are nowhere near [as high] as those of Shanyin and Guiji, our affairs are in greater disorder? It is because we have distanced ourselves from the past's virtuous customs. Our group likes to argue. Arguing, we cannot reach agreement; not reaching agreement, everyone is necessarily angry; anger breeds slander, and it is indeed difficult to save the situation. I now fear our gazetteer cannot be finished.[35]

Zhang Yuanyi described his reaction to Lü's statement:

> When I heard the Minister of War, I was upset. I examined his words in light of everyone's mood and indeed it was as he said. In discussing borders,

31. Ibid., prefaces, 12b.
32. Ibid., prefaces, 4b–5b, 13a.
33. *XCXZ* (1579), prefaces, 12b–13a.
34. Ibid., prefaces, 17b.
35. Ibid., postfaces, 5b.

they argue [the districts] of Tai versus Shan.[36] In discussing chronology, they argue Song versus Yuan. In discussing civil service examinations, they argue vacuity versus substance. In discussing the term "surname," they argue which character should come first, "*shi* 氏" or "*xing* 姓." In discussing scenic sights, they argue commemorative inscriptions versus narrations. In discussing social status, they argue number one versus number two. In discussing historic residences, they argue tablets versus plaques. In discussing predecessors' graves, they argue epitaphs versus memorials. In discussing dynasties, they argue projected power versus actual accomplishment. In discussing agriculture, they argue [the schools of] "wealth studies" (*fuxue* 富學) versus "success writings" (*gongwen* 攻文). In discussing womanly virtue they argue for [women like] Mencius's mother, and those who do not, argue for [women like] Gong Jiang 共姜.[37] If one example is raised, they argue over one. If one hundred examples are raised, they argue over one hundred. Without exception it is so, and thus the Minister of War said, "Arguing we cannot reach agreement . . . Will this gazetteer ever be finished?"[38]

After a month spent discussing the draft, the compilers could not overcome their differences and Zhang Yuanyi sought the magistrate's permission to quit, asking, "How can I end their quarrels and calm their anger?"[39] The magistrate reassured Zhang, who agreed to stay. Prefect Jia Yingbi also visited Magistrate Tian, reviewed the collected documents, and again explained the order to compile a gazetteer.[40] This led Magistrate Tian to take personal charge and he ordered a new draft, assigning some people to the initial drafting, some to discussion, and some to revision.[41] Magistrate Tian obtained the biographical materials from Lü Guangxun and had them checked and corrected by Lü Guanghua 呂光化, Guangxun's lineage cousin descended from Guangxun's great-

---

36.   Tai and Shan are literary names for the areas from which Xinchang County was carved out as a new administrative unit in the Liang dynasty Kaiping reign (907–10).

37.   Mencius's mother epitomized the role of mothers as educators of sons; Gong Jiang personified widow chastity.

38.   Zhang Yuanyi, *XCXZ* (1579), postfaces, 5b–6a.

39.   Ibid., 6a.

40.   *XCXZ* (1579), prefaces, 17b.

41.   Ibid., prefaces, 17b, postfaces, 6b.

great-grandfather.[42] According to the 1587 *Shaoxing fu zhi*, most biographies were written by Lü Guangxun.[43]

Many were abridged genealogy biographies. For example, an untitled gazetteer biography of two virtuous women is an abridged version of Pan Sheng's *Shuang jiefu zhuan* 雙節婦傳 (Biography of two virtuous women), which appears in the *Nanming Zhang Shi zongpu* 南明張氏宗譜 (Genealogy of the Nanming Zhang lineage).[44] In the gazetteer there is no mention of the story's origin, but the genealogy version states that a Zhang told the story to Pan Sheng, who wrote it down. The original biography was 319 characters long, while the gazetteer version was just 89, a reduction of 72 percent. The editors cut some parts, summarized others, eliminated grammatical particles and long titles, but retained keys words and phrases.

Lü Guangxun, Lü Guanghua, Pan Sheng, and Lü Ruoyu critiqued and verified the biographies by comparing them to Zhang Yuanyi's materials. Lü Jiru 呂繼儒 then worked behind the yamen's main hall to compare the two drafts and verify that names were accurate and dates correct. Two other government students did proofreading. Magistrate Tian further edited the materials and prodded the students to copy over narrations of old events and to "arrange and verify that new items had no private purpose."[45]

When the new draft was complete, Magistrate Tian "solicited corrections from the men of the countryside and the scholars of the city." All said the draft was accurate. Tian then polished it a bit more, hired craftsmen to cut printing blocks, and divided supervisory authority between the vice magistrate and clerk. According to Tian, "the scholars were happy at the county chronicle's continuation and joined in to complete the work."[46]

---

42. Ibid., prefaces, 18a.

43. *Shaoxing fu zhi* (1587), 3339.

44. *XCXZ* (1579), 12.5b–6a; Pan Sheng, n.d., "Shuang jiefu zhuan" 雙節婦傳, in *Nanming Zhang Shi*, 21a–b.

45. *XCXZ* (1579), prefaces, 18a.

46. Ibid., prefaces, 18a–b.

Claims of Historical Accuracy

Magistrate Tian's commendation mattered because local history writing was a contested process that could result in recriminations and editors needed to protect themselves. A handwritten anecdote appended to the National Central Library's imprint of the 1539 gazetteer of Changshu 常熟, Nanzhili, suggests that compiling a gazetteer not only involved political risk but could even endanger one's life. It states that the compiler, Deng Fu 鄧韍, was pressured by a vice censor-in-chief to change his draft and had to seek support of the grand coordinator and regional inspector. He also left out two chaste widows, with unfortunate consequences: "In his old age Fu, while walking alone in the market, was greeted at the side of the road by the two [widows], who were wearing mourning clothes. They said, 'Master, what made you think we were not chaste? Please ask the dead.' This horrified Fu and caused him to sicken and die."[47]

To preempt such criticism, the 1579 *Xinchang xian zhi* editors made a concerted effort to present the gazetteer as a model of historical integrity. As Magistrate Tian explained: "Gazetteers are nonetheless histories and thus that which was not of a public nature was not made central, that which had not been verified was not included."[48] Tian continued:

> Nevertheless, I was filled with trepidation. Confucius was a sage but in writing the *Spring and Autumn Annals* he still worried that others would criticize him. How much the more [was I concerned] for I am not even the Sage's disciple and have no special talent! At the time that Mo Dan 莫旦 compiled the [Xinchang] gazetteer in the Chenghua era [1465–88], all of the scholars praised it as well documented, but ever since some have criticized it for "conspiring to gain through the written word." I was afraid this [might happen again]. Therefore, I solicited numerous famous officials and outstanding scholars to consider as a group the pros and cons, verify what was extant and lost, and decide what to include and exclude. From [the gazetteer's] beginning to end there were no mistakes. If you

47. *Changshu xian zhi*, inside back cover. Also see Feng Fujing, *Ming Changshu xian xian*, 159–61.

48. *XCXZ* (1579), prefaces, 17b.

gentlemen have anything you wish to affirm or refute, be diligent and raise it now for public discussion and judgment. Do not be like those who criticized Mo's gazetteer one hundred years after [its completion]. This is good. This is good.

Zhang Yuanyi proclaimed that the compilers' "judgments were as accurate as those of the *Zuo Commentary* and the *Records of the Historian* and their records were as systematic as those of Sima Qian," that "those of today will trust [the gazetteer], those of tomorrow will transmit it," and that "in my view, readers of this gazetteer should not call it 'Xinchang County's gazetteer,' rather they should call it 'Xinchang County's *Rites of Zhou*.' They should not call it 'one county's little history,' rather they should call it 'one county's *Spring and Autumn Annals*.' "[49]

Pan Sheng noted in his preface that the ruler's knowledge of the realm necessarily starts from local gazetteers and thus "county gazetteers must not be one family or one township's private history."[50] Pan declared the gazetteer to be carefully researched and "refined to the point that it became the words of a single school.[51] It may supplement what was left out of the dynastic histories in order to complete the Sagely Emperor's selections; how could it merely be a case of one family or one township's private servants building a hodgepodge house on the side of the road?!"[52]

Avenues of Influence

The editors' loud protestations of integrity invite us to ask whether the gazetteer was precisely what Pan Sheng said it was not: one family or one township's private history. By comparing the 1579 gazetteer to the preceding edition published in 1477, we can see a process of consolidation of family power in Xinchang that created opportunities to shape the

49.　Ibid., postfaces, 7a–b.

50.　Ibid., prefaces, 8b–9a.

51.　The phrase "words of a single school" alludes to the *Han shu* 漢書 (Record of the Han) biography of the historian Sima Qian.

52.　*XCXZ* (1579), prefaces, 10b.

gazetteer's content. The process was already under way by 1477, but by 1579 power had become highly concentrated. Two places to look for mechanisms by which the power holders could exercise undue influence on the gazetteer are the project's finances and the compilers' relationships with one another.

Magistrate Tian did not say how he paid for the block cutting and printing, but as will be shown in chapter 5, gazetteers were often financed with donations by locals and resident officials. The money for printing the 1477 *Xinchang xian zhi* came from a fundraising drive initiated by the magistrate's and prefect's personal donations and filled out with local donations.[53] Thereafter, "donations of silver came like swarming ants, contributions like a bubbling spring. Small donors did not mind giving one or two coins; large donations did not exceed five or ten piculs of grain."[54] Genealogies show that most—and probably all— donors other than the resident administrators were local.

Donations may have influenced content. The 1477 gazetteer lists by style name seventy-four donors who had twenty different surnames.[55] Many were members of the same lineages, and people from those lineages are the subject matter of a large percentage of the gazetteer's biographies. Of the twelve donors surnamed Lü, seven are listed in the *Lü Shi zongpu* 呂氏宗譜 (Lü lineage genealogy) as belonging to a single lineage branch, and four of the five others likely were as well, based on the lineage's naming patterns for style names.[56] Likewise, for the eleven donors surnamed Yu, three were first cousins and the style names of seven of the other eight correspond to the same lineage's style-name pattern.[57] These Lü and Yu lineage branches were the same ones involved in compiling the 1579 gazetteer. Comparing the subjects of the gazetteer entries to the donor list, one finds a rough correspondence. For example, fifteen of the sixteen surnames listed in the 1477 gazetteer's lineages section are among the twenty donor surnames. More than one-third of the donors

53. *XCXZ* (1477), preface, 2a–b, Li Ji postface, 1b.
54. Ibid., preface, 2a–b.
55. Ibid.
56. *Lü Shi zongpu*, You 友 and Mu 睦 branches (*LSZP-YM*).
57. Yu Shuxing 叔行, Shu'an 叔安, and Shuguang 叔光. *Yu shi Xizhai Shide*, 3.2a–b. Six donors' style names began with Ting 廷 or Yong 用, which were used in the Yu lineage's twenty-fourth and twenty-fifth generations. *YSJA, juan* 4.

had one of the three surnames listed first in the lineages section—Shi 石, Lü 吕, and Yu 俞.[58]

Entries in the 1579 gazetteer reflect changes in the lineages that had examination success after the 1477 gazetteer's publication, including the decline of the Shi lineage.[59] In the century prior, more lineages shared in examination success than in the century after. From the Ming founding in 1368 through 1477, people surnamed Lü, Pan, Yu, and He 何 had official success, but others did too. Only 8 of 19 Xinchang *jinshi* were surnamed Lü, Yu, Pan, or He. But from 1478 to 1579, these surnames' share increased to 13 out of 14.[60] Likewise, in the earlier period they had only 19 of 51 *juren*, but in the later period 19 of 25. The count for tribute students went from 10 of 85, to 37 of 63.[61] In the earlier period, 14 different surnames were represented on the list of *jinshi*, while in the later, there were just 4. For *juren*, the number of surnames dropped from 22 to 8; and for tribute students from 25 to 14.

Not only had the Lü, Pan, Yu, and He lineages produced the most degrees after 1477, they also had produced the highest-ranking officials: He Jian 鑑 (1442–1522) was minister of war, Yu Zhenqiang 振強 (1470–1540) was vice director of the Ministry of Works, Yu Chaotuo 朝妥 (1488–1539) was supervising censor in the Office of Scrutiny for Rites, and Yu Zequan 則全 (1509–72) was an investigating censor.[62] Lü Guangxun and Pan Sheng had risen higher in the Ming bureaucracy than any other living Xinchang men.[63] In fact, their positions were so high that none of their descendants was likely to surpass them. Thus,

58. *XCXZ* (1477), 11.

59. Totals are given by surname because some people cannot be definitively placed in a particular lineage from available sources. However, for members of the Xinchang local elite, the 1477 and 1579 gazetteers equate surname and lineage.

60. The list of Ming *jinshi* in the 1579 *XCXZ* appears to be accurate. All listed *jinshi* also appeared on the *timing beilu*. Zhu Baojiong and Xie Peilin, eds. *Ming-Qing jinshi*. Searchable databases did not reveal any omitted Xinchang *jinshi* and *juren*.

61. *XCXZ* (1579), *juan* 10.

62. Yu Jingming, "Wufeng Yu shi," 92–93; *XCXZ* (1994), 667.

63. I am not counting retired grand secretary Lü Ben, who was known as Li Ben until he changed his surname to Lü in 1570. Lü Ben, who was registered in nearby Yuyao County, "recovered" his surname after he retired from office, claiming that he actually was a member of Lü Guangxun's lineage. See Dennis, "Mingdai daxueshi Li Ben."

with Lü in retirement and fast approaching his death in 1580, and Pan serving as minister of rites, 1579 was an opportune time for them to shape their legacies by compiling a gazetteer.

The contributors' family relationships can be reconstructed from the gazetteer itself, by consulting Xinchang genealogies and by using Xinchang lineage naming practices.[64] Doing so shows that most, and possibly all, forty-six contributors except for Magistrate Tian and Zhang Yuanyi were related by blood and/or marriage.

Eight Xinchang people played key roles in compiling the 1579 gazetteer: the six-person editorial committee consisting of Lü Guangxun, his brother Lü Guangyan 光演, Lü Guanghua, He Jiong 絅, He Chang 裳, and Yu Bangshi 邦時, plus Lü Ruoyu and Pan Sheng, who critiqued and verified the biographies.[65] All eight were relatives. The four Lüs were members of a single lineage branch and were related to the other four by marriage: Lü Guangxun's third daughter married Pan Sheng's eldest son, Lü Guangxun's brother Guangbi 光泌 married Pan Sheng's cousin, Guangbi's daughter married He Chang's son.[66] Lü Ruoyu married He Chang's first cousin's granddaughter and He Chang himself married a Lady Lü.[67]

Committee member He Jiong was in the same lineage branch as He Chang; their common ancestor was He Chang's great-great-grandfather.[68] He Jiong also married a Lü woman, and their eldest daughter was Pan Sheng's first wife.[69] Two of He Jiong's three daughters and his eldest sister married men of Lü Guangxun's lineage branch, and He Jiong's mother was born in committee member Yu Bangshi's lineage branch.[70]

---

64. Lineages in Ming China often had all members of the same generation use the same character or radical in their given names.

65. *XCXZ* (1579), prefaces, 14a.

66. *LSZP-YM*. The Xinchang Lü lineage originally had six branches, each descended from a grandson of the Xinchang Lü first ancestor, Lü Yi, who came to Xinchang in the Song dynasty. By the time of the Ming, only three branches remained. Zhang Yuanbian, "Wozhou Lü Gong," 4.5a; Lü Ben, "Guanglusi shucheng," 4.17a; *HSZP*, 4.14b.

67. Lü Ben, "Guanglusi shucheng," 4.11b–14b.

68. Ibid., *juan* 4.

69. Ibid., 4.34a. The daughter (Pan Sheng's first wife) had died by the time the gazetteer was published. *XCXZ* (1579), 2.11a.

70. *HSZP*, 4.33b–34a; *LSZP-YM*, 7.96–102. Lü Yingkui 應奎, who married He Jiong's second daughter, descended from Lü Guangxun's great-grandfather. Lü Mengyan 夢言, who married He Jiong's fourth daughter, and Lü Guangjin, who married He

Yu Bangshi's lineage branch also had intermarried with Lü Guangxun's lineage branch for generations.[71] Yu's cousin married Lü Guangxun's brother Guanglong 光瀧 and Yu's second sister married Lü Guangxun's cousin.[72] Yu's eldest sister married Pan Xianchen 憲臣, who, based on his name, likely was Pan Sheng's lineage great-uncle.[73] Pan Sheng's second wife was surnamed Yu. Yu Bangshi and Lü Guangxun had been friends since their youth, and the *jinshi* Lü Nai 鼐, Lü Guangxun's lineage uncle, married a Yu woman and taught Yu Bangshi's father, the *jinshi* Yu Zhenqiang.[74]

Looking at all contributors' family relationships makes it even more clear that they were an extended family composed of paternal, maternal, and affinal relatives. Of the forty-six contributors, thirty-three were from a few branches of the Lü, Pan, Yu, or He lineages, and most were also related through their maternal lines and by marriage.[75] Twelve of the fifteen contributors surnamed Lü were descended from Lü Guangxun's great-great-grandfather. In addition to editorial committee members Guangxun, Guangyan, and Guanghua, these included Guangyan and Guanghua's sons, Guangxun and Guangyan's nephew, two cousins, and four grandnephews.[76]

Jiong's sister, both descended from Lü Guangxun's great-great-grandfather. *HSZP*, 4.33a; *YSJA, juan shou*, 8; *Yu shi Xizhai Shide*, 3.1a.

71. *LSZP-YM*; *YSJA*.

72. Yu's cousin, the granddaughter of Yu Zhengming, married Lü Guanglong. *LSZP-YM*, 3.129a; 7.104a; *YSJA*, 4. Yu's sister married Lü Yunjin. *YSJA, juan shou*.22a; *LSZP-YM*, 7.90a.

73. *YSJA*, 22a; Pan Biaohui, "Unpublished notes."

74. *YSJA*, 16a, 26a–b.

75. Contributor He Jiugong 九功 was He Jiong's nephew, and both descended from He Jiong's grandfather, Minister of War He Jian. Jiugong's granddaughter married Lü Guangxun's grandson Chenglin. *XCXZ* (1919), 1280. Lü Guangxun's son-in-law, He Jiuwan 九萬, also was He Jian's great-grandson. *HSZP*, 4.35a. Yu Banghu's daughter's son married Pan Sheng's nephew's daughter. *XCXZ* (1919), 1291. Lü Guangyan married Yu Zhi 治, granddaughter of Vice Minister of Rites Yu Qin. *LSZP-YM*, 4.13. The mother of Lü Guangxun's nephew, the contributor Mingtai, was surnamed Pan. *LSZP-YM*, 4.28. His son married the niece of contributor Yu Yingshan. *LSZP-YM*, 4.27; *YSJA*, 4.24b. Lü Jipian's daughter married Pan Sheng's grandnephew, his son Tiankuang married He Jian's great-granddaughter, his granddaughter married He Jian's great-great-grandson. *LSZP-YM*, 4.43–45

76. *LSZP-YM, juan* 4.

The remaining three Lüs were descended from Guangxun's sixth-generation ancestor and were the great-grandsons of the Xinchang *jinshi* Lü Xian 獻.[77] Lü Jiru 繼儒 and Jiqiao 繼橋 were first cousins, and Jipian 繼梗 was their second cousin.[78] Jiru's mother, and Jiru and Jipian's paternal grandmother were both surnamed Yu. Jiqiao's mother was the *jinshi* Yu Qin's 欽 granddaughter.[79]

The six contributors surnamed Pan included Pan Sheng, his brother, and his father's brother.[80] As for the remaining three, based on naming patterns it is probable that one was Pan Sheng's cousin and that two were Pan Sheng's nephews.

The eight contributors surnamed Yu were members of the same lineage branch.[81] Yu Bangshao 邦詔 was committee member Bangshi's brother and Banghu's cousin; Binghu 秉瑚 was father of Yingsu 應肅, lineage uncle of Yingshan 應山, and cousin of Bingzhong 秉中.[82]

Most, and possibly all, of the eleven contributors to the gazetteer who were not surnamed Lü, Yu, Pan, or He were related to them and to each other.[83] In sum, most, and possibly all, forty-six gazetteer contributors, except for Magistrate Tian and Zhang Yuanyi, were related by blood and/or marriage.

Elite endogamy within the county was the norm in fifteenth- and sixteenth-century Xinchang, and even national-level figures like Lü Guangxun and Pan Sheng married locally. The 1477 and 1579 gazetteers both stated that members of "old families and ancient clans" married

---

77. Ibid., 4.40.
78. *Lü Shi zongpu, Xu*, 7.41b–43b.
79. Ibid., 7.43a.
80. Pan Biaohui, "Unpublished notes."
81. The Xinchang Yu shared a common Tang dynasty ancestor then split into three branches. The gazetteer compilers surnamed Yu are all from the Jing'an Fang branch. Yu, "Wufeng Yu Shi," 86–106.
82. *YSJA, juan shou*.22a, 1.9b.
83. Dennis, "Between Lineage and State," 82; *Nanming Zhang Shi*, 66a–71b. Lü Guangxun's fourth daughter married Chen Shibin 陳世彬, son of Chen Zicheng 子誠. *LSZP-YM*, 4.5. Contributor Yu Banghu's daughter married Chen Shizhang 世彰, who probably was a brother or cousin of Shibin. *XCXZ* (1919), 1291. The daughter of Lü Guangxun's maternal cousin Zhang Jingchuang 章景床 married Chen Zice 陳子策. "He Yunfeng Gong ji Liang Anren liuxun shuangshou xu" 賀雲峰公暨梁安人六旬雙壽序, in *Xinchang Banzhu Zhang Shi*, unnumbered.

only those of equal status and did not marry those from wealthy but lower-status families.[84] "Old families and ancient clans" were defined as "those having a genealogy that proves the family's continuity of official rank."[85]

The 1579 gazetteer does not list families that had such genealogies, but the graves (*fenmu* 墳墓) section implies a list (fig. 2.1). The graves section is composed of thirty subsections, each titled with a surname, and a final section labeled "various surnames."[86] Each surname's section lists the first-migrant ancestor. If a surname had multiple descent groups, the graves section distinguishes by both locality and ancestor. When people who shared a common ancestor resided in separate localities within the county, the graves section named the person who moved to the new locale. For example, the Zhang 章 subsection states that the surname's first-migrant ancestor was Zhang Mu 木, who moved from Fujian to Xinchang's Huaqiang Village 花牆村 in the Shaoxing period of the Song Dynasty (1131–63), and that the Banzhu 班竹 Zhangs descended from Zhang Yao 耀, who moved from Huaqiang to Banzhu later in the Song. Such information most likely came from genealogies, and its specification in the gazetteer created a rough county genealogical map. All thirty of the listed surname groups had produced Ming officials prior to the gazetteer's publication, and they are listed in an order that appears to combine the number and rank of officials having that surname.

The graves section surname order implies a social ranking based on examination and official success, particularly since the publication of the 1477 gazetteer. First is the surname Shi. According to the gazetteer, Xinchang County had 47 *jinshi* surnamed Shi during the Song and early Ming, making it by far the dominant lineage in those periods. Second is Lü, with 28. Third is Yu, with 14. Fourth is Pan with 5, including Minister of Rites Pan Sheng. Fifth is He with 2, including Minister of War He Jian.

Extant Xinchang genealogy descent charts, biographies, and prefaces confirm the endogamous marriage pattern described in the gazetteers. Lü Guangxun's lineage branch genealogy and Lü Guangxun's wife's natal lineage's genealogy reveal a dense web of relationships between Lü

84.　*XCXZ* (1477), 4.4a; *XCXZ* (1579), 4.2b.
85.　*XCXZ* (1477), 4.4a.
86.　*XCXZ* (1579), 2.10a–14a.

宗昭塋大嶺頭 ○倩武郎悅可塋真覺寺東山

太常簿豁塋臨海縣雲溪 ○縞儋斗文塋鼓山後

十六都霧後山 ○孝子永壽塋三

○呂氏墓 本宋宰相端之後 始祖大理評事億

以父由誠死節贅來氏 封初品官宜塋之蒼恩 始居新昌塋 之後贈

王無愁塋龍潭 ○氏始居新昌塋 長壙前都指揮使定塋甘棠四都

都指揮使集塋杜潭 封長壙前都指揮使退塋甘棠四都 ○指揮使推步官頭大亨

○王無愁塋龍巖 陳秉巖塋節度白竹隱步頭 ○訓導

馬家坑○塋龍巖 農卿塋陳秉巖塋節南塋節度白竹隱士九導

不孝子升塋蘇師山行 孝子珮塋施家塋長壠與化知縣童九

蓮金庭塋杜山○ 人孝子忍塋家壠壠○○侍卽獻塋白芳童西

成塋蘭庵衍○ 敎諭使塋許家長壠隱存茂塋小石佛西塢西

塋蝙蝠庵訓導宗信塋察使昌塋耆隱○○

舉塋訓導宗信○贈 信塋雪塘○書廷安塋甘棠域之

孝子好和同男贈尚 尚書廷安塋甘棠附壽域于此

尚書世良塋皇渡尚 書呂光洵塋

○餘姚大學士呂本七世祖珣塋唐末○○○

俞氏墓 拜劍令橐官居邑之五峯 始祖驕龍斬

Guangxun's lineage branch and the descendants of Zhao Jing 趙經, the great-great-grandfather of Lü Guangxun's father-in-law, Zhao Tianyu 天與.[87] Not only did Lü Guangxun marry a Lady Zhao, his adopted son married his brother-in-law's daughter, Lü's brother-in-law's adopted son's mother was the granddaughter of Lü Guangxun's great uncle, Lü Guangxun's sister-in-law married his second cousin, and Lü Guangxun's brother-in-law and father-in-law's wives were women of Lü Guangxun's lineage branch.[88] Such dense marital webs appeared throughout the compilers' lineage genealogies.

Over time, members of lineages having different surnames might through persistent intermarriage become more closely related to each other, in the biological sense, than to more distant members of their own lineages. This was the case for many of the gazetteer contributors. These cross-surname relatives also had close social relationships that are evidenced by numerous epitaphs, genealogy biographies, prefaces, and other materials. For example, Lü Guangxun recorded his New Year's visit to his maternal relatives, the Banzhu Zhangs, with whom Lü's lineage branch had intermarried for generations.[89] Tang Shunzhi's biography of Lü Guangxun's mother, Zhang Bao 寶, explained that after her marriage she lived in the Lü home with her mother-in-law, a woman of her own lineage to whom she was related by both blood and marriage.[90]

The gazetteer editors from Xinchang clearly had the opportunity to shape the content, but that still leaves the question of why the magistrate would accept their version of Xinchang history and society. Katherine Carlitz's study of mid-Ming Jiangnan shrines suggests one possible answer. Carlitz found that when sojourning magistrates cooperated with local notables in building shrines, "they were (consciously or unconsciously) manipulating the state-sanctioned canons of virtue to legitimate the claim that they and men like them were the appropriate shapers of policy for the empire" and that for a magistrate it was a way to "position oneself

---

87. *LSZP-YM; Xinchang Caiyan Zhao Shi.*

88. *Xinchang Caiyan Zhao Shi, Li* no. 188. (The genealogy is arranged by characters that signify a given ancestor's line, and numbers that identify the descendants' place in that line.)

89. *Xinchang Banzhu Zhang Shi,* preface.

90. *LSZP-YM,* 3.131–32.

advantageously for promotion."[91] Like shrine building, gazetteer compilation could be undertaken as a cooperative effort between members of a local elite and the magistrate to consciously enhance their status at the county and higher levels.

The editors already had high status locally, but that status needed reification in order to be passed on to new generations. David Faure explained that because "a written genealogy could not be readily updated and because the written word conferred legitimacy, the written genealogy, like the ancestral hall of the official style, objectified lineage history."[92] Gazetteers provided an avenue to objectify extended-family histories that lineage genealogies did not.

The county gazetteer also provided an avenue for enhancing status at the prefectural, provincial, and national levels because county gazetteers were key sources for higher-level gazetteers and dynastic histories. The 1587 *Shaoxing fu zhi* contains materials from the 1579 *Xinchang xian zhi*—for example, three chaste widow biographies of women married to men of the Yu lineage.[93] But the prefectural gazetteer lacks a genealogical organizing principle similar to the county gazetteer, because one extended family did not dominate the entire prefecture or control the compilation. Nevertheless, the editors did include some material for personal reasons: compiler Zhang Yuanbian's biography of Lü Guangxun provided a version of the fighting at Wuding that supported Zhang's attempts to clear his father's name and restore his rank.[94]

Magistrate Tian had much to gain and little to lose by ceding control over the gazetteer project. Pleasing Minister of Rites Pan Sheng was a better option for Tian than the mere possibility of offending the Shaoxing prefect or some other official. The story of the building of Xinchang's city wall, recounted in the next section, further shows that Tian needed the local leaders' cooperation to perform his job. There was no point in offending them, especially because with them on his side he could include his own administrative accomplishments.

91. Carlitz, "Shrines, Governing-Class Identity," 625.
92. Faure, "Lineage as Cultural Invention," 8.
93. *XCXZ* (1579), 12.9a–11a; *Shaoxing fu zhi* (1587), 47.23b–25a.
94. *Shaoxing fu zhi* (1587), 41.57b–59a.

Genealogy as Community Building

Lü Guangxun and Pan Sheng saw genealogy writing as a technique for building social cohesion, ordering social relationships, and cultivating morality. Such cohesion had practical effects, including the ability to protect one's family. If we extend their reasoning about genealogies to gazetteers, we could see gazetteer compilation as a way to build cohesion among county-level political actors. The compilation process brought them together physically, allowed them to work through issues as a group, and created a book that illustrated cooperation between an intermarried leadership. This "objectified history" reinforced the expectation of future cooperation. Many scholars have examined community compacts as organizing tools; here we can see the *Xinchang xian zhi* project as another form of interlineage cooperation.

Lü's interest in genealogy and lineage organization began in his youth and may have come from his father, Lü Shiliang 世良, who helped rebuild the Lü lineage temple in 1522.[95] As a young man in 1536, Lü Guangxun compiled his lineage genealogy, and late in life he wrote genealogy prefaces.[96] Pan Sheng's interest in genealogy is suggested by his service as imperial genealogy reviser, his genealogy prefaces, and other genealogical writings.[97]

Lü and his relatives had a golden opportunity to shape the 1579 gazetteer because he supplied the biographies. Biographical materials are found in almost every section of the gazetteer, not just the formal biography sections such as "virtuous women" and "local worthies." Lü and Pan's writings on genealogy stress security and morality, which were central concerns in Ming Xinchang. The gazetteer compilation provided them an opportunity to associate Xinchang's dominant families with these politically attractive issues.

95. *LSZP-YM*, 2.2b.
96. Ibid., 2.4; *Xinchang Banzhu Zhang Shi*, preface; *Xinchang Caiyan Zhao Shi*, preface.
97. *XCXZ* (1579), 10.15a; Pan, "Chongxiu Xinchang Caiyan Zhao"; Pan, "Zheng shi kao."

Security

Security was tenuous in mid-sixteenth-century Xinchang. Pirate attacks, bandits, feuds, and lawsuits all were potential dangers. Ninety pirates attacked Xinchang in the winter of 1555–56 as they retreated from Tiantai 天台 to Shaoxing, killing or injuring more than 110 people. A few days after the attack, Lü Guangxun, Pan Risheng 日升 (Pan Sheng's father), Yu Zequan, and Magistrate Wan Peng 萬鵬 tried to organize the construction of a city wall. Before the attack Magistrate Wan had raised the idea but found that "most commoners feared corvée labor" and so it had not been built.[98]

After the attack, Magistrate Wan simply ordered the people to build the wall, but they refused until Lü Guangxun and other local leaders from the great lineages intervened.[99] David Faure argues that the need to organize local defense was one reason lineage came to be the normative form for village organization in the Pearl River delta during the fifteenth to eighteenth centuries.[100] In Xinchang there were already many lineages before the pirate attack, but they were not up to the task of defending the county against ninety pirates, despite a registered population of more than 13,000. What the county needed was higher-level, interlineage organization. The consolidation of power from 1477 to 1579 in the hands of fewer, but densely intermarried, lineage branches created an elite extended family that served as a foundation for such organization.

In addition to pirates, the gazetteer described other dangers stemming from the lack of social cohesion. In the customs section, Magistrate Tian wrote that a divide existed between those living in the county seat and those in the mountain valleys. In his view the townspeople were noted for their honesty and simplicity, although customs were deteriorating.[101] In the mountain valleys, however, many people were bandits.[102]

---

98.   *XCXZ* (1579), 1.2b, 1.4b.
99.   *XCXZ* (1579), 9.9b–10b.
100. Faure, "Lineage as Cultural Invention," 4.
101. *XCXZ* (1579), 4.1b–2a; 6a.
102. James Cole points to extensive banditry and other criminal activity in the Shaoxing countryside in the late-nineteenth and early-twentieth centuries. Cole, *Shaohsing,*

To deal with these dangers, Lü Guangxun and Pan Sheng promoted family strength. After retiring to Xinchang and before editing the gazetteer, Lü Guangxun visited his maternal relatives, examined their genealogy, and in 1574 wrote a preface, translated below, for their forthcoming revised edition:[103]

> Because Xinchang is an isolated southeastern mountain town that has rarely suffered the destruction of war, there are many old families and great clans, each of which has a genealogy describing its descendants. Of late, many are not updating their genealogies. Among them, how could we discover all the illegitimate heirs?[104]
>
> When I was a government student I put my heart into matters of genealogy, but after removing commoner's clothes and walking the path of an official I did not have free time. Now, however, I am temporarily returned from Yunnan, enjoying the forest of repose, and may indulge my desire to revise my genealogy.
>
> At the New Year I passed Mt. Tianmu 天姥 on my way to pay respects at my father's grave. Below Tianmu's peak is Banzhu Township, where the Zhang family has flourished for several hundred years. They have intermarried with my family for generations. Once, when I was resting at their forest retreat, people such as Masters Zhu'an 竹庵 and Yunfeng 雲峰 showed me the family genealogy because they were favorably disposed toward me. They were about to revise it and entreated me to write a preface. This is deeply connected to my interests, but the Zhang descent charts already have prefaces written by eminent forefathers. [Thus] I will not repeat their narration [of the line of descent], rather [I will discuss why] their genealogy compilation project indeed deserves respect and imitation.
>
> When people of today meet a stranger, they do not necessarily have a sense of affinity, but among lineage members there is a sense of kin affection. Most of those who take care of each other in times of trouble, through thick or thin, are not forced to do so. Indeed, the ancestor's unique essence silently unites them. Yet if the duty of uniting the lineage is taken lightly, then compilation work is not esteemed and genealogies are not

---

64, citing *Jiangnan shangwu bao* #33, Guangxu 26 (1900), eleventh lunar month, twenty-first day, "shang qing" section 3b.

 103. *Xinchang Banzhu Zhang Shi* (unnumbered).

 104. This refers to unorthodox adoptions. For discussion, see Waltner, *Getting an Heir*, 75.

compiled. [As a result] there are some who do not know their lineage members and some who know their lineage members but are unclear about their generation and age order. This is no different from being strangers. Does not looking upon lineage members as strangers compound the loss of the ancestor's sense of kin affection? If this is the case, how can we obtain filiality toward parents? How can we obtain deference to elders?

Now, filial piety and brotherly deference are our innate moral compasses, but we also rely on genealogies to cultivate critical aspects. How could they be treated lightly?! Therefore, we know that when genealogies are compiled, the invigorated filial and brotherly mind will persist and cannot lapse. [Compilation] is indeed praiseworthy.

People are of different minds just as they have different faces. Lineages have many people, and of course they cannot all be similarly virtuous. Some, because they are miserly, take no delight in compiling a genealogy. But how could it be that [compilers] alone have filial and brotherly minds? This bears thinking about at length. We still should encourage them. I am devoted to my own genealogy project and soon will complete the work. Thus I make clear my ideas and the splendor of the Zhang family genealogy revision. This responds to their request. Moreover their genealogy revision creates an example of responsible action distinct from other lineages and may be taken as a model. I await its completion and will request to read it again, taking it as the standard.

At the hour of dawn on the day of the new moon of the first month of the second year of the Wanli era [January 23, 1574].

Preface by Bestowed *Jinshi*, First Rank Minister of War and Works, Wozhou Lü Guangxun.

Lü Guangxun's concerns were largely about cultivating Confucian morality, but he also points to enhancing security via lineage building: those with a sense of kin affection cared for one another in times of trouble. Therefore it was critical for lineages to cultivate that affection among their members and to create a clear record of who should provide protection and be protected.

Like Lü Guangxun, Pan Sheng saw genealogy compilation as a way to enhance the group solidarity needed to protect one's family. In Pan's preface to the *Xinchang Caiyan Zhao Shi zong pu*, he wrote the following:

In today's world it is easy to know the temple order of famous and power-ful families from the first-generation ancestor to the second and third gen-erations. But after five generations, familial affection dissipates and the mourning relationship is extinguished, or the descendants disperse or move around keeping no permanent residence. If there is no genealogy to con-nect them, they will not think twice and will regard each other as if they were strangers on the road. Alas!

Now, being born as a human one is different than the multitude of crea-tures, and if one acts as a gentleman one is different than the common folk. But if a gentleman cannot recover the strayed and gather the scattered in order to protect his family, that is his shame. If a family's rise and fall depend on the times, if poverty or wealth comes from fate, if wisdom or foolishness, good or evil, comes from social practices, how can recording things in a genealogy put one's mind at ease? By completing knowledge of the Way for relatives to act as relatives—t̲h̲a̲t̲ is how! How can we say that genealogies may only be written once the fallen flourish, the rich are ennobled, and the wise and virtuous have kept others from foolishness?[105]

From these writings we can see that ministers Lü and Pan viewed genealogy writing as an organizational tool. Gazetteer writing was an extension of this, a tool for enhancing elite social cohesion. One way in which it did so was by promoting customs that would reduce conflict. According to Magistrate Tian, customs in Xinchang had degenerated since the early Ming.[106] Weakened morals led to increasing discord. The gazetteer customs section tells that the sons of old families liked to sue and that if they had even slight animosity toward someone, they poured out their grievances, spread rumors, and posted notices on walls or put them in bamboo tubes and secretly threw them into the yamen.[107] Mag-istrate Tian's commentary accords with James Cole's observation that Shaoxing had a reputation for litigiousness.[108]

Although Magistrate Tian blamed the elite, saying, "What those above do, those below imitate," he also looked to them for the solution.[109]

---

105. Pan, "Chongxiu Xinchang Caiyan."
106. *XCXZ* (1579), 4.1a–b.
107. Ibid., 4.1b.
108. Cole, *Shaohsing*, 131–38.
109. *XCXZ* (1579), 4.7a.

The gazetteer editors used the customs section to highlight their efforts at ritual reform. The capping section stated that the "three cappings ceremony" (*san jia li* 三加禮) had long been discontinued but Yu Zhenqiang was the first to bring it back when he capped his sons.[110] This led his son "Yu Bangshi's generation to also follow this practice. Now there are those among the gentry households who perform it."[111]

The wedding section claimed that Lü Guangxun, Pan Sheng, and Yu Bangshi introduced proper wedding ritual:

> A man of the county, the titled gentleman Lü Shiliang ordered his son Lü Guangxun to begin carrying out the "welcoming the bride ceremony," and Minister Pan Sheng carried it out when he was a government student. Government student Yu Bangshi always followed the *Family Rituals* when conducting engagements and marriages for his junior male relatives. Today, most surnames have those who follow this practice.[112]

In a passage cited earlier, Lü Guangxun confessed that even though Xinchang's taxes were lower than those of Shanyin and Guiji, its problems were greater due to Xinchang's degenerate customs.[113] The confessional tone is surprising, but it makes sense if we understand Lü to be positioning himself as an honest mediator capable of harmonizing governmental and local interests and leading the locals in the self-improvement that will bring about a cohesive society.

The "Xinchang xian zhi" as a Public, Extended-Family Genealogy

By 1477 we can already see the consolidation of official power that would intensify through 1579. Genealogy and family status are prominent in the 1477 edition of the gazetteer authored by Xinchang County Confucian

110. For more on capping, see Ebrey, *Chu Hsi's Family Rituals*, 35–47.
111. *XCXZ* (1579), 4.2b.
112. Ibid., 4.2b–3a.
113. Ibid., postfaces, 5b.

school assistant instructor Mo Dan. The gazetteer contains an entire section called "lineages" (*shizu* 氏族), a local worthy section that documents lineage origins, discussions of lineage villages and gravesites, and biographies that narrate family relationships. The lineages section stresses the importance of lineage in Xinchang society, with Mo Dan's introduction to the section offering another hint of the politics of gazetteer compilation:

> Lineages are that which society esteems, not only because of their wealth and status, prominence and strength, but also because they have worthy ancestors who founded them in the past and worthy descendants who will continue them into the future. They accumulate benevolence, sow righteousness in the netherworld, transmit their good names, and extend their good fortune in the registers of this world. This is what is called "old family" (*gujia* 故家), this is what is called "venerable lineage" (*shizu* 世族).
>
> The common ignorant people look upon those whose prominence over the generations has been due to their wealth or status as "old families and venerable lineages," but if one examines such families' genealogies to see whether they had ancestors who transmitted the Confucian classics and morality, they completely lack verifiable, substantial traces. Even so they want to be included in the array of lineages [in this gazetteer chapter]. How could this not be difficult?![114]

Documenting imperial lineage was an important part of dynastic histories beginning in antiquity. In gazetteers, the earliest-known *shizu* section is in the 1379 gazetteer of Suzhou 蘇州, which has entries arranged under thirty-seven surname headings. These narrate Suzhou families' origins and migration to Suzhou, with much of the material drawn from genealogies and other genealogical works, such as *Qian xing bian* 千姓編 (Compilation of one thousand surnames) and *Xing yuan* 姓苑 (Garden of surnames).[115] Such sections continued throughout the Ming. The 1627 gazetteer of Pinghu 平湖, Zhejiang, has elaborate lineages and family temples (*jiamiao* 家廟) sections as part of the "customs" chapter.[116] These reprint texts about first-migrant ancestors, which tell how a particular lineage came to be established in a locale, name prominent descendants,

---

114.   *XCXZ* (1477), 11.1.
115.   *Suzhou fu zhi* (1379), 16.10a–15a.
116.   *Pinghu xian zhi*, 597–644.

and document lineage charitable estates and other genealogical information. First-migrant ancestor stories also can be found in the "visitors and sojourners" (*liuyu* 流寓) section.

Mo Dan's interest in using gazetteers to record the histories of prominent local lineages can be seen in his native place gazetteer, the late-fifteenth-century *Shihu zhi* 石湖志 (Shihu gazetteer), which Mo Dan co-authored with his father, Mo Zhen 震.[117] Figure 2.2, from the *Shihu zhi*, shows a late-fifteenth-century birthday celebration at the Mo family temple and multiple generations of Mo family members.[118] The gazetteer draws heavily upon the Mo genealogy and narrates Mo family history. For example, the gazetteer has a "gardens and residences" section that contains an entry for the Mo family home that recites the story of the Mo's first-migrant ancestor.[119]

Like the *Shihu zhi*, the lineages section of the 1477 *Xinchang xian zhi* narrates lineage origins and names first-migrant ancestors. Furthermore, as with the graves section in the 1579 edition, the 1477 gazetteer contains an implied ranking of families.[120] However, the ranking changed from 1477 to 1579. The Pans are not even on the 1477 list but appear fourth after Shi, Lü, and Yu, in the 1579 list.[121] Based on the gazetteer's examination tables, the Shi had declined by the early Ming, but they were probably left in first place to honor their Song dominance.

The 1477 gazetteer pays much more attention to villages than does the 1579 gazetteer, and most of the seventy entries in the villages section (*cun xu* 村墟) give information on the lineages residing therein. For example, the entry for Dieshi Village states, "Dieshi Village: Eighty plus *li* east of the county yamen. The old Wu lineage has lived there for generations."[122] Many have poems about the village, and some record families that resided there. In contrast, most of the 1579 gazetteer's village entries just give the location.[123] This deemphasis paralleled the spatial

---

117. Shihu was in Wujiang County, Suzhou Prefecture.
118. *Shihu zhi*, 1.14b–15a.
119. Ibid., 3.1–5.
120. *XCXZ* (1477), 11.1a–5b.
121. *XCXZ* (1579), 2.11a.
122. *XCXZ* (1477), 8.4.
123. *XCXZ* (1579), *juan* 2.

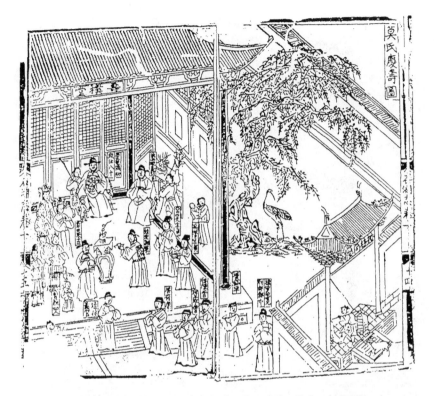

FIGURE 2.2. Birthday celebration at the Mo family temple. *Shihu zhi* (National Library of China).

change in locus of power from lineage-dominated villages to the extended-family-dominated county seat.

The 1477 gazetteer is full of biographies of people from successful lineages, and they tend toward lavish praise. The 1994 *Xinchang xian zhi* criticizes its distant predecessor for "making great efforts to exaggerate family status."[124] Examination success, however, was more dispersed before 1477 than after, and those lineages' elite members did not appear to have coalesced into the kind of densely intermarried extended family seen in the 1579 edition. If the donors were able to influence Mo Dan, it seems that they were more interested in promoting their own lineages

124. *XCXZ* (1994), 751.

than in portraying the associations and cooperation between members of any elite extended family. By 1579 the consolidation of power is reflected clearly in gazetteer biographies. In the following paragraphs I will illustrate the genealogical organizing principle that runs through the gazetteer by examining the Lü biographies and biographical notes appended to various sections.

Lü Guangxun used his position as editor-in-chief to trace his patriline back far enough in time to establish a common ancestor for every Ming dynasty Xinchang Lü *jinshi*, thereby textually indicating a common descent group. Each man in Lü Guangxun's patriline back seven generations had at least one gazetteer biography, and each Lü *jinshi* descended from one of these men. In all, the gazetteer established the nine most recent generations of Lü Guangxun's direct patriline, three generations of his mother's family, his paternal adoptive grandmother and her father, his paternal great-grandmother, famous Song dynasty ancestors, and multiple generations of the branch Lü lines. All of the lines were tied to Lü Ji, the first common ancestor of all Ming dynasty Xinchang *jinshi* degree holders surnamed Lü, and then to Lü Yi 億, the ancestor who first migrated to Xinchang.[125]

The degree of biographical detail and number of biographical entries generally is inversely related to the subject's distance from Lü Guangxun's patriline. Lü Guangxun himself, his immediate family, and his grandparents on both sides are the most extensively described. There are several dozen entries about Lü Guangxun's career, garden, homes, poems, and ancestral hall, temples to which he donated, his leadership in ritual reform, and auspicious portents connected to him. Most of these contain additional genealogical or associational information.

Readers are repeatedly informed that Lü Shiliang was Lü Guangxun's father: their relationship is specified in the sections on literature, customs, prestige titles, and graves. Lü Shiliang's biography names and specifies the relationships of seven members of Lü Guangxun's family: his

---

125. Lü Yi married uxorilocally to a Xinchang native, Lady Yuan, in the Southern Song. *XCXZ* (1579), 2.10b; *LSZP-YM*, 1.2b. Lady Yuan was the daughter of Yuan Tangwei, an eighth-generation descendant of Yuan Yi, who served as Xinchang magistrate after passing the *jinshi* examination in 996. *Yuan shi zongpu*, 2.9a. The *Yuan shi zongpu* states that Lady Yuan "married" (*shi* 適) Lü Yi rather than that Lü Yi married her uxorilocally (*zhui* 贅). *Yuan shi zongpu*, 2.9a.

father, himself, three brothers, his mother, and maternal grandfather.[126]
It also establishes Lü Shiliang's ritual authority, scholarly ability, and
generosity. The biography further explains that Lü Shiliang built the ancestral hall, distinguished the major and minor lineage branches, and
established lineage fields.

A biography of Lü Guangxun's paternal grandmother through adop-
tion, the Lady Zhang, is found in the virtuous women section and explains
that she was married to Lü Ting'an 廷安, Lü Shiliang's paternal uncle.[127] Lü
Ting'an died without sons, and so Lü Shiliang's biological father, Lü
Tinggui 廷圭, ordered that his youngest son, Shiliang, be Ting'an's heir.
The biography also names Lady Zhang's father and describes her virtue:

> One night a fire started in Lü Shiliang's uncle's rooms. Lady Zhang told
> the maidservants to bring water to put out the fire and it was soon extin-
> guished. [Another] time there was a flood. The townspeople struggled to
> escape. Lady Zhang locked her door, sat erect, and said, "I am a widow,
> where would I go in the middle of the night?" It can be said that having
> walked through fire and water she remained [chaste] unto death. The
> magistrate Song Xian petitioned for an official to be sent to verify the
> story and a memorial arch was built in her honor.

The biography of Lü Guangxun's brother Guangbi describes his and
his wife's filial act of going to the capital to petition for imperial com-
memoration of his deceased grandmother, the Lady Zhang above. While
they were on the journey, Guangbi's father (Lü Shiliang) became sick
back in Xinchang. Guangbi's wife, the Lady Pan, returned and day and
night gave Shiliang soup and medicine, prayed at the City God Temple,
donated lands as an offering for Guangbi's mother, and bought fields to
support ancestral sacrifices to Guangbi's maternal grandfather.[128]

Lü Guangxun's sixth-generation lineage ancestor, Lü Sheng 升, is the
subject of one of the gazetteer's longest biographies, found in the "filial
and brotherly" section.[129] Read with other passages, it establishes the

126.   *XCXZ* (1579), 11.55a–b.
127.   Ibid., 12.6b.
128.   Ibid., 10.30a.
129.   Ibid., 11.29b–30b.

common ancestry of all Ming dynasty Lü *jinshi*. The biography goes on to explain that Lü Sheng taught Lü Guangxun's great-great-great grandfather Lü Jiucheng 九成 and his brother Lü Buyong 不用, that Lü Pei 珮 was Sheng's eldest son, that his second son was Lü Lian 璉, and that Sheng's son by a concubine was sent away but secretly raised by Lü Pei.

In addition to inserting into the gazetteer numerous biographies of his own lineage members' households, Lü Guangxun also included biographies of his affinal relatives. For example, the "virtuous elders" section has a biography of Lü Guangxun's father-in-law's great-great-grandfather, Zhao Jing 經.[130] It tells how at age ten Zhao Jing sucked pus from his father's wounds and cared for his arthritic mother until her death. The end of the biography states that Zhao Tianyu 天與, Lü's father-in-law, through diligence enriched his family for generations. This biography appears to have been inserted to create a status marker for Lü Guangxun's affinal relatives and the multiple members of Lü's own lineage who had married Zhao Jing's descendants.

Monopolization of Gazetteer Entries

Examining in their entirety those portions of gazetteer sections pertaining to events subsequent to the 1477 gazetteer's publication gives a better sense of the degree to which the compilers were writing their own family history on top of basic gazetteer information. Consider, for example, the auspicious portents (*xiangrui* 祥瑞) and gardens sections:

The "auspicious portents" section contains the following seven post-1477 examples:[131]

- In the winter of the ninth year of Jiajing's reign (1530–31), five stalks of lingzhi fungus grew from Lü Ting'an's grave.[132]
- In the nineteenth year (1540–41), Pan Sheng's family water crock sprouted several lotus plants.

130.   Ibid., 11.67a.
131.   Ibid., 13.13a–14a.
132.   Lingzhi is a dark brown-purple, hard, lustrous fungus that is said to possess supernatural powers.

- In the twentieth year (1541–42), Camel Mountain called out.
- In the *bingyin* year (1566–67), sweet dew descended on Yu Zequan's garden. The drops looked like beautiful pearls, the flavor was clean and pure. The droplets dissipated only after four or five days.
- During the Jiajing reign, Lü Guangqian 光遷 and Lü Guangxin 光新 corralled clouds into a pavilion. The Chinese redbud tree's irregular branches became regular. Many famous Yue scholars sang its praises.[133]
- In the third year of Wanli's reign (1575–76), a golden pheasant came from the south, stopped at the Ritual Gate, and flew into the yamen hall, where it perched as a guard on top of the placard of successful examination candidates. Magistrate Tian Guan caught it and released it into the mountains.
- In the *bingzi* year (1576–77) Yu Yingsu's family silkworms chirped.

Of the seven recorded post-1477 portents, one involved Pan Sheng, two involved the Yu lineage, one involved Lü Guangxun's grandfather, Ting'an, and another Lü Guangxun's lineage cousins.[134] Magistrate Tian was involved in one, and no person was clearly associated with the one concerning Camel Mountain, although that was the location of Yu Zequan's garden.[135]

Most of these portents should be understood as foretelling examination success. The families of Lü Guangxun, Pan Sheng, Yu Zequan, and Yu Yingsu each had an auspicious portent in the year of, or year prior to, their passing the provincial or metropolitan examination. Magistrate Tian's portent was explicitly connected to exam success, and an undated earlier entry for Yu Seng 僧 states that because his gravesite's feng shui was unusual and efficacious, each examination period one rock fell from the mound in front of his grave and one descendant passed the examination.[136] Not every post-1477 *jinshi*, however, was foretold and recorded. For example, comparing the examination list to the portent list reveals

133. A poem by Xu Wei is attached to this portent.

134. Guangqian and Guangxin both descended from Lü Guangxun's great-grandfather. *LSZP-YM*, 4.100a–109a. Guangqian's first wife, Lady Zhao, was Guang-xun's wife's first cousin. *Xinchang Caiyan Zhao Shi*, 3.48; *LSZP-YM*, 7.109. Guangqian's second wife was Lady Pan. *LSZP-YM*, 4.109a.

135. *XCXZ* (1579), 2.22b.

136. Ibid., 13.13a.

that Liu Zhongqi 忠器, Hu Rui 胡汭, and other Lü and Yu *jinshi* holders had degrees but no recorded portent.[137]

As they did the portents section, the Lü, Yu, Pan, and He lineages dominated the gazetteer's gardens section.[138] These four lineages received nine of twelve entries and sixty-eight out of seventy-four lines of text. A description of Lü Guangxun's garden fills nearly half of the entire section. Four of the other eight entries are for gardens that belonged to the gazetteer's editors, one belonged to a contributor, and the remaining three belonged to his lineage members. These garden entries provide family information, such as Lü Ruoyu's entry telling how he built his garden next to his father Lü Yizong's 益宗 grave, and Lü Guangxun's stating that his younger brother wrote a poem about the garden and that his father and brothers enjoyed it. The entries also tell of elite associations by recording their exchanged garden writings. For example, one entry reveals that Lü Ruoyu wrote a poem for Yu Yingsu's garden, which was built by his father, the gazetteer contributor Yu Binghu.

Reviewing the entire 1579 *Xinchang xian zhi*, and reading it in light of the 1477 edition, clarifies that the majority of biographies were included due to the subject's relationship to one or more of the compilers. Entries regularly specified family relationships, which taken together reveal a conscious effort to publicly establish the compilers' patrilines, affinal relatives, and community connections. On top of this genealogical framework, the compilers wrote a myriad of late-Ming status markers. Thus, if we extend to the gazetteer genre David Faure's analysis of genealogies as constructions of agreed-upon lineage history that could confer important rights within a village, we could view the 1579 *Xinchang xian zhi* as an agreed-upon extended-family history that conferred important rights within the county. The nature of those rights is suggested by the types of stories the gazetteer tells: the right to lead countywide projects, to be the moral exemplars who guide the reformation of customs, to shape and judge aesthetic values, to receive and interpret auspicious portents. If we take Ueda Makoto's notion of recognized family history as the basis for future cooperation, then we could see the gazetteer as laying a foundation for continued intermarriage and cooperation between the compilers' descendants.

---

137. Ibid., 10.13a–15b.
138. Ibid., 3.21b–23a.

Ming Readings of the "Xinchang xian zhi"

The above interpretation is based on the gazetteer contents and knowledge of the compilers' family relationships. But to what extent did readers at the time also understand the gazetteer as a public genealogy? In positing public genealogy as an agenda for gazetteer compilation, I left open the question of whether readers in Xinchang actually read the gazetteer through a genealogical lens. The following section examines reader responses and other records of actual readings to explore the ways in which Ming readers shared this understanding. The first set of Ming readings are by members of the Huang lineage who took issue with the 1477 and 1579 gazetteers' portrayal of their place in Xinchang's social hierarchy. By closely examining their reception of the *Xinchang xian zhi*, connections between gazetteers, status, and the exercise of power in local communities become visible.

Mo Dan and the Huang Lineage

When Confucian school assistant instructor Mo Dan compiled the 1477 *Xinchang xian zhi*, he presented a lengthy history of the school, consisting of his own narration supported by copies of school-related inscriptions and documents. Mo wrote about the school's founding in 1121, its destruction in a rebellion, reconstruction in 1144, and subsequent renovation and expansion.[139] It is a tale of Confucian progress. One inscription Mo entered into the gazetteer, the *Chong jian dachengdian ji* 重建大成殿記 (Record of the reconstruction of the Hall of Great Accomplishment), written in the early 1200s by Huang Xiang 庠, appears to be a straightforward narration of the school's early history.[140] Nothing about it seems controversial. Huang Xiang's descendants, however, saw things very differently. They wrote two detailed responses to Mo Dan's version of the school history and other parts of the gazetteer, and placed their

139. *XCXZ* (1477), 5.2b–24b.
140. Ibid., 5.7a–b.

responses in their lineage genealogy. The responses, titled *Fuzai xinjian Dachengdian ji fu lu* 附載新建大成殿記附錄 (Addenda to the attached "Record of the New Construction of the Hall of Great Accomplishment") are not dated, but the first, by Huang Zhenzhi 振治, appears to have been written shortly after the 1477 gazetteer, because it discusses Mo Dan as if he were still alive and records a conversation with him.[141] The complete response states:

> In the thirteenth year of the Ming Chenghua era [1477], a man surnamed Mo from Wujiang was the Xinchang County Confucian school instructor. He wanted to expand the school's grounds and destroyed our first ancestor's grave. Lineage member Huang Rui was livid and rushed to bring a lawsuit. The court ruled that the grave was to be preserved and ordered Mo to restore and return it. Mo Dan came close to being punished, but he was lucky to bribe his way out of it.
>
> When Dan later recompiled the county gazetteer he omitted reference to the Huang family ancestral grave, removed the road to it [in the illustration of the school], and only preserved one or two out of ten names of Huang family members who were on the registry of officials (fig. 2.3).[142] When he came to Huang Xiang's *Record of the Newly Built Hall of Great Accomplishment*, he changed "Newly Built" to "Rebuilt" and cavalierly changed other words' meanings.
>
> Another example of Mo's [malevolence] is his inconsistent treatment of grants of degrees through exceptional petitions.[143] When a Shi family

141. *MDHS*, 3.3–4. For more on Mo Dan, see Chen Guangyi, *Zhongguo fangzhi xue*, 148.

142. This refers to the 1477 gazetteer's illustration of the Confucian school. The illustration shows something labeled "ancient graves" northwest of the main hall, where the Huang graves were located, but the label does not include the Huang surname. The school grounds surround the graves and no road to them is shown, even though other roads through town are shown. The 1477 edition has a graves section, but unlike the 1579 edition, it does not contain a section for the Huang family graves. The 1477 edition's graves section, however, is far more limited than that of the 1579 edition. In the 1579 edition, there is a subsection titled "Huang Family Graves," which states: "The first ancestor, Fan, originally came from Jianning's Pucheng. During the Five Dynasties period, he moved from Shan to Xinchang. He is buried in the Huang Family Garden." *XCXZ* (1579), 2.12a. So the Huangs were at least partially successful in restoring their family's coverage in the 1579 edition.

143. This contrasts with the standard petition submitted for final imperial approval upon passing the highest civil service exam.

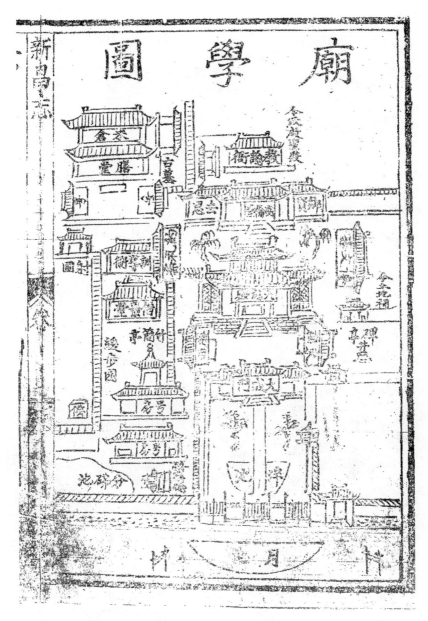

FIGURE 2.3. Illustration of the Xinchang County Confucian school in the 1477 *Xinchang xian zhi*, showing the Huang lineage first ancestor's grave (Xinchang County Archives).

member received such a degree, he praised it as a glorious event. But when a Huang family member received one he used taunting words, saying: "In Li San's group of graduates the person who placed last on the list of presented scholars was unhappy and said, 'Raising my head I cannot see [the optimus] Wang Shi, but if I stretch my toes, I can still trample on Li San' And an exceptional petition is not even as good as a standard petition."[144] Mo Dan further said, "Do we know whether Huang Zhan[145] [received his degree by] exceptional petition?" (He did.)

When Mo Dan came to Huang Yudong, the Gentleman for Fostering Uprightness, the previous gazetteer had praised him saying, "His body and name are dead, but his mind and righteousness all live on."[146] Mo, however, said, "I do not know who he is [and cannot include him in the gazetteer]." These examples suffice to show that he destroyed the public way and nourished private resentments.

I recall that in the past, ancestor [Huang] Ying lived in Pujiang and paid for the construction of the county yamen's foundation. The Pujiang gentry respected the gentleman's virtue and had a shrine to him built outside the Ceremonial Gate and commissioned a portrait that was placed

---

144.   The top person on the exceptional petition list was still beneath the bottom person on the regular list. In 1157 Wang Shipeng placed first among regular candidates, Wu Yizheng placed last among regular candidates who passed, and Li Sanying placed first among candidates by exceptional petition. The exceptional petition pass list was appended to the regular pass list and Wu Yizheng wrote a poem containing the phrase "raising my head I cannot bear to look at Wang Shi, turning my head I can still enjoy seeing Li San." Zhou Bida, *Erlaotang shi hua*, 3.95.

145.   The list of Song Dynasty *jinshi* in the 1579 gazetteer is divided into "regular" and "exceptional." The entry for Huang Zhan states: "Huang Zhan: Exceptional petition in the tenth year of the Xining era (1068)." *XCXZ* (1579), 10.7b. According to the 1477 edition, the Optimus Memorial Arch west of the county seat reveals that Huang Zhan was the exceptional appointments optimus. In the Huang genealogy, Huang Xuanxian's epitaph states, "Zhan had literary merit and was granted the office of Yizhou Litterateur through exceptional petition. Most of his disciples became officials and famous people." *MDHS*.

146.   Xinchang County had gazetteers before 1477, but none are extant. The first known gazetteer was the *Shan Dong lu* 剡東錄 (Record of Eastern Shan) by Yu Rui, a 1235 *jinshi*. The *Xinchang zhi* by Liang Xiyi appears in the Song dynastic history literature section. The compilers of the 1994 *Xinchang xian zhi* believed that Mo Dan used an incomplete copy of a Yuan dynasty edition in compiling the 1477 edition. An early-Ming manuscript gazetteer was submitted to the palace library prior to publication of the 1441 catalog. The manuscript likely had been submitted in response to one of the early-Ming compilation orders discussed in chapter 1.

therein. The shrine's lintel was inscribed, "General Huang's Shrine." Later a Pujiang magistrate scraped off the Huang surname. That person then spat out crazy words and suddenly died. Now, Mo is even worse than the Pujiang magistrate, I wonder what will become of him? Thus, I specially raise this issue and record it to inform people of later times.

—Recorded by twentieth-generation descendant Zhenzhi

The second response, by Huang Mouqing 懋卿, which was likely written in the late sixteenth century, follows below:[147]

First Ancestor [Huang Fan] moved from Shan County, Double Well Village, to live separately in Stone Ox Fort. In the second year of the Latter Liang dynasty's Kaiping era (908 CE), Prince Qian of Wu Yue cut off District Thirteen of Shan County [which contained Stone Ox Fort] to create Xinchang County. Thus, Fan is considered our first Xinchang ancestor. For generations our lineage lived by the North Gate behind the present yamen. Our female forbearers, the Lady Yu and the Lady Wu, had three male children, the eldest was Xiang, the next was Gun, and the youngest was Yan. Their graves are in the Huang Family Garden behind Number Five Hill, northwest of the Confucian school's lecture hall.

It so happened that in the Chenghua era (1465–88) Confucian school instructor Mo dug up our ancestors' graves to expand his vegetable garden. Ancestor Rui sued him, so when Mo revised the county gazetteer he largely omitted our Huang family. For example, he said of Optimus Memorial Arch, "It was said in olden days that it was built for Huang Chen but we do not know if this is the case." He said of Beautiful Brocade Memorial Arch, "It was erected by the Shi Family." He said of Qianshangen Village, "The Chen family lives there." Now who doesn't know that Optimus Memorial Arch, Cultural Prosperity Memorial Arch, Beautiful Brocade Memorial Arch, and Qianshangen Village have since olden days belonged to the Huang family?

When he came to the righteous scholar Huang Yudong, Mo Dan said, "I do not know what kind of person he was." Yet Elder Yungu (Huang Yudong) is recorded in the following books: the *Nanming Gazetteer*, the

147. Huang Mouqing is not listed in the genealogy descent charts, which are incomplete. Most of the members of the twentieth generation whose dates of death are recorded died in the sixteenth century, and Huang's text mentions the 1579 gazetteer.

Huang Family Genealogy, the *Singing Earthworm Collected Works*, and Huang Du's *Commentary on the Book of Odes, Commentary on the Book of Documents*, and *Commentary on the Rites of Zhou*. It is written in all of the histories and collected works that our cultured and virtuous ancestor was a mirror for governance and that the Emperor Renzong followed his advice to record the military fields to enhance border defense across the ages. The venerable texts do not record this under any other surname or lineage. The books also record that so-and-so served in such-and-such office and that our lineage has had successful examination graduates and serving officials since the Song dynasty Zhiping era (1064–67), yet *that person* obscured them and failed to record them.

Mo wrote about the graves of other surnames—he only failed to write about the Huangs' graves because of our lawsuit over his violation of our first ancestor's grave taboo. Alas! Who knew that after the lawsuit we would we have to let out such a long sigh?

And as for great families, we only make way for the Shi, Lü, and Yu surnames; the others all belong behind the Huang. Is it not the case that without exception we Huangs have been considered a great family?! For example, in the Song dynasty, Mr. Chen Zhizhai's grave epitaph of Chen Yan, which was written on behalf of the Lady Lü, says, "among Xinchang surnames, Shi, Lü, and Huang are great," the *Record of the Shrine to the Worthies of Old* by Master Huang of Jinhua says, "the two surnames Shi and Huang are especially famous," and the Yuan, Huang, Lü, and Shi surnames appear everywhere in Mr. Lü Xiaozhi's poems.[148] Public opinion (*gong lun* 公論) already regards [the Huangs as a great family]; we cannot countenance a cover-up.

Tian Guan's [1579] gazetteer followed the records in Mo Dan's [1477] gazetteer; we were unable to get them corrected. His gazetteer went even further and placed us behind the Pan and He families in the list of local lineages. Alas! We cannot be placed behind them; although they are now flourishing, they do not have a long history of official rank. I do not know who should fight to reveal these deficiencies and extol our worthy ancestors, so I, Mouqing, narrate the story of our first ancestor's grave to thoroughly refute the two gazetteers, which insufficiently evidence our own talented worthies. We must remember them.

—Recorded by twentieth-generation descendant Mouqing.[149]

---

148. Lü Xiaozhai was Lü Sheng, who lived in the fourteenth century. Lü Sheng's wife was surnamed Huang and from Qianshangen Village. *Lü Shi zongpu, Xu*, 7.22.
149. *MDHS*, 3.5a–b.

These two passages reveal much about Chinese gazetteers. First, they show local people reading and critiquing gazetteers. Huang Zhenzhi and Huang Mouqing, neither of whom was an official or had a civil service degree, carefully examined the gazetteers and argued that their lineage should have been featured more prominently. Although Mo Dan steered readers to understand the Confucian school's history as a tale of progress, Huang Zhenzhi read it through the eyes of someone whose ancestral graves had been desecrated by the author.

Second, the passages provide a clear example of gazetteer compilation politics. Mo Dan undercut his local enemies by minimizing coverage of their famous ancestors and the Huangs responded to the slights by writing critiques. In addition, the Huangs did not contribute to the gazetteer's publication costs. They either boycotted the publication as a lineage or Mo Dan excluded them from participation. The seventy-four people on the donors list had twenty different surnames corresponding to all known major Xinchang lineages except for the Huangs.[150] In 1477 some Huangs were certainly capable of donating to the publication: Huang women were marrying top members of the local elite, and just twelve years earlier the lineage had published a genealogy with a preface written by the chancellor of the Nanjing Directorate of Education.[151] Considering that some donors gave only a few coins, financial incapacity cannot have been the reason the Huangs did not contribute.

Huang Mouqing's argument that the Huangs should not have been placed behind the Pan and He lineages demonstrates a contemporary reader's understanding that a gazetteer was a text that portrayed relative family status in local society. The gazetteer's ranking of lineages, and Huang Mouqing's criticism of it in his lineage genealogy, shows that gazetteers and genealogies were arenas for elite discourse on social issues, in this case, the debate was over the appropriate criteria for ranking local lineages. Huang argued that his lineage deserved to be placed ahead of the Pan and He lineages because of the Huang's longer history of official

---

150. *XCXZ* (1477), preface.

151. Prominent local men who married Huang women include Lü Feng, a 1460 *jinshi* who served as vice director in the Nanjing Ministry of Works; Ding Chuan, a 1464 *jinshi* and assistant censor-in-chief; Yu Zhencai, a 1475 *jinshi* and Huguang surveillance vice commissioner; and Yu Zhenying, a 1484 *jinshi* who became chief of the Imperial Seals Office. *MDHS*, prefaces, 8a–b, 1.10b; *XCXZ* (1579), 10.13b–14a, 11.42b, 11.50a.

service, whereas the gazetteer editors ranked the Pan and He lineages higher because they had recently produced high-ranking officials.

The Huangs were not the only people in Xinchang who read the gazetteer as a text documenting social status. In a 1519 birthday composition for Ding Haohe 丁好和, Gao Tai 高臺 (1493 *jinshi*) wrote: "The Dings are an esteemed Xinchang lineage that has for generations lived in Caiyan [Village], which is famous throughout the land for the beauty of its mountains and rivers. The Ding's culture and service are arrayed in the county gazetteer; in assessing the great lineages east of the Zhe River we must place the Ding at the head."[152] Such references to gazetteers as proof of elite status were common in imperial China.

The story of Mo Dan and the Huangs shows that conflict over gazetteer content did not end upon publication. If we think of gazetteers as sites of struggle for social and cultural capital, then publication was merely the first battle's conclusion. Compilers signaled how they expected readers to read, but readers were free agents who could ignore or seek to overturn the compilers' desired outcomes. By recording their dispute with Mo Dan in their genealogy, the Huangs perpetuated their own version of their family history and made it available to future gazetteer compilers. The Huangs, although participants in a dominant discourse of status, were not passive recipients of their portrayal in the official county history; in the act of consumption they resisted that history and produced an alternative.

Returning to agendas for compiling gazetteers, this story reveals revenge and "reversing the verdict" as two motivations. Both Mo Dan and the Huangs expected that readers would perceive relative local status through the gazetteer, and it mattered to the Huangs that they be portrayed as a great lineage. The Huang's dragging Mo into court for destroying their ancestral grave gave him motive for revenge. Compiling the gazetteer gave him opportunity. In writing critiques of Mo Dan's gazetteer and the subsequent edition, the Huangs expressed their desire to inform future generations of the "true history" of the Huangs in Xinchang County. As we have seen, powerful families could influence a gazetteer's content during the compilation process, but these reading responses show that, failing that, a lineage could write its own version of local history

152.   Gao Tai, "Zeng Xinchang Haohe Ding."

in its genealogy and hope to get their revisions incorporated into future editions.

Conclusion

By understanding the gazetteer as, like a genealogy, embodying a concept of kinship, setting forth the relationships that counted in the kinship group and providing a model for how people in the group should act, we raise a number of further questions. First, this view suggests that when considering lineage-building activities, we should broaden our examination to include the activities of "extended families" such as the *Xinchang xian zhi* compilers. The compilers teamed up, not only with members of their own patrilineal lineage branches, but also with their maternal and affinal relatives. Thus, in considering concepts of kinship in Ming China, we should not be blinded by the dominant discourse of patrilineality and ignore cross-surname kinship ties created through persistent elite endogamy. In Xinchang, cross-surname lineage branches coalesced at the apex of local society, socializing with each other, acting in concert, and mediating between lineages and the magistrate.

James Cole's monograph on nineteenth-century Shaoxing describes the countryside as being controlled by powerful lineages that acted as quasi governments performing a wide range of functions. He also examined lineage and class-based competition and cooperation in core and peripheral counties, and argued that in Shaoxing's core, competition and cooperation occurred along both the vertical bonds of lineage and the horizontal bonds of class, and that class cooperation varied directly with proximity to the core.[153] Applying Cole's hypothesis, the peripheral Xinchang would have competition between lineages, cooperation within lineages, and limited class consciousness. The evidence examined in this study complicates Cole's model by positing an elite extended family operating above the lineages at the county level.

The 1579 *Xinchang xian zhi* also raises questions about the relationships between dynastic histories, gazetteers, and genealogies. Although

153. Cole, *Shaohsing*, 13.

Sima Qian 司馬遷 consulted genealogies in writing the *Shiji* 史記 (Grand Scribe's records) and genealogies were sources for county gazetteers, which in turn were sources for higher level histories, genealogy has generally been viewed as a separate genre. For example, the Qing *Siku quan shu* 四庫全書 (Complete books of the Four Treasuries) history classification (*shi* 史) excluded genealogies but included gazetteers. In catalogs of Ming private book collections there was no agreement on how to categorize either gazetteers or genealogies. More often than not, both were included under *shi*, but some collectors gave them separate headings. For example, the Wanli-era (1573–1620) *Hongyulou shumu* 紅雨樓書目 (Catalog of the Hongyulou), by Xu Bo 徐燉, placed both under *shi*, with separate subheadings, *jiapu* 家譜 (genealogies) and *fensheng* 分省 [*zhi* 志] (gazetteers arranged by province).[154] In contrast, the Jiajing-era (1522–67) *Chao shi baowentang shumu* 晁氏寶文堂書目 (Catalog of the Chao family Baowentang), by Chao Li 晁瑮, excluded both from *shi*.[155]

As seen above, there could be tremendous tension between public and private interests in gazetteer publication, in part because people did not agree on what was public and what was private. Power in imperial China derived from both heredity and merit, and working out the relative scope of each is reflected in gazetteer production. One area of disagreement among gazetteer compilers was over whether to include imperial edicts related to individuals, such as those granting titles to the parents of officials. Many *fanli* prohibited them. For example, the 1541 gazetteer of Xuzhou 許州, Henan, *fanli* state, "A locale having a gazetteer is for documenting the locale. It is not for families' private records. Records of imperial edicts conferring offices, titles, posthumous names, and praise are for genealogies. Do not include any herein."[156] The compilers of the 1556 gazetteer of Guangshan 光山, Henan, went even further and cut out all such texts that had been included in the previous edition, saying, "The old gazetteer recorded gentry families' prestige titles, received edicts, poetry and prose writings, and even included imperial edicts for posthumous names and praise.

154. Xu Bo, *Hongyulou shumu*, 263–92.
155. Chao Li, *Chao shi*, 18–27.
156. *Xuzhou zhi* (1541), *fanli*, 15b.

These, however, belong in genealogies. Today, we expunge them from the gazetteer."[157]

Another type of often-excluded genealogical record was grave epitaphs (*muzhiming* 墓誌銘). The *fanli* of the 1541 gazetteer of Changyuan 長垣, Beizhili, state, "The included writings document administration, teaching, and transformation of customs, and are all connected to governance. In the old gazetteer, epitaphs also were included, but those belong in family genealogies; [their inclusion] is not loving the people according to what is right. Today please correct it. This will also be a kindness to the former magistrate."[158] In this case we can see that compilers of successive editions of a particular gazetteer did not necessarily agree on the principles of compilation. This could lead to different coverage and uses of sources. Removal of such "private records" may have reflected a weakening of formerly dominant lineages, or a strengthening of local representatives of the central government.

Sometimes the compilers made a strong statement against the inclusion of genealogical materials, but then ignored their own rule. The *fanli* of the 1553 edition of the gazetteer of Cizhou 磁州, Beizhili, say that because writings of a private, family nature belong in genealogies, the current compilers were cutting out such materials that had been included in the previous edition.[159] Nevertheless, they still included grave epitaphs of officials' wives and mothers.[160]

In the above examples, we can see that the reasons given for rejecting certain types of records were phrased in terms of separate genres, not only in terms of public and private. The "separate genres" argument is made clear in a 1564 gazetteer from Henan, which says the compilers feared that edicts and epitaphs "belong to the genre of genealogy; they are not records of the county's affairs."[161] Similarly, the *fanli* of a 1634 gazetteer from Shandong prohibited the inclusion of edicts and epitaphs in order "to distinguish the county gazetteer from a family genealogy."[162]

157. *Guangshan xian zhi, fanli*, 2a.
158. Ibid.; *Changyuan xian zhi, fanli*, 1b.
159. *Cizhou zhi*, 798.
160. Ibid., 1123.
161. *Yancheng xian zhi* (1637), *fanli*, 499.
162. *Yuncheng xian zhi*, 40. Also see *Quwo xian zhi*, 270–71.

Although the above compilers rejected use of genealogies, in whole or in part, many explicitly allowed them.[163] The postface to the 1525 gazetteer of Chaling 茶陵, Huguang, explains that biographies were selected according to public opinion and from those recorded in the local gentlemen's collected works and in the great families' genealogies.[164] Mo Dan wrote in the *fanli* of the 1477 *Xinchang xian zhi* that he was using biographies from genealogies. Not only did he use genealogies for the biography sections of the gazetteer, he also used them as sources for writing nonbiographical sections. In fact, many gazetteer compilers mentioned using genealogies.

Some *fanli* allowed use of genealogies but urged caution. The 1553 gazetteer of Jianyang 建陽, Fujian, *fanli* say, "Record the stories of those left out of the old gazetteer if they can be proven by examination of various gazetteers, genealogies, and the collected works and biographies of past worthies so that the traces of people past will not be extinguished. As for those stories found [only] in genealogies, although they are trustworthy based on what the county's people have heard and seen, or [appear] to be true but have not circulated widely, you dare not enter them in haste. Put them in the 'collecting the omitted' (*shi yi* 拾遺) section to await further research." This section was generally tacked on to the end of the main text and contained things that did not fit the gazetteer's categories or had been omitted from the main text for various reasons, but that the compilers still wished to include.

There are several reasons that gazetteer compilers looked to genealogies for materials. One is that a large portion of most late imperial gazetteers consists of biographies of famous local people, and those biographies had to come from somewhere. In addition, it was common for people who contributed to local gazetteers to have also compiled their family genealogies. Writing gazetteers and genealogies provided a literary outlet for people who were not currently holding office due to leave, retirement, or failure to obtain office in the first place. A retired official would often start by compiling his genealogy and then contribute to the local gazetteer. The two genres were closely linked, and genealogy writing often began

163.   See, e.g., *Sinan fu zhi*; *Shangcheng xian zhi*; *Taiping fu zhi*.
164.   *Chaling zhou zhi*, 1085.

with research in gazetteers to find long-lost relatives, a topic that will be developed further in chapter 7.

While the connections drawn between genealogies and gazetteers in prefaces are often stated in broad, abstract terms, and the *fanli* are merely statements of what compilers were supposed to do, examining the contents of gazetteers reveals more detail about how genealogies were actually used and confirms that gazetteers drew a tremendous amount of material from them. Occasionally it is obvious that genealogies were used because their titles are included in lists of works consulted or given in a citation to a particular record.[165] Access to genealogies is also demonstrated by the common practice of reprinting genealogy prefaces in literature chapters.[166]

The examples discussed above are almost all from the fifteenth, sixteenth, and seventeenth centuries, but there were genealogical aspects to gazetteers in earlier times. In the preface to the 1288 gazetteer of Jiaxing 嘉興, in modern Zhejiang, the author complains that the earlier lack of a gazetteer was a problem for three reasons, one of which was that descendants of worthies lacked a resource for investigating their ancestry. The compiler of the 1357 gazetteer of Zhuji wrote in his preface that he consulted genealogies. But beginning in the late 1400s there was an extensive, explicit discussion and debate over of the nature of the relationship between genealogies and gazetteers. Many compilers looked down on genealogies as sources, but even more compilers openly embraced them, the result being that a majority of Ming gazetteers have a significant genealogical aspect.

If we imagine Ming China as a "family-state," then to what extent might we also view the three genres—genealogies, gazetteers, and dynastic histories—as expressions of the family-state concept but at different administrative levels? To answer this we can compare them in terms of both "family" and "state." Many prefaces in Ming and Qing gazetteers and genealogies compare the three genres. For example, the preface to the 1501 gazetteer of Yongping 永平, Beizhili, says, "A prefecture or county having a gazetteer is like a family having a genealogy and a state

165. *Songjiang fu zhi*, 19.
166. *Neihuang xian zhi*, 7.36a.

having a history; only their scale is different."[167] The postface to the 1549 gazetteer of Weishi 尉氏, Henan, states, "A county having a gazetteer is like a family having a genealogy and a state having a history. The sources, the lines of descent, the warp and weft, the affairs of the day; how can we just one day discard them?"[168] Although many genealogy prefaces of the early Ming compare state histories and genealogies, it is only in the late fifteenth century that explicit analogies of all three genres are drawn. I have found no evidence of this prior to the Ming.

But in what senses are the three genres alike? If in the *Xinchang xian zhi* we can see "family" in what we think of as being "state," then we should also examine genealogies to analyze the extent of "state" in what we think of as being "family." The most cursory examination of lineage genealogies reveals that many are much more than descent charts; they often contain extensive materials about administration, including donations to lineage halls, educational endowment lands, grave maintenance and land division contracts, records of lawsuits against surname interlopers, and more.

The Wanli *Xinchang xian zhi* also raises methodological questions. Knowing that an extended family was able to dominate much of a gazetteer's compilation process, what does that imply for how we use gazetteers as historical sources? Would knowing that most chaste widows in a given gazetteer were related to each other affect our interpretation? If local gentry were strong enough to control gazetteer biographies, to what extent might they also have been able to alter tax and population figures?

One may be tempted to speculate that the *Xinchang xian zhi* is unusual or unique due to the two powerful ministers' personal roles in providing and editing materials, but that is not the case. Many other gazetteer compilations were dominated by powerful local families and contain extensive genealogical materials.[169] The *Xinchang xian zhi* should therefore be viewed as a compelling and revealing lesson on the importance of considering gazetteers as unified works.

---

167. *Yongping fu zhi*, 6.
168. *Weishi xian zhi*, postface, 1b.
169. See, e.g., *Dacheng xian zhi*; *Cheng'an yi sheng*.

PART II

Production Process

CHAPTER 3

Editorial Process

Before we can go beyond case studies to draw general conclusions about the rise of local history, we must first consider the ways in which gazetteer compilation varied by time and place. Scholars have spent decades cataloging extant gazetteers, compiling references to lost ones, and attempting to calculate production rates. As we saw in chapter 1, there is wide agreement that gazetteers emerged as a distinct genre in the Southern Song and were universalized down to the circuit level by central government edict in the Yuan and to county level in the early Ming. In 1958 Aoyama Sadao 青山定雄 counted 343 Song gazetteers in contemporary bibliographies.[1] In 1962 Zhang Guogan 張國淦 published references to about 2,000 Song and Yuan gazetteers and geographical works, mostly from Song, almost all of which are now lost.[2] In 1986 Liu Weiyi 劉緯毅 argued that "in the 320 years of the Song Dynasty, there were 1016 distinct gazetteer editions published in the entire country."[3] Excluding the forty comprehensive gazetteers included in Liu's list, this total of 976 local gazetteers would average out to 3.1 titles per year for the entire Song. If Liu's figures had been broken down by Northern Song (960–1127) and Southern Song (1127–1279), the Southern Song figure would be higher. For the much shorter Yuan dynasty (1279–1368), Timothy

1. Aoyama, *Tō Sō chihōshi mokuroku*.
2. Zhang Guogan, *Zhongguo gu fangzhi kao*.
3. Liu Weiyi, "Song dai fangzhi," 129–39.

Brook and Jun Fang found references to only "about 200" gazetteers, or about two per year.[4]

For the Ming, in 1988 Ba Zhaoxiang 巴兆祥 published his research categorizing 2,892 extant and lost Ming administrative-unit gazetteers by reign period and place of publication.[5] Although Ba acknowledged that his data was incomplete, his figure became the standard for the next decade. Ba's work was reproduced in *Fangzhi xue* 方志學 (Gazetteer studies), the authoritative 1993 volume edited by Huang Wei 黃葦 and widely cited in other scholarly works.[6] Ba's periodization divided Ming gazetteer compilation into four eras: "beginning," "vigorous development," "flourishing," and "gradual decline." For the first period, the Ming founding through the Tianshun reign (1368–1465), Ba identified 257 datable gazetteers and argued that this meant there was an annual compilation rate of less than three per year in the entire Ming state. This would be comparable to the Song and Yuan figures cited above. For the second period, the Chenghua through Zhengde reigns (1465–1522), Ba identified 460 gazetteers, a rate of about eight per year. During the third period, the Jiajing and Wanli eras (1522–1620), Ba identified 1,622 gazetteers, or more than sixteen per year. Ba argued that in the last period, the Tianqi and Chongzhen eras (1620–44), gazetteer production declined. Only 66 gazetteers were compiled, or less than three per year.

In 2000 Zhang Sheng 張升 challenged Ba's figures and his characterization of the early Ming as a time with few gazetteers. Zhang argued that Ba had ignored hundreds of Ming gazetteers copied into the *Yongle dadian* 永樂大典 (Great encyclopedia of the Yongle Era), more in the Wenyuange 文淵閣 imperial collection, ones produced by guard units, and others compiled in response to early-Ming edicts, and as a result, the total number "far, far, exceeded 2892."[7] The *Yongle dadian* was a massive work of 22,937 chapters, of which fewer than 5 percent survive, but in 2004 Wang Duanlai 王端來 and Liu Xian 柳憲 examined what remains to identify approximately 900 gazetteers used in the compilation. Most, they argued, dated to the period between 1368 and 1408.[8]

4. Brook, "Native Identity," 236.
5. Ba Zhaoxiang, "Mingdai fangzhi," 152–62.
6. Huang Wei, *Fang zhi xue*.
7. Zhang Sheng, "Mingdai fangzhi," 64–67.
8. Wang and Liu, *Yongle dadian fangzhi*, 3.

The 1441 *Wenyuange shumu* 文淵閣書目 (Wenyuange book catalog) cited by Zhang divided local gazetteers into "old gazetteers" and "new gazetteers," and listed 600 of the former and 568 of the latter, but it did not define its categories or date the gazetteers.[9] If one included gazetteers from these sources, Zhang argued, there were "certainly 1,000 or more gazetteers compiled" in the Ming prior to 1441.[10]

In response to Zhang's critique, Ba did additional research and in 2004 published an increased figure, 3,470 editions, of which he was able to date 2,972 by reign period.[11] The 3,470 editions consisted of 73 provincial gazetteers, 622 prefectural, 421 subprefectural, 2,225 county, 49 village, 53 guard unit, and 27 border pass gazetteers. Ba acknowledged that he had not accounted for all early-Ming titles, but argued that Zhang had overstated the number because many titles found in the *Wenyuange shumu* and *Yongle da dian* cannot be dated and were likely from Song or Yuan, or were duplicates. Thus, Ba did not revise his periodization of Ming gazetteers.

Table 3.1 presents Ba's revised figures by reign period and adds a calculation of the number of gazetteers produced per year. Using these revised figures to calculate yearly averages for Ba's four periods yields 5.0 gazetteers per year from 1368–1465, 8.9 per year from 1465–1522, 17.4 per year from 1522–1620, and 10.7 per year from 1620–44.

Considering these figures on their own terms, one number is striking: In Ba's original periodization, the rate of compilation during the period of "gradual decline" (1620–44) was less than half the rate found in the period of "vigorous development" (1465–1522). But using Ba's revised numbers, the rate of compilation in 1620–44 was higher than in 1465–1522, despite the fact that much of north, central, and southwest Ming was consumed by the rebellions of Li Zicheng 李自成, Zhang Xianzhong 張獻忠, and others from 1628 to 1644.

In the following pages I will argue that the disagreement between Ba Zhaoxiang and Zhang Sheng stems from their failure to address a fundamental question: What is a "gazetteer" (*zhi* 志)?

9.   Yang Shiqi, *Wenyuange shumu*, 183–216.
10. Zhang Sheng, "Mingdai fangzhi," 2000, 64.
11. Ba, *Fangzhi xue xin lun*, 47–49. Ba does not include the six empire-wide gazetteers in his total. Li Yanqiu, "Mingdai Wenyuange."

Table 3.1
Number of gazetteers by Ming reign period and per year

Reign Period	Extant	Lost	Total	Years	Number per year
Hongwu (1368–99)	4	280	284	31	9.2
Jianwen (1399–1403)	0	0	0	4	0
Yongle (1403–25)	6	58	64	22	2.9
Hongxi (1425–26)	0	1	1	1	1.0
Xuande (1426–36)	1	22	23	10	2.3
Zhengtong (1436–50)	9	30	39	14	2.8
Jingtai (1450–57)	3	45	48	7	6.9
Tianshun (1457–65)	4	27	31	8	3.9
Chenghua (1465–88)	18	129	147	23	6.4
Hongzhi (1488–1506)	51	132	183	18	10.2
Zhengde (1506–22)	66	112	178	16	11.1
Jiajing (1522–67)	351	351	702	45	15.6
Longqing (1567–73)	33	53	86	6	14.3
Wanli (1573–1620)	358	561	919	47	19.6
Taichang (1620–21)	1	0	1	1	1.0
Tianqi (1621–28)	27	41	68	7	9.7
Chongzhen (1636–44)	72	126	198	17	11.6
Date unclear	10	488	498	276	1.8

This turns out to be a complex question. Should we count an unpublished compilation put together by a local scholar on his own initiative and kept in his home? Or a retained copy of materials submitted by a county clerk to prefectural officials for use in compiling a new prefectural gazetteer? Neither Ba nor Zhang defined the thing they were counting.

If one accepts a broad definition of "gazetteer" that includes quickly assembled, marginally edited texts, private compilations, and manuscript texts that were submitted to superior administrative units for use in a higher-level gazetteer compilation, then the number of Ming gazetteers would indeed "far, far, exceed" even Ba's expanded count. Such quick gazetteers were not always printed separately and the locally held manuscript copies were often soon lost and forgotten. But if one construes "gazetteer" more narrowly to include only mature texts that were extensively researched and carefully edited, then even though the total number doubtlessly exceeds Ba's count, his general point that the genre flourished in the period from 1522–1620 still makes sense.

Before proposing my own periodization for gazetteers, I will first discuss the editorial process. Doing so will make it possible to better understand, and partially reconcile, Ba and Zhang's findings, and to propose a more accurate and useful periodization, one that takes account of the various ways in which gazetteers were initiated in different times and places and that does not privilege Ming as a discrete period, as in Ba's work.

Gazetteers as Living Documents

As the gazetteer genre became well established during the Southern Song, compilers began to conceive of their texts as both individual editions and parts of ongoing studies of particular places that transcended dynastic changes. Authors of the time used the word *zhi* to refer to both discrete compilations and sets of compilations for a locale, which included an original plus supplements made in later years. The ideal gazetteer was a "complete book" (*quan shu* 全書) or a "full compilation" (*da bei* 大備), that is, one that had appropriate coverage and was not out of date.[12] The idea of the "complete book" can be seen in Zhou Yinghe's 周應合 1261 preface to his gazetteer of Jiankang 建康, in which he recalls his discussion with prefect Ma Guangzu 馬光祖. Zhou said to Ma: "That which is recorded on the 280 blocks of the old gazetteer 舊志 stops at the Qiandao era [1165–73]. That which is recorded on the 220 blocks of the supplemental gazetteer 續志 stops at the Qingyuan era [1195–1200]. In making a [new] supplement I dare not treat in a cursory manner those matters that should be included for the more than sixty years from Qingyuan to today, yet I also dare not discard the earlier gazetteer 前志." Ma responded: "The two gazetteers of the Qiandao and Qingyuan eras have parts that are detailed and parts that are sketchy and much is not in accord with the *Liu chao shi ji* 六朝事跡 (Traces of matters of the Six Dynasties) and *Jiankang shilu* 建康實錄 (True record of Jiankang). Now you should collate and unify them. Where the previous gazetteers have omissions, supplement them; where they have errors, correct them; for

12. *Jiayu xian zhi*, 2nd preface, 1b; *Jiankang zhi*, 1329; *Qiandao Siming tu jing*, 4874; *Wujun zhi*, 693.

undocumented matters from after Qingyuan, record them. Only then will it be a complete book."[13]

In this preface, separate editions are identified, but the gazetteer is also treated as a complete book composed of an original and two supplements. Even though changes and additions had been made to the gazetteer over the course of a century since its original publication, the 1261 edition still used *Jiankang zhi* as the title.

The term "edition" is problematic when discussing gazetteers and requires clarification. Not only were gazetteers repeatedly supplemented and recompiled, but after they were completed local officials and scholars regularly added new materials, such as the accomplishments of new magistrates, in the form of handwritten additions or supplemental woodblocks for xylographic printing. Compilers planned for such additions. One technique was to include blank sheets in the original bound volume, which is described in the compilation notes of the 1261 *Jiankang zhi*: "At the end of every chapter and section, blank, lined pages have been inserted to await supplements and additions; we dare not consider it a finished book."[14]

Another technique for ongoing supplementation can be seen in the gazetteer of Linding 臨汀, Fujian. In 1258 Prefect Hu Taichu 胡太初 recompiled the gazetteer because the previous edition, published sixty years earlier, was incomplete. In his preface Hu emphasized the ongoing nature of the gazetteer project, expressing his hope that like-minded gentlemen of the future would "supplement it without end." Hu simultaneously compiled a separate local literary anthology and "left the back covers off of both works to await supplements by those who come in the future."[15] In the above cases, the living nature of the gazetteer was expressed in both discourse and material form.

Whether or not we should consider a supplemented gazetteer to be a new "edition" depends on the extent of the supplements. The updating done between the original gazetteer and the next recompilation could range from simple handwritten entries on blank lines to entirely new chapters. It is appropriate to treat major supplements as new "editions" because gazetteer compilers, readers, and collectors talked about them

---

13. *Jiankang zhi*, 1329.
14. Ibid., 1331.
15. Wang and Liu, *Yongle dadian fangzhi jiyi*, 1467.

as distinct works, and the word *xu*, meaning "supplement" or "continuation" was usually inserted into the title. A supplemental gazetteer was a major milestone even as contemporaries recognized the ongoing nature of local history and expected further additions. Minor additions, however, did not result in new titles, and contemporaries did not treat them as separate works even though such additions caused individual imprints to have different content.

Such modifications are visible in many Ming gazetteers. The Tianyige Library's copy of the *Ruzhou zhi* 汝州志 (Henan) is a modified reprint of the 1506 edition. In 1510, four months after An Shixian 安世賢 became the Ruzhou magistrate, he had a new block cut to include himself and a new judge in the list of officials. This forced an awkward renumbering of the folios.[16] Inserted and renumbered blocks are often identified as such. The blocks for the gazetteer of Hezhou 河州, Shaanxi, were originally cut in 1546 but supplemented at least twice before the printing of an extant copy. The result was an original page 18 followed by a "newly added 18" 新增十八, which included officials who took office between 1546 and 1571 as well as a Hezhou garrison commander who took office in 1436 but was left out of the original gazetteer.[17] Supplemental blocks were typically labeled *zeng*, *you* 又, *bu* 補, or *xu*, meaning "added" or "supplemented," and sometimes inscribed with separate dates. Folios of the 1616 *Shandong tong zhi* 山東通志, which supplemented and reprinted the 1533 edition, have the phrase "supplemental cutting in Wanli *bingchen*" (1616) in each new folio's "white mouth" (the typically blank area along the fold). Such minor updating was a way for a new official to ensure that his service was recorded and in keeping with the sense that gazetteers, like genealogies, were living documents and cumulative records of places, just as genealogies were cumulative records of families. Thus, when thinking about the length of time between editions, it is important to keep in mind that there could be multiple reprints with minor modifications between major revisions.

Not only did new editions change after their initial publications, but texts that are considered to be original editions were often preceded by other works. This is illustrated by the compilation of the Zhengtong-era

16. *Ruzhou zhi* (1506), postface, 2b.
17. *Hezhou zhi* (1546), *TGQ*, 178.

(1436–48) gazetteer of Xincheng 新城, Jiangxi. Two locals, Zhu Hui 朱徽 and He Cheng 何澄, were friends who lived together at the local Confucian school in their youth.[18] He Cheng was interested in gazetteers and regretted never having seen the old gazetteer of *Xujiang* 盱江, a twelfth-century gazetteer that encompassed Xincheng and three neighboring counties.[19] In 1393 He Cheng passed the *juren* exam and went away for many years, including two years spent working on the *Yongle dadian*, which, as noted above, was compiled from 1403 to 1408. Early in the Yongle era (1403–25), Zhu Hui finally got a printed copy of the Xujiang gazetteer from someone in Huixi 匯溪. Zhu went through it, copied out materials on Xincheng, and planned to turn them into a gazetteer to be called *Lichuan zhi* 黎川志 (Li River gazetteer).[20] Zhu wanted He Cheng to make corrections, but he was in the capital. While awaiting his return, Zhu collected more materials and completed a manuscript, but it was not yet polished and he "dared not show it to anyone." Zhu put covers on his manuscript and stored it in his family school.[21] At this point, we can say that he had a "gazetteer," even though he hoped to improve it in the future.

In 1418 the Xincheng County Confucian school instructor received the imperial edict to submit a gazetteer to the court, and he put Zhu Hui in charge of the project. Zhu copied his manuscript and submitted it to the palace library, where it was "not easy for people to see."[22] Zhu worried that after time passed the gazetteer would be lost, so he wanted to publish a facsimile edition 似本.[23] Zhu thought the gazetteer he had submitted to the court was still rough, a common complaint about gazetteers done in response to the Hongwu and Yongle edicts that had strict deadlines for submission.[24]

In 1423 Zhu finally passed the *juren* exam and was appointed assistant instructor of the neighboring Guangze County 光澤縣, just across

18.   *Xincheng xian zhi*, 821, 829.

19.   *Xincheng xian zhi*, 829. Ma Duanlin, *Wenxian tongkao*, 1701–2, lists the *Xujiang zhi* as having been compiled in 1158 and supplemented in 1199.

20.   The Li River flows through Xincheng. The Xu River is the same river, but the name applies to the section below the prefectural seat of Jianchang.

21.   *Xincheng xian zhi*, 830.

22.   Ibid., 826.

23.   Ibid., 824, 827.

24.   Ibid., 830; *Jiayu xian zhi*, Mo Zhen preface, 1b.

the border in Fujian.[25] In 1429 Zhu Hui's son Zhu Ding 朱鼎 and four other local scholars asked Xincheng County Confucian school instructor Shangguan You 上官祐 to edit Zhu Hui's manuscript and "print and disseminate it to people" 刊布於人.[26] Shangguan worked on it but did not print it. In 1438 He Cheng returned to Xincheng and reviewed the manuscript. Sometime between 1438 and 1448 Zhu Hui wrote, "This year, having now completed and published the *Guangze Gazetteer*, I again picked up the Xincheng gazetteer manuscript corrected by the two gentlemen, He Cheng and Shangguan You, obtained the labor of block cutters, and had it cut on red jujube 華棗."[27]

Understanding the living nature of gazetteers affects how we think about gazetteer counts. Ba Zhaoxiang's figures give the impression that in any given year almost no Ming jurisdictions were engaged in gazetteer compilation. In fact many jurisdictions that already had a gazetteer were incrementally adding materials, trying to maintain it as a "complete book." The Xincheng example reveals two additional problems. First, the 1448 printed edition had two early-fifteenth-century manuscript incarnations, one kept in the compiler's family school and an updated version submitted to the central government. An accurate count would include all three as separate titles, but finding such references and determining how the various texts related to each other requires extensive searching and careful reading of prefaces, *fanli*, authors' collected works, and other sources.

A second problem is accounting for all of the gazetteers produced in response to orders from the court or superior administrative units, the problem raised by Zhang Sheng. National-level gazetteer projects were repeatedly started in the early Ming, and each one triggered another round of local gazetteer compilation. For the 1370 *Da Ming zhi shu* 大明志書 (Gazetteer of the Great Ming), the central government collected materials from over 1,100 administrative units down to the county level, but it is unclear how many units compiled new gazetteers for this project.[28] In the spring of 1376 the central government again collected

25. *Xincheng xian zhi*, 534.

26. Ibid., 831. Zhu Hui may have known Shangguan You from his time in Guangze, because Shangguan was a Guangze native.

27. Ibid., 831.

28. *Ming shilu* (Taizu), 59.2a–b, third year, twelfth month, *xinyou* day. The *Da Ming zhi shu* is no longer extant.

local gazetteers, this time through provincial administration commissions. In Huguang Province the commission opened a provincial gazetteer compilation office and ordered each prefecture to compile a gazetteer with maps by using "all of its old gazetteers" updated with new information. The order assumes that old gazetteers were available to each prefecture. In Yongzhou 永州 Prefecture, the compilers worked quickly and submitted the completed manuscript to the commission in the first month of the summer of 1376. The prefect then had woodblocks cut from a retained copy to keep in the yamen.[29] It is not clear how many counties and subprefectures compiled new manuscripts for this project, and how many simply sent loose materials to the prefecture.

The best-documented early-Ming national-level gazetteer project was the one begun in 1418. The Ministry of Rites was ordered to dispatch officials to "visit locales everywhere to widely collect traces of events and old gazetteers," and the minister of revenue and two members of the Hanlin Academy directed the project.[30] As the order came down to the locales, it required new compilations based on the *fanli* translated in chapter 1.[31] From extant prefaces we know that counties across the realm compiled and submitted gazetteers, but it is not clear where they went. The Xincheng gazetteer was sent to the palace library, and the gazetteer of Chaoyang潮陽, Guangdong, was "submitted to the Heavenly court" 貢天府.[32] The 1441 Wenyuange catalog does not list either title, so it is possible that the gazetteers were sent to one of the ministries or elsewhere.[33] Thus, the problem of counting gazetteers is not simply one of dating the titles found in the *Wenyuange shumu* and *Yongle dadian*. It goes much deeper. We must accept that there were thousands of manuscripts produced in response to these and other imperial edicts (discussed in chapter 1) of which there is now no trace.

29.   *Yongzhou fu zhi* (1383), 3a–4a.

30.   *Ming shilu* (Taizong), 2089; *Shenxian zhi*, preface, 3a, *fanli*, 1a–3b.

31.   *Chaoyang xian zhi*, 1419 preface (old prefaces, 7b).

32.   Ibid.

33.   The catalog does list two texts titled *Xincheng xian zhi*, but they appear to have been gazetteers of counties of the same name in Beizhili and Zhejiang.

Private Gazetteers and Official Gazetteers

Another factor to consider in thinking about the meaning of "gazetteer" is compilers' categorization of their works into two types, official and private, distinguished by editorial process. An official gazetteer was one that was initiated by and recognized as such by the local government. "Official" was the default category. There was no common term for "official gazetteer" analogous to "official book" 官書, "official edition" 官板 or 官本, or "official printing" 官刻, which regularly appear in late imperial sources referring to books printed by government offices in contrast to those printed by commercial presses 坊刻 and households 家刻.[34]

Gazetteer compilers denoted their work's official status in two main ways: in statements in the prefaces that the resident administrator had initiated and approved the project, and by creating a threshold of interpretation using paratextual elements. Some Song, Yuan, and Ming gazetteers, and many Qing gazetteers, also contain a petition to superior officials requesting permission to compile and print the gazetteer and its approval. Together these elements pushed readers to understand gazetteers as authoritative, orthodox monographs on locales, produced through the diligent efforts of non-native resident officials in cooperation with key representatives of local society. The statements of official initiation, sponsorship, or approval were the most important signifiers of official status. Titles were also important. The standard title format of official local gazetteers consisted of (1) place, (2) administrative unit, and (3) "gazetteer," as in "*Suzhou fu zhi* 蘇州府志" (Suzhou Prefecture gazetteer). Titles of provincial gazetteers almost always consisted of the province name followed by "comprehensive gazetteer" (通志 or 總志).[35] Such a short, direct title portrayed the book as authoritative. Titles could take the modifiers "recompiled," "supplemented," or "new," to indicate that the work was not a jurisdiction's first compilation. Occasionally compilers of official gazetteers omitted the administrative unit name in the title

34. For use of *guan ban* and *fang ban*, see the *Xinzhou zhi*, 1.22b–23a. For use of *guan ben*, see *Dezhou zhi* (1570s), 5.2b. For further discussion of this division, see Chia, *Printing for Profit*, 6–7.

35. An exception is the Jiajing-era *Jiangxi sheng da zhi*.

or used an old place name with a rich history, as in the 1542 *Weiyang zhi* 惟揚志, the gazetteer of Yangzhou Prefecture 揚州府.

As with other book genres, gazetteer titles were inscribed in multiple places. Even when a gazetteer came in a box with a title block on the cover, the title was typically repeated in a separately printed block affixed to each fascicle, in prefaces and postfaces, the principles of compilation, the table of contents, the first folio of each chapter, and in each folio's fold. Titles also often appeared on a separate title page following the cover, on the last column of the last folio of each chapter, and along the bottom edge.

Subtle clues in the historical record suggest that local elites occasionally compiled and printed a local gazetteer using the standard official title without first obtaining permission from the local magistrate or prefect. In 1544 Zou Tingji 鄒廷濟 supplemented the official 1480 gazetteer of Gong'an 公安, Huguang, and published it under the same title, yet there is no mention in the gazetteer's paratext that the magistrate was involved or gave permission. Zou, however, had official status through a hereditary title and was a National University student in Nanjing. Even so, he was careful to point out in his postface that he had discussed the project with four National University classmates and had the support of three Gong'an natives who were ranked officials.[36]

"Private gazetteers" (私志, or 私乘), were generally compiled by a single local person working, at least initially, without support or recognition from the local administration. Private gazetteers had titles such as *Shanju yezhi* 山居野志 (Unofficial gazetteer from a mountain abode), which uses *yezhi*, a term analogous to *yeshi* 野史, the standard term for "unofficial dynastic history;" *Yongfu zheng qi lu* 永福正氣錄 (Record of the true essence of Yongfu), *Shouning daizhi* 守寧待志 (Shouning gazetteer-in-waiting), and *Liangzhou fu zhi bei kao* 涼州府志備考 (Preparatory studies for the Liangzhou Prefecture gazetteer).[37]

As the last two titles suggest, private gazetteers could become official gazetteers, and administrators could put private persons in charge of official compilations. Compiling a substantial gazetteer was time consuming,

---

36. *Gong'an xian zhi* (1543), postface. Compilers of the 1874 edition were unaware of Zou Tingji's edition. *Gong'an xian zhi* (1874), *fanli*.

37. *Liyang xian zhi*, 264; *Yongfu xian zhi*, 353; *Liangzhou fu zhi bei kao*.

and if a magistrate waited too long, it was unlikely to be finished unless it drew heavily on preexisting work. Because gazetteers were not usually started until well into a local administrator's term in office, and most administrators served only one or two three-year terms, many projects were not finished before the official was transferred. Due to the law of avoidance, which prohibited service in an official's native province, resident administrators generally needed to work closely with native scholars. Sometimes magistrates simply printed as official gazetteers the privately compiled manuscripts that local scholars presented to them, either as submitted or after having the author update or revise selected parts.[38] This is what happened in the Xincheng case discussed above.

More commonly magistrates used private gazetteers as foundations for official gazetteers and brought in additional editorial personnel to make updates and changes. A typical case is that of Zhou Wanjin 周萬金, an out-of-office provincial graduate from Neihuang 內黃, Beizhili, who spent years working alone on a county gazetteer without managing to finish. In 1523 he showed his work to the magistrate, who then opened an office to compile an official gazetteer, hired Zhou, and brought in the Confucian school instructor and students to help Zhou complete the project.[39] Not all authors of private gazetteers were selected to work on the official editions, even when their work was the foundation. Local community school teacher Liao Benxiang 廖本祥 compiled a private gazetteer of Chaling 茶陵, Huguang, in the Zhengde era (1506–22), but his work became merely one source for the official 1525 edition and he was not involved in its compilation, perhaps because of his low status.[40]

Editorial Personnel

Identifying the types of people involved in gazetteer compilation is important to understanding the genre. Throughout the period covered by this book, most people who worked on gazetteers were resident administrators

38. *Tiantai xian zhi*, old preface, 2a.
39. *Neihuang xian zhi*, preface, 4b–5b.
40. *Chaling zhou zhi*, 1085.

(prefects, magistrates, and subordinate ranked officials), Confucian school teachers stationed outside their native places, or locals who were current, retired, or aspiring officials.[41] But within this broad generalization there were noticeable differences in who contributed to gazetteers in core and peripheral regions.

Details about editorial personnel and their roles in compiling and publishing gazetteers can be gleaned from gazetteers' prefatory matter, especially contributor lists and prefaces.

Contributor lists typically appear under the headings "compilers names" 纂修姓氏 or simply "names." They most commonly follow the prefaces, but the exact placement varies. Lead compilers' names may also appear on each chapter's first page and the book's last page. Lists vary in coverage, but generally proceed in status order, beginning with honorary participants and supervisory officials; continuing with editorial personnel, who determined categories if they had not already been decided at a higher level, drafted text, gathered sources, and checked facts; and concluding with production supervisors and craftsmen. In addition to each person's name, lists typically note offices held, status as a local person, and sometimes the native places of outsiders, degree dates, and style names. An example list, from the 1568 gazetteer of Chuxiong 楚雄, Yunnan, follows:[42]

Names

Compilation advocates 議修:
Zhu Kui, Lancang Military Defense Circuit Vice Commissioner
Zhang Yue, Concurrent Erhai Branch Circuit Assistant Administration
  Commissioner
Ceng Yijing, Erhai Branch Circuit Assistant Administration
  Commissioner

Compilation directors 總修:
Xu Shi, Yunnan Surveillance Commissioner
Ren Weidiao, Erhai Branch Circuit Assistant Surveillance Commissioner

Compilers 纂修:
Zhang Ze, Chuxiong Prefecture Prefect

41.   For a detailed study correlating roles in the compilation of Ming dynasty gazetteers of Nanzhili with official positions and status, see Zhang Yingpin, *Mingdai Nanzhili*, 123–31.
42.   *Chuxiong fu zhi*, prefatory matter.

Ma Wenbiao, Chuxiong County Magistrate
Chen Ce, Dingyuan County Magistrate
Ju Fu, local person, administrator
Ju Yiren, local person, secretary
Xie Zan, local person, judge
Yu Ruqin, local person, provincial graduate
Ju Yizheng, local person, provincial graduate

Collators 校修:
Chen Mo, Dali Prefecture Prefect
Yuan Liang, Lijiang Prefecture Prefect
Zhang Taiheng, Chuxiong Prefecture Vice Prefect
An Yu, Chuxiong Prefecture Judge
Liu Sumin, Chuxiong Prefecture Confucian School Instructor
Wang Bingzhong, Chuxiong County Confucian School Instructor
Li Yangdong, Guangtong County Confucian School Instructor

Supervisor of printing craftsmen 督理刻匠:
Tang Qin, Chuxiong County Clerk

Copyist 書寫:
Bai Shibian

This list reveals several common aspects of personnel lists: First, non-natives and natives are identified as such. Creating an impression that resident administrators and local elites cooperated in producing the gazetteer and reached consensus on the final product was critical to projecting its authoritative status. Second, the list suggests how hard it can be to determine a primary compiler. Most gazetteers were group projects, lists contain names of people who did little or no work, and overlapping and ambiguous terms were used for editorial roles. Yunnan Surveillance Commissioner Xu Shi 徐栻 wrote in a preface that a censor inspecting Chuxiong ordered the branch surveillance official, Ren Weidiao 任惟釣, to organize and oversee a compilation and that soon thereafter the Chuxiong prefect, two county magistrates, and local literati began collecting and editing materials. The surveillance commissioner proofread the text, and Ren wrote a postface. None of the three officials listed as "compilation advocates" appear to have been involved in the actual work; their listing was honorary. The two "compilation directors," Xu and Ren, had actual oversight and limited editorial duties. Following the supervisors were editorial personnel in two categories: eight compilers, consisting of three officials and five locals. The seven collators were officials from Chuxiong and neighboring prefectures, and three Confucian school instructors.[43] Of the eight listed compilers, none is described as a primary compiler, although the Chuxiong prefect is listed first due to his status. Most likely, the five local literati did most of the collecting, arranging, writing, and editing.

As a result of such ambiguity, catalogers of major gazetteer collections often disagree on a gazetteer's primary compiler and author searches can be ineffective. If one searches for the Chuxiong gazetteer in current library catalogs, Xu Shi and Zhang Ze 張澤, the Chuxiong prefect, appear in the author field. Sometimes Xu comes first and sometimes Zhang, but in fact it was co-edited by multiple people. Although such ambiguity is the norm, in some gazetteers a primary compiler is identified. For example, the editorial participant list in the 1585 gazetteer of Tengxian 滕縣, Shandong, begins, "written and arranged 撰次 by townsman Wang Yuanbin 王元賓," then lists eight "collective readers" 同閱, and one "researcher" 採訪.[44] Editorial personnel terms were often modified by *fen* 分, indicating that the work was divided, usually by chapter; *xie* 協 or *can* 參, indicating assistant status; and *tong* 同 indicating that a group performed the named function.

From such lists and prefaces it is clear that most gazetteers were compiled by local literati and supervised by resident administrators. The head territorial administrator typically approved the project, but the Confucian school instructors, local people, and yamen staff did most of the work. Local degree holders residing in their native places were the most important category of editorial personnel. Some were aspiring officials studying for higher-level exams or waiting for their first official posts, others were between assignments, on sick leave, or retired, had been stripped of office, or were on mourning leave, as in the case of Wan Hao 萬浩, a compiler in the Historiography Institute who compiled the 1563 *Jinxian xian zhi* 進賢縣志 at home following his mother's death.[45] Mandatory

43. Ibid., *xingshi*, 4.

44. *Tengxian zhi*, 5.

45. *Jinxian xian zhi*, preface. For other examples, see: *Jingxian zhi*, 415; *Wujiang xian zhi*, preface; *Yanping fu zhi*, preface; *Yongping fu zhi*, 24; *Neihuang xian zhi*, preface, 4b–5b.

mourning periods were opportunities for men who had spent years away from home to reconnect with their families, friends, and other members of the local elite. To reconnect with family, an off-duty official could compile a genealogy, and to reconnect with local literati, he could compile a gazetteer. Gazetteer writing reintegrated out-of-office officials into the local scene, refreshing old connections and establishing new ones, while giving an official something to do and perhaps some income.

In 1524–25 Zheng Qingyun 鄭慶雲, a native of Yanping 延平, Fujian, edited a gazetteer while home on sick leave from his post as a supervising secretary in the Ministry of Rites in Nanjing.[46] At the time, Zheng's classmate 同年, the Yanping prefect, visited Zheng's home to ask him to edit the gazetteer. Zheng accepted. Soon thereafter his father died and he extended his sick leave with mourning leave, giving him plenty of time to finish the project. In fact, he was gone so long that a central government official impeached him, unsuccessfully, for circumventing the three-year time limit for returning to work.[47]

Scholarly locals without degrees or current student status participated in some compilations, but rarely, at least in literati centers, were they chief editors. Zhang Yingpin's study of Ming gazetteers of Nanzhili (Southern Metropolitan Region) found that twenty-six of thirty-nine lead editors held the *jinshi* degree, one held the *juren* degree, five were government students, and seven were Confucian school instructors. An exception to this general pattern is a gazetteer of Shangyu 上虞, Zhejiang, from the Yongle era (1401–24), which was drafted by Yuan Hua 袁鏵, a "local commoner" 邑民, and polished by his elder brother, Yuan Xuan 袁鉉, a teacher of children.[48]

Resident administrators' involvement varied. Some took great interest and established editorial principles, wrote introductions to chapters and prefaces, and polished the entire work. Some simply approved the work of others, and a few took credit but used ghostwriters. At one end of the spectrum was Feng Weixian 馮惟賢, the magistrate of Lucheng 潞城, Shanxi, who personally edited the manuscript for the 1591 gazetteer to

46. *Yanping fu zhi*, preface.

47. *Ming shilu* (Shizong), 2555–57. Zheng's extended leave triggered a widespread investigation of sick leave abuse by officials and new metropolitan graduates.

48. *Shangyu xian zhi jiao xu*, 3810–11. Neither appears on lists of local graduates.

prevent the problem of "one sheep and nine shepherds," a common flaw of group compilations.[49] At the other end was Yi Shizhong 易时中 (style name Kuixu 愧虚), the magistrate of Xiajin 夏津, Shandong, who had the well-known essayist Wang Shenzhong 王慎中 (1509–59) ghostwrite his 1540 preface to the Xiajin gazetteer. The preface does not reveal that it was ghostwritten, stating, on the contrary, "written by Yi Shizhong."[50] But in Wang's collected works the preface appears under the title "Preface to the Xiajin County Gazetteer, Written on Behalf of Mr. Yi Kuixu."[51] Wang, an official from Yi Shizhong's hometown of Jinjiang 晋江, Fujian, wrote additional parts of the gazetteer, and other Jinjiang natives wrote much of the rest.

One reason magistrates hired ghostwriters was to finish the gazetteer during their term in office. Compilations frequently spanned multiple administrations because administrators tended to start gazetteers only after they had served long enough to have accomplishments worth recording and promoting, and editorial personnel often changed. In addition to transfers, personal tragedies forced contributors to drop out. During compilation of the 1320 *Siming zhi* 四明志, Wang Housun 王厚孫 was assigned to collect documents on all the temples in Changguo 昌國 County. Unfortunately for Wang and the gazetteer, his daughter died after he had researched only one temple and he quit the project. No one took over his work, and the gazetteer simply omitted the county's other temples.[52]

Supervisors of gazetteer projects generally preferred to recruit local editorial talent, but in peripheral areas with few educated Chinese residents this could be difficult. Thus, as we saw earlier, in Chuxiong, a highland area populated by Yi and Zhuang people, vice prefects of two neighboring prefectures helped collate the gazetteer.[53] Wang Chongxian 王崇獻, the compiler of the 1514 gazetteer of Xuanfu Garrison 宣府鎮, near the Great Wall, explained that the project was difficult because many garrison officials were soldiers and few books were available.[54] He noted,

49.   *Lucheng xian zhi*, postface.
50.   *Xiajin xian zhi*, 5.
51.   Wang Shenzhong, *Zunyan ji*, 9.15b.
52.   [*Zhizheng*], *Siming xu zhi*, 6668.
53.   *Chuxiong fu zhi*, xingshi, 4.
54.   *Xuanfu zhen zhi*, 16b.

"Some prefectural and county officials are able to make a record of their locale; but few military men in the border regions can do it." Not only were military affairs pressing, said Wang, but soldiers' scholarship was not outstanding, and thus, "how could they set their minds to it?"[55]

But lack of scholarly resources was not confined to Ming border regions and areas populated by people who were not culturally and linguistically Chinese. In the traditional Chinese heartland, the Central Plains 中原, a region that by the Ming had been passed up economically by Jiangnan, finding literati could be difficult in some locales. Timothy Sedo, in his study of the 1506 gazetteer of Linzhang 臨漳, Henan, draws on Roger Des Forges's work to argue that in the Ming, most locales in North China lacked the resources enjoyed by southern literati, such as corporate lineage lands that supported high-achieving students pursuing civil service examination degrees.[56] Lineages were far less organized in North China, and land there was more likely to be farmed by owner cultivators taxed directly by the state rather than by tenants who rented land from lineage estates.

As a result of lineage support, southerners dominated the exams in the early Ming and the government created a quota system guaranteeing a fixed percentage of *jinshi* degrees to candidates from the North and Southwest.[57] A mature quota was promulgated in 1427. It reserved 35 percent of degrees for candidates from northern provinces (Shandong, Henan, Shanxi, Shaanxi, and Beizhili), 10 percent for those from southwestern provinces (Sichuan, Guizhou, Yunnan, and Guangxi), and the remaining 55 percent for southerners (Nanzhili, Zhejiang, Fujian, Guangdong, Huguang).[58]

In Linzhang, a town that had few examination graduates, Magistrate Jing Fang 景芳 dominated the gazetteer compilation and wrote it with a "statist" orientation rather than a "localist" orientation like that seen in the 1579 *Xinchang xian zhi* discussed in chapter 2. His only editorial help was from two local community school students, one of whom was so poor that Jing Fang gave him money so that he could marry.[59] The

55. Ibid., preface, 3b.
56. Des Forges, *Cultural Centrality*.
57. Sedo, "Linzhang County," 198, 203.
58. Elman, *A Cultural History*, 95–96.
59. Ibid., 227.

resulting gazetteer had few biographies of local people and many records of Jing's success at rebuilding the county's cultural and governmental infrastructure.[60] Sedo argues that the Linzhang gazetteer reflects a more activist central government in North China, compared to the gentry-dominated South. Records of reconstructing Linzhang's public buildings did not list gentry donors, as was common in the South; instead, the gazetteer credited the magistrate.[61] Jing was able to use the gazetteer to document his successes in governing Linzhang because there were no powerful local families to resist his efforts. He also emphasized Linzhang's ancient connection to activist government by foregrounding coverage of Ximen Bao, the fifth century BCE tamer of floods.[62] Sedo concluded that the gazetteer attempted to bring Linzhang back into the Chinese cultural mainstream by raising awareness of its cultural centrality even though it had been bypassed economically.

Sedo's study highlights the opposite end of the continuum of local elite participation in gazetteer compilation from that seen in the 1579 *Xinchang xian zhi*. But Linzhang should not be taken as characteristic of all northern gazetteers in the Ming. In fact, as in the South, compilation of many gazetteers was dominated by local elites, and many northern locales produced gazetteers upon local initiative.

In the Ming, the number of gazetteers produced in the North, South, and Southwest roughly paralleled the distribution of the registered population. Ba Zhaoxiang's data (table 3.2), which is arranged by the modern provinces, municipalities, and autonomous regions used to organize the *Zhongguo difangzhi lianhe mulu* 中國地方志聯合目錄 (Union catalog of Chinese gazetteers), show that 38.6 percent of known Ming gazetteers were from the North, 52.8 percent were from the South, and 8.6 percent were from the Southwest.[63] These figures are remarkably close to population figures from the 1586 *Da Ming huidian*, which record 40.8 percent of the population as living in the North, 50.9 percent in the

60.   Ibid., 102.
61.   Ibid., 187.
62.   Ibid., 62.
63.   Zhuang et al., *Zhongguo difangzhi*, 47–49.

Table 3.2
Number of Ming gazetteers by modern province or municipality

Province, municipality, or autonomous region	Total gazetteers	Extant gazetteers	Lost gazetteers
Zhejiang	348	118	230
Hebei	275	89	186
Shandong	273	77	196
Henan	271	99	172
Jiangsu	232	107	125
Jiangxi	229	51	178
Anhui	227	73	154
Shanxi	217	56	161
Hubei	202	37	165
Fujian	200	84	116
Guangdong	194	50	144
Shaanxi	172	46	126
Hunan	168	31	137
Sichuan	86	23	63
Yunnan	81	9	72
Guangxi	67	10	57
Guizhou	64	8	56
Beijing	55	7	48
Gansu	45	15	30
Shanghai	32	14	18
Tianjin	12	1	11
Ningxia	11	6	5
Liaoning	8	3	5
Qinghai	1	0	1
Totals	3,470	1,014	2,456

South, and 8.3 percent in the Southwest.[64] It is also close to the 35:55:10 *jinshi* ratio.

Modern administrative units do not match those of the Ming, and organizing the data by Ming units produces a different rank order (table 3.3). Modern Anhui and Jiangsu Provinces were combined as Nanzhili in Ming; Hunan and Hubei formed Huguang; Gansu, Ningxia, and Qinghai were

64. van der Sprenkel, "Population Statistics," 300–301. These figures were the registered populations. Actual populations were significantly higher in many areas, especially in parts of the Southwest.

Table 3.3
Gazetteers arranged by Ming province

Province	Total	Extant	Lost
Nanzhili	491	194	297
Huguang	370	68	302
Zhejiang	348	118	230
Beizhili	342	97	245
Shandong	281	80	201
Henan	271	99	172
Shaanxi	229	67	162
Jiangxi	229	51	178
Shanxi	217	56	161
Fujian	200	84	116
Guangdong	194	50	144
Sichuan	86	23	63
Yunnan	81	9	72
Guangxi	67	10	57
Guizhou	64	8	56
Totals	3,470	1,014	2,456

in Shaanxi; Beijing, Tianjin, and Hebei made up Beizhili; and Liaoning was part of Shandong. In this arrangement, the large provinces that were later broken into two or more parts rank higher. Nanzhili had the most gazetteers, about one-third to two-fifths more than the next three provinces, Huguang, Zhejiang, and Beizhili, but its population was double that of each of those provinces.

The regional distribution of gazetteers tracks the distribution of administrative units less closely than it does population. The Southwest had more administrative units per registered person than did the North and South, reflecting the difficulties of governing borderlands. The Southwest had 23.6 percent of administrative units for 8.6 percent of the population, the North had 38.0 percent of units for 40.8 percent of the population, and the South had 38.4 percent of the units for 50.9 percent of the population. From this perspective, a southern administrative unit was somewhat more likely to produce a gazetteer than was a northern unit, and much more likely to produce one than was a southwestern unit in the Ming.

In the Song, the regional distribution of gazetteer production was much different from that in the Ming. Liu Weiyi's data (table 3.4),

Table 3.4
Number of identified Song dynasty gazetteers
by province

Province (modern)	Total	Extant	Lost
Sichuan	180	0	180
Zhejiang	141	14	127
Jiangxi	100	0	100
Guangdong	84	0	84
Jiangsu	81	9	72
Guangxi	64	0	64
Hubei	63	0	63
Hunan	60	1	59
Anhui	57	1	56
Fujian	52	2	50
Shaanxi	28	2	26
Henan	23	0	23
Gansu	15	0	15
Shanxi	9	0	9
Shandong	8	0	8
Hebei	6	0	6
Guizhou	3	0	3
Yunnan	1	0	1
Xinjiang	1	0	1
Total	976	29	947

arranged by modern provinces, shows that Sichuan was the leading center, but by the Ming it was far down the list.[65] This is not surprising, considering the devastation of the Mongol conquest and subsequent depopulation. There were few northern gazetteers because the North was lost to the non-Chinese Jin state just as gazetteers were emerging as a distinct genre.

Payments to Editorial Personnel

Throughout the country, editorial work on gazetteers was a mix of paid and volunteer labor. Because many of those who worked on gazetteers

65. Liu Weiyi, "Song dai fangzhi," 129–30.

were already on salary at the local yamen or school, or from well-off families, in all likelihood many worked for free. Others, however, were paid, and local gazetteer projects were a way for officials to provide meaningful work and income to educated men with time on their hands. Payments for editorial work can be traced back to at least the early fourteenth century, with numerous examples from the sixteenth century on.

A typical case is the 1574 gazetteer of Wuxi 無錫, Nanzhili. In 1572 Zhou Bangjie 周邦傑 became Wuxi magistrate and was upset about the poor-quality local gazetteer. So he visited Qin Liang 秦梁 (1515–78), a retired official, presented money, and asked him to revise it. Qin accepted, and the project began.[66] Payments could be made in a lump sum called "book money" 書幣, "writing fee" 筆札之費, or "honorarium" 禮幣, or as a salary for the duration of the project.[67] In 1585 the magistrate of Tengxian, Shandong (discussed earlier in this chapter), set up an office in the yamen, and provided writing implements and salaries to the "Confucians" working on the county gazetteer.[68] These included editor Wang Yuanbin 王元賓, a retired official and book collector; eight local readers, five of whom had previously held office and three who had juren degrees but had not yet been appointed to office; and one researcher, a student at the Confucian school.[69]

Preface authors included a variety of people, and like editorial staff, some were paid. Generally, lead compilers, sponsoring local officials, superior officials, and officials from the subject locale wrote prefaces, but often an outside literatus wrote one as well. It is this last type of person who was most likely to be paid. One such author was Su You 蘇祐 (jinshi 1526), a retired governor-general. A compiler of the 1564 gazetteer of Bozhou 亳州, Nanzhili, passed through Su's hometown of Puyang 濮陽, Beizhili, while traveling on business and presented Su with a copy of the gazetteer, along with book money provided by the Bozhou magistrate. The compiler asked Su to write a preface, which he did.[70] Payments could be made not only to outsiders, but also to local school officials.

66. *Wuxi xian zhi* (1574), 2.
67. *Pengcheng zhi*, Song Ji preface; *Jiading xian zhi,* 659.
68. *Tengxian zhi*, 1.5a–b.
69. Ibid., table of contents, 3a, 1.5a.
70. *Bozhou zhi* (1564), preface. Another example is He Tang (1474–1543), who was paid for his preface to the *Xiuwu xian zhi.* He Tang, *Bozhai ji*, 5.8a.

Assistant Confucian school instructor Feng Bo's 馮伯 postface to the 1504 gazetteer of *Yanshi* 偃師, Henan, records that the magistrate "sent money over to the school office and asked me to write a postface." While it is well known that literati were paid to write prefaces for other types of publications, Feng was a currently serving local school official. It is not clear whether such payments were common, but this case does suggest that magistrates could supplement instructors' low salaries by paying for literary work.

If an instructor did not finish a gazetteer before his term in office was complete, his superior could retain him to finish it before moving on to his next post. In 1551 Sheng Ji 盛繼, an instructor at the county school of Xingning 興寧, Guangdong, was promoted to a position elsewhere before he finished the county gazetteer. Magistrate Huang Guokui 黃國奎 had arrived in the fall of 1550 and wanted Sheng to finish, so the county clerk petitioned the provincial superintendent of schools for permission to keep Sheng on, not as the instructor but as a local gazetteer compiler. The superintendent agreed and ordered that Sheng be given a quiet office in the county yamen, treated "generously according to guest ritual," and supplied with "necessities, money, paper, woodblocks, etc."[71]

Outside literati were sometimes hired to compile gazetteers, and some were involved in multiple projects. Those hired tended to come from the same general area as the subject locale. Fame and distance traveled were correlated. For example, Zhang Yuanyi 張元益, a student of Tang Shunzhi 唐順之, had a local reputation as a capable scholar, but he repeatedly failed the civil service examinations.[72] The native of Shanyin County, Shaoxing Prefecture, was hired to polish the 1579 gazetteer of Xinchang (discussed in chapter 2), another Shaoxing county. After it was finished, Zhang worked as a collator on the 1587 prefectural gazetteer.[73] The better-known Deng Fu (discussed in chapter 2) traveled farther afield for a job: After the magistrate of Puzhou 濮州, Henan, sent a letter and book money to Deng's home in Changshu, Deng traveled 600 kilometers

71. *Xingning xian zhi*, prefatory matter, 1a–4b, 4.9b.

72. *Shanyin Baiyutan Zhang Shi zupu* (Shanyin Baiyutan Zhang lineage genealogy), ed. Zhang Yuanshu, biography of Zhang Yuanyi (unpaginated, biographies of the thirteenth generation).

73. *Shaoxing fu zhi* (1587), 17.

to compile the 1527 gazetteer.[74] Prominent literati who traveled long distances, as Deng did, probably commanded higher fees than lesser locals.

The above examples are from the sixteenth century, and one might assume that paid editorial work on gazetteers was part of the late-Ming (1570–1644) "commodification of writing" described by Kai-wing Chow, but glimpses of a similar phenomenon can be observed centuries earlier.[75] For Zhang Zhe 章嚞, who was active in the first half of the fourteenth century, compiling gazetteers was a large part of his work for nearly two decades. Prior to 1307 Zhang compiled one of his native place, Yongjia 永嘉, while serving as the Confucian school instructor.[76] Yongjia was part of Wenzhou Circuit 溫州路 (modern Zhejiang), and after Zhang finished the Yongjia gazetteer, the Wenzhou government hired him to compile the gazetteers of two other subordinate territories, Pingyang 平陽 (completed in 1307) and Rui'an 瑞安 (ca. 1307). He also compiled the circuit gazetteer, which he finished in 1310. In the Yanyou period (1314–20) Zhang compiled another gazetteer of Wenzhou, the *Dong'ou zhi* 東甌志. Zhang apparently did a good job, because he was then hired by Taizhou 台州, the circuit to the north of Wenzhou, to compile a gazetteer of Tiantai 天台, a subordinate county, circa 1323.[77] These were major projects and probably brought him a substantial portion of his income during these years. While Zhang is an early example of a repeat gazetteer compiler, this phenomenon became more common as the surplus of educated men increased in the fifteenth and sixteenth centuries and gazetteer compilation was universalized down to the county level.

Spaces for Editorial Work

Private gazetteers were usually compiled by a single scholar working at home, whereas official gazetteers were compiled by groups of varying

74. *Puzhou zhi* (1527), 276, 732. Another example is Wang Tinggan, who was hired to compile the history of Jingxian. *Jingxian zhi*, 415.

75. Chow, *Publishing, Culture, and Power*, chap. 3.

76. Some sources call Zhang a Pingyang native. Pingyang was about 35 kilometers from Yongjia.

77. Zhang Guogan, *Zhongguo gu fangzhi kao*, 387, 406–9.

sizes working in government buildings or other spaces. Once a resident administrator decided to compile a gazetteer, a compilation office was set up, typically in the local yamen or Confucian school.[78] Space was an important consideration, especially for large groups such as the fifty-seven people who worked in the prefectural school on the 1521 gazetteer of Shangyuan, Nanzhili, one of the gazetteers demanded by the Zhengde Emperor.[79] Both yamens and schools had space, but each had distinct advantages. Working in yamen offices gave compilers easier access to government records, while working in a school was convenient for school instructors and students, who did much of the research and writing, and for access to key reference works in school libraries.[80]

Yamens and schools were not the only editorial spaces. Several provincial gazetteers were compiled and edited in the civil service examination halls 貢院, which were excellent venues for large editorial projects because they were designed to hold numerous test takers, were used for exams only once every three years over the course of seven days in the eighth lunar month, and included work areas for the copyists, woodblock cutters, and printers who reproduced examination answers.[81] For the *Nanji zhi* 南畿志 (Southern Capital Region gazetteer) published in the 1530s, the education intendant set up an office in the examination hall for twenty-seven people to review sources.[82] Such compilations could be done either between exams or around them. The 1533 gazetteer of Shandong Province was compiled between the 1531 and 1534 exams; work on the 1556 gazetteer of Henan Province straddled the 1555 exam.[83]

Territorial-unit gazetteers were occasionally compiled at Daoist, Buddhist, and other religious sites. This is not surprising, because religious buildings were used for various secular activities in late imperial China: Buddhist monasteries rented rooms and served meals to travelers, and as Anne Gerritsen has shown, Confucian debating groups in Jiangxi

---

78. *Wujiang xian zhi*, preface. Examples of gazetteers compiled in yamen compounds include the 1169 *Siming tujing*, 1261 *Jiankang zhi*, and many others.

79. *Shangyuan xian zhi*, old preface, 12.62.

80. *Wuding zhou zhi* (1548), postface.

81. Miyazaki, *China's Examination Hell*, 39; Elman, *A Cultural History*, 178.

82. *Nanji zhi*, 35.

83. *Shandong tong zhi*, 17; *Henan tong zhi*, prefaces.

met therein.[84] The range of religious institutions used can be seen in the examples below:

- The 1550 gazetteer of Tianchang 天長, Nanzhili, was compiled in the Daoist Xuanmiao Abbey 玄妙觀. The yamen or school was not used, even though the editor was an active official who had stopped in his native place to visit his mother while traveling on official business.[85]
- The 1591 gazetteer of Hongdong 洪洞, Shanxi, in the Jade Peak Daoist Monastery (*Yufeng Daoyuan* 玉峰道院).[86]
- The 1454 gazetteer of Wujiang 吳江, Nanzhili, was compiled at the Chan Buddhist Shengshou Temple 聖壽寺.[87]
- The 1503 gazetteer of Xinghua 興化, Fujian, was compiled in the Nanshan Monastery 南山僧舍.[88]
- The 1542 gazetteer of Sichuan Province was compiled in the shrine to Song Lian 宋濂 and Fang Xiaoru 方孝孺 inside the Jingju Temple 靜居寺 in Chengdu.[89]
- The 1556 gazetteer of Xiangshan 象山, Zhejiang, was written by three government students at the shrine for a mountain god, the Great Lord of Round Peak 圓峰大帝, in the Round Peak Temple 圓峰廟.[90]

Gazetteer work was also done in miscellaneous other spaces. The fine copy for the 1497 gazetteer of Taizhou, Zhejiang, which would be pasted and transferred to woodblocks for cutting and printing, was written out by scribes assembled in the Fangyan Academy 方岩書院, which was established by the family of gazetteer compiler Xie Duo 謝鐸 (1464 *jinshi*) and located in Taiping 太平, about 70 kilometers from the prefectural seat.[91] In 1577 a resident of Zhending 真定, Beizhili, met the county magistrate at an inn to exchange drafts of local gazetteers they had been writing, neither of which was a gazetteer of Zhending. The local person was

84. Gerritsen, *Ji'an Literati*, 212–17.
85. *Tianchang xian zhi*, 1.10b, 3.10a–b, 7.3b.
86. *Hongdong xian zhi*, preface, 3b.
87. 1488 *Wujiang zhi*, Mo Dan preface, 7–8.
88. *Xinghua fu zhi*, prefaces, 1a.
89. Yang Shen, *Shen'an ji*, 2.32a; *Sichuan zong zhi*, 5.
90. *Xiangshan xian zhi* (1556), 432.
91. *Chicheng xin zhi*, 200, 265.

working on a gazetteer of Chun'an 淳安, Zhejiang, and the magistrate was working on one of Hengshan 衡山, Huguang.[92] This shows that not all gazetteer writing was done locally. Once local sources were collected, compilers could finish a manuscript elsewhere if needed.

Source Materials

Obtaining access to needed sources was an initial problem in compiling local gazetteers. Because compilers had varying degrees of success in collecting sources, the scope of materials used varied tremendously. Some gazetteers are spare lists of basic data drawn from government records, while others are rich texts based on extensive research. More ambitious compilers pursued multiple avenues to obtain sources, with public solicitation being among the most important. For the 1552 gazetteer of Xingning (discussed earlier in this chapter), the provincial education intendant ordered the magistrate to do the following:

> First issue a big-character proclamation 大字告示 to clearly notify the entire county's scholars and commoners that those who know of local people—past or present—who possess unused talent, or who were virtuous or righteous in poverty or adversity and have yet to be commemorated, or who know which current government policies should be followed and which should be changed, are to forthwith submit reports to the instructor's office in the county yamen to serve as documentation for carrying out the compilation.[93]

Proclamations were typically posted on the yamen gate for everyone to see, and many kinds of people could submit materials. In a proclamation about the compilation of the 1779 gazetteer of Ganzhou 甘州, Gansu, Prefect Zhong Gengqi 鐘賡起 asked for materials from "the entire body of people: gentry, students, scholars, merchants, soldiers, and commoners"

92. *Zhending xian zhi*, second preface.
93. *Xingning xian zhi*, prefatory matter, 2a.

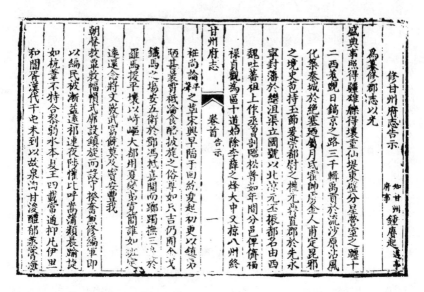

FIGURE 3.1. Proclamation soliciting source materials for the 1779 gazetteer of *Ganzhou fu zhi* (Harvard-Yenching Library).

紳衿士商軍民人等一體 (fig 3.1).[94] Such proclamations suggest that at least some gazetteer compilers were willing to accept sources from almost anyone, even if in fact most gazetteers contain only materials on subjects that were part of dominant discourses and excluded many topics of interest to common people.

In addition to soliciting materials through public notices, researchers solicited directly from individuals, consulted books held by local libraries and yamens, conducted interviews, copied texts, and located information about the locale in nonlocal sources. Textual sources were essential, especially previous editions of the local gazetteer, gazetteers from superior and inferior territorial jurisdictions, genealogies of local lineages, literature by or about local persons, stone inscriptions, and government records. The compilers of the 1564 *Bozhou zhi* noted that Bozhou had no book collectors, so they relied on books that a former magistrate placed in the Confucian school in the 1520s.[95]

94. *Ganzhou fu zhi* (1779), prefatory matter, 3a.
95. *Bozhou zhi* (1564), *fanli*.

That some gazetteer compilers consulted large numbers of works can be seen in lists of references (fig. 3.2). The 1494 gazetteer of Xuzhou 徐州, Nanzhili, lists 107 source books; the 1474 gazetteer of Hangzhou 杭州, Zhejiang, lists 62.[96] Even a supplement could draw from numerous sources: In 1616, there were 1,745 names and biographies drawn from 101 sources that were added to the 1533 edition of the Shandong provincial gazetteer. The sources included forty-two gazetteers of Shandong prefectures, subprefectures, and counties, twenty gazetteers from outside of Shandong, two mountain gazetteers, four rolls of successful examination candidates, and two stelae listing government officials. The rest were primarily works on history, geography, and government.[97]

Most of what gazetteer compilers used was available free of charge. Government records could be copied from the yamen and schools, books could be borrowed, and donated materials received. Because most compilers were educated, many had personal copies of important historical, literary, biographical, and geographic works—and many had substantial book collections. Wang Yuanbin, editor of the 1585 *Tengxian zhi*, let his fellow compilers use over one thousand *juan* from his personal collection.[98] As members of the elite, compilers could draw on networks of friends and colleagues to obtain unpublished manuscripts by local authors, genealogies, and other rare materials.

Gift giving and lending were important means of circulating books in late imperial China, and this is true of books used in gazetteer compilation.[99] Joseph McDermott stressed that book collectors did not freely lend their books.[100] But for the purposes of compiling their local gazetteer, many were willing to share. Compilers regularly approached book collectors and authors, and many, like Wang Yuanbin, allowed access to their collections and manuscripts. Genealogies were routinely shared because locals wanted their families documented in the gazetteer. Local literati used lending and gifts of local gazetteers to make connections

---

96. *Xuzhou zhi* (1494), *fanli*, 2–4; *Hangzhou fu zhi*, prefatory matter. Other substantial lists of works consulted are found in the *Ningxia xin zhi*, *Yexian zhi*, and *Songjiang fu zhi*.
97. *Shandong tong zhi*, 10.155.
98. *Tengxian zhi*, 1.
99. On books and gift giving, see McDermott, *A Social History*, 84–94.
100. Ibid., 134–42.

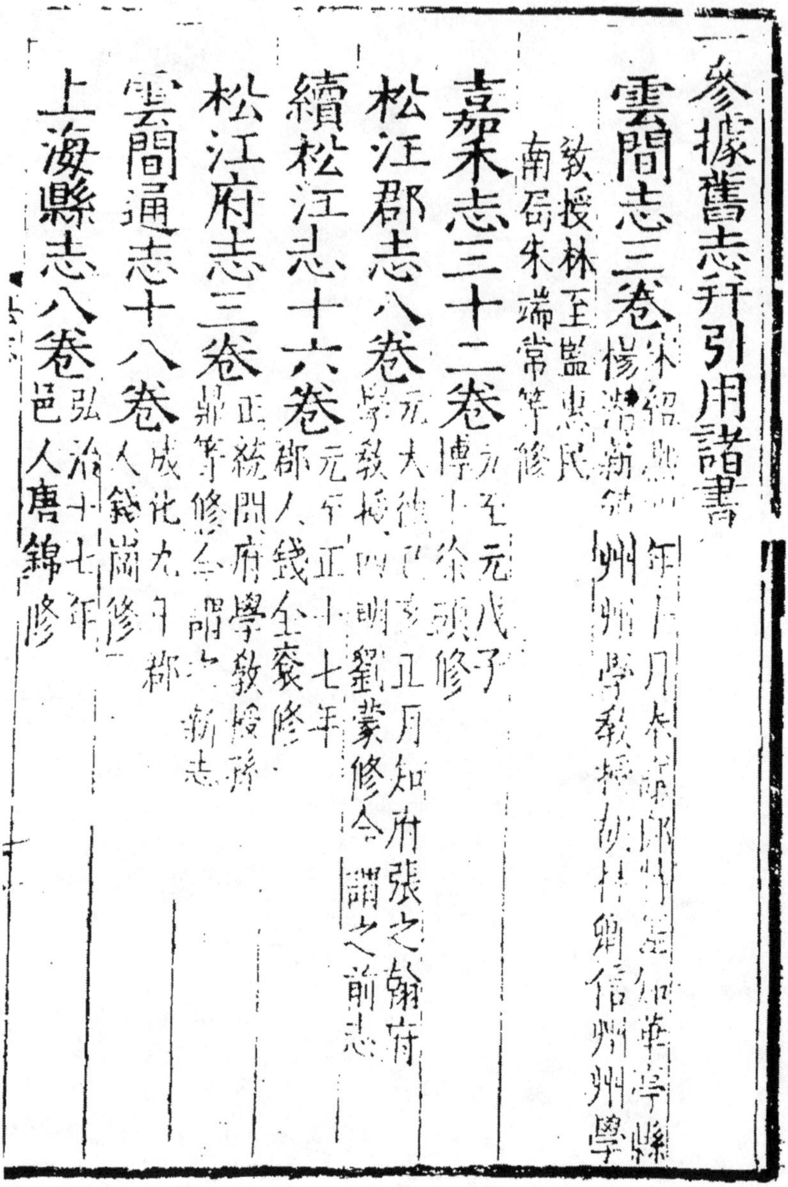

參據舊志幷引用諸書

雲間志三卷 朱紹熙
致授林至監惠民
南碣朱端常等修
年十月本縣邯州冠知華亭縣
州州學教授胡村鄉信州州學

嘉禾志三十二卷 博士徐碩修 元戊了

續松江志十六卷 郡人錢全裒修 正十七年

松汪郡志八卷 縣教授 元大德 正月知府張之翰府學教授孫 劉蒙修今謂之前志

松江府志三卷 正統間府學教授孫 郡人新志

雲間通志十八卷 成化九 人錢崗修

上海縣志八卷 邑人唐錦修 弘治十七年

FIGURE 3.2. List of works consulted in compiling the 1512 *Songjiang fu zhi* (Tianyige Library).

with administrators and other scholars and to get texts connected to friends and relatives into gazetteers. Compilation of the 1351 gazetteer of Xianyou 仙游, Fujian, began when local scholar Fu Yucheng 傅玉成 presented himself to the touring assistant surveillance commissioner, Tian Jiujia 田九嘉, gave him a copy of the 1257 edition as a gift, and requested that the gazetteer blocks be recut in the county Confucian school. County magistrate Daolasha 倒剌沙 then compiled a supplement and the commissioner donated money for printing.[101] In 1547 Jiao Xicheng 焦希程 (1519 *juren*) was compiling a gazetteer of Dengzhou 登州, Shandong, and wrote a letter to Cong Pan 叢磐 (1485–1510) asking for old county gazetteers. Cong, a native of Wendeng 文登, a county in Dengzhou, had his son put a cover on a manuscript gazetteer compiled by his father and deliver it to Jiao.[102] In compiling the 1542 gazetteer of Yangzhou, the prefectural government collected multiple private gazetteers.[103] In 1533 the printed edition of the Song dynasty Jiading-era (1208–24) gazetteer of Luhe 六合, Nanzhili, was no longer extant, but compilers of a new edition got a handwritten copy from a book collector.[104] The compiler of the 1637 gazetteer of Tangyin 湯陰, Henan, got an old manuscript gazetteer from the home of a deceased local *jinshi* who had been killed by bandits in 1621.[105] When compilers of the 1671 gazetteer of Hengzhou Prefecture 衡州府, Huguang, were looking for old editions, a student at the Hengyang 衡陽 County Confucian School gave the prefect a copy of the 1593 edition, which he had bought and "kept as a treasure" in his home.[106] Lending gazetteers could be reciprocal, because compilers often got to know each other and developed networks through the compilation process.[107]

When donations were not forthcoming, books and documents had to be copied or purchased. Hand copying of entire works or selections was common. When compilers began work on a gazetteer of Wujiang, Nanzhili, in response to the 1454 imperial edict, they made hand copies

101. *Xianxi zhi*, 8269.
102. *Ninghai zhou zhi*, 873.
103. *Weiyang zhi*, postface, 1.
104. *Luhe xian zhi*, 718.
105. *Tangyin xian zhi*, 402–6.
106. *Hengzhou fu zhi* (1671), 2–3, 6–7, 856.
107. *Ningzhou zhi*, 2, 8–10, 849–51, 858.

of two short manuscript gazetteers completed in 1378 and 1418.[108] The
purchase of materials for use in local gazetteers can be traced back to the
late thirteenth century. When Feng Fujing 馮福京 compiled the 1298
Changguo zhou tu zhi 昌國州圖志 (Illustrated gazetteer of Changguo
Prefecture), he bought materials from local commoners 里民 and gathered sources from the prefectural school.[109] Because old gazetteers or
unpublished private gazetteers were critical sources for new editions, if
a compiler or his descendant was unwilling to freely share the manuscript, magistrates tried to buy them.[110]

There was a secondhand market for local gazetteers. Cao Xuequan
曹學佺 (1547–1646) wrote that he bought secondhand gazetteers in Henan
and Huguang.[111] The descendants of Guo Nan 郭南 (retired 1447) even
used imprints of their ancestor's 1441 gazetteer of Shangyu as loan collateral, which suggests that the imprints had a substantial monetary value.[112]
They were valuable because book collectors wanted them, they documented
rights in local society (which will be discussed more in chapter 7), and
subordinate officers had to provide copies to superiors.[113]

Even though there was a market for gazetteers and compilers were
willing to pay, compilers were not always able to acquire a desired text. A
compiler of the 1552 gazetteer of Lüeyang 略陽, Shaanxi, wrote that an
earlier edition existed but he could not consult it because it was "secreted
away by a selfish person."[114] Such a refusal was the exception, probably
due to official pressure to allow access and the opportunity to help shape
the representation of one's native place and people. In other cases, invasion, rebellion, banditry, natural disasters, and fire destroyed gazetteers,
a topic discussed further in chapter 4.

Compilers sometimes had to search for key sources outside of their
immediate areas. The richest collection of old gazetteers in the Ming was
in the palace library, first in Nanjing, then in Beijing after the capital

108. *Wujiang zhi*, Mo Dan preface.
109. *Changguo zhou tuzhi*, 6061.
110. *Chaoyang xian zhi*, old preface, 1b, 3a.
111. Cao Xuequan, *Da Ming yitong mingsheng zhi*, 234–38.
112. *Shaoxing fu zhi* (1587), 3338.
113. *Xinchang xian zhi* (1579, 1618), "Xin zhi xu xiaoyin" (A short introduction to
the continuation of the Xinchang Gazetteer); *Ganzhou fu zhi* (1621, 1660), preface.
114. *Lüeyang xian zhi*, Gu Yan preface, 6a.

moved in 1421. Those who could use the collection did. For example, in the in the Hongwu era (1368–99), Ma Tao 馬濤 (dates unknown), a native of Xingguo 興國, Huguang, made a complete copy of the early-thirteenth-century Xingguo gazetteer held in the palace library in Nanjing. He needed it for work on a new edition.[115] Other compilers looked to officials and book collectors in other regions for particular texts. The compiler of the 1640 gazetteer of Licheng 歷城, Shandong, bought many books for the project locally but had to get a copy of the *Qi sheng* 齊乘 (Qi chronicle), a Shandong gazetteer first published in 1351, from Shangqiu 商丘, Henan, about 200 kilometers southwest of Licheng, and a copy of the *Jinyu ji* 金輿集 (Collected works of Jinyu), written by a Licheng native, from the Jin 晉 region west of Shandong.[116] Compilers could learn of potentially useful sources from reference works, as did the compiler of the 1531 gazetteer of Jianping 建平, Nanzhili, who learned of a relevant 1232 local gazetteer from the *Wenxian tong kao*, which was published in the early 1300s and circulated widely.[117]

Reference works like those discussed above covered only a small number of elite people and institutions, mostly in the administrative seats. Some compilers supplemented them with field research to cover a greater range of social classes, locales, and topics. For ambitious compilers, gathering records from government offices and books was just the beginning. Serious researchers conducted interviews and collected inscriptions in villages and mountains far from the county and prefectural towns. The compilers of the 1548 gazetteer of Ninghai, Shandong, claimed that they interviewed recluses, gentry, patriarchs, old fishermen, village elders, mountain monks, Daoists, cart drivers, and artisans.[118] The compilers of the 1572 gazetteer of Linjiang 臨江, Jiangxi, "went everywhere interviewing virtuous scholar gentry, mountain people 山氓 and elders."[119] The researcher for the 1585 Tengxian gazetteer traversed the county recording inscriptions and interviewing gatekeepers and old people, then gave his notes to the editor.[120] A compiler of a 1749 gazetteer of Liangzhou

115. *Xingguo zhou zhi*, postface.
116. *Licheng xian zhi*, postface, 2.
117. *Jianping xian zhi*, postface.
118. *Ninghai zhou zhi*, 663–64.
119. *Linjiang fu zhi* (1572), preface, 2a.
120. *Tengxian zhi*, 4.

涼州, Gansu, even claimed to have recorded words spoken by children.[121] Some illustrators who prepared drawings of famous scenic sights, temples, academies, yamens, and schools also worked on-site. For the 1642 gazetteer of Wuxian 吳縣, Nanzhili, Xu Mu 徐霖, a local commoner 布衣, spent two months traveling around the county, sketching while on a boat, and preparing final drawings after his return.[122] In 1582 Ai Mu 艾穆, a cashiered official, was traveling to Xi'an 西安 and stopped on the way to visit an acquaintance, Yang Sanping 楊三平, who was serving as magistrate of Ruzhou, Henan. Yang happened to be revising the Ruzhou gazetteer and showed his manuscript to Ai, who put it in a small box and took it with him as he continued west, visiting places described in the local gazetteer and making revisions and additions along the way. When Ai came back east through Ruzhou, he returned the manuscript to magistrate Yang with his changes, and it was published.[123]

Arranging Materials

Once materials were collected, compilers had to decide how to arrange them. If the local project was part of a superior territory's project, categories would generally be determined at the higher level. If not, local compilers could decide. Huang Wei divides Song to early-Qing gazetteer formats into seven main types:[124]

1. Independent-categories format 平目體. In this format, each topic appears as a separate *juan*, and typically there were twenty or more *juan*, as with the 1418 *fanli* translated in chapter 1. This format predates the Song and was common through the early Qing.
2. Categories-with-subcategories format 綱目體. Here topics are grouped under general headings, such as government buildings, and have subsections, which could include administrative offices, schools, civil service examination hall, granaries, shrines to local worthies, and

121.   *Wuliang kao zhi*, preface, 2b.
122.   *Wuxian zhi*, 164.
123.   *Ruzhou zhi* (1506, 1510), 301.
124.   Huang Wei, *Fang zhi xue*, 311–21.

more. This format began in the Southern Song and was common by the mid Ming. *Pingmu* and *gangmu* were the two most common late imperial gazetteer formats.

3. Annals-biographies format 紀傳體. Many compilers emphasized the historical nature of their works, but a smaller number adopted the format of standard dynastic histories. Such works were organized into sections of annals 紀, tables 表, treatises 志, grouped biographies 列傳, and occasionally, hereditary houses 氏家. Works in this format are common throughout the late imperial period, beginning with the 1261 *Jingding Jiankang zhi* 景定建康志 (Jingding-era Jiankang gazetteer).

4. Chronological format 編年體. Although most gazetteers are arranged chronologically within topic headings, in this format there are no topic headings and chronology organizes the entire gazetteer. Huang dates this seldom-used format to the Ming Jiajing period (1522–66).

5. Three-treasures format 三寶體. Entries are grouped under land, people, and administration, following the statement in *Mencius* that these are a lord's three treasures. This format is rare, but examples can be found throughout the late imperial period.

6. Administrative-text format 政書體. This format is confined to several examples from the mid Ming. Each is arranged according to the six ministries (Personnel, Revenue, Rites, War, Punishments, and Works) and focuses on administrative matters.

7. Two-part format 兩部體. In this format, according to format creator Chen Fei 陳斐 (1535 *jinshi*), the first part consists of material-oriented topics, such as mountains, schools, and temples, while the second part consists of action-oriented topics, such as service in office, passing the examinations, and customs.

Choice of format was influenced by the compilers' views on the nature of gazetteers. By organizing the text under the headings of the six ministries, a compiler emphasized the gazetteer's connection to administration. By writing in the format of a dynastic history, but for a locale, the compiler emphasized the gazetteer's role as a form of historical writing.

Compilers also had to decide which information would be presented in which level's gazetteer. Generally speaking, the higher in the nested hierarchy of territorial units one went, the less detail was included. Phrases such as "see county gazetteer" were commonly used in prefectural and provincial gazetteers as a way of limiting their size.[125] The 1560 gazetteer of Pingliang Prefecture 平涼府, Shaanxi, omitted the roster of Confucian scholars from Ganzhou, its subordinate territory, because it was already in Ganzhou's gazetteer.[126] Similarly, lists of school property and villages were generally omitted from provincial gazetteers.

The rigorous editing process used for many gazetteers is illustrated by the 1622 gazetteer of Quzhou 衢州, Zhejiang. Because drafts of gazetteers typically consisted of sheets of text with notes, corrections, and insertions written in the margins, a clean copy needed to be made before proofreading. When Ye Bingjing 葉秉敬 completed his draft for the Quzhou gazetteer, he gave it to copyists, but they could not read his "grass-style" handwriting, so his younger brother and grand-nephew wrote out the text and read the copy aloud against the original draft 對讀. Ye then made corrections to this second draft and gave it to three copyists, who read it aloud and corrected several thousand words. Ye then gave the third draft to a calligrapher, who made a fine copy, which was read aloud a third time and several hundred words were corrected. The fourth draft went to the block cutters. After the blocks were cut, a proof imprint was made. The proof was read aloud, the fourth reading, and several dozen words were corrected on the blocks, which could be done by scraping down wrong words and adding plugs with the correct words.[127] Printing a proof was a common practice for gazetteers.[128]

A final step for some gazetteers was approval by superior officials. As we saw in chapter 1, in a few cases members of the imperial family destroyed or shelved gazetteers because of their content, but generally speaking the central government did not attempt to censor gazetteers. As Timothy Brook has argued, the Ming and Qing occasionally banned particular books or insisted that offending passages be removed; however, there was not widespread prepublication review or state censorship as in modern China.[129] There are, however, many records of resident administrators and higher-level territorial officials granting permission

125.   *Baoning fu zhi*, 3.23a.
126.   *Pingliang fu zhi*, 7.32a.
127.   *Quzhou fu zhi* (1622), 65–66.
128.   Cheng Minzheng, *Huangdun wenji*, 29.5a.
129.   Brook, *The Chinese State*, 118–36.

to compile a gazetteer: Compilation of the 1344 gazetteer of Jinling was approved by the Jiangnan branch censorate, and the 1552 gazetteer of Xingning was approved by six different offices: the prefecture, the provincial surveillance commission branch office, the provincial administration commission's main and branch offices, the regional inspector, and the grand coordinator.[130] This path through the bureaucracy was relatively short compared to that for the 1597 gazetteer of Fu'an 福安, Fujian, which was approved by twelve different offices and officers.[131] But we should not think of these approvals as censorship: petitions and orders related to gazetteer compilation focus on financing, not content, and most gazetteers were approved before compilation began, not after the text was finished. There are only a few Ming records of manuscripts submitted for prepublication review. In 1528 the magistrate of Dezhou 德州, Shandong, submitted a manuscript to the circuit intendant, who found it to be poorly organized and sent it back for revision.[132] Even though there was no dedicated censorship office, resident administrators were careful in what they wrote because their finished gazetteers were sent to superior officials. Gazetteers do not directly challenge core government policies.

Gazetteers could be major projects, and like many other kinds of projects in imperial China, rituals were associated with them. Auspicious starting and ending dates could be determined through divination, and upon completion, literati might mark the occasion with an exchange of poems about their experience.[133] On the completion of the 1565 gazetteer of Qingzhou 青州, Shandong, Li Panlong 李攀龍 (1514–70) wrote one poem for the Qingzhou prefect, Du Si 杜思, and another for Xue Chen 薛晨 (*zi* Zixi 子熙), a student from Ningbo, Zhejiang, who worked on the gazetteer and was about to return to the South to visit the famous scholar Wang Shizhen 王世貞 (1526–90).[134] The poem for Xue follows:

130. *Jinling xin zhi*, 5278–82; *Xingning xian zhi*, 959–65.
131. *Fu'an xian zhi*, 110–11.
132. *Dezhou zhi* (1528), 521; *Fengyang xian zhi*, 6.60a.
133. *Changyuan xian zhi*, preface, 6a.
134. Li Panlong, *Cangming ji*, 10.4a–b.

The *Qingzhou Prefecture Gazetteer* is Complete, Student Xue Again
Visits Me to Say Goodbye. He Is Off to Visit Yuanmei.[135]
I Write This Poem as a Gift.

A student from Yue to Jixia comes,[136]
The Wu Palace reading platform resurrected.[137]
Mr. Xue's scholarship reveres the classics,
The Qi guest's legacy is an historian's talent.
He blows across the North Sea on Heaven's throne,
Mt. Yunmen's fall beauty reflecting in the lake.[138]
When common folk ask I will say,
To see the dragon he's on his way.

Editorial and Printing Process Case Study: The 1537 Hengzhou Prefecture Gazetteer

Detailed records of Chinese book editing and printing are rare prior to
the late Qing. In previous scholarship, the most commonly cited sources
on book production issues have been Jesuit missionary Matteo Ricci's
observations, made before his death in 1610, and those of an anonymous
author, likely William Medhurst, published in 1834 in the *Chinese Repository*, a missionary journal, which compares the costs of printing Chinese Bibles by various methods.[139] Neither source, however, discusses the
editorial process in conjunction with the printing process.

The 1537 gazetteer of Hengzhou Prefecture, Huguang, however,
contains the editor's notes, which provide a rich description of the

135.   Wang Shizhen and Li Panlong collaborated on literary projects. Wang had
served as surveillance vice commissioner in Qingzhou beginning in 1557, but returned
to his home in Taicang before the gazetteer project began. This poem was translated
with Gu Yang of the University of Wisconsin–Madison.

136.   Ningbo is part of the Yue region. Jixia refers to the area near the west gate of
Linzi, which was the Qi capital during the Warring States period, and to a famous gathering of scholars there. The site of Linzi was close to the Qingzhou prefectural town.

137.   Wugong was the Qi palace.

138.   Mount Yunmen is located in Qingzhou.

139.   Ricci, *China in the Sixteenth Century*, 21; Brokaw and Chow, *Printing and Book
Culture*, 9; Heijdra, "Technology, Culture, and Economics," 230; Anonymous, "Estimate of the Proportionate Expense," 246–52.

complexities affecting book production, such as managing recalcitrant contributors, gathering materials from distant locations, retaining a competent editorial staff, navigating local politics, dealing with illiterate block cutters, and the technical problems of woodblock printing.[140] Because the notes predate Matteo Ricci by more than a half century, are made by an insider rather than a foreign observer, and address issues not discussed by Ricci and Medhurst, they are an important source for Chinese book history and will be partially translated and analyzed below. This case study will serve as both a conclusion to this chapter and an introduction to issues to be explored further in chapter 4 on the printing of gazetteers.

When Yang Pei 楊佩 became prefect of Hengzhou in 1536, he wanted to read about its previous administration in the local gazetteer. Unfortunately the yamen no longer possessed the two fifteenth-century editions.[141] He asked local book collectors for them but found only a short Chenghua-era (1465–88) edition of the provincial gazetteer.[142] Prefect Yang criticized it, saying things that should have been recorded—schools, the civil service examinations, defense, natural disasters, and portents—were left out. He decided to recompile the Hengzhou gazetteer and obtained permission from a senior censorial official. Prefect Yang discussed the idea with his fellow officials, who all said, "We should talk to Yueting."[143] The Master of Yueting 岳亭子, was Liu Fu 劉軾, who passed the *jinshi* examination in 1517, began his career in the Messenger Office, was beaten with eighty strokes of the heavy stick and demoted for criticizing the Zhengde Emperor's 1519 southern tour (discussed in chapter 1), was rehabilitated by the Jiajing Emperor, rose to be an investigating censor, and then retired in Hengzhou.[144]

Prefect Yang repeatedly met with Liu to persuade him to take on the project. Liu finally agreed, in part because he thought the yamen staff was not up to the task. Liu explained:

140. *Hengzhou fu zhi* (1537), 9.8a–14a.

141. Ibid., 1.14b, 15b, 19b. The previous editions of the *Hengzhou fu zhi* were compiled in the Zhengtong era (1436–50) and Chenghua era (1465–88).

142. The gazetteer was published by Hengzhou prefect He Xun. Ibid., 1.16b.

143. Ibid., preface, 2a.

144. Ibid., 5.7b. Zhu and Xie, *Ming-Qing jinshi*; *Hengzhou fu zhi* (1671), 16.23a–25b; Jiao Hong, *Guochao xianzheng lu*, 65, 77.

The prefecture has already lacked a gazetteer for one hundred years and Prefect He published the provincial gazetteer fifty years ago. Although Prefect He did so, the provincial gazetteer was not a continuation of [the earlier prefectural gazetteer]. But having your office compile [a new] prefectural gazetteer would be ineffectual and the gazetteer would not be completed; those who would lift their brushes would not know what to select and what to discard and the officers would all look upon it as their least important duty. We now want to plan for the gazetteer's continuing vitality after a long period of neglect.[145]

Prefect Yang then appointed Liu editor and publisher and justified his decision not to have his yamen officials compile the gazetteer:

Regular officers compiled ancient states' histories, yet from time to time a worthy also did one. Some acted out of self-interest and made selections from their own writings, glorifying their names and ignoring the facts. Such works could not transmit the historical record.

The *Book of Documents* says, "in administration, consistency and constancy are valued; in declarations, completeness and brevity are esteemed. There should not be the love of the unusual." This too is what is said of gazetteers. If later compilers are diligent and maintain [these qualities], drive out self-interest and uphold public interest, add from the past that which has not yet been included, provide for the future that which has not yet been compiled, then will not the historical record be forever transmitted?[146]

Prefect Yang's statement reveals that he did not care whether a current official or a "worthy" compiled the gazetteer as long as it was done correctly.

After Prefect Yang hired Liu, Hengzhou's one subordinate subprefecture and nine subordinate counties compiled local materials. Liu, who called his operation the "Yueting Bookroom" 岳亭書屋, then spent two months editing the text, cutting the 244 blocks in his home, and making imprints.[147]

Getting desired information was Liu's main editorial problem. Because the prefectural gazetteer was based on materials supplied by

---

145. *Hengzhou fu zhi* (1537), Yang Pei preface, 2a.
146. Ibid., 2b–3a.
147. Ibid., 2b.

administrators of subordinate territorial governments, Liu was dependent on their assistance. Not all cooperated. The Guiyang 桂陽 County magistrate did not update the old gazetteer, so recent Guiyang materials were omitted.[148] Hengyang County magistrate Chen Qi 陳琦 was responsible for gathering materials in his county, but soon after the project began he learned from the government newsletter 邸報 that he was about to be transferred. Chen then stopped work on the county gazetteer, which caused Liu Fu to leave large gaps on Hengyang County in the prefectural gazetteer. Hengyang, however, encompassed the prefecture's main urban area and could not be completely ignored. Liu said he "could not take lightly the [figures for the] land taxes, population, tribute, etc.," and so as a substitute for the county's missing numbers he copied figures from the prefectural revenue office.[149] Liu, however, omitted recent biographies of county officials and worthies because they were only recorded in the Hengyang County yamen. Liu apparently lacked either access to the yamen or time to go there, or did not care if those biographies were left out.

Liu also disagreed with a magistrate over the proper categories of materials to include in the gazetteer. In large part Liu simply had to merge, cut, and polish materials submitted by magistrates in predetermined categories, but unfortunately for Liu, Linwu 臨武 County magistrate Guo Hongde 郭宏德 compiled and printed a new gazetteer of Linwu arranged by titles of the six ministries of Ming government. He excluded literature, explaining, "In striving for the true record 實錄 we need not know literature." Liu criticized Guo, saying that because he left out Linwu County's literature, his work was not a "gazetteer."[150] These omissions may have led Liu to include his compilation notes in the published gazetteer to deflect future blame for its incompleteness.

Guo Hongde represents one extreme in the debate over literature in gazetteers, but most compilers took an intermediate position between including all kinds of literature and including no literature at all, and typically framed their positions in terms of public versus private. The *fanli* of the 1560 gazetteer of Rugao 如皋, Nanzhili, state, "Poems and prose writings to be selected for inclusion in the gazetteer are those about

148. Ibid.
149. Ibid., 9.12b–13a.
150. Ibid., 9.12a–b.

the county. Some pieces record its buildings, some document people who passed through. Private family poems and prose writings shall not be included. Epitaph inscriptions shall not be included."[151] The *fanli* of the 1577 gazetteer of Suqian 宿遷, Nanzhili, state, "Only those biographies, records, poems, and prose writings that are connected to administration, transformation of customs, and scenic sites are to be collected and recorded. Do not include private family records, prefaces, poetry, and prose writings."[152] Literature and, as discussed in chapter 2, genealogical materials, were not the only disputed materials. Gazetteer compilers also disagreed about including biographies of living people, religious institutions that were not on the list of the official sacrifices, portents and strange phenomena, people who were not culturally Chinese, and other topics.

Creating a perception that their gazetteer was an orthodox work was important to most compilers. Thus, they often wrote in conspicuous places that their work covered only appropriate topics, even when they in fact covered topics they knew some literati would consider inappropriate. The reasons for including or excluding particular topics were often addressed in the *fanli*, introductions to *juan* or subsections, compilers' notes, and prefaces. For example, the *fanli* of the 1658 gazetteer of Qishan 岐山, Shaanxi, state, "The literature section only records poems and essays that relate to the transformation of customs and commemorative records of public works old and new; the heterodox and crude are not recorded."[153]

In Liu Fu's gazetteer, additional lacunae were caused by institutional record-keeping practices. Liu wanted to list all students selected for the national universities from the prefectural school during the Ming dynasty, but said that he had nowhere to get the names. Apparently the prefectural school itself did not maintain a running list. Liu noted that at the rate of one tribute student per year, there should have been more than 160 students since the Ming founding, and even more if one included students selected outside the annual quota. Liu, however, had records for only twenty and some. He thus asked a magistrate and local elders for more names, but none reported back to him. He then asked a medical officer, Liu Zhengjing 劉正經, who was able to write from

151.   *Rugao xian zhi, fanli*, 18.
152.   *Suqian xian zhi, fanli*, 846.
153.   *Chong xiu Qishan xian zhi, fanli*, 1b.

memory the names of more than twenty students and the offices in which they served. Liu Fu noted that Liu Zhengjing's practice of medicine had sharpened his memory.[154]

Liu Fu omitted many stone inscriptions because he could not travel to distant parts of the prefecture to copy them. Instead he did what he could, as in the case of a former prefect's record of Mount Yumu 雨母山, which was inscribed in stone on the mountain. Liu wrote that he had once visited Mount Yumu, read the inscription, and wrote a few sentences recording its main idea upon descending the mountain. He used his trip notes to summarize the record for Mount Yumu's gazetteer entry and left it to later compilers to get the full record.[155]

From collected records, selections had to be made, conflicting accounts reconciled, and texts verified. For example, Liu included the wife of Jiang Chang 蔣閭, a *juren* from Leiyang County 耒陽縣, in the virtuous and filial section 節孝. Liu found, however, that the two extant editions of the Leiyang gazetteer disagreed on her story's details. The earlier edition said that Jiang Chang's wife, the Lady Li 李氏, remained chaste after Jiang died prematurely, but the later edition said that Jiang Chang's wife, the Lady Zheng 鄭氏, carried her husband's coffin home from Lingnan 嶺南, where he had died in office, then hung herself. Both versions cited the same source, which Liu did not have, so he chose the earlier version and said that future gazetteer compilers would have to check the original source to resolve the issue.[156]

Liu Fu criticized materials from several counties. Some provided too much material or types of materials that Liu Fu considered inappropriate. Leiyang County submitted a manuscript that listed shrines that had not been approved for inclusion in the official sacrifices.[157] Liu stated that those shrines should be excised before publishing the gazetteer of Leiyang County, and Liu's published prefectural gazetteer lists only orthodox shrines 祀典祠宇.[158] But Liu praised other counties' compilations as being

154. Ibid., 9.12a.

155. Ibid., 9.13b.

156. Ibid., 6.10b, 9.10b. Of course, both stories could have been correct if Jiang Chang had more than one wife.

157. Ibid., 9.12b.

158. Ibid., 4.9a–20a. For more on "improper shrines," see Schneewind, "Competing Institutions."

so good that they could be published separately as county gazetteers
with only minor revisions.[159]

Compiling and editing was not the end of Liu's difficulties. He hired
eleven craftsmen: three copyists, Ma Yongzhang 馬永章, Li Cheng 李成,
and Zhu Shixiang 朱時相; two calligraphers, Yin De 殷德 and Ma
Yongcheng 馬永成; and six block cutter/printers 刊匠, Hu Xian 胡憲, Fu
Yongji 傅永繼, Li Shiwei 李世偉, Li Shihua 李世華, You Shen 游深, and
You Hu 游湖, who had trouble printing the book.[160] Liu Fu describes his
troubles as follows:

> Printing a book is rather troublesome. Even after [the text] has been ac-
> curately copied and collated, once the craftsmen put ink and paper on the
> block and press, when the words appear, every block turns out to be miss-
> ing several characters, or characters are missing dots or strokes. When the
> cutting is finished, it is necessary to print [a proof] to look for omissions
> and fix them. When each chapter is completed you then need to make
> corrections. If there are too many blocks they get mixed up and it is hard
> to find [the correct block]. Moreover, this time the pear woodblocks were
> freshly cut and still damp. Every time we pressed, the wood and paper did
> not stick together and we lost several columns. The manuscript for this
> book should have been given to the yamen for cutting, but I was afraid it
> would have been difficult for the functionaries to fill in missing words be-
> cause they would not have understood the principles of language in the
> original draft. Moreover, walls separate the yamen and outside world and I
> could not have collated [the blocks]. Thus, we decided to have them cut in
> my humble home. Only after the cutting began did I realize what trouble
> it was, but I could not face stopping midway.[161]

This passage is a rare description of the intersection of the editorial
and printing processes. It is worth reading it next to Matteo Ricci's
description of xylographic printing one-half century later:

> Their method of printing differs widely from that employed in Europe,
> and our method would be quite impracticable for them because of the

   159.   *Hengzhou fu zhi* (1537), 9.12b.
   160.   Ibid., 9.14b.
   161.   Ibid., 9.13a–b.

exceedingly large number of Chinese characters and symbols. At present they cut their characters in a reverse position and in a simplified form, on a comparatively small tablet made for the most part from the wood of the pear tree or the apple tree, although at times the wood of the jujube tree is also used for this purpose.

Their method of making printed books is quite ingenious. The text is written in ink, with a brush made of very fine hair, on a sheet of paper which is inverted and pasted on a wooden tablet. When the paper has become thoroughly dry, its surface is scraped off quickly and with great skill, until nothing but a fine tissue bearing the characters remains on the wooden tablet. Then, with a steel graver, the workman cuts away the surface following the outlines of the characters until these alone stand out in low relief. From such a block a skilled printer can make copies with incredible speed, turning out as many as fifteen hundred copies in a single day. Chinese printers are so skilled in engraving these blocks, that no more time is consumed in making one of them than would be required in setting up a form of type and making the necessary corrections.[162]

Matteo Ricci's explanation of Chinese woodblock printing describes part of the process, compares it to European printing, and praises its efficiency and speed. Liu Fu's description, in contrast, describes technical, cultural, and governmental problems connected to printing. Liu tells us of insufficiently cured woodblocks, the low literacy of government functionaries, and his restricted access to the yamen. Printing topics will be developed further in the next chapter.

Conclusion

From the above cases it is clear that there was a continuum of involvement in gazetteer compilation between local scholars and resident administrators. It was equally unlikely that an administrative unit gazetteer would be compiled without the involvement of local scholars or the blessing of the local government. It is also clear that official gazetteers routinely drew on privately compiled gazetteers. In centers of literati culture,

162. Gallagher, *China in the Sixteenth Century*, 20–21.

there were often multiple private gazetteers available. Thus, in thinking about the number of gazetteers compiled, it is critical to recognize these foundational works. Those discussed in the prefatory matter of extant gazetteers are usually described as manuscripts kept in someone's home, and titles are rarely mentioned, but they were distinct from the official gazetteers that drew upon them. Most privately compiled works do not appear in the gazetteer counts discussed above, and this further skews our view of the rate of gazetteer production.

By understanding the various ways in which gazetteer projects were initiated, the living nature of gazetteers, and the editorial process, we can synthesize Ba Zhaoxiang's and Zhang Sheng's arguments. Ba's count favors mature texts, developed over a long period, carefully edited and printed. The gazetteers that Zhang would like to add to Ba's count are mostly early-Ming manuscript gazetteers compiled for use in imperial gazetteers. Both arguments treat the Ming as a discrete unit. It would be better, however, to frame the rise of local history more broadly as a long-term trend that tracks the expansion of local literati culture in South China during the Southern Song dynasty and in more locales in the Ming and Qing dynasties. This long-term trend stemmed from the "localist turn" and was further stimulated by imperial compilation projects and intellectual changes, such as the expansion of "evidential learning" in the late Ming and Qing. In the Yuan, gazetteer production was universalized down to the circuit level, and in the early Ming, down to the county level. Even though every Ming locale was required to compile gazetteers in response to edicts, locales with weak literati cultures were less likely than literati centers to maintain and improve their gazetteers after submission to the court, and more likely to lose them. As the Ming enjoyed renewed prosperity beginning in the late fifteenth century, the number of gazetteers initiated by local literati steadily increased. In times of war, such as the collapse of the Yuan and the Ming, gazetteer compilation contracted, but it quickly rose again upon the founding of the new dynasties. Thus, the long-term picture of gazetteer production is a steady rise in numbers and geographical scope from Northern Song through the Qing, with peaks resulting from imperial edicts, the flourishing of local literati scenes, and the rise of evidential learning, and troughs resulting from economic downturns and wars.

CHAPTER 4

Publishing Gazetteers

Our understanding of the geography of book publishing in late
imperial China has been heavily influenced by Zhang Xiumin's
Zhongguo yinshua shi 中國印刷史 (History of Chinese printing). In Cynthia Brokaw's introduction to her and Kai-wing Chow's important volume, *Printing and Book Culture in Late Imperial China*, she summarizes
the state of the field on this topic and notes that based on Zhang's count
of the number of *shufang* 書房 (print and book shops) in various locales
and the number of imprints attributable to them, publishers in Jianyang, Fujian, and the Jiangnan cities of Nanjing, Suzhou, Hangzhou,
Huizhou, and Huzhou 湖州 dominated the industry in the late Ming.[1]
Publishing centers in Jiangxi Province formed a second tier, while Beijing and the remaining provinces published comparatively few titles.
Beijing, according to Zhang, was a lesser publishing center in the Ming,
with only thirteen *shufang* compared to ninety-three in Nanjing alone.
Zhang argued that Beijing could not compete in book publishing with
the South because paper cost three times as much in the north. His rank-
ing changed after the Manchu conquest; Jianyang publishing collapsed,
Beijing rose, and Nanjing, Hangzhou, and Huizhou lost their leading
roles. By the mid and late Qing, commercial publishing was growing in
Sichuan, Guangdong, and smaller intermediate-level publishing centers.
Brokaw points out, however, that this picture is tentative and that we do

---

1. Brokaw and Chow, *Printing and Book Culture*, 26–30.

not yet understand migrations of print craftsmen or how migration related to regional or national publishing networks.

Zhang's study was limited in critical ways, and we cannot assume that it presents a full and accurate picture of the geographic distribution of late imperial publishing. The first major problem is that he did not account for movements of craftsmen and texts in how he assigned titles to locales. He did not provide information on whether a title was sent to a major publishing center or printed locally, and if it was printed locally, whether it was printed by local or nonlocal craftsmen. The second major problem is that his title count tracks *Gujin shuke* 古今書刻 (Published books old and new), a late-sixteenth-century work by the official Zhou Hongzu 周弘祖 (1529–95) that records titles published by central and local government offices, arranged by locale. Cui Wenyin 崔文印 argues that Zhou compiled the work while stationed in Nanjing from 1579–84.[2] Thus, the work does not include books from the last sixty years of the Ming. But an even bigger problem is that *Gujin shuke* was far from comprehensive even for the early and mid Ming. Its incompleteness can be understood by comparing its lists to those found in local gazetteers from the same locales: *Gujin shuke* lists only one title published by Yongzhou Prefecture, Huguang, the prefectural gazetteer, presumably the 1571 edition. But that gazetteer contains a list of thirteen titles published by Yongzhou prefects and subordinate magistrates between 1494 and 1570, all of which as of 1571 were extant and held in the prefectural yamen storeroom.[3] Apparently Zhou Hongzu recorded the Yongzhou gazetteer title but did not read it to learn of the other titles published in Yongzhou. The problem caused by the *Gujin shuke* coverage ending in the 1580s can be seen in its record for Jinan 濟南 Prefecture, Shandong, which lists only one title. A 1640 gazetteer, however, lists seventeen titles published by the yamen.[4] These are not isolated examples: In 1573 Zhangzhou 漳州 Prefecture, Fujian, had newly cut blocks for eleven titles, but *Gujin shuke* recorded only one of them.[5] In 1608 the Baoding 保定 Prefecture yamen had eighteen sets of woodblocks, while *Gujin shuke* recorded

2. Cui Wenyin, "Gujin shuke qian shuo," 4. Zhou was chief minister of the Seals Office and Court of State Ceremonial in Nanjing. *Ming shilu, Shenzong shilu*, 1896, 2121.

3. Zhou Hongzu, *Gujin shuke*, 371; *Yongzhou fu zhi* (1571), *juan* 12.

4. *Licheng xian zhi*, *juan* 15, folio numbers illegible.

5. *Zhangzhou fu zhi*, 209.

thirteen. Local yamens all around the country published books, but Zhou Hongzu did not learn about most of them from his residence in Nanjing. Instead, books that were readily available in Nanjing are over-represented in *Gujin shuke*. This includes books published in Nanjing and nearby Jiangnan cities, and those from Jianyang, whose publishers marketed their books in Nanjing.

Studying the printing of gazetteers will allow us to reanalyze the geography of Ming book publishing and add a dynamic aspect to it. The craftsmen who produced gazetteers are sometimes listed in the front matter along with the editorial personnel, on the last folio, or in the white mouth area along the centerfold, and are often identified by hometown. Because gazetteers are connected to identifiable locales and contain more detailed information on their production than do other book genres, they make it possible to link movements of texts, craftsmen, and materials, identify craftsmen business zones and regional publishing centers, and begin to explore craftsmen networks.

William Skinner argued that China's late imperial economy comprised eight regional economies with relatively little interaction.[6] In recent years scholars have begun to look closely at transregional and international trade before the modern era and qualified Skinner's model. Examining craftsmen business zones shows that craftsmen worked locally, regionally, and nationally, with some traveling long distances for jobs. For print craftsmen who worked on gazetteers, both Beijing and Nanjing were central nodes in publishing networks that stretched across the country. This contrasts with Zhang Xiumin's portrayal of Beijing as only a minor publishing center in the Ming. The data presented below will also reveal that craftsmen traveled widely to print gazetteers, allowing many to be published in remote locales. Printing technology and labor were widely dispersed throughout the Ming state.

Before going further it is important to examine underlying terminology. I follow book historian Lucille Chia's use of the term "publisher" to mean an individual or entity that is in charge of selecting, preparing, and marketing the books produced.[7] A gazetteer could be published in either manuscript or print form, but printing was normative. Almost

6. Skinner, *Marketing and Social Structure.*
7. Chia, *Printing for Profit,* 321–22 n. 6.

all official gazetteers were first published by territorial administrations, but materials presented in this book reveal substantial variation in the degree of government involvement in initiating, supervising, editing, printing, and distributing gazetteers. Thus, although it is often convenient to designate a unit of government, such as a county, as a gazetteer's publisher, such a designation may obscure important details of the actual production.

The Norm of the Printed Gazetteer

The emergence of local gazetteers as a distinct genre coincided with the Song dynasty expansion of printing, and from the beginning compilers and local officials expected, or at least hoped, that their gazetteers would be printed. The earliest known printed local gazetteer is the *Taiyuan shiji ji* 太原事迹記 (Record of the traces of the matters of Taiyuan), published by Taiyuan Prefecture in the Zhiping era (1064–67).[8] As discussed in chapter 1, map guides, the precursors to gazetteers, were printed even earlier, at least by 1011.[9]

Compilers came to consider it their duty not only to compile a gazetteer in manuscript form but also to print it. This is clearly expressed in Tang Tianlin's 唐天麟 preface to the 1288 gazetteer of Jiaxing 嘉興 (modern Zhejiang), in which he argues that even though circuit officials read and praised the gazetteer upon its completion in manuscript form, "compiling but not printing this gazetteer would be like not compiling it at all."[10] This emphasis on the importance of print is echoed by Feng Fujing, who was serving as assistant magistrate of Yueqing 樂清 (modern Zhejiang) in 1304.[11] He compiled and printed a gazetteer, explaining that because the country was now unified under a new regime (the Yuan), information on the scope of Yueqing's territory, duties of the various offices, local agricultural products, and advantages and disadvantages of government policies since the Yuan founding should be compiled and

8. Zhang Guogan, *Zhongguo gu fangzhi kao*, 138.
9. Chen Zhensun, *Zhizhai shulu jieti*, 430.
10. *Jiahe zhi*, 4414.
11. Zhang Guogan, *Zhongguo gu fangzhi kao*, 408.

"printed as a gazetteer" to "complete the collecting and recording of the Son of Heaven's history office." These comments show that compilers considered gazetteers to be essential local documentation that deserved to be printed. The norm of printing gazetteers extended to all corners of the Ming state, transmitted by resident administrators sent by the central government.

Compilers preferred print over manuscript because they thought it enhanced fixity, survivability, convenience, and audience size. Although manuscript and printed gazetteers could be subjected to equally rigorous proofreading in their initial compilation, in subsequent hand copying even careful copyists could make errors that compounded as copies were made of copies and originals disappeared. In 1404 the prefect of Chuzhou 滁州, Nanzhili, read a handwritten copy of the Song dynasty Chunxi-era (1174–89) manuscript gazetteer but lamented the lack of a printed edition because errors had been made in recopying the text.[12] In 1410 the newly arrived magistrate of Gong'an 公安, Huguang, went to the county school and asked about famous local people and events. A student brought the magistrate a hand-copied gazetteer 藁帖 that was full of mistakes, so he formed a group to update and collate it, had a student copy out the resulting text, and ordered craftsmen to cut woodblocks.[13]

Once the blocks were cut, fixity could be further promoted by keeping gazetteer woodblocks under lock and key in the yamen or Confucian school to prevent alterations. The earliest known record of this is the 1261 gazetteer of Jiankang 建康 (Nanjing). The prefect overseeing the work wanted the gazetteer printed before he left office, but because time was running out, as soon as each section of the manuscript was finished in the Hall of Book Editing in the prefectural yamen's garden, artisans cut woodblocks, made imprints, and presented them to the emperor. The 994 double-sided blocks were then locked up in five cabinets in the yamen, and a clerk was appointed to take charge of their opening and closing.[14]

Compilers recognized that printing enhanced their gazetteer's long-term chances of survival. A stock phrase in gazetteer prefaces was that the text was being "cut into wood to perpetuate its transmission" (鋟梓以永

---

12. Ibid., 310.
13. *Gong'an xian zhi* (1548), Yongle-era preface, 1a.
14. *Jiankang zhi*, 1331, 1711.

其傳 or 鋟梓以壽其傳).¹⁵ When the manuscript gazetteer of Changzhou 常州, Nanzhili, was finished in 1515, the compiler asked the prefect to "please keep it in a bamboo box in the yamen storehouse," but the prefect responded, "Yes, we can do that, but it might become worm eaten. What better way to long preserve it than by printing it?"¹⁶

Printing enhanced survivability by increasing the number of copies in circulation. Many gazetteers were acquired by people who were in a locale for only a short time and requested a copy. Making a handwritten copy was often impossible due to lack of access or time.¹⁷ As government student Zhang Bangqi 張邦奇 explained in 1577, "Our county has long had a gazetteer, but the problem is that making a hand copy is extremely inconvenient. Fortunately, Magistrate Zhu contributed from his salary to have it printed."¹⁸ Compilers expected this convenience to increase readership. A 1363 postface to the gazetteer of Changshu (modern Jiangsu), noted that there was a rough compilation in 1196 but that it was only in 1210 that county magistrate Ye Kai 葉凱 became the first to "broaden its transmission" 廣其傳, that is, print it.¹⁹ That this phrase refers to printing can be inferred from the subsequent statement that "the old blocks were gone." This meaning was made explicit in Yu Qian's 1351 preface to the Qi sheng. Yu wrote that he "ordered workers to cut blocks to broaden its transmission" 命工鏤板以廣其傳.²⁰ Like "perpetuate its transmission," "broaden its transmission" was a stock phrase used to discuss printing. Once officials or local donors had paid for block cutting, printing one copy on demand years later was much cheaper and faster than hiring someone to make a complete hand copy, because the labor required was so much less. Publication costs will be discussed in detail in chapter 5.

If yamen imprints were lost or taken away, more could be made from blocks, and if the blocks were lost or worn down, new blocks could

15. See, e.g., the 1376 *Sanyang tu zhi*, reprinted in Wang and Liu, *Yongle dadian fangzhi jiyi*, 2775; *Jiayu xian zhi*, 2a.

16. *Changzhou fu zhi*, old prefaces, 9, 27.

17. *Wujun tujing xu ji*, Zhu Anshang postface. See McDermott, *A Social History*, for discussion of access to libraries.

18. *Xingxian zhi*, postface.

19. *Qinchuan zhi*, 1309.

20. *Qi sheng*, 511.

be cut from an imprint. Often some blocks were damaged but others remained usable. It is not unusual to find extant imprints that were made from a mix of original and recut blocks. The 1565 preface to the gazetteer of Taizhou, Zhejiang, records that many of the woodblocks for the 1497 edition had been damaged by insects, rot, and fire and the Taizhou prefect ordered craftsmen to cut more than 260 replacement blocks from a high-quality copy 善本. An inscription at the start of each chapter records the number of replacement blocks in that chapter. For example, the household register chapter 版籍 says "seven replacement folios cut" 補刻七張 on the first folio, and "replacement cut" 補刻 in each replacement folio's white mouth. Additional replacement blocks were cut in 1627, and these can be identified by the inscription "Replacement cut in the sixth year of the Tianqi era" 天啓六年補刻.[21] In some cases gazetteers used the term *bu* 補 when adding new materials, but that was not the case here.

Gazetteer compilers feared loss for good reason. There are only a few dozen relatively complete extant Song and Yuan local gazetteers, even though, as discussed in chapter 3, they were produced in large numbers.[22] Song dynasty losses can be seen in a book list from the gazetteer of Jiujiang 九江, Jiangxi, circa 1235. The compiler was unable to locate four earlier Jiujiang gazetteers and three map guides.[23] The scope of Yuan losses can be seen by comparing the number of identified Yuan titles to the number of Yuan administrative units. Timothy Brook and Jun Fang identified "about 200" extant and lost Yuan gazetteers, but there were more than a thousand counties and several hundred higher-level units in the Yuan, many of which had multiple compilations within this short dynasty.[24]

War, rebellions, and banditry led to the destruction of many gazetteers, and losses through violence were substantial even by the Southern Song, especially in the north. The postface to the 1494 gazetteer of Baoding states that it had earlier gazetteers but that one was burned in the "Khitan's aggression" and another was lost in the Zhenyou period (1213–17), when the Jin moved its capital south and the Mongols took Baoding. The

21. *Chicheng xin zhi*, preface, 5.1, 5.10.
22. *Song Yuan fangzhi congkan* is the main collection of Song and Yuan gazetteers.
23. Wang and Liu, *Yongle dadian fangzhi jiyi*, 1544–45, 1555–56.
24. Brook, "Native Identity," 236; Fang, "A Bibliography," 123.

1527 gazetteer of Neihuang, Beizhili, blamed the lack of local gazetteers first on the Khitans, because they forced Song local officials to focus on military matters, and then on the Jin and Yuan occupations.[25] Violence that destroyed gazetteers and libraries included not only invasions by external powers but also internal revolts and banditry.[26] Even when gazetteers were not physically destroyed in an attack on a yamen or school, war could indirectly cause their disappearance. The Jin invasion in the 1120s delayed the printing of the gazetteer of Tong'an 同安, located just north of the Yangzi River. It was compiled in 1123 but not printed until 1143.[27] Such delays probably led to the loss of many manuscript gazetteers. Centuries later compilers were still expressing bitterness about missing gazetteers and the local history they embodied.

Gazetteer woodblocks also fell victim to natural disasters and fires. The blocks for the early sixteenth-century gazetteer of Puzhou 蒲州, Shanxi, were destroyed when the yamen collapsed in a 1555 earthquake; the blocks and all but a few imprints of the 1559 gazetteer of Fu'an, Fujian, were swept away in a 1581 flood.[28] The 1546 gazetteer of Changle 昌樂, Shandong, notes that there was an old manuscript edition stored in the Confucian school, but it was burned in a fire.[29] Fire was a significant threat to wooden school libraries, and more than a few burned down.[30]

We have so far considered only unidirectional cases—from manuscript to print. But not infrequently a previously printed gazetteer was lost except in a handwritten copy. These could be brought back into print, either directly or in updated form. In the early 1500s the blocks for the 1218 gazetteer of Luhe, Nanzhili, were worn down and no printed copy survived, but a collector had a hand copy 寫本 that served as the foundation for a new printed edition.[31] Similarly, a preface to the 1343 gazetteer of Chengdu, Sichuan, said the previous edition's woodblocks had been destroyed in fighting and a Sichuan censor had the blocks recut

25. *Neihuang xian zhi*, preface.

26. Wang and Liu, *Yongle dadian fangzhi jiyi*, 2971–72; *Wenxian zhi* (1702), 3.3b–4a.

27. Zhang Guogan, *Zhongguo gu fangzhi kao*, 289.

28. *Puzhou zhi* (1559), preface, 1; *Fu'an xian zhi*, 7a–b.

29. *Changle xian zhi*, prefaces, 2a, 533.

30. See, e.g., the 1499 burning of the Jiangle, Fujian, library. *Jiangle xian zhi*, 5.5a.

31. Zhang Guogan, *Zhongguo gu fangzhi kao*, 232.

from handwritten copies.[32] Gazetteers could also be recovered from imprints after blocks were destroyed. Facsimile blocks could be cut by transferring ink from an extant work *fanke* 翻刻, as was done with the 1190s gazetteer of Xinghua, Fujian, in the 1310s.[33]

Circulating copies also served as foundations for works that were updated before reprinting. Chaozhou 潮州, Guangdong, had a gazetteer during the Song and Yuan that "left out nothing." Its blocks were stored in the prefectural school library and survived the Mongol invasion of 1278, but some were destroyed when the Yuan fell less than a century later. The gazetteer was restored and reprinted after assistant censor Zhao arrived in 1375. He wanted to understand local customs, summoned students to the Confucian school, and asked them about the prefectural gazetteer. When he learned that it had been damaged, he made its restoration an "internal government project" 公内事. The compilers searched for complete imprints and found a few held by commoners. Chaozhou native Lin Shiyou 林仕猷 complained that the scarcity resulted from officials serving in Chaozhou, who always took imprints with them when they left. Although this practice may have caused local shortages when blocks became unusable, in the long run it increased survivability.[34]

The recompilation and printing of the Chaozhou gazetteer likely resulted from the early-Ming edict to recover the realm's "essential documentation" 典故. In 1376 Jiangyin 江陰 County magistrate Rao Yuande 饒元德 joined this effort but found that Jiangyin's "bookcases and libraries" were empty due to the war that accompanied the Yuan collapse. He then gathered elders in the school to reconstruct what was lost and supplement what survived. He asked several families for old gazetteers, got thirteen chapters from Zhang Yanxiang's 張彥翔 collection, gathered elders and scholars in the Confucian school to collate the text, copied out a new manuscript, and had blocks cut.[35]

Our knowledge of pre-1400 gazetteer printing is limited by the small number of extant gazetteers, most of which were transmitted as

32. Zhou Fujun, *Quan Shu yiwenzhi*, 30.27b.
33. *Xinghua fu zhi*, 2nd preface, 3a.
34. Wang and Liu, *Yongle dadian fangzhi jiyi*, 2699, 2704–6, 2774–75.
35. *Jiangyin xian zhi* (1640), old prefaces, 12.

incomplete hand copies. The best information on gazetteer printing, when it exists, is found in notes following the prefaces, administrative orders, or lists of contributors, on the last folio, or in the white mouth area along the centerfold. This type of paratextual material, however, was almost never reproduced in later editions or compilers' collected works, and relatively few examples survive. Prefaces, however, also contain information on printing, and hundreds of these have survived.[36] Unfortunately it was typical for only one gazetteer preface, if any, of an original set to discuss the printing, and production-oriented prefaces were less likely to survive than more literary prefaces. The ones most likely to give production details are secondary prefaces written by low-ranking contributors, such as Confucian school instructors and students. Lead prefaces tended to be written by high-ranking administrators or famous scholars who were less familiar with, or less interested in discussing, production details. It was these literary prefaces that were often copied into later editions and collected works. Thus, if you read a single surviving preface that does not mention printing, you cannot conclude that the gazetteer was not printed.

The complex transmission of Song and Yuan gazetteers can be seen in the gazetteer of Guiji, Zhejiang. In 1510 the prefect of Shaoxing (Guiji county's superior prefecture) reconstructed and reprinted the 1202 gazetteer and its 1226 supplement. First the prefect worked with subordinate officials to locate old editions. They found four: From the home of Commander Feng, they got an incomplete imprint of a 1339 edition published by a Shaoxing Circuit Confucian school instructor who had hand-copied the old texts and reprinted them. From National University student Tao Zhi 陶秩 they obtained a copy of the supplement; from scholar Zhang Chuanshi 張傳世 they got a copy that was missing the first volume; and from scholar Luo Qi 羅頎 they got a handwritten copy made long before from a copy in the prefectural yamen.[37] None of the four versions, however, was a complete text printed from the original blocks, so the prefect had a local scholar, Wang Yan 王綎, reconstruct the gazetteer

---

36. Zhang Guogan's work is the largest collection of surviving Song and Yuan prefaces. Users should be aware, however, that many are abridged and others are omitted. Portions of other gazetteers, including some prefaces, can be found in Wang and Liu, *Yongle dadian fangzhi jiyi*, and Ming and Qing gazetteers.

37. *Guiji zhi* (1201, 1510) (*Siku quanshu zhenben* edition), postface, 1a–2b.

and its supplement, taking the Confucian school official's imprint as the most reliable.

Although information on pre-1400 gazetteers is sparse, examining what does exist reveals much about the relationship between manuscript and print culture. But in thinking about this relationship it is important to keep in mind that local gazetteers were living texts with complex life cycles, as discussed in chapter 3. We cannot simply identify titles and label them "manuscript" or "imprint," count up numbers, and use the totals to argue that gazetteers were mostly one or the other. First we must consider how they were compiled, printed (or not), circulated, recompiled, lost, and discarded. All gazetteers started out as manuscripts, some were eventually printed, but not always immediately upon completion, and most that were printed continued to exist in the original manuscript plus additional handwritten copies. Many thousands of short manuscripts were compiled by local governments as part of gazetteer projects of the court or superior territorial administrative units. When this was done, a manuscript copy was generally held locally, and although many of these were not printed, some eventually served as foundations for revised, expanded, and printed gazetteers.

When we know that a printed edition was made, it can be tempting to think of the manuscript as simply a stage in the production process leading to printing, and to compress in our minds the time frame between completion of the manuscript and cutting the blocks. If a manuscript was printed, block cutting was usually done immediately upon completion. But sometimes there was a time lag of years. If we think of gazetteers as living documents, we can see that while gazetteers all started out in handwritten form, even after initial printing, handwriting still played important roles in the lives of individual gazetteers. Handwritten notes, prefaces, and colophons supplemented printed editions, and these were often later cut into blocks and inserted into the text. Copies of individual sections or the entire work were made by hand, and sometimes it was only these that perpetuated the gazetteer during times of war or neglect.

Examining gazetteer life cycles can contribute to the debate over when the printed book replaced the manuscript book in China. Joseph McDermott recently argued, based on studies by Inoue Susumu 井上進 and Katsuyama Minoru 勝山稔, that in most of China, for most types of literati books, the imprint was not ascendant over the manuscript until the sixteenth century.[38] Inoue and Katsuyama examined changes over time in the ratio of manuscripts to imprints in catalogs of library and private book collections.[39] Book catalogs, however, inconsistently recorded whether a given gazetteer was a manuscript or an imprint. Even Chen Zhensun's relatively detailed thirteenth-century *Zhizhai shulu jieti* 直齋書錄解題 (Catalog of books with explanatory notes of the Zhi Studio) is misleading. Because Chen's catalog sometimes states that a gazetteer was printed, one might be tempted to infer that when it does not state this, there was no printed edition. But that would not be a safe assumption. Chen's entries on the 1223 *Chicheng zhi* 赤城志 and its 1227 supplement, the *Chicheng xu zhi*, did not identify either manuscript or print, but a Ming edition of the *Chicheng zhi* noted that it was first printed in 1223 and that the palace library had imprints of both Song editions.[40] As Hilde De Weerdt's analysis has shown, many titles in Song private book catalogs that were not described as imprints had printed editions.[41]

If one wanted to do a study similar to Inoue's and Katsuyama's for gazetteers, calculating a ratio between imprints and manuscripts at various points in time, a central problem would be deciding what counts as a "gazetteer," as discussed in chapter 3. If one accepts a broad definition that includes quickly assembled, marginally edited texts, and private compilations, then a majority of gazetteers down to the twentieth century were in manuscript form. But that does not mean we should think of gazetteers as a manuscript genre. Instead we should keep in mind the gazetteer life cycle. Most gazetteers submitted in response to higher-level collection projects were not compiled first as independent works. Rather, they were put together quickly by local officials, often under a tight deadline, for the express purpose of the larger project.[42] Such quickly composed gazetteers generally were not printed separately, and many of the locally held manuscript copies were soon lost. But if one construes "gazetteer" more narrowly to include only mature texts that were extensively researched and carefully edited, then by the Southern Song printing was the norm. Nevertheless, despite print's normative power, even in

38.   McDermott, *A Social History*, 49.
39.   Inoue, "Zōsho to dokusho."
40.   *Chicheng xin zhi*, 202, 349.
41.   De Weerdt, "Byways," 178–84.
42.   *Pengcheng zhi*, Song Ji preface.

the late Ming some magistrates reported that their locale had never had a printed edition.[43]

Another way to look at this question would be to ask whether readers were more likely to encounter handwritten or printed local gazetteers. The answer would vary by the type of reader and whether the locale had a printed edition. In places with only one or two manuscript copies in the yamen and school, officials, teachers, and students, but probably few others, read them. However, in locales that had printed editions, outside readers would have been more likely to read the gazetteer. Calculating the actual number of printed and manuscript gazetteers is impossible, but it is clear that printing gazetteers was common in many parts of China before the late Ming, the period McDermott identifies as the start of print's dominance. Timothy Brook and Fang Jun found that almost all of a group of 173 Yuan dynasty local gazetteers they studied were produced in printed form.[44] Some centers of literati culture printed multiple gazetteers in short spans of time. For example, three fourteenth-century editions of the Jiangyin gazetteer were printed in a span of twenty-eight years: 1363, 1376, and 1391.[45]

Technologies of Print

Almost all pre-Qing gazetteer imprints were made from cut woodblocks rather than movable type. Woodblocks were preferable for three main reasons: First, as will be discussed further in chapter 6, gazetteers were printed on demand for interested individuals and offices, often decades after the first printing, and this could not be done if movable-type forms were broken down after the initial print run. Second, gazetteers were frequently updated, and inserting a few new blocks was much easier than recomposing an entire updated text. Finally, magistrates usually served in their locales for just three or six years and would not want to pay the paper, ink, and binding costs for imprints that would be distributed

43. *Wenxian zhi* (1577), preface, 1a.
44. Brook, "Native Identity," 239; Fang, "A bibliography."
45. *Jiangyin xian zhi*, old prefaces.

long after they had left office. Xylography allowed magistrates to keep the cost of future copies off their current budgets. In addition, xylography was a simple and widely dispersed technology in China, compared to printing with metal type.

A few gazetteers were printed with movable type prior to the seventeenth century, and more thereafter, but xylographic printing remained standard until the late nineteenth century. The oldest-known movable-type gazetteer is the 1298 edition of Jingde 旌德 (modern Anhui), printed with wooden type by Wang Zhen 王禎 (fl. 1290–1333), a Yuan dynasty official. It contained more than sixty thousand characters and required less than a month to print one hundred copies.[46] About twenty years later, Ma Chengde 馬稱德 made a set of one hundred thousand wooden types and compiled the gazetteer of Fenghua 奉化 (modern Zhejiang).[47] It is not clear, however, that he used his movable type to print the gazetteer, which is no longer extant. At least one Ming gazetteer, the 1521 gazetteer of Dongguang 東光, Beizhili, was printed with movable copper type: The vice minister of personnel in Beijing, Liao Ji 廖紀, compiled the gazetteer of his hometown while serving in Beijing. He took the manuscript with him when he was promoted to minister of personnel in Nanjing in February 1521 and asked An Guo 安國 (1481–1534) of Wuxi (about 130 kilometers from Nanjing), who had begun printing with movable copper type around 1512, to print it.[48]

Woodblock quality affected the crispness of prints. Hardwoods that would not easily warp were best, especially jujube 棗, catalpa 梓, pear 梨, apple 平果, camphor 樟, acacia 皂莢, boxwood 黃楊, and gingko 銀杏.[49] Jujube is a drought-tolerant tree that grew widely in a broad range of climates from the semi-arid and cold Loess Plateau in the north to the moist subtropical south.[50] Other hardwoods had narrower ranges.

Although some areas were deforested by the Ming, most regions still had enough forest to supply woodblocks, although not necessarily of the

46.　　Wang Zhen, *Nong shu*, 538. *Nong shu* is one of the most famous books printed with movable wooden type. Zhang Xiumin, *Zhongguo yinshua shi*, 549.

47.　　Ibid., 550.

48.　　*Ming Shilu, Wuzong shilu*, 3650; *Dongguang xian zhi*, old prefaces, 4a. Zhang Xiumin, *Zhongguo yinshua shi*, 562.

49.　　Bussotti, *Gravures de Hui*, 23; Gallagher, *China in the Sixteenth Century*, 21.

50.　　Ma Lihui, "Spatial Distribution of Roots," 57–68.

highest quality.[51] In those that did not, publishers who wanted impressive gazetteers needed to obtain blocks from outside their local areas. Pear woodblocks for the 1600 gazetteer of Huairen, a poor, dry county in northern Shanxi, were purchased 700 *li* (about 370 kilometers) away with money donated by the magistrate.[52] Although the place of purchase was not recorded, Beijing was approximately 700 *li* from Huairen via the Sanggan River. When the manuscript for the 1637 gazetteer of Lianzhou 廉州, Guangdong (now Hepu 河浦, Guangxi), was completed, "pear and jujube were gathered in Gaoliang 高涼; block cutters were called in from Yangcheng 羊城" (Guangzhou 廣州).[53] Mount Gaoliang was about 200 kilometers east of Lianzhou, and Guangzhou, the provincial capital, was more than 500 kilometers away.[54] Lianzhou was a coastal town near the Vietnam border with a registered population of 15,467 in 1630.

Paper quality also affected printing. Many extant Ming and Qing gazetteers were printed on relatively cheap bamboo paper, but some used higher-quality papers.[55] The Tianyige Library's copy of the 1525 gazetteer of Chaling, Huguang, discussed in chapter 3, was printed on white mulberry bark paper 白桑皮紙, and its copy of the 1556 gazetteer of Xiangshan, Zhejiang, was printed on white cotton paper 白棉紙.[56]

Craftsmen

In all Yuan, Ming, and early-Qing dynasty cases for which I have clear information, woodblocks for first editions of local gazetteers were cut by hired craftsmen, not yamen staff or corvée laborers. Administrative orders

51. Elvin, *Retreat of the Elephants*, 84–85.
52. *Huairen xian zhi*, postface, 2a–2b.
53. *Lianzhou fu zhi*, 1. Lianzhou was in Guangdong during the Ming, but it is now in Guangxi.
54. Mount Gaoliang is 35 kilometers north of the modern city of Maoming.
55. Chia, *Printing for Profit*, 328 n. 9; *Xiangshan xian zhi* (1556), 431.
56. *Chaling zhou zhi*, handwritten note appended to postface; *Xiangshan xian zhi* (1556), 431. The Tianyige in Ningbo, Zhejiang, holds more than one-fourth of all extant Ming gazetteer titles.

related to publication of local gazetteers often refer to craftsmen's wages, a topic explored further in chapter 5. In addition, print craftsmen are almost never found on lists of local government employees. A rare exception is one staff printing position 刷匠 in the Guizhou provincial administration commission branch office in Pu'an Subprefecture as of 1565.[57] Nothing, however, shows that this person printed the 1565 Pu'an gazetteer. The only clear evidence of a first-edition local gazetteer printed by yamen staff craftsmen comes from the early 1200s. The gazetteer of Anxi 安溪, Fujian, was printed by the yamen's own "book printing office" 印書局 during the tenure of magistrate Zhou Jin 周珒 (served 1216–23).[58]

Even in the early Ming, donations funded the printing of local gazetteers. Officials donated from their salaries to print the 1368 gazetteer of Wuzhou 梧州, Guangxi, the 1383 gazetteer of Yongzhou, Huguang, and the 1413 gazetteer of Xuzhou, Henan, and no staff or corvée printing craftsmen were mentioned.[59] In fact, the craftsman corvée system was in severe decline by the mid Ming.[60] The 1572 gazetteer of Linjiang, Jiangxi, explains that at the Ming founding there were 10,786 registered craftsmen households in Linjiang, but that only 3,774 households remained on the registers. The rest either had no heirs and their households were "extinguished," or had fled, or had found another way to be removed in the intervening two centuries.[61] According to an order regarding publication of the 1542 gazetteer of Gushi, Henan, the blocks were cut locally by hired craftsmen. This happened even though the county had print craftsmen on the household registers who owed labor service.[62] The gazetteer's "Military and Craftsmen" section listed them and explains why they were recorded in the gazetteer: "The state uses the military when the emperor is insulted, and craftsmen for the skilled arts 精藝, so a clear accounting is necessary. As their heavy labors accumulate, they use one

57. *Pu'an zhou zhi*, 32a.
58. *Anxi xian zhi*, 3.6a, 8.73a.
59. Wang and Liu, *Yongle dadian fangzhi jiyi*, 2971–72; *Yongzhou fu zhi* (1383), prefaces, 6; *Yingchuan jun zhi*, postface. Yingchuan was the Han dynasty name for Xuzhou in Kaifeng Prefecture, Henan.
60. Chen Shiqi, *Mingdai shougong*, 71.
61. *Linjiang fu zhi* (1572), 7.56a.
62. *Gushi xian zhi* (1542), prefatory matter, 8a–b, 4.15b–29b.

hundred schemes to escape their registration and have long found numerous ways to disappear. We should record them in order to prevent their treachery."

The section then listed 1,792 military men and 188 craftsmen, out of a total registered county population of 42,186. Each craftsman was listed by administrative community, name, and type of craft.[63] Four, Yan Xiang 鄢祥, Wang Guanyinbao 王官音保, Hu Wenjing 胡文敬, and Hu Ziming 胡子名, were printers, and all were registered in Huiguang 會光, 40 kilometers southwest of the county seat.[64] The labor service these printers owed would have been to the central government, not the local government, and if they had printed the gazetteer, they would have been hired to do so.

It is of course possible that in some cases the magistrates used free labor. Most gazetteers do not reveal the craftsmen's names, hometowns, or employers, so it is possible that the cutters and printers of such "silent" gazetteers were more likely to have been government staff craftsmen or conscripted labor. Some gazetteer prefaces contain magistrates' statements that they "ordered craftsmen" 命工 to cut the blocks.[65] But this does not necessarily mean that the magistrates did not hire and pay them, as will be discussed further in chapter 5. The weight of the evidence is that gazetteers in the Ming were cut and printed by hired craftsmen.

Production Spaces

Cutting woodblocks, printing folios, collating, folding, and binding required a work space, often for several months. The amount of space needed varied with the number of craftsmen used and the gazetteer length. Some gazetteers were cut by a single person, others by many; some were a single, thin volume, others were dozens of thick volumes.[66] Previous scholarship has not fully answered the question of where gazetteer woodblocks were cut and imprints made. Zhang Xiumin 張秀民 argued that

63. Ibid., 4.15b–29b.
64. Ibid., 4.26a.
65. *Xuanping xian zhi*, postface, 1a; *Chicheng xin zhi*, preface.
66. The 1735 *Shaanxi tong zhi* was bound in one hundred volumes.

almost all Ming gazetteers were cut and printed on-site in the administrative unit that was the subject of the gazetteer, and Hou Zhenping's 侯眞平 study of the 1632 Fujian provincial gazetteer, *Min Shu* 閩書, supports Zhang's position.[67] Hou showed that multiple teams of block cutters from various parts of Fujian came to a central site; manuscript chapters were not sent out to cutters working elsewhere. The approximately 118 cutters were organized into teams by place of origin. Each team cut one chapter, more or less. Hou's proof that the teams came to a single site was that some chapters' blocks were cut by more than one cutting team, and a member of one team sometimes appeared on another team's chapter. Hou asserts that this pattern was the typical way in which production of provincial gazetteers was organized.[68] Provincial gazetteers, however, were generally much larger than county, subprefectural, and prefectural gazetteers, and his findings of teams organized by locale does not necessarily apply to gazetteers of smaller territorial units or even to other provincial gazetteers. In addition, neither Zhang nor Hou studied the types of spaces in which the work was done.

In her study of Fujian commercial publishers, Lucille Chia noted that although block cutters often traveled to jobs, they may also have received work at established printing centers, with the cut blocks and unbound sheets sent back to the places of "publication." This would have been especially true in locations with ready access to water transport.[69] Gazetteers, a noncommercial book genre, provide evidence of movement in both directions. Although most gazetteers were cut and printed on-site with craftsmen, local or nonlocal, brought to the yamen, school, or other work site, sometimes a manuscript was delivered to distant craftsmen.

Explicit statements in gazetteers often reveal where the blocks were cut. Some have frontispieces such as that found in the 1485 gazetteer of Neixiang 內鄉, Henan, seen in figure 4.1.[70] It states, "In the eleventh month of winter of the Chenghua *yisi* year, magistrate Wo Pan ordered craftsmen to cut [the blocks] in the Neixiang government office." The

67. Zhang Xiumin, *Zhongguo yinshua shi*, 325.
68. Hou, "Ming mo Fujian banke," 217–18.
69. Chia, *Printing for Profit*, 190, 376–77 n. 142.
70. *Neixiang xian zhi*, frontispiece.

1551 gazetteer of Badong 巴東, Huguang, states, "cut into wood at the county offices."[71] Over the course of the late imperial era, such statements became more common, and by the late Qing most gazetteers had title folios that specified where the blocks were cut and stored (fig. 4.2).

Even when a gazetteer does not explicitly identify the block-cutting location, local cutting can often be inferred. Many note that after the text was finished, craftsmen were "summoned" (徵匠, 召匠, 招工, etc.) or "gathered" 募工 by the magistrate. Upon completion of the manuscript for the 1588 gazetteer of Wuding 武定, Shandong, "donations were made, materials bought, craftsmen summoned, and an office opened."[72] The 1544 gazetteer of Yongfeng 永豐, Jiangxi, was printed locally as a preliminary step in compiling the prefectural gazetteer. Each magistrate was ordered to open a compilation office and upon completion of the manuscript to "gather craftsmen to cut the blocks" 募工刊刻.[73] Similar statements appear regularly in Song, Yuan, Ming, and Qing gazetteer prefaces. Pre-Ming examples include the 1230 gazetteer of Ganshui 澉水 (modern Zhejiang), which says that craftsmen were "hired and gathered to cut and print" the gazetteer 售募鐫行, and the 1300 gazetteer of Nanfeng, Jiangxi, which says, "Craftsmen were gathered to cut it into catalpa" 募匠刻諸梓.[74] Such statements do not always reveal the precise location in which the work was done or the cutters' hometowns, but they do demonstrate that blocks were cut locally.

In other cases we can infer local cutting because local people were involved in production.[75] The 1527 gazetteer of Yangwu 陽武, Henan, states that townsmen Zhang Zuo 張佐 and Zhao Tang 趙堂 "wrote out the text and cut it into wood"; the 1627 gazetteer of Pinghu, Zhejiang, records that a local named Zhang Qianxian 張啓賢 was both the calligrapher and the block cutter.[76] Many gazetteers list yamen functionaries or local people as "production supervisors" 督工, "printing supervisors" 督梓, or copyists 騰寫書手, or variations thereof. The most common supervisors were yamen clerks 典史, subbureaucratic functionaries 吏, and

71.   *Badong xian zhi*, 1200.
72.   *Wuding zhou zhi* (1588), preface.
73.   *Yongfeng xian zhi*, prefatory matter, *xiuzhi shiyou*, 3a.
74.   *Ganshui zhi*, 4659; Zhang Guogan, *Zhongguo gu fangzhi kao*, 561.
75.   *Pujiang zhi lüe*, postface, 2b.
76.   *Yangwu xian zhi*, 923; *Pinghu xian zhi*, 42.

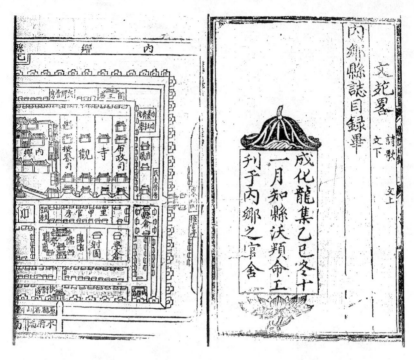

FIGURE 4.1. Frontispiece of the 1485 *Neixiang xian zhi* recording its production in the county yamen (Harvard-Yenching Library).

school instructors. A functionary in the yamen's rites section oversaw printing of the 1541 gazetteer of Yaozhou 耀州, Shaanxi.[77] The prefectural record keeper 照磨 and jail warden 司獄 oversaw printing of the 1572 gazetteer of Yanzhou 兗州, Shandong.[78] Locals from outside the yamen or school also acted as production supervisors. The 1546 gazetteer of Zichuan 淄川, Shandong, lists by name four "county elders" 邑耆 as printing supervisors, none of whom had a degree or tribute student status.[79] "Elder Yuan Fang" 老人袁方, who also had no degree, supervised production

77. *Yaozhou zhi*, 125.
78. *Yanzhou fu zhi*, vol. 1, 28. Record keepers were responsible for the maintenance of documentary files in various government agencies and in some cases held civil service rank of 8a to 9b. Hucker, *Dictionary of Official Titles*.
79. *Zichuan xian zhi*, postface, 2a

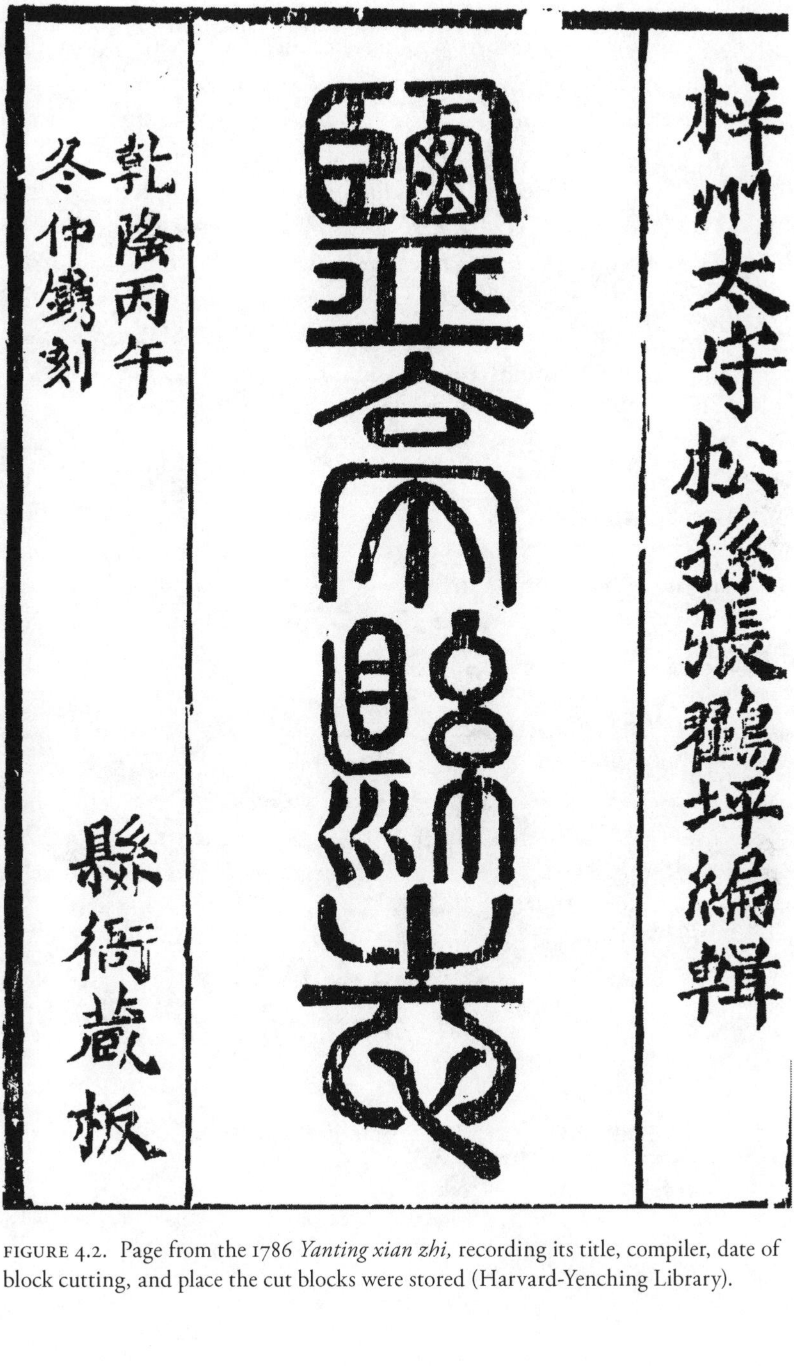

梓州太守松孫張鶴坪編輯

鹽亭縣志

乾隆丙午
冬仲鐫刻

縣衙藏板

FIGURE 4.2. Page from the 1786 *Yanting xian zhi,* recording its title, compiler, date of block cutting, and place the cut blocks were stored (Harvard-Yenching Library).

of the 1537 gazetteer of Sinan 思南, Guizhou.[80] Because it is unlikely that elderly supervisors and yamen personnel would travel to distant sites for extended periods to supervise block cutters, we can assume local cutting when a printed gazetteer names local production supervisors.

The local yamen was the default location to cut the blocks, even in the Song dynasty.[81] As Liu Fu explained when he had difficulties printing the 1537 *Hengzhou fu zhi* in his home, "The manuscript for this book should have been given to the yamen for cutting." The yamen had supervising officials, scribes who could copy out the text, and space for craftsmen to work. Among gazetteers printed in yamens, most were the gazetteers of that yamen's territorial unit, but occasionally a yamen printed a subordinate unit's gazetteer. In the Ming, Baoding Prefecture printed its own gazetteer and those of two subordinate departments, Qizhou 祁州 and Anzhou 安州.[82]

Schools were the other common site for printing gazetteers. Like yamens, they were spacious, the proofreaders were often teachers and students, and school libraries frequently ended up storing the cut blocks. In every case for which I have information, the woodblocks for Song and Yuan dynasty gazetteers were cut and stored in the local yamen or Confucian school, and this remained the norm throughout the late imperial period. The 1177 *Piling zhi* 毗陵志 was reprinted in 1315 in conjunction with the rebuilding of a school library destroyed in the Mongol conquest of 1275. An education official told an instructor, "The library is finished and other books can be bought if you have the money, but the prefectural gazetteer cannot." They got an imprint from a Shandong man who had been an official in Changzhou 常州 (Piling was an old name for Changzhou), assembled artisans on the library's top floor, and used the imprint to cut new blocks.[83] In 1333 the Zhenjiang 鎮江 prefectural Confucian school held 2,007 woodblocks for two editions of the local

80.   *Sinan fu zhi*, end matter.

81.   *Wujun tujing xu ji*, 688; Zhang Guogan, *Zhongguo gu fangzhi kao*, 241; *Xinding xu zhi*, 4.11b–14a.

82.   Zhou Hongzu, *Gujin shuke*, 8.

83.   Other pre-1400 map guides and gazetteers cut in Confucian schools include: *Yanzhou tujing*, *Yanzhou xu zhi*, 4383; *Yufeng zhi* (*SYFZ* ed.), 1051–52; *Lianjiang zhi* (in Zhang Guogan, *Zhongguo gu fangzhi kao*, 421); and *Gu Teng jun zhi*, (in Wang and Liu, *Yongle dadian fangzhi jiyi*, 3032).

gazetteer.[84] The 1341 gazetteer of Dongyang 東陽, Zhejiang, was cut in the county Confucian school. Four local schools divided up the manuscript of the 1344 *Jinling xinzhi* 金陵新志 for printing, each being responsible for three to five chapters.[85]

Beginning in the sixteenth century, however, there are also instances of blocks being cut and stored elsewhere. Provincial surveillance commissions 提刑按察使司 and administration commissions 承宣布政使司 printed most provincial gazetteers in their yamens, but as discussed in chapter 3, examination halls were also used. Work was likely done in other government-owned spaces as well. The 1552 gazetteer of Chongyi 崇義, Jiangxi, was cut by Liao Can 廖燦, a student at the county Yinyang 陰陽 school, although it is not clear where he did the work.[86] The school was located near the yamen and of modest size; it had a quota of fifteen students and one unranked instructor.[87]

Woodblocks were occasionally cut or stored in a compiler's home. Many compilers were retired officials who lived in large compounds that had space for craftsmen to work. The blocks for the 1537 *Hengzhou fu zhi*, discussed in chapter 3, were cut and stored in the compiler's home, and the blocks for the 1530 gazetteer of Qizhou 蘄州, Huguang, were stored in the home of the compiler, Gan Ze 甘澤, after one Confucian school student and four community school students wrote out the text and the magistrate had the blocks cut.[88] After Liu Da'en 劉大恩 (*juren* 1543) compiled the gazetteer of his native place, Xincai 新蔡, Henan, in 1574, he died and the sponsoring magistrate transferred before having it printed. When a new magistrate arrived, he was shown the manuscript by Liu's son, Liu Zhounan 劉周南 (*juren* 1570), who asked him to publish it, but the magistrate was too busy setting up his new administration. So Liu ordered his two younger brothers to copy out the text, prepare the needed money, and bring in more than ten skilled block cutters. The Xincai gazetteer was

84. *Zhenjiang zhi*, 2945.

85. *Jinhua fu zhi* (*SKCM* ed.), 453; Brook, "Native Identity," 240, citing *Jinling xin zhi*, preface.

86. *Chongyi xian zhi*, postface.

87. Ibid., 38b.

88. *Hengzhou fu zhi*, 9.13a–b; *Qizhou zhi*, 9.72a.

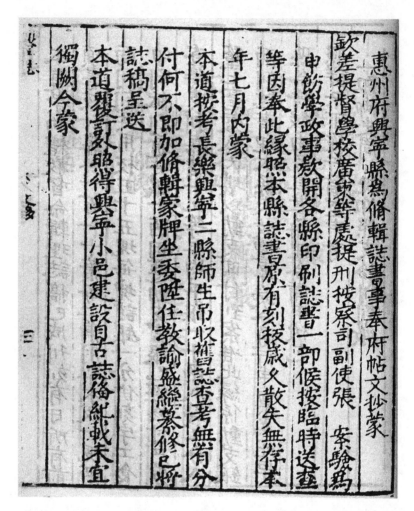

FIGURE 4.3. Order from the Guangdong provincial education intendant granting permission to print the 1552 gazetteer of Xingning, Guangdong (Tianyige Library).

printed in 1579.[89] Liu Fu, Gan Ze, and Liu Da'en were all retired officials, and all received the resident administrator's permission to print (fig. 4.3).

Manuscripts could also be sent to local commercial print shops for block cutting. In 1576 Zheng Tianzuo 鄭天佐, the magistrate of Taoyuan

89. *Xincai xian zhi* (1579), preface, 1a; *Xincai xian zhi* (1795), 477–82.

桃源, Huguang, was approached by Li Zheng 李徵, a local retired official who had inherited a gazetteer that had been hand copied by his ancestor. Li wanted to update and publish it, but the magistrate responded, "This is my responsibility." He worried, however, about the expense of bringing in craftsmen, and instead gave the manuscript to the local Zhangjiang Book Room 漳江書屋 (also written 漳江精舍), for block cutting.[90] This suggests that having a print shop do the work could be cheaper than opening an office in the yamen and bringing in craftsmen, at least in Taoyuan. For the 1621 gazetteer of Ganzhou 贛州, Jiangxi, a transport supervisor took the manuscript 300 kilometers to the provincial capital, Nanchang, where document clerks wrote out the text. The sheets of the fine copy (also called the "printer's copy") were assembled into volumes, shipped back to Ganzhou, and given to a print shop head, Mr. Yu 堂長余公, for block cutting.[91]

Commercial publishers reprinted a few local gazetteers from previous dynasties. In the early 1600s the Mao Family Jiguge 毛氏及古閣 publishing house in Suzhou reprinted the *Qinchuan zhi* 琴川志, a gazetteer of Changshu, Suzhou, originally compiled in the 1250s.[92] In 1613 Lin Cai 林材 reprinted the *Sanshan zhi* 三山志, a twelfth-century local gazetteer of Fuzhou 福州, Fujian, put the blocks in Fuzhou's Fahai Chan Buddhist Temple 法海禪寺, and had the head monk keep them to "make it convenient for those who were interested to print it."[93] The national gazetteer, the *Da Ming yitongzhi*, was also commercially reprinted in 1505 by Liu Hongyi's Shendu Book Studio 劉弘毅慎獨書齋, and by the Yang Family's Guiren Studio 楊氏歸仁齋, in Jianning, Fujian, in 1559 and 1588.[94]

90.   *Taoyuan xian zhi*, 389, 395. My identification of the print shop as local is based on the use of *Zhangjiang*, a name used in many Taoyuan institutions. Li Zheng's biography appears on p. 436.

91.   *Ganzhou fu zhi* (1621), preface. It is not clear whether Yu was related to the Yu publishers of the same surname in Jianyang studied by Lucille Chia.

92.   Mao Jin, *Jiguge jiaoke shumu*, 24.

93.   Xu Bo, *Hongyulou shumu*, 2049.

94.   Zhou Hongzu, *Gujin shuke*, 28–30; Xie Shuishun, *Fujian gudai keshu*, 314–15; National Library of China Catalog, nlc.gov.cn.

Printing Craftsmen and Their Business Zones

Previous studies of printing craftsmen have begun to uncover the ways in which woodblock cutters organized their work, but we still have relatively few details, especially on the zones in which they operated and how they got work. Li Guoqing 李國慶 compiled a name index of block cutters in the Ming dynasty that allows us to associate names with texts, and occasionally a hometown, but he rarely records the text's origin. Thus, although the index is useful, it can present only a static picture.[95] Cynthia Brokaw's study of the Sibao 四堡, Fujian, book trade in the Qing and Republican periods shows that Sibao commercial publishers used block-cutting specialists from their own lineages, but also hired professional cutters from outside their lineages who lived and ate with the publisher. They may also have used cutter-monks or itinerant cutters who resided at a local temple.[96] Soren Edgren examined a block cutter involved in a lawsuit in the late 1100s who worked in four towns in the Jiangnan region: Guangde 廣德, Mingzhou 明州, Taizhou, and Ningbo, and argued that many block cutters were itinerant workers.[97] Michaela Bussotti, in her study of Huizhou, argued that block cutting was a secondary winter activity for farm families, including women and children, and that some Huizhou cutters carried movable wooden type and cutting tools from village to village to print genealogies. Busotti further argued that traveling to work outside Huizhou was a local cultural practice that went well beyond Huizhou's famous traveling merchants.[98]

Gazetteers can help us create a more dynamic and detailed picture of the block-cutting business because the production sites are generally known and craftsmen's names and hometowns are sometimes recorded. This makes it possible to reconstruct craftsmen's movements and their business zones. By "business zone" I mean the geographic area from which a block cutter either received manuscripts or traveled to jobs. Aggregating and analyzing this information makes it possible to identify previously unknown regional printing centers. Earlier studies focusing

---

95. Li Guoqing, *Mingdai kangong*.
96. Brokaw, *Commerce in Culture*, 97–102.
97. Edgren, "Southern Song Printing," 46–54.
98. Bussotti, *Gravures de Hui*, 283.

on well-known printing centers had relatively little to say about how people outside these centers could publish a book or other text. Gazetteers were published throughout the country, a fact that makes it possible to explore this important question. Printed texts were key carriers of core aspects of Chinese culture, therefore understanding the publishing industry and book trade, even in remote regions, is critical to understanding late imperial society and economy. The data presented in the following pages will show that even in isolated county towns, officials could hire block cutters and publish books, and that some print craftsmen were highly mobile, operating both regionally and nationally.

Acceptable block cutters were often available at relatively short distances, especially for locales close to major printing centers.[99] But even in remote areas, magistrates often did not need to look far to find block cutters. The blocks for the 1525 gazetteer of Chaling 茶嶺, Huguang, a mountainous border region 150 kilometers southeast of Changsha 長沙, were cut by Long Sheng 龍盛 of Yongxin 永新, Jiangxi, 70 kilometers east of Chaling.[100]

Even though local craftsmen could be found far from China's major cultural centers in the sixteenth century, skill and graphic style mattered, and as a result publishers sometimes brought in outsiders or sent their manuscripts out to calligraphers and cutters. The magistrate of Huixian 輝縣, Henan, hired Mr. Chu 褚 from Kaifeng, the provincial capital 100 kilometers away, to polish the manuscript and write out the text of the county gazetteer.[101] A high-quality fine copy for transfer to the woodblocks was a prerequisite to printing an attractive book. Good calligraphy was an important status marker for officials, a fact that is most apparent in prefaces, which were generally written by high-status individuals in a better hand than the main text. New editions sometimes even included facsimile reproductions of old prefaces, especially if the person was well known. The 1541 gazetteer of Xuzhou, Henan, reprinted two handwritten prefaces to the previous edition dated 1493, one by Li Dongyang 李東陽 (1447–1516), the famous official and calligrapher, and one by the former magistrate (fig. 4.4). The compilers transferred ink

99. *Taicang zhou zhi*, 69.
100. *Chaling zhou zhi*, 928.
101. *Huixian zhi*, 273.

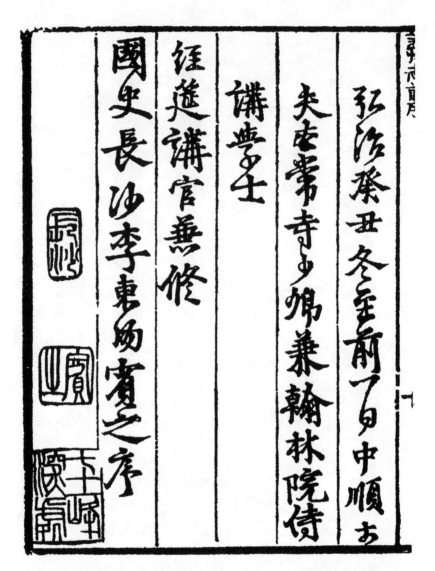

FIGURE 4.4. Facsimile copy of Li Dongyang's 1493 preface to the *Xuzhou zhi*, reprinted in the 1541 edition (Tianyige Library). The preface was reprinted in facsimile in order to preserve the beauty of the original calligraphy.

directly from the old prefaces 翻刊 to new blocks in order to "preserve the subtle beauty of the writing."[102]

Although many gazetteer publishers wanted elegant calligraphy, others either did not care or could not afford it. An administrator could save money by having yamen functionaries, students, or cheap laborers write out the text.[103] The fine copy of the 1554 gazetteer of Anqing 安慶, Nanzhili, was made by five farmers 農民 and three yamen functionaries (fig. 4.5). The farmers' calligraphy was acceptable, yet inelegant. Farmer Zhu Gao's 朱誥 characters often drift from side to side as the folio progresses, are unbalanced, and contain tentative strokes (figs. 4.6 and 4.7).[104] The farmers had five different surnames and thus do not appear to have been part of a lineage-based block-cutting business. A yamen clerk and two "commoners of the neighborhood" 街民 did the mediocre calligraphy of the 1554 gazetteer of Yancheng 郾城, Henan.[105]

Like calligraphy, gazetteer maps and illustrations were sometimes done locally, as seen in chapter 3, and sometimes not. The city wall illustration in the 1608 gazetteer of Huanggang 黃岡, Huguang, was done by a local, Zheng Zhongyuan 鄭仲元,[106] whereas the numerous illustrations in the 1505 gazetteer of Qufu 曲阜, Shandong, were done by Xiong Neng 熊能 of Jinan, the provincial capital 120 kilometers north of Qufu.[107]

Craftsmen could be recruited either by letter or in person. After the manuscript for the 1549 gazetteer of Longqing 隆慶, Beizhili, was completed, the magistrate dispatched someone to Beijing, about 60 kilometers to the south, to summon cutters 召鐵筆者 and brought back six "Beijing block cutters" 北京刊字匠.[108] When the manuscript for the 1585 gazetteer of Qingyun 慶雲, in the southeast corner of Beizhili, was finished, the magistrate wanted high-quality block cutting 繕刻, but in his view the county had no skilled craftsmen 良匠. Thus, he sent a letter and

102. *Xuzhou zhi* (1541), prefaces, 13b.
103. *Ruizhou fu zhi*, 1324; *Hezhou zhi* (1579), 369; *Yaozhou zhi*, 124.
104. *Anqing fu zhi*, 270, 486, 724, 1038, 1222, 1369, 1494, 1678.
105. *Yancheng xian zhi* (1554), 938.
106. *Huanggang xian zhi*, illustrations.
107. *Queli zhi*, 1.36b.
108. *Longqing zhi*, Su Qian's postface, 4a, 10.77a–b. Longqing's name was changed to Yanqing in 1567 because of a name taboo during the Longqing era.

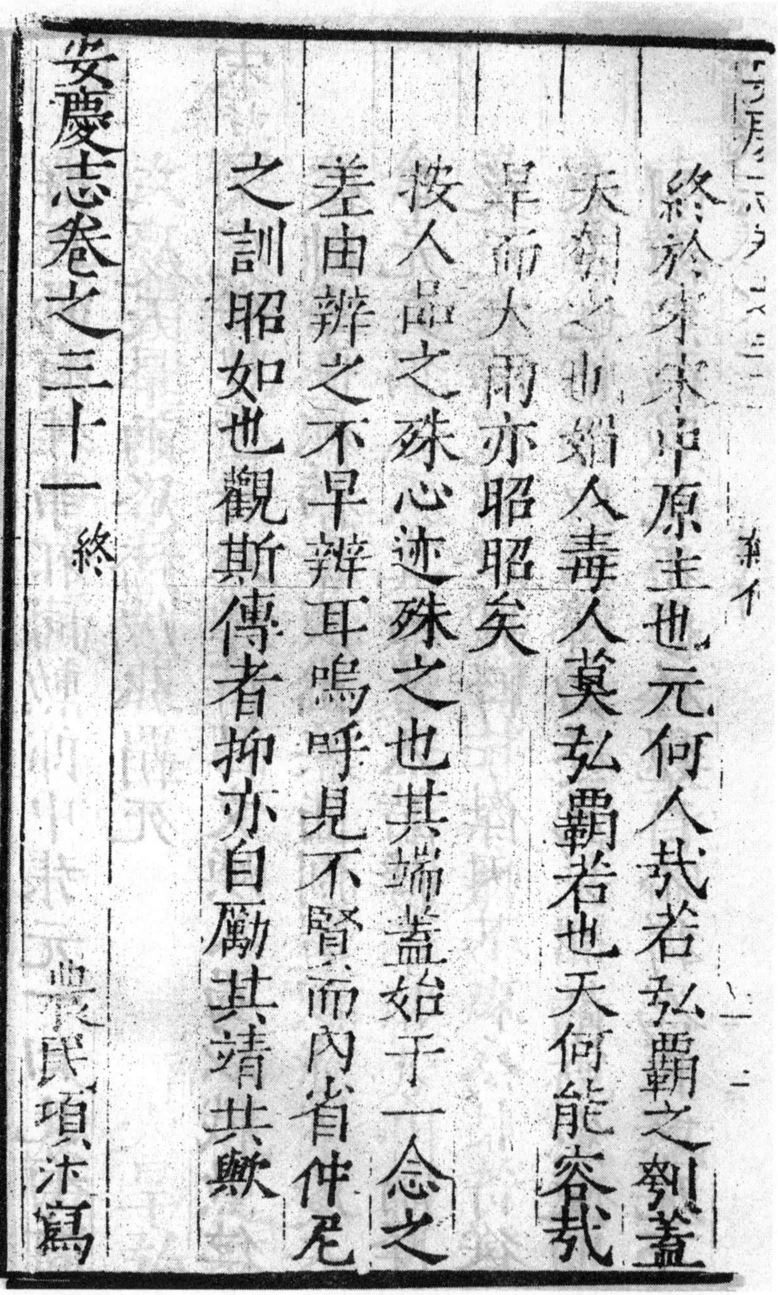

安慶志卷之三十一　終

農民項沭寫

終於身宋中原主也元何人哉若弘覇之劄蓋

天朝之也媚人毒人莫弘覇若也天何能容哉

早而大雨亦昭昭矣

按人品之殊心迹殊之也其端蓋始于一念之

差由辨之不早辨耳嗚呼見不賢而內省仲尼

之訓昭如也觀斯傳者抑亦自勵其靖共歟

FIGURE 4.5. Calligraphy by farmer Xiang Bian for the 1554 gazetteer of Anqing, Nanzhili (National Central Library).

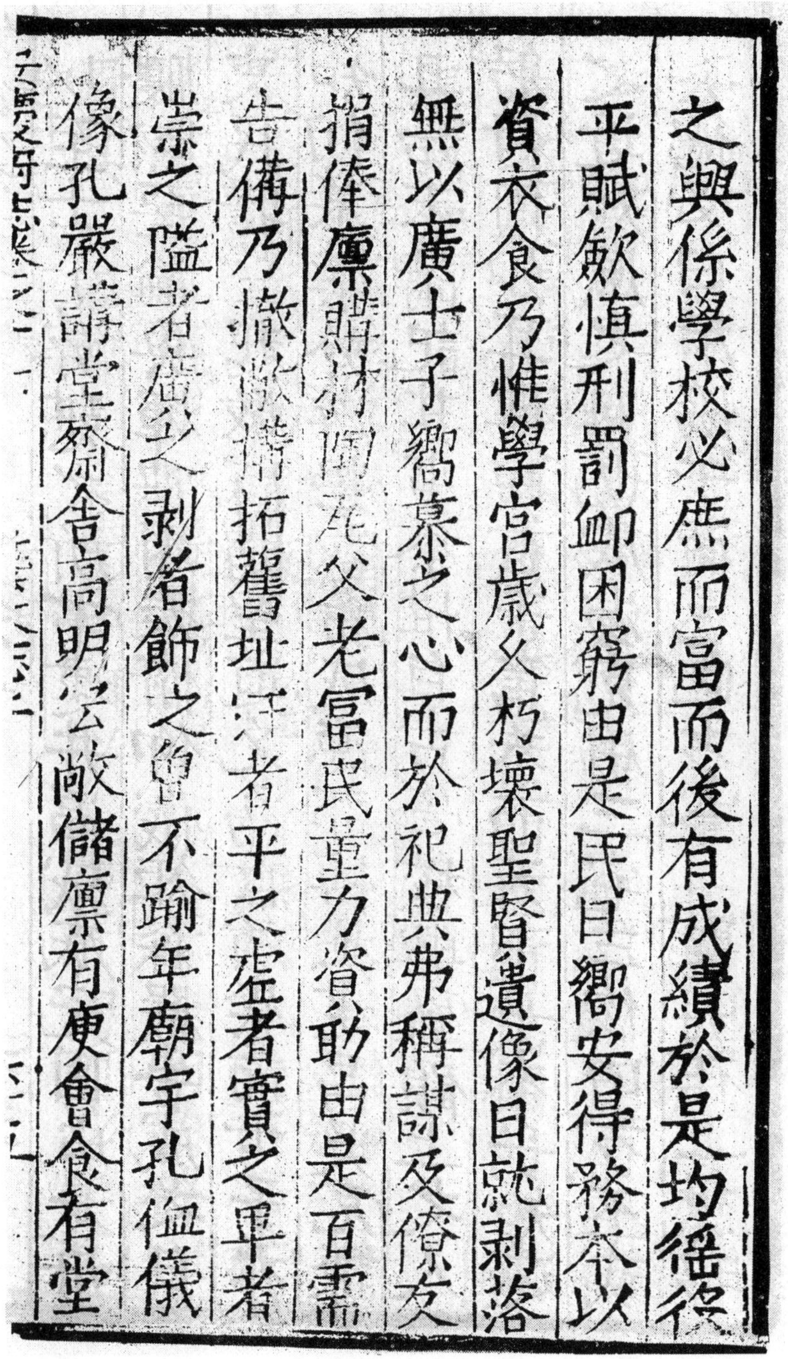
之興係學校必庶而富而後有成績於是均徭役
平賦斂慎刑罰卹困窮由是民日嚮安得務本以
資衣食乃惟學宮歲久朽壞聖賢遺像日就剝落
無以廣士子嚮慕之心而於祀典弗稱謀及僚友
捐俸廩購材同心父老富民量力資助由是百需
告備乃撤敝構拓舊址汙者平之虛者實之卑者
崇之隘者廣之剝者飾之曾不踰年廟宇孔侐儀
像孔嚴講堂齋舍高明宏敞儲廩有庾會食有堂

FIGURE 4.6. Calligraphy by farmer Zhu Gao for the 1554 gazetteer of Anqing, Nanzhili (National Central Library).

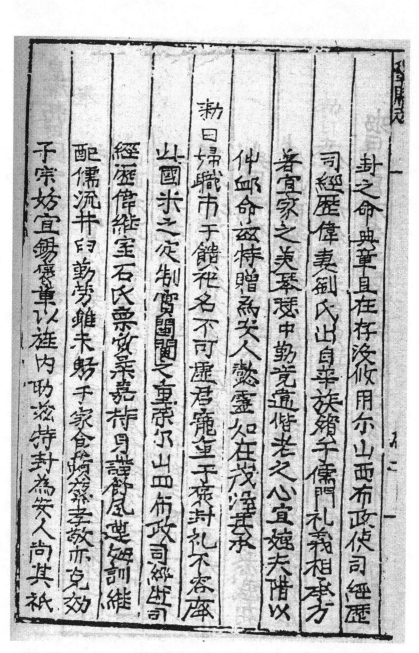

FIGURE 4.7. Unbalanced, poorly composed calligraphy in the 1555 gazetteer of Gongxian, Henan (Tianyige Library).

money to an official he knew who was serving in Tianchang, Nanzhili, asking him to hire craftsmen. Tianchang was located 50 kilometers north-west of Yangzhou and 600 kilometers from Qingyun, but they were linked by river and the Grand Canal.[109]

JIANGXI BLOCK CUTTERS

In the Ming dynasty, Nanchang 南昌, Jiangxi's provincial capital, and Ji'an 吉安 were important centers of literati culture, and the province as a whole was relatively prosperous (map 4.1).[110] Print craftsmen could be found across the province, and Jiangxi block cutters can be connected to gazetteer projects in both their local regions and distant locales. We have already discussed two cases in this chapter, one from Yongxin, and one from Ganzhou. In addition, cutters from Fengxin 奉新, 50 kilometers west of Nanchang, and Jinxian 進賢, 50 kilometers southeast of Nan-chang, worked on multiple gazetteer projects, and cutters from Nanchang, Ji'an, and Gao'an 高安 can be connected to at least one.

Fengxin cutters worked on projects in northern Jiangxi and eastern Huguang, all within 150 kilometers of Fengxin. Blocks for the 1518 gazet-teer of Ruizhou 瑞州 Prefecture, Jiangxi, 30 kilometers north of Fengxin, were cut by craftsmen from Fengxin, and Gao'an, Ruizhou's urban county (table 4.1).[111] Two Fengxin craftsmen cut blocks for the 1530 gaz-etteer of Qizhou, Huguang, 140 kilometers to the north via Lake Poyang and the Yangzi River.[112] Many blocks of the Jiajing-era (1522–66) gazetteer of Yuanzhou 袁州, Jiangxi, were likely cut by Fengxin cutters. The three Fengxin cutters of the Ruizhou and Qizhou gazetteers were surnamed Zhai 翟, Chen 陳, and Yu 余, as were five cutters of the Yuanzhou gazet-teer.[113] Zhai is a relatively rare surname, and from Fengxin to Yuanzhou was only 140 kilometers. A 1604 edition of the *Bencao gangmu* 本草綱目 (Great pharmacopeia), published in Nanchang by the Jiangxi provincial administration commission, also had two block cutters surnamed Zhai

109. *Qingyun xian zhi*, preface, 3b.
110. Dardess, *A Ming Society*; Gerritsen, *Ji'an Literati*.
111. *Ruizhou fu zhi*, 1324.
112. *Qizhou zhi*, 9.71b.
113. *Yuanzhou fu zhi*, 607, 609, 738, 740, 745.

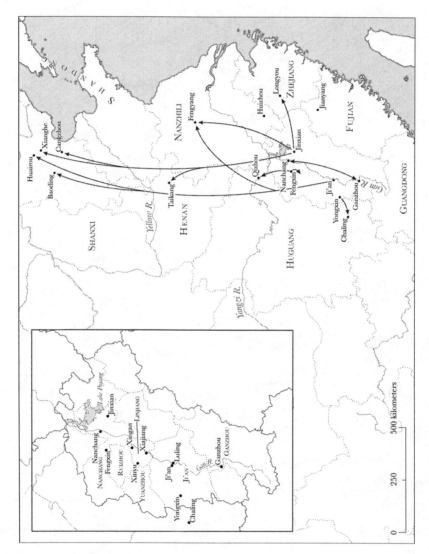

MAP 4.1 Jiangxi block cutter business zones

and five surnamed Yu.[114] Together, these records suggest that Fengxin was a regional block-cutting center.

A second Jiangxi block-cutting center was Jinxian. Gazetteer records document Jinxian cutters working farther from home than Fengxin cutters. Five worked on the 1524 gazetteer of Taikang 太康, Henan, along with four cutters from four places in Henan: Taikang itself; Guide, 75 kilometers northeast of Taikang; Jiyuan 濟源, 200 kilometers northwest; and Qixian 杞縣, 50 kilometers north.[115] Jinxian, which abuts the southern edge of Lake Poyang 鄱陽湖, was about 600 kilometers south of Taikang, although the most likely route by water doubled the distance. There is no information on how the Jinxian cutters came to be in Taikang, but one might speculate that the local cutter, Ge Jin 葛金, was related to, and contacted, the Jinxian carver of the same surname, who then recruited the other Jinxian cutters. Jinxian cutters also worked on the 1488 gazetteer of Fengyang, more than 650 kilometers north of Jinxian; the 1603 gazetteer of Cangzhou 滄州, Beizhili, a town on the Grand Canal approximately 1,300 kilometers north of Jinxian and 200 kilometers south of Beijing; and the 1612 gazetteer of Longyou 龍游, Zhejiang, over 300 kilometers east of Jinxian.[116]

Like Jinxian cutters, ones from Nanchang and Ji'an also worked on gazetteers in distant locales. Nanchang craftsman Guo Tingfeng 郭廷鳳 was both a calligrapher and a block cutter for the 1620 gazetteer of Xianghe 香河, near Beijing, and was joined by another Nanchang cutter.[117] A cutter from Luling 廬陵 (Ji'an) worked on the 1488 Fengyang gazetteer with the Jinxian cutter discussed above.[118] A Ji'an craftsman cut the 1604 gazetteer of Huairou 懷柔, near Beijing.[119] Liu 劉 of Ji'an, and at least four other Jiangxi cutters, worked on the 1608 gazetteer of Baoding along with cutters from Zhenjiang and Ningguo 寧國, Nanzhili.[120]

Other locales in Jiangxi also had print craftsmen. The 1572 gazetteer of Linjiang 臨江 Prefecture, between Nanchang and Ji'an, records registered

114. Li Guoqing, *Mingdai kangong*, 351.
115. *Taikang xian zhi*, 822.
116. Li Guoqing, *Mingdai kangong*, 321, 326; *Zhongdu zhi*, 448–49.
117. *Xianghe xian zhi*, prefaces, 1.1.
118. *Zhongdu zhi*, 448–49.
119. *Huairou xian zhi*, preface.
120. *Baoding fu zhi*, 11–16, 21, 23, 35, 37, 41, 124–26, 732, 733, 737.

Table 4.1
Jiangxi block cutters who worked on gazetteers

Date and title	Place of publication	Block cutter origin	Block cutter name(s)
1488 *Zhongdu zhi*	Fengyang, Nanzhili	Jinxian, Jiangxi Luling, Jiangxi	Wu 吳 Wang Zhen 王珍
1518 *Ruizhou fu zhi*	Ruizhou, Jiangxi	Gao'an, Jiangxi Fengxin, Jiangxi	Liu Xing 劉興 Zhai Xian 翟賢
1543 *Yuanzhou fu zhi*	Yuanzhou, Jiangxi	Fengxin, Jiangxi?	Chen Yang 陳洋 Yu Jing 余景 Zhai Xian 翟顯 Zhai Yi 翟義 Zhai Zhi 翟智
1525 *Chaling xian zhi*	Chaling, Huguang	Yongxin, Jiangxi	Long Sheng 龍盛
1530 *Qizhou zhi*	Qizhou, Huguang	Fengxin, Jiangxi	Chen Luan 陳欒 Yu Jie 余節
1524 *Taikang xian zhi*	Taikang, Henan	Jinxian, Jiangxi	Ge Jingchang 葛景昌 Gong Long 龔龍 Liang Benshi 梁本實 Qi Zhengxiang 齊正祥 Zhou Mei 周美 (with Henan cutters: Ge Jin 葛金 Sang Youzhu 桑有柱 Zhang Jingfu 張景福 Zhang Kui 張魁)
1603 *Cangzhou zhi*	Cangzhou, Beizhili	Jinxian, Jiangxi	Lu Kecheng 魯克程
1604 *Huairou xian zhi*	Huairou, Beizhili	Ji'an, Jiangxi	Peng Zuo 彭佐
1608 *Baoding fu zhi*	Baoding, Beizhili	Ji'an, Jiangxi Jiangxi (locale unspecified)	Liu 劉 Fu 付 Gong 貢 Zhang 張 Zheng 正
1612 *Longyou xian zhi*	Longyou, Zhejiang	Jinxian, Jiangxi	Wan Deng 萬燈 Wan Qi 萬祈
1620 *Xianghe xian zhi*	Xianghe, Beizhili	Nanchang, Jiangxi	Guo Tingfeng 郭廷鳳 Shen Xingbing 沈性炳

artisan households in the prefecture's four counties. The most recent census prior to the 1572 publication, done in 1526, recorded 135,872 households and 473,211 people in the prefecture. Of these, 21 households were registered as block cutters and 43 as printers subject to the labor service levy. Seven households of block cutters and one household of printers from Qingjiang 清江, the prefecture's urban county, were required to provide resident labor service in Beijing government offices. The others were required to do rotating labor service in Nanjing for one season every four years. All four of Linjiang's counties had registered block-cutter households: seven in Qingjiang, one in Xingan 新淦, three in Xinyu 新喻, and three in Xiajiang 峡江. Three of the four counties had registered printer households: twenty-six in Qingjiang, eight in Xingan, and nine in Xinyu.[121] Because cutters worked with members of their extended families, many of whom would not have been registered as artisans, these figures do not tell us the total number of people involved in block cutting and printing in Linjiang. Nevertheless, they do suggest a floor and reveal that every county in the prefecture had some print craftsmen. The Linjiang labor service information also suggests a mechanism whereby print craftsmen could form national networks: they could meet other craftsmen during their labor service in the capitals and draw on those networks when projects arose. This makes it easier to understand how some magistrates hired cutters from multiple locales.

BEIJING BLOCK CUTTERS

The Ming had a dual-capital system beginning in 1421, and both Beijing and Nanjing were publishing centers. The two cities were filled with officials who had connections in the provinces from which to draw publishing business. They were furthermore centers of literati culture and religious, educational, and government organizations, all of which printed numerous texts. In addition, print craftsmen did labor service in both capitals, and students studied, took examinations, and bought books in the capitals.[122] Gazetteers from inside and outside of the capital regions

---

121. *Linjiang fu zhi* (1572), 7.1a–b, 7.56a–58a.

122. On Nanjing commercial publishers, see Chia, "Of Three Mountains Street," 107–51.

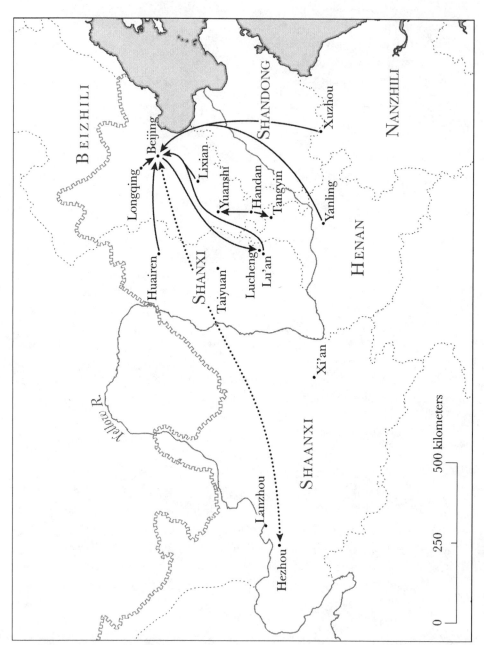

MAP 4.2 Beijing and Handan block cutter business zones

were printed therein, often through official or personal connections.[123] The 1537 gazetteer of Yanling 鄢陵, Henan, was printed in Beijing, a distance of more than 700 kilometers (map 4.2). An official from Yanling, Liu Ren 劉訒, compiled the gazetteer while home on mourning leave. When Liu finished, the magistrate said to him, "In the capital, none of the scholars' calligraphy and block cutters' graphic styles are not excellent. I am willing to donate from my salary to help have it cut." Thus, Liu took the manuscript with him back to Beijing for block cutting when he returned to work.[124]

After Ma Tun 馬暾 finished the manuscript for the 1494 gazetteer of his native place, Xuzhou, Nanzhili, magistrate He Bangzhi 何邦治 "sealed and delivered it to skilled craftsmen 良工 in the capital for cutting" and requested a preface of Lin Han 林瀚 (1434–ca. 1519). "Capital" refers to the northern capital, Beijing, where Lin was chancellor of the Directorate of Education.[125] In 1495 the same Ma Tun had become prefect of Lu'an 潞安, in southeastern Shanxi, and compiled its gazetteer. When finished, he sent a copy of the text with a letter over 600 kilometers to his close friend in Beijing, Cheng Minzheng 程敏政, and asked him to write a preface and have it printed.[126] A century later the movement was in the other direction, from Beijing to Lu'an. The 1591 gazetteer of Lucheng 潞城, one of Lu'an's subordinate counties, was cut onsite by six Beijing craftsmen.[127] These gazetteers were cut by outsiders even though local block cutters were almost certainly available. The 1513 gazetteer of Zhangzi 長子, another county in Lu'an, was cut by five locals, Shen Bin 沈斌, Shen Ming 沈銘, Shen Yu 沈鈺, Shen Xuan 沈鉉, and Shen Mei 沈枚 (table 4.2).

Two other gazetteers from outside Beijing can be identified as cut by Beijing craftsmen through the place name "Jintai 金臺" that precedes their names. Jintai was the capital of the state of Yan 燕, and appears on two Beijing print/book shop names identified by Zhang Xiumin, "Jintai Yue Family" 金臺岳家 and "Wang Liang's Jintai Book Stall" 汪諒金臺書

123. Farmer, *Early Ming Government*.

124. *Yanling zhi*, 8.95a–97a.

125. *Xuzhou zhi* (1494), preface, 3–4; Zhang Tingyu, *Ming shi*, 4428; *Ming shilu*, *Xiaozong shilu*, 921.

126. Cheng Minzheng, *Huangdun wenji*, 32.38a.

127. *Lucheng xian zhi*, 75.

Table 4.2
Beijing block cutters who worked on gazetteers

Date and title	Place of publication	Block cutter origin	Block cutter name(s)
1534 *Lixian zhi*	Lixian, Beizhili	Beijing	Huang Lu 黃祿 Shou Tianfu 守天福
1549 *Longqing zhi*	Longqing, Beizhili	Beijing	Deng Ji 鄧紀 Huang Ming 黃明 Ji Hao 紀毫 Ji Jin 紀縉 Xu Luan 徐欒 Zhang Long 張龍
1591 *Lucheng xian zhi*	Lucheng, Shanxi	Beijing	Pei Guocui 裴國翠 Pei Guoming 裴国明 Pei Jiugai 裴九垓 Pei Jiuqian 裴九乾 Pei Yi'e 裴一鶚 Pei Yiyuan 裴一元

鋪, both of which were located near Beijing's Zhengyang Gate. The 1534 gazetteer of Lixian 蠡縣, Beizhili, 200 kilometers southwest of Beijing, was cut by two Jintai craftsmen, and the 1546 gazetteer of Hezhou, Shaanxi (modern Gansu), 1600 kilometers west of Beijing, was cut by the "Jintai Liu Family Shiyoutang" 金臺劉氏仕優堂.[128]

NANJING AND OTHER JIANGNAN BLOCK CUTTERS

The pattern of officials using connections in Beijing to print their gazetteers appears similar for Nanjing. In 1497 Wu Wendu 吳文度, the prefect of Tingzhou 汀州 in southwestern Fujian, sent his manuscript more than 1,000 kilometers to Nanjing where his *jinshi* classmate, Liu Zhen 劉震, was serving as chancellor of the Nanjing Directorate of Education, and asked him to have it printed (map 4.3).[129] Wu presumably could have had it cut on-site by Fujian or Jiangxi block cutters. By that date there even may have been a commercial publishing industry in

128. *Lixian zhi*, 504; *Hezhou zhi* (1546), 174.
129. *Tingzhou fu zhi*, old preface.

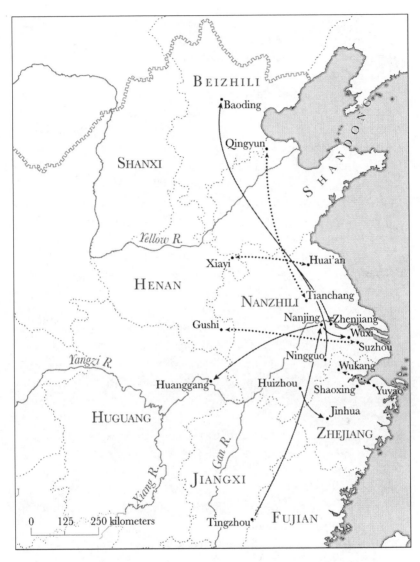

MAP 4.3 Jiangnan block cutter business zones

Sibao, the village in Tingzhou studied by Cynthia Brokaw.[130] But by sending the gazetteer to Liu, he probably expanded his readership to colleagues and students in Nanjing.

130. Brokaw, *Commerce in Culture*, 79–93.

The Nanjing Directorate of Education published multiple gazetteers. The *Gujin shuke* lists seventeen gazetteers it published in the early through mid Ming: Four were reprints of Song and Yuan dynasty gazetteers—three of the Nanjing area and one of Chang'an 長安—three were gazetteers from Guangxi; and the others were from Guangdong, Sichuan, Jiangxi, Shaanxi, and Shandong.[131] As we saw above, *Gujin shuke* omits many titles, and the Tingzhou gazetteer is not on the list, either because the chancellor did not print it at the Directorate, it was lost, or he did not keep the blocks at the Directorate. Not all gazetteers that were sent long distances for printing went to the capitals. A Ming gazetteer of Yicheng 翼城, Shanxi, was printed approximately 800 kilometers away in Lintao, Shaanxi, but almost the entire distance could have been covered by boat.[132]

When woodblocks for gazetteers were cut outside of the subject locale, they were probably shipped back, with or without imprints, because the primary market for local gazetteers was in the subject locale and the local administrators who sponsored the project would have wanted the blocks. Cynthia Brokaw's interviews with descendants of Sibao publishers revealed that shipping blocks from Guangxi and Guangdong to Fujian was not a problem in the late nineteenth and early twentieth centuries. In fact, publishers contracted block cutting to poor women in Shunde 順德, Guangdong, and shipped the blocks back to Sibao. Because gazetteers were official projects, magistrates could use the postal system, which helps explain why magistrates would have been willing to have their gazetteers printed in distant locales.

Like cutters from other areas, Nanjing cutters worked on gazetteer projects far from home. For the 1608 gazetteer of Huanggang, Nanjing cutter Zhang Guifang 張桂芳 joined eight cutters from Jiangxia, the urban county of the Huguang provincial capital, 70 kilometers west of Huanggang, and other cutters of unknown origin.[133] Huanggang was 500 kilometers southwest of Nanjing. The 1531 gazetteer of Ningguo County 寧國縣, Nanzhili, was cut by Duan Hui 段輝, of

131. *Gujin shuke*, in Gao Nuo, *Baichuan shuzhi*, 321; Miao, *Mingdai chuban shi*, 29.

132. Zhou Hongzu, *Gujin shuke*, 382. Yicheng is 250 kilometers south-southwest of the Shanxi provincial capital, Taiyuan.

133. *Huanggang xian zhi*, 8.7a, 8.40a, 8.41a, 8.42a, 8.45a, 8.50a, 8.51a, 8.54a, 9.3a, 9.10a, 9.64a.

Shangyuan, the urban county of Nanjing, approximately 200 kilometers by water.[134]

Jiangnan craftsmen from outside of Nanjing also cut gazetteers from around the region, as well as those of distant places. A 1501 preface found in the 1550 gazetteer of Wukang 武康, Zhejiang, was cut by a craftsman from Yuyao 餘姚, Zhejiang. Wukang was in Huzhou Prefecture, while Yuyao was in Shaoxing Prefecture. The total distance of approximately 150 kilometers could be covered mostly by boat. Two Yuyao cutters worked with a Suzhou cutter and others on the 1587 gazetteer of Shaoxing, Yuyao's superior unit. The 1597 gazetteer of Gushi, Henan, was cut by craftsmen from Wumen 吳門 (Suzhou),[135] about 800 kilometers from Gushi by boat along the Huai River and Grand Canal, and the 1545 gazetteer of Xiayi 夏邑, Henan, was cut by a craftsman from Huai'an 淮安, Nanzhili, 300 kilometers southeast of Xiayi.[136]

Unlike the case of the *Min Shu*, the Fujian provincial gazetteer studied by Hou Zhenping, in which all cutters were from Fujian, Jiangnan cutters sometimes worked on a gazetteer with cutters from other regions. The 1578 gazetteer of Jinhua, Zhejiang, records names of thirty-three craftsmen who cut its blocks. Some were from Huizhou and some from Fujian: Huang Zhongwen 黃仲文 was from "Xindu 新都" (an old name for Huizhou), as was Huang Ruqing 黃汝清.[137] Three others were from Fujian: Yu Jinxiu 余錦秀, Zhu Zhen 朱珍, and Liu Hongzai 劉弘宰.[138] Jinhua was about 150 kilometers from Huizhou, and 300 kilometers from Jianyang, the closest major Fujian publishing center. Based on naming patterns, cutters Huang Zhongmeng 黃仲孟 and Huang Zhongwu 黃仲武 likely came with Huang Zhongwen, and some of the four other Huangs may also have been relatives. How the Huizhou and Fujian cutters came to Jinhua is not recorded, but their presence highlights the mobility of craft labor in Ming China. It is unlikely that the Jinhua prefect would have recruited labor in two

134. *Ningguo xian zhi*, postface, 10.9b.

135. *Gushi xian zhi* (1659), 15.

136. *Xiayi xian zhi*, preface, 3a.

137. For more on Huizhou cutters, see Bussotti, *Gravures de Hui*; Zhang Xiumin, *Zhongguo yinshua shi*; and Bao Guoqiang, "Ming ke Huizhou," 299–301.

138. *Jinhua fu zhi*, SKCM reprint: table of contents, 2a–3b, 2.4, 3.1; ZSX reprint: 13, 17.

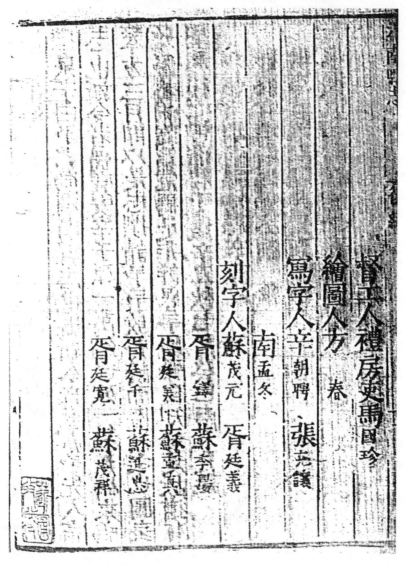

FIGURE 4.8. Names of block cutters, copyists, illustrator, and production supervisor for the 1541 gazetteer of Weinan, Shaanxi (Harvard-Yenching Library).

separate locales, so the more likely explanation is that at least some of them were already in the region for other jobs, or that some were recruited through family or craftsmen networks. Some evidence suggests that family networks of print craftsmen could persist for decades. Pairings of surnames on multiple projects could be such an indicator. For example, the 1541 gazetteer of Weinan 渭南, Shaanxi, were all surnamed Su 蘇 or Xu 胥, and four cutters named Su and nine named Xu worked together on the 1581 *Ji qian jia zhu Du gongbu shi ji* 集千家註杜 工部詩集 (One thousand schools' collected commentaries on Du Fu's collected poetry) (fig. 4.8).[139] Su and Xu are relatively rare surnames, and one would not expect to see them working together often by chance, so this may indicate a network connection. Such networks could be mapped from collections of craftsmen names from multiple book genres.

JIANYANG BLOCK CUTTERS

Jianyang, Fujian, had a large commercial publishing industry from the Song through Ming and Jianyang craftsmen cut at least two Fujian gazetteers outside the Jianyang region. Lucille Chia, in her study of Jianyang publishers, argued that there were probably a few hundred block cutters in the area at any given time in the mid-sixteenth century, piecework was probably the norm, and cutters traveled throughout the country.[140] The 1548 gazetteer of Zhangping 漳平 was cut by the "Jianyang cutters Zou Wu 鄒五, et al."[141] Zhangping was approximately 300 kilometers from Jianyang, most of which could be covered by boat. The Hongzhi-era (1488–1506) gazetteer of Xinghua, Nanzhili, was cut by Zhang Hao 張好 and Liu Chengqing 劉成慶 of Jianyang, approximately 400 kilometers from Xinghua.[142]

139.   *Weinan xian zhi*, postface; Li Guoqing, *Mingdai kangong*, 59, 157, 402.

140.   Chia, *Printing for Profit*, 38–39.

141.   *Zhangping xian zhi*, 1168.

142.   Miao, *Mingdai chuban shi*, 87; Zhang Xiumin, *Zhongguo yinshua shi*, 387; Li Ruiliang, *Zhongguo chuban biannian shi*, 439–40.

HANDAN BLOCK CUTTERS

Two late-Ming gazetteers, the 1637 gazetteer of Tangyin, Henan, and the 1642 gazetteer of Yuanshi 元氏, Beizhili, were cut by craftsmen from Handan 邯鄲, Beizhili (map 4.2, table 4.3).[143] Handan was close to the Henan-Beizhili border, about 70 kilometers north of Tangyin, and 130 kilometers south of Yuanshi. Although there was a water route from Handan to Tangyin, overland travel was the only option for traveling from Handan to Yuanshi. The cutter of the Tangyin gazetteer, Pei Sanyue 裴三岳, was probably related to some or all of the cutters of the Yuanshi gazetteer, who were surnamed Pei and Jia 賈, and possibly related to the Beijing Peis who cut the 1591 gazetteer of Lucheng, discussed above.

Not all gazetteers from the Handan area were cut by Handan cutters. The 1567 gazetteer for Zhaozhou 趙州, Beizhili, was cut by "Luo Nangong" 羅南宮, which suggests that he was either on staff at the Ministry of Rites in Beijing, or from Nangong County.[144] Zhaozhou was about 130 kilometers north of Handan, 275 kilometers south of Beijing, and 70 kilometers northwest of Nangong.

The above cases show that some cutters' business zones ranged hundreds of kilometers from their homes. In all cases in which gazetteer blocks were cut by craftsmen who lived more than 150 kilometers from the subject administrative unit, the craftsmen's hometowns were close to water routes that could take them to the gazetteer cutting site or bring the manuscript to them. This data reveals the tremendous mobility and range of craftsmen and manuscripts in Ming China. The fact that multiple gazetteers were cut by Fengxin and Jinxian natives raises the possibility that certain cutters or locales might have specialized in, or at least regularly cut, gazetteers. In Huizhou and Shaoxing, there were "genealogy craftsmen" who specialized in cutting and printing genealogies.[145] Of course, there were fewer gazetteers printed than genealogies, and it seems unlikely that many cutters could be supported solely through cutting gazetteers. Gazetteers were, however, large projects that employed

---

143. *Tangyin xian zhi*, 52; *Yuanshi xian zhi*, 160.
144. *Zhaozhou zhi* (1567), 10.5b.
145. Miao, *Mingdai chuban shi*, 98; Xu Xiaoman, "Preserving the Bonds of Kin."

Table 4.3
Handan block cutters who worked on gazetteers

Date and title	Place of publication	Block cutter origin	Block cutter name(s)
1637 *Tangyin xian zhi*	Tangyin, Henan	Handan, Beizhili	Pei Sanyue 裴三岳
1642 *Yuanshi xian zhi*	Yuanshi, Beizhili	Handan, Beizhili	Jia Jinxiao 賈進孝
			Jia Shouzong 賈守宗
			Pei Gaoge 裴高閣
			Pei Gaolou 裴高樓
			Pei Wensui 裴文燧

multiple cutters over a period of several months. It may have been the case that certain craftsmen or publishing houses became popular among magistrates who were producing gazetteers and that gazetteers became a significant part of their businesses.

Conclusion

In this chapter I have argued that printing of gazetteers was normative, even in the Song Dynasty, and even in isolated regions. Compilers believed that print was superior to manuscript because it increased circulation and survival. Print was particularly useful for gazetteers because imprints could be made quickly on demand for officials and others passing through a locale. Block cutting was usually done on-site in the local yamen or school, using hired craftsmen, local or not, but manuscripts were sometimes sent out for printing.

Second, I have argued that because gazetteers are connected to known locales and we often have information on their production process, studying them creates a more detailed and dynamic picture of Ming publishing than has heretofore been possible. Although from Zhou Hongzu's *Gujin shuke* we know that many local governments published books, it gives us a distorted image of the geography of Ming publishing. His catalog is heavily weighted toward Jiangnan and Jianyang publishers, probably because he compiled the catalog while working in Nanjing. Examining local gazetteers from places Zhou covered reveals that there were far more titles published outside of major Jiang-nan and Fujian publishing centers than Zhou recorded. In fact, Beijing and Jiangxi were rich in print craftsmen, and craftsmen lived in many areas that we think of as being peripheral. This finding is important be-cause it affects our understanding of the spatial dimensions of the late imperial economy. It reveals that people who lived in areas far from ma-jor cultural centers were still able to publish books and other texts and participate in the dominant literary culture, and that print craftsmen business zones could be interregional in scope.

CHAPTER 5

Financing Gazetteers

How much books cost to produce in imperial China and how those costs were paid are important questions in book history and social history. Understanding the financial aspects of publishing is critical to determining affordability and mapping readership, which are in turn important to understanding the significance of books in Chinese society and culture. Unfortunately, financial data is rare, and what little exists is difficult to interpret. These problems have led scholars to opposite conclusions. In early work based on limited price data, Wilt Idema and Chun Shum (Shen Jin) suggested that books were too expensive for most people to afford.[1] More recently, Kai-wing Chow, Joseph McDermott, and Cynthia Brokaw have argued that by the late Ming books were affordable to a broader reading public, which Chow characterizes as including not only officials and merchants but also a wide range of skilled workers.[2] Chow stresses that production costs dropped in the late sixteenth century due to near-universal adoption of the "craftsman script" typeface and cheap bamboo paper, and that because of book market segmentation a person of moderate means could afford a variety of inexpensively printed books. Although Chow's economic analysis is the most substantial to date for the Ming, his conclusions are based on a small

1. Idema, *Chinese Vernacular Fiction*, lviii–lix; Idema, "Review," 322; Shen, "Mingdai fangke tushu," 101–18; Chia, *Printing for Profit*, 190–92.
2. Chow, *Publishing, Culture, and Power*, chap. 1, 302; McDermott, *A Social History*, 25–31; Brokaw, *Commerce in Culture*, 552.

number of sources. To put such arguments on a firmer foundation, more data is needed. This chapter will add to the store of data and examine the significance of this new information to the ongoing debate. The data is both qualitative and quantitative, and relates to both the editing and the physical production of local gazetteers.

Using financial information found in local gazetteers to understand the publication of other types of books does require caution. After all, local gazetteers were noncommercial books, at least in the sense that making a profit from sales was not the primary motivation for publishing them.[3] Economic calculations for a county magistrate who had government funds, willing or unwilling donors, space in the yamen for compilation and printing offices, volunteer scholarly labor, and clerks who could write out the text and supervise block cutting, were different from those for commercial publishers. Nevertheless, much of the information presented herein can inform our understanding of the broader publishing world of commercial, family, and religious publishers. Publishers of local gazetteers, like other publishers, bought source materials and production supplies, paid editorial personnel and craftsmen, fed workers, gave gifts to those who assisted in the compilation or wrote prefaces, and incurred incidental expenses such as transportation and storage. Some expenses, such as those for hiring and feeding block cutters, were monetized and generally unavoidable; others, such as salaries for editorial personnel, could often be limited or avoided altogether by recruiting volunteer labor.

Although the local gazetteer appeared as an important genre in the Southern Song, most of the financial data I have found comes from the Ming, because only a few surviving Song and Yuan gazetteers contain any financial information. As we saw in chapter 4, some information can be gleaned from Song and Yuan prefaces reprinted in later editions and authors' collected works, which survive in substantial number. Thus, although a limited study of the financing of Song and Yuan gazetteers is possible, the Ming sources are far richer.

This chapter is divided into two parts, beginning with a discussion of methods for financing the expenses incurred in producing a local

---

3. For discussion of the noncommercial nature of local gazetteers, see Heijdra, "Town Gazetteers and Local Society," 1–53.

gazetteer. The second part presents quantitative information on costs and compares it to similar information found in other sources.

Categories of Expenses and Financing Methods

There is no single local gazetteer from the time period of this study for which the documentation fully describes the expenses involved. Instead it is necessary to sift through the voluminous but fragmentary record, sampling broadly and deeply across time and space, to create a composite picture. In this section I will use qualitative sources to describe the various labor and material inputs, before turning to quantitative sources in the next section. Qualitative description is required because numerical records are limited to figures for woodblocks, paper, craftsmen's wages, and board costs. Other expenses were also incurred and also need to be discussed.

To understand the economics of local gazetteers, we need to know who paid for them, not just how much they cost to produce and purchase. Superior government officers often ordered subordinates to compile local gazetteers, but they rarely funded them. Almost all first editions were published by local governments with funds raised in a variety of ways. Most commonly local administrators and compilers donated money, but government funds were also used, especially money from fines, litigation fees, and programs designed to cover magistrates' office expenses. In some cases one or more local individuals donated, and in others money was raised through the *lijia* 里甲 (administrative community) and most likely lineage organizations, which often overlapped with *lijia* units.

Compilation or updating a local gazetteer was widely recognized as one of a local official's duties, but there was little agreement on how to pay for production costs. This issue can be seen in the 1536 reprinting of the 1530 gazetteer of Qizhou, Huguang. After the original blocks were cut, the magistrate stored them in the compiler's home, but within a few years someone took away seventeen blocks. The new magistrate had the missing blocks recut from an original imprint, paying for it out of his salary, even though, in the words of a postface author, "those who discuss it say, 'this certainly cannot be viewed as being outside the scope of his official duties.'"[4]

Local officials were concerned enough about financing that they sought permission before spending government money on gazetteers. Assistant Magistrate Lü Jingmeng wrote in his postface to the 1536 gazetteer of Yingzhou 潁州, Nanzhili:

> Getting the production money was troublesome. I submitted a request to the military defense circuit for the craftsmen's wages only and spent twenty-one taels of this subprefecture's unrestricted government silver, but the craftsmen required twice as much for their daily food and drink. Thus I took some extra money from my own salary and made arrangements for a very small amount of other money; I did not ask the administrative community units for it.[5]

Military defense circuits were multiple-prefecture jurisdictions for military affairs. Benjamin Elman has argued that there was a link between military needs and local gazetteer production, which may explain the defense circuit's willingness to support the project, if only in part.[6]

In some cases an official simply declared that the local gazetteer was a government project and used unspecified funds.[7] Superiors also could allow local officials to use whatever funds they had that were not otherwise spoken for. The grand coordinator of Huguang Province let the prefect of Changde 常德 use "unrestricted government funds" 無碍官錢 to compile and publish the 1538 gazetteer. The grand coordinator simply required an expense report and list of compilers.[8] The magistrate of

---

4. *Qizhou zhi*, 9.72a.

5. *Yingzhou zhi*, 1110.

6. Elman, "Geographical Research," 1–18.

7. *Sanyang tuzhi*, reconstructed in Wang and Liu, *Yongle dadian fangzhi jiyi*, 2699–2755.

8. *Changde fu zhi*, 20.18a–19b. The administrative order regarding the local history's financing is dated 1534. In another case, the Beizhili grand coordinator allowed a magistrate to use "unencumbered silver" to publish the local gazetteer. *Huairou xian zhi*, compilation order, 3a.

Shangyuan, Nanzhili, collected "leftover funds" 遺貲 from local officials to print the 1593 gazetteer.[9]

More commonly, however, when the government paid, funds came from named sources. Publication of the 1552 gazetteer of Xingning 興寧, Guangdong, was financed by "equalization silver" (*jun ping yin* 均平銀). The Xingning magistrate requested and received permission to spend the money, writing, "It is on the record that there is an internal account balance of 10.8987 taels and a bit from the equalization silver for the nineteenth year of the Jiajing era (1540) and other years."[10] "Equalization" was a program designed to simplify tax payments, cover the magistrate's office expenses, and replace some of the *lijia* requisitions.[11]

Categories of expenses covered by equalization silver are listed in the 1547 gazetteer of Zhangping, Fujian, and included paper, brushes, ink, and seal mud, as well as wages, food, and drink for copyists and craftsmen. The *Zhangping xian zhi* records that the amount of equalization silver collected from the *lijia* in the year of publication was 349 taels of silver, of which 149.5 taels had not yet been allocated.[12] Such an amount would have been more than enough to pay publication costs. In the absence of equalization silver or a similar program, the *lijia* was often directly responsible for covering these types of expenses.[13] This, plus the fact that some magistrates proudly recorded that they did not bother the *lijia* or "the commoners" 民 to finance the local gazetteer, suggests that others did.[14]

One clear case in which *lijia* units were assessed for publishing a local gazetteer is the 1618 reprinting of the 1579 *Xinchang xian zhi*. Because the old woodblocks had burned, Xinchang magistrate Zheng Dongbi 鄭東壁 decided to have new blocks cut from an extant imprint. He calculated the number of characters, divided the cost equally among Xinchang's thirty

9. *Shangyuan xian zhi*, first postface, 2a.

10. *Xingning xian zhi*, prefatory matter, 3b–4a.

11. Heijdra, *Socio-Economic Development* (1994), 175–77, and "Socio-Economic Development" (1998); Huang, *Taxation and Governmental Finance*, 86–87.

12. *Zhangping xian zhi*, 5.7a–b.

13. Littrup, *Subbureaucratic Government in China*, 55–56.

14. *Tongling xian zhi*, 1b; *Yingzhou zhi*, 1110; *Yanshi xian zhi*, postface.

administrative communities, and called in craftsmen. The cost to each *li* was "two and some *qian*" 錢, or a total of 6 and some silver taels.[15]

In addition to direct assessment, administrators could also tap *lijia* funds that had already been collected. The magistrate of Fengrun 豐潤, Beizhili, received permission to spend up to 42.856 taels of "assignable reserve silver" 派剩銀 for cutting and printing the 1570 gazetteer. Assignable reserve silver was money set aside by the *lijia* to meet unexpected taxes.[16]

Money collected by magistrates in local court cases was a major source of funding. Publication of the 1530 *Qizhou zhi*, discussed earlier in this chapter, was paid for with "the document, board, and other fees from the criminal Zhang Quan 張全 et al."[17] The magistrate of Chaoyang, Guangdong, described his financing plan for the 1572 gazetteer as follows: "I plan to use confiscated ill-gotten gains and fines collected in cases under my sole jurisdiction 自理詞訟贓罰 for the expenses: monetary gifts of encouragement to local scholars, labor of Confucian students and copyists, and the various supplies, craftsmen, etc."[18] By "cases under my sole jurisdiction" the magistrate meant minor cases that were not normally subject to appellate review. Although he determined punishments in the underlying cases, he still needed permission to spend money derived from them.[19]

Magistrate Su Minwang 蘇民望 financed the 1594 gazetteer of Yong'an 永安, Fujian, with 90 strings of cash paid into the county treasury for the redemption of crimes.[20] Su transferred the money to the assistant magistrate and clerk for use in the project. Similarly, the 1544 gazetteer of Guangxin 廣信, Jiangxi, was financed with fines paid to redeem crimes and "confiscated illicit profits and similar monies."[21]

Money collected from tax cheats was used to pay for the 1597 gazetteer of Fu'an 福安, Fujian. Magistrate Lu Yizai's 陸以載 petition

---

15. *Xinchang xian zhi* (1579, 1618), prefatory matter; *Xin zhi xu xiaoyin,* 2a.

16. *Fengrun xian zhi,* 519; Hoshi, *Chūgoku shakai keizaishi goi,* 1, 335.

17. *Qizhou zhi,* 70.

18. *Chaoyang xian zhi, xiu zhi yi wen,* 1b.

19. The 1563 *Tongling xian zhi* also was financed with funds recovered in cases under the magistrate's sole jurisdiction. *Tongling xian zhi, gong yi,* 1b.

20. *Yong'an xian zhi,* 6.

21. *Yongfeng xian zhi,* prefatory matter, 1a–4b. Another local gazetteer funded with fines was the 1639 *Dangshan xian zhi. Dangshan xian zhi,* 385.

explains that a 1581 flood swept away the 1559 edition's blocks and all but a few imprints. He described his plan to finance the recompilation: "Production materials can be supplied from excess document paper. Other expenses can be paid from [funds collected from those who] cheated on their cultivated field, garden, or other taxes; we will not bother the commoners with an additional burden."[22]

Rents newly assessed against home owners who had encroached on the neighboring Confucian school grounds covered a portion of the expenses for the 1600 gazetteer of Gutian 古田, Fujian. When county magistrate Liu Riyi 劉日暘 was recompiling the gazetteer, he discovered the encroachment. About a century earlier a local person had been given a piece of land cut from the school archery grounds in exchange for land needed for a new town wall. Subsequent owners of the parcel built numerous small homes on the adjacent school property. Instead of having them demolished, the magistrate ordered compensation, some to be paid as rent to the school and some to be paid to the yamen to support the local gazetteer project.[23] Before finding this source of funds, the magistrate wrote that he did not dare take the money from the treasury or assess the people, so his only choice was to donate from his salary, and use money from redemption of crimes and excess stored grain.[24]

The 1544 gazetteer of Yongfeng 永奉, Jiangxi, provides evidence of two types of funding: money collected in the magistrate's court and contributions by officials. Yongfeng was subordinate to Guangxin, which was compiling a prefectural gazetteer. The Yongfeng magistrate gathered materials and submitted them to the prefecture. The Jiangxi grand coordinator ordered the Guangxin prefect to use fines paid to redeem crimes for the compilation and publishing costs. As with the *Fu'an xian zhi*, the local people were not to be bothered with a levy, in order to "further demonstrate the government's sympathy for the people." The grand coordinator's order came down via the assistant surveillance commissioner, who broadened the financing language to include not only fines, but also confiscated illicit profits and similar monies 人犯贓贖等銀 held by

22. *Fu'an xian zhi*, 7a–b.
23. *Gutian xian zhi*, 8.6b.
24. Ibid., 14.2b.

the prefecture and the subordinate county governments.[25] After submitting materials for the prefectural gazetteer, the county magistrate turned them into a manuscript for a county gazetteer, and he, along with the vice magistrate, Confucian school instructor, and assistant instructor, paid for its publication out of their own salaries. Apparently all of the county's money from fines had already been spent on the prefectural gazetteer.[26]

These examples of local officials using money from named sources outside of general revenues shows that local funds were not fungible. Most local administrators did not use general revenues or special levies to finance local gazetteers. Instead they sought funds collected from wrongdoers. This practice was not confined to local yamens; the Southern Imperial Academy had a system in which fines received from officials and students were used to repair and supplement woodblocks used to print a variety of texts.[27]

The most commonly mentioned financing method was donation from salary by one or more officials currently serving in the locale that was the subject of the gazetteer. An example is the 1300 gazetteer of Nanfeng, Jiangxi, which was compiled by order of Prefect Li Yi 李彝. When it was finished, Li wrote, "I donated from my salary to bring in craftsmen to cut the blocks. My colleagues were of like mind and happily contributed."[28] The additional donors were Vice Prefect Alaowading 阿老瓦丁 ('Alā-al-Dīn), Assistant Prefect Chang Tai 常泰, and Chief of Police Wang Yi 王沂. The *darughachi* (overseer) Boyanchaer 伯顏察兒 "guided" the project but was not mentioned as a donor. Even though it is clear in this case that an official put up his own money, it is unknown whether he could recover any of it through sales of imprints or other means.[29] When Wenzhou Circuit, Jiangzhe, ordered compilation of the 1307 gazetteer of Pingyang, it contributed nothing. Instead Pingyang

25.   *Yongfeng xian zhi*, prefatory matter, 1a–4b.

26.   Ibid., 4a–b.

27.   Miao, *Mingdai chuban shi*, 51, citing Ye Dehui, "Ming nanjian fakuan xiu ban zhi miu," in *Shulin qinghua*.

28.   Zhang Guogan, *Zhongguo gu fangzhi kao*, 561–62.

29.   Additional examples include: 1469 *Gushi xian zhi*, 1469 preface reprinted in *Gushi xian zhi* (1542), 10.39a–b (folio 39 follows folio 43 in the reprint); 1552 *Jingxian zhi*, preface; 1555 *Gongxian zhi*, 950; 1577 *Xingxian zhi*, postface; 1637 *Wucheng xian zhi*, 225; 1591 *Putai zhi*, postface.

assistant magistrate Pi Yuan 皮元 provided the editor, Zhang Zhe, a salary, an office, and writing supplies. After the manuscript was done, newly arrived magistrate Xie Zhensun 謝振孫 raised funds for block cutting by donating from his own salary as an example for others to follow.[30]

Although there are numerous examples of financing by a single magistrate or prefect, the cost of producing a local gazetteer could be more than a magistrate or prefect's annual salary, and many sought donations from their colleagues.[31] According to the 1587 *Da Ming hui dian*, a county magistrate's annual salary was only 27.49 taels and a prefect's annual salary was 62.05 taels, but sixteenth-century county gazetteer production costs ranged from 10 to 90 taels, and one large work published in 1640 cost more than 298 taels.[32] However, few officials lived on their salaries alone, and clearly many local officials could afford either to pay for the local gazetteer or to front the money and be reimbursed from sales, donations, or levies. Some officials may have even profited from publishing local gazetteers. An administrative order contained in the 1530 *Qizhou zhi* warns local officials that they must not use the local gazetteer project to extort money from the local people, so perhaps such extortion was not unknown.[33]

Lack of financial capacity to publish a gazetteer was a bigger problem for lower-ranked compilers. In the fall of 1368, the year of the Ming founding, Chi Liangxin 赤良心 was transferred from Fujian to serve in the Wuzhou, Guangxi, registry office. The day after he arrived, Chi asked the Confucian school students if the area had a recent gazetteer. He learned that there had once been a printed edition, but the blocks had been burned by "Yao bandits" 猺寇. He inquired of surviving elders and obtained pieces they had copied, though at first he was not able to publish his reconstructed gazetteer. However, two new officials soon arrived in Wuzhou and asked Chi about the prefecture's maps, books,

---

30. Zhang Guogan, *Zhongguo gu fangzhi kao*, 409.

31. See, for example, the 1404 *Yingchuan jun zhi*, postface; 1456 *Jingzhou fu zhi*, preface reprinted in 1532 edition; 1484 *Xuanping xian zhi*, preface reprinted in 1546 edition, 4.34; 1499 *Suzhou zhi*, postface; 1525 *Chaling zhou zhi*, 1085; 1544 *Yongfeng xian zhi*, prefatory matter, 4a–b; 1560 *Pingliang fu zhi*, 121; and 1577 *Yingtian fu zhi*, preface, 5.

32. Huang, "The Ming Fiscal Administration," 152; Li and Shen, *Da Ming huidian*, 39.1a–7b.

33. *Qizhou zhi*, 9.69a.

records, and customs. Chi told them about his gazetteer, at which point one of them, Assistant Prefect Fan Wenli 范文禮, offered to give up his salary to have it printed.[34]

In many cases in which a magistrate donated, he did not cover the entire production cost. His donations simply led off a fundraising campaign that spread the cost among local officials and gentry, or covered limited expenses, such as those for recutting a few blocks, or unbudgeted expenses. For example, an assistant prefect paid out of his salary those expenses that exceeded the government funds allocated for publishing the 1556 gazetteer of Huizhou 惠州, Guangdong.[35] Excess costs were probably incurred because approved expenditures were based on estimates submitted to higher officials before cutting began and did not always reflect actual costs.

Because gazetteers were commonly finished in the later years of an administrator's term or after he left, printing was sometimes financed by successive administrations. The 1201 gazetteer of Huzhou was financed by two prefects. The first, Li Langzhong 李郎中, "entrusted money for cutting the wood to Gui'an 歸安 County magistrate Zhou" (Gui'an was a subordinate county whose yamen was located in the prefectural town). Shortly thereafter Prefect Li was recalled and the new prefect, Fu Sizheng 富寺正, "donated additional funds to complete it."[36] This suggests that funds could be disbursed as the project progressed rather than paid up front in a lump sum.

In times of local budgetary distress, official donations were the most likely funding method. Such distress could come from rebellions, natural disasters, or persistent poverty.[37] When Shangyuan magistrate Bai Siqi 白思齊 wanted to print the gazetteer for the Zhengde Emperor, the county had no money for printing because, he claimed, public funds had been exhausted by the suppression of the Prince of Ning's rebellion. So Bai asked each of his colleagues to donate.[38] In Jiangning, Nanjing's other urban county, Magistrate Wang Gao paid to publish the gazetteer, saying,

---

34. *Cangwu jun zhi*, in Wang Duanlai and Liu Xian, *Yongle dadian fangzhi jiyi*, 2971–72.

35. *Huizhou fu zhi* (1556), postface, 1b.

36. *Wuxing zhi*, 4679.

37. *Xiong sheng*, preface.

38. *Shangyuan xian zhi*, 12.63a–64b.

"Even if my wife and children were hungry and cold I would have no regrets."[39] In the early 1200s the magistrate of Haiyan Garrison 海鹽鎮 ordered Chang Tang 常棠, a local, to compile the gazetteer of Ganshui (modern Zhejiang). When the magistrate's term was up, the book was still rough and seven or eight administrations passed before Chang finally had it right. A new magistrate, Sun Ribian 孫日邊, arrived, and after his administration was in order he "donated from his own salary to hire workers to cut and print" the gazetteer 爰割己俸售募鐫行. Sun's act was praised by Haining Naval Station commander-general Yuan 袁, who noted that the magistrate was able to print this book even though the local tax coffers were depleted. Yuan then donated wood and materials, and the printing was done in 1230 in a garrison office building.[40] Yuan's comment about "tax coffers" suggests that it was not uncommon to use government funds to print gazetteers. Such donations were a relatively painless way for magistrates to do a documented good deed that would reflect well on their administration.

Superior administrative units also could obtain contributions from subordinate units. The 1503 gazetteer of Fuzhou 撫州 Prefecture, Jiangxi, was published with money and woodblocks provided by magistrates of Fuzhou's subordinate counties.[41] The reverse, however, does not seem to be true. There is no known evidence of superior units paying to print subordinate units' local gazetteers.

When officials were not willing to donate their own money or use government funds for printing, compilers and members of local society paid. Yang Qian 楊潛, the magistrate of Huating, wrote that when the local "erudite gentlemen" completed the manuscript for the 1193 gazetteer, the county government's funds were exhausted and could not support its publication. Thus, "worthy county gentry" paid.[42] By using the term "exhausted" the magistrate implies that printing with government funds would have been possible at other times. The 1355 edition was also financed by locals.[43]

39. *Jiangning xian zhi*, preface, 1; postface, 5.
40. Zhang Guogan, *Zhongguo gu fangzhi kao*, 342; *Ganshui zhi*, 4659.
41. *Fuzhou fu zhi*, 3.
42. *Yunjian zhi*, Yang Qian preface.
43. Zhang Guogan, *Zhongguo gu fangzhi kao*, 260, citing the 1630 *Songjiang fu zhi*.

Donating money to print a gazetteer was considered to be a meritorious act that deserved recognition. Zhuji County literatus Luo Xiangxian 駱象賢 compiled and published the 1453 gazetteer of Zhuji, Zhejiang, "without bothering others for production costs." Upon publication, "everyone" visited Luo bringing meat and wine, but he declined the gifts. In 1456 Luo's generosity was recorded in a postface to a poetry collection assembled by his son, Luo Danian 駱大年.[44]

The compiler of the 1441 gazetteer of Shangyu, Zhejiang, expanded and published a manuscript drafted in the Yongle era (1401–24) by a local commoner, Yuan Hua 袁鏵, and polished by his elder brother Yuan Xuan 袁鉉, a teacher of children. The compiler, Guo Nan, a retired assistant prefect, obtained the manuscript, collated it, added an account of the Ming soldiers' entrance into the county at the fall of the Yuan, and then paid for the cutting and printing with his own money.[45]

When a group of scholars jointly compiled a local gazetteer, they all might donate for its publication. The 1457 gazetteer of Huizhou, Guangdong, was first drafted by Deng Lian 鄧璉, the Confucian school instructor, in response to the 1454 imperial edict to recompile local gazetteers. After sending the completed manuscript to the court, Deng and several local scholars decided to expand and print it. When the additions were finished, they all donated money for publication.[46] A compiler's family members might also contribute.[47]

Compiler Yu Jishan 余繼善 (1580 *jinshi*) paid to cut the 1597 gazetteer of Gushi, Henan, during a time of crisis. Yu's addendum to his 1597 preface explains why he did not ask the magistrate to pay: "The gazetteer is complete, ordered, and error free. I want to give it to Suzhou block cutters and have calculated the workers' costs to be about sixty taels of silver. Because over the last year the locale has been repeatedly invaded and its material resources declared 'diminished,' I dared not bother the government [purse] and so donated half of a year's income to complete the gazetteer."[48] Not all local donors were compilers. A single local man,

44. Bai Gui, "Shu zhuzhai xiansheng shi ji" 書竹齋先生詩集, in Wang Mian, *Zhuzhai ji*, postface.

45. *Shangyu xian zhi jiao xu*, 3810–11; *Shangyu xian zhi* (1891), 186–87.

46. *Huizhou fu zhi* (1542), 5.

47. The Wanli-era gazetteer of Xincai, Henan, was published by the compiler's three sons. *Xincai xian zhi*, 1.1a–b.

48. *Gushi xian zhi* (1659), 15.

Zou Xian 鄒賢 (1431–98), paid the entire cost of cutting the thirty-six-*juan* 1496 gazetteer of Wuxi, Nanzhili. The preface described Zou as a "local learned man," but he had no degree.[49] In fact, Zou was a wealthy grain merchant and art collector.[50] Xu Zhidao 徐志道, an elderly local commoner, paid to publish the 1515 gazetteer of Dantu 丹徒, Nanzhili.[51] Several prominent individuals paid a portion of the publishing costs for the 1542 edition of the *Gushi xian zhi.*[52] Its compilation was initiated by order of the Henan grand coordinator to Runing 汝寧 Prefecture, Gushi's superior administrative unit, which ordered its subordinate counties and subprefectures to deliver copies of published local gazetteers and "sages and worthies' writings of ancient times or today."[53] Those like Gushi that had no published local gazetteer were to immediately submit a compilation plan to the education circuit intendant's office, and when the work was complete, send a printed copy to the prefectural yamen. Though Gushi County lacked a published gazetteer, nine years earlier its magistrate had hired prefectural Confucian school student Ge Chen 葛臣 (*juren* 1528) to compile one. Before the manuscript was finished, the magistrate left office and as a result the gazetteer was not published. When Magistrate Zhang Ti 張梯 took office, he sought out the local gazetteer, learned that Ge Chen still resided in the county and had his original work. Magistrate Zhang wanted to finish the project, and "prepared book money to hire Master Ge, a fine man, to help do it."[54] In 1541 the work was completed and the Confucian school submitted an expense report to the education intendant, stating:

We invited with due propriety the county's students and officials [to participate]. We began [compiling the local gazetteer] on the first day of the third month, and finished on the fifteenth day of the fourth month. When done, we had it cut. The fine copy was written out by Document Clerk Xu Bing 徐昺 and four others. The host official 引禮官 Yang Sui

---

49. *Wuxi xian zhi* (1574), old preface, 5a.

50. Cheng Mingzheng, *Huangdun wenji*, 207–8; Liu Rihua, *Liuyanzhai biji*, vol. 3, 4.31a–b; Wang Shu, *Wang Duanyi zou yi*, 5.40a–45b.

51. *Dantu xian zhi*, 4.19b.

52. The Tianyige's copy of the *Gushi xian zhi* was printed sometime after 1552 when fifty new blocks were cut to replace missing blocks. *Gushi xian zhi* (1542), *mulu*.2b.

53. Ibid., prefatory matter, 8a–b.

54. Ibid., postface.

楊璲 and others voluntarily took care of the craftsmen's food and expenses. Only the workers' wages 工價 and cost of wood for blocks are included in this calculation, which is for thirty-four taels of silver.[55]

A postface gives more information on the local gazetteer's financing:

> How is it that in the past the Gushi gazetteer was neglected yet today it comes together? The group of gentlemen gathering was the confluence of people. Completing the project in two months was the confluence of time. The appearance one after another of those who donated money out of devotion to duty was the confluence of financing. When the three confluences combined, the gazetteer was completed. The esteemed participants' names are recorded in the prefaces, but we cannot leave out the names of the humble toilers. The host official Yang Sui took care of feeding the craftsmen. National University student Yi Cunxu 易存緒 and host officials Yi Xi 易諿 and Peng Weiyan 彭危言 fed the copyists.[56]

Additional money was sometimes needed to replace blocks. A decade after the Gushi gazetteer was published, a new magistrate, Shi Huai 師槐, found that fifty blocks were missing and paid to recut them from an existing imprint. Shi's blocks are identifiable by their inscription, "Mt. Huang Academy" 黃山書院, which refers to his native place, Huangshan Village, Dong'e 東阿 County, Shandong, whereas Zhang Ti's original blocks are inscribed "Nanjiong's Rustic Hall" 南坰草堂, following his style name.[57]

Another technique for dividing expenses was for a donor to pay for printing a designated number of blocks, or specific blocks. The 1505 gazetteer of Jiangle 將樂, Fujian, was paid for by two "righteous commoners" 義民 and the county administrators. The two commoners, Weng Jing 翁璟 and Yu Sheng 余盛, each paid for the cutting of twenty blocks, and Magistrate He Shilin 何士麟 and other officials paid for the rest.[58]

55. Ibid., prefatory matter, 8a–b.
56. Ibid., Cai Jin postface.
57. Ibid., 5.5a; table of contents, 2b. In some cases the recut blocks contain new entries, such as updated lists of county officials.
58. *Jiangle xian zhi*, 9. The gazetteer contains no other information on the two commoners, although Yu Sheng had the same surname as two local *juren*, Yu Lian and Yu Tai.

In at least one case, that of the 1621 gazetteer of Ganzhou, Jiangxi, discussed in chapter 4, a print shop covered printing costs. After the fine copy was written out in Nanchang, it was returned to the Ganzhou printer, who gave it to his block cutters and covered the cost. Mr. Zhu of the revenue office 司儲 provided food for all of the assembled artisans, and the work was finished in four months.[59]

It was also possible to fund a local gazetteer with small donations from many donors. Typically the administrator would make the first contribution, to encourage other contributions. For publication of the 1488 gazetteer of Wujiang 吳江, Nanzhili, the magistrate, three vice magistrates, the assistant magistrate, and the clerk "each donated from his salary as an encouragement, and local supporters were all happy to help out."[60] Forty-nine people contributed to the publication of the 1641 gazetteer of Yongnian 永年, Beizhili. Of them, forty-eight were officials, from families on the official register, or students, while only one was described as a "commoner" 布衣.[61] Fifty-four people contributed to the 1585 gazetteer of Changshan 常山, Zhejiang.[62] For publication of the 1348 gazetteer of Shangyu, Zhejiang, the magistrate collected donations from a broad range of people. He noted, "All of the county functionaries, scholars, commoners, Buddhists, and Daoists contributed and I ordered artisans to finely cut it to perpetuate its transmission."[63] As mentioned in chapter 2, seventy-four local donors, plus the Shaoxing prefect and Xinchang County magistrate, financed the 1477 *Xinchang xian zhi* (fig. 5.1).[64]

The relative sizes of donations are visible in a donations list from the 1640 gazetteer of Jiangyin, Nanzhili. Three officials and eleven local gentry donated a total of 298 taels. The amounts of the donations from another five people on the list had been blackened out, perhaps for nonpayment. The officials gave 112 taels, and the local gentry gave 186 taels. Two hundred taels, about two-thirds of the total, were given by just two people, the magistrate and a local. From these records we can see that

59. *Ganzhou fu zhi* (1621), preface.
60. *Wujiang zhi*, 3.
61. *Yongnian xian zhi*, 27–32.
62. *Changshan xian zhi*, 15.40a–b.
63. *Shangyu xian zhi jiao xu*, 3808.
64. *Xinchang xian zhi* (1477), preface.

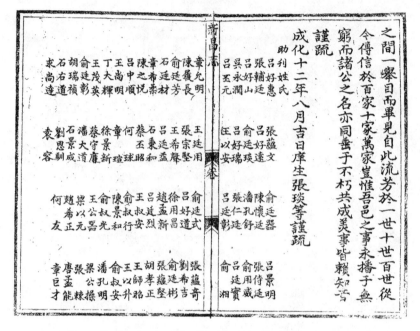

FIGURE 5.1. Donor list for the 1477 *Xinchang xian zhi* (Xinchang County Archives).

local gazetteer projects, like many local infrastructure projects in late imperial China, were financed jointly by administrators and locals.

Numerical Data on Production Costs

Having surveyed various costs for which we have no hard figures, I will now turn to those for which we do. Table 5.1 summarizes numerical information on local gazetteer production costs. To supplement the table I provide details from an analysis of the data and comparison to information on xylographic printing costs presented by Kai-wing Chow in his 2004 book, *Publishing, Culture, and Power in Early Modern China,* and Martin Heijdra in his 2004 article, "Technology, Culture, and Economics: Movable Type versus Woodblock Printing in East Asia."[65]

65.   Heijdra's figures come from an anonymous article, "Estimate of the Proportionate Expense."

Publishing costs for woodblock-printed books can be divided into onetime expenses and recurring expenses. The main one-time expenses were for acquiring or compiling a text, buying woodblocks, and paying copyists and block cutters' wages and board. The main recurring expenses were for buying paper and ink, and also paying printers and binders' wages and board. To date, scholars have a limited understanding of these costs, separately and in total, across space and time. Reconstructing costs and comparing them to incomes and the costs of other goods and services will give us a better understanding of the business of publishing and the affordability of books.

Chow brought together some of the limited available information and estimated that late-Ming block-cutting costs were between 0.10 to 0.15 taels per folio page.[66] His figure was based on numbers found in two books. The first was a 1554 edition of *Yuzhang Luo xiansheng wenji* 豫章羅 先生文集 (Collected works of Mr. Luo of Yuzhang), by Luo Congyan 羅從 彥 (1072–1135), printed in Shaxian 沙縣, Fujian. It required eighty-three blocks for 161 folio pages, and cost 24 taels for "high-quality cutting" 繡梓.[67] That comes to about 0.15 taels per folio page. The second source for Chow was *Linzi quanji* 林子全集 (Complete works of Master Lin) by Lin Zhaoen 林兆恩 (1517–98). According to the text, its blocks were cut in Nanjing in 1629–31 and cost 300 taels for "over 1,500 blocks," and "nearly 3,000 folio pages," or about 0.1 taels per folio page with double-sided cutting.[68] The text is actually a little under 2,500 folio pages, and thus, assuming that the 300 taels was not a rough figure as well, would have cost about 0.12 taels per folio page. These two figures, although important, are separated by seventy-five years of time, come from different regions, and do not break down the costs of wages, board, and woodblocks.

Table 5.1 provides more detail on specific costs and is a step toward filling in gaps in the larger picture of publishing costs. In evaluating

66. Chow, *Publishing, Culture, and Power*, 37.

67. Ye Dehui, *Shulin qinghua*, 186. Ye's account differs from that in Du Xinfu's *Mingdai banke zonglu*, which records eighty-three blocks and 141 folio pages. Using this figure would give a per-page figure of 0.17 taels. Du records that each half-folio consisted of thirteen columns with space for 23 characters, or a total of 598 characters per folio page. *Mingdai banke zonglu*, 7.9a.

68. Chow, *Publishing, Culture, and Power*, 37, citing Lin Zhaoen, *Linzi quanji*, 1240–41.

Table 5.1
Local gazetteer production costs

Date, title, and province	Total listed cost	Items included in the total cost	# of blocks	Cut on 1 side or 2	Folio pages in text
1510 *Guiji zhi* Zhejiang	110 taels	"wages, board, etc."	515	2	1,030
1530 *Qizhou zhi* Huguang	38.56 taels	"wood for blocks, craftsmen's wages and board, printing paper, etc."	214	1	214
1536 *Yingzhou zhi* Nanzhili	63 taels	wages, "daily needs," drink, food	?	?	302
1542 *Gushi xian zhi* Henan	34 taels	"only the craftsmen's wages, wood for blocks"	?	?	207
1552 *Xingning xian zhi* Guangdong	10 taels	pear woodblocks, "cutters' wages, food, printing paper"	55	2	110
1570 *Fengrun xian zhi* Beizhili	Up to 42.85 taels	"paper, wages, food"	?	?	206
1588 *Nanchang fu zhi* Jiangxi	150 "and some" taels	compilation costs and supplies, including paper	722	528 on 2, 194 on 1	1,251
1594 *Yong'an xian zhi* Fujian	nearly 90 strings of cash	project costs	?	?	206
1597 *Gushi xian zhi* Henan	about 60 taels	Suzhou block cutters' costs	?	?	?
1640 *Jiangyin xian zhi* Nanzhili	298 taels	donations for unspecified costs	?	?	903
1642 *Wu xian zhi* Nanzhili	370 "and some"	compilation, illustrations, calligraphy, block cutting	2200 "and some"	1	2200 "and some"

NOTE: The less-than symbol (<) in the column "Per-page block-cutting cost" indicates titles that included paper or unnamed costs among the listed costs. For the 1542 *Gushi xian zhi*, the greater-than symbol (>) indicates titles for which the craftsmen's board was donated, thereby reducing the total cost.

Cost per wood block	# of block cutters	Work days	Wage costs	Board costs	Per-page block-cutting cost
?	15	1600	?	?	<0.107 taels
?	?	?	?	?	<0.180 taels
?	?	?	21 taels	42 taels for "daily needs, drink, food"	0.209 taels
?	?	?	?	copyists and cutters' "food and necessities" were donated	>0.164 taels
1 *fen* (0.1 taels)	?	?	?	?	<0.091 taels
?	?	?	?	?	<0.208 taels
?	?	?	?	?	<0.12 taels
?	?	?	?	?	<0.437 taels
?	?	?	?	?	?
?	?	?	?	?	<0.330 taels
?	?	?	?	?	<0.162 taels

these figures, however, we must keep in mind that four of the eleven figures explicitly included paper costs, and others may have, but none revealed how many copies were printed or the cost of the paper. This introduces a potentially large margin of error, because the larger the run, the higher the paper cost. The biggest print run for most local gazetteers would have been the first run, when imprints were made for people and offices connected to the project and interested locals.

The only known print run for a pre-Qing local gazetteer is the one hundred copies made by Wang Zhen for his 1298 movable wooden-type gazetteer of Jingde.[69] Because movable type is disassembled and reused, this figure likely approximates the number of copies Wang expected to give away or sell, if not immediately, then within a reasonable time. If the text had been printed from cut blocks, the initial run could have been smaller, because more copies could have been printed quickly in case of greater-than-expected demand. Although this figure suggests a ceiling for initial print runs in counties similar to Jingde in 1298, over the course of the Ming the potential audience grew due to the expanding educated population and the genre's deeper penetration into local society. The number of local gazetteers being produced began increasing in the Southern Song, though compilation of local gazetteers down to the circuit level only became mandatory in 1296 under the Yuan. In the Ming, periodic edicts beginning in 1376 required compilation all the way down to the county level. This stimulated publication and increased interest.[70]

Some evidence, however, suggests that the margin of error introduced by the unspecified paper costs was not large enough to render the figures in table 5.1 unusable. Most important are sources implying that people with no connection to a local gazetteer project paid for their own copies. If that was the case, then the cost of such copies would not have been included in the figures taken from prepublication petitions, the sources for most figures in table 5.1. After an initial print run, cut blocks were stored and local gazetteers were printed on demand, a topic addressed in detail in chapter 6. The magistrate would not have paid for such copies. A record in the 1536 *Yingzhou zhi* notes that the cut blocks

69.   Zhang Xiumin, *Zhongguo yinshua shi*, 550; Wang Zhen, *Nong shu*, 538.
70.   Brook, "Native Identity," 241; Bol, "The Rise of Local History."

were put in the Confucian school library and that "when worthy scholar gentry who travel through here or who live here want copies, the paper's [cost] should be calculated and craftsmen ordered to print it."[71]

Assuming that unaffiliated individuals paid for their own copies, that still leaves an unknown number of imprints made for compilers, donors, government offices, officials, schools, and preface authors. Most county gazetteers list no more than a dozen editorial personnel, but that number could be several dozen for provincial gazetteers. In addition, some local gazetteers list dozens of donors. If each contributor and donor received one free copy in the initial run, then these copies, plus those sent to government offices, the local Confucian school, and preface authors, probably added up to between twenty and one hundred free copies in most cases. A few people, such as the magistrate, main author, and major donors, may have received additional free copies. To reflect this ambiguity, I have used a less-than symbol (<) in the "per-page block-cutting cost" column of table 5.1 for those titles that included paper or unnamed costs among the listed costs. For the 1542 *Gushi xian zhi*, I have used a greater-than symbol (>) because the craftsmen's board was donated, thereby reducing the total cost.

If we assume various numbers of imprints included in the figures, then rough estimates of paper costs can be made by using paper prices and sheet sizes found in other sources. There was a great range in paper prices in the mid and late Ming, but common bamboo printing paper was relatively cheap, and as Lucille Chia has observed, many late imperial local gazetteers were printed on bamboo paper rather than on more expensive papers such as mulberry or cotton.[72] Kai-wing Chow's summary of known paper prices lists the kind of bamboo paper used by commercial publishers in the 1640s as costing 0.026 taels of silver per one hundred sheets.[73] Chow's figure comes from Ye Mengzhu 葉夢珠 (b. 1623), who, writing in the 1690s, recalled that in his youth in Shanghai bamboo paper was sold in seventy-five-sheet reams 刀 at a price not exceeding 0.02 taels.[74] Ye did not record the size of the sheets.

71. *Yingzhou xian zhi* (1536), 1110.
72. Chia, *Printing for Profit*, 328, note 9.
73. Chow, *Publishing, Culture, and Power*, 35.
74. Ye Mengzhu, *Yueshi bian*, 182.

There is, however, other evidence of common dimensions. The 1587 edition of the *Da Ming huidian* notes that 1.2 million sheets of civil service examination paper 榜紙 were requisitioned decennially and that the required dimensions were 4.4 *chi* 尺 by 4 *chi* (150 cm by 136 cm).[75] A 1580 memorial written by Minister of Works Zeng Shengwu 曾省吾 (b. 1532, retired 1582), lists sheet sizes for three types of paper the ministry requisitioned: large white civil service paper 大白榜紙 was 4.65 *chi* by 4.5 *chi* (158 cm by 153 cm), white, large/medium pressed paper 白大中夾紙 was 3.9 *chi* by 3.8 *chi* (133 cm by 129 cm), and white, large, Kaihua paper 白大開化紙 was 5.05 *chi* by 4.45 *chi* (172 cm by 151 cm).[76]

Cynthia Brokaw found that publishers of woodblock-printed books in Sibao, Fujian, in the early twentieth century bought sheets of paper the size of door leaves by the *dao*, a one-hundred-sheet ream. The paper was cut one *dao* at a time into eight, twelve, eighteen, or twenty-four sections based on the size needed for a particular imprint. The twenty-four-cut paper produced a half-folio page roughly 16 centimeters high by 11 centimeters wide.[77] Adding margins of 14 percent to the width and 19 percent to the height would mean a full-folio measuring 19 cm by 25 cm. Twenty-four such pages could be cut from a sheet 150 cm by 76 cm. Illustrations in the 1637 *Tian gong kai wu* 天工開物 (Devices for the exploitation of nature) show papermakers drying sheets that look to be approximately this size, and using frames that appear slightly shorter, but wider.[78]

If we assume that publishers of local gazetteers in the Ming used similar-sized sheets of paper, then we can use actual page sizes and book lengths to calculate the approximate number of sheets needed for each imprint. The average measurements of fifty-nine local gazetteers from 1510 to 1642, listed in table 5.2, were 25.2 cm by 33.2 cm, including the blank spaces for the margins. The printed area averaged 21.1 cm high by 29.2 centimeters wide. Thirty such folio pages could be cut from a sheet of paper 172 cm by 151 cm, twenty-four from a sheet 158 cm by 153 cm,

75.   Li and Shen, *Da Ming huidian*, 2645. One *chi* was about 34 cm. Luo Zhufeng, *Hanyu da cidian*, index volume, 6.

76.   *Jiangxi sheng da zhi*, 13–22.

77.   Brokaw, *Commerce in Culture*, 121–22.

78.   Song, Sun, and Sun, *Technology in the Seventeenth Century*, 226, 228, 229.

Table 5.2
Size of printed area per half-folio page (centimeters)

Date	Title	Province	Height	Width
1500	*Huangzhou fu zhi*	Huguang	22.0	14.5
1501	*Ningxia xin zhi*	Shaanxi	21.0	15.6
1513	*Kuizhou fu zhi*	Sichuan	21.5	14.6
1514	*Yuanzhou fu zhi*	Jiangxi	21.5	14.8
1515	*Guanghua xian zhi*	Huguang	20.8	14.3
1517	*Jianchang fu zhi*	Jiangxi	22.3	14.5
1521	*Huating xian zhi*	Nanzhili	20.0	12.7
1524	*Dongxiang xian zhi*	Jiangxi	19.8	13.9
1525	*Yanping fu zhi*	Fujian	20.8	14.5
1526	*Pujiang zhi lüe*	Zhejiang	19.2	14.8
1528	*Hui da ji*	Guangdong	20.0	13.5
1529	*Qizhou zhi*	Huguang	20.8	15.0
1530	*Hui'an xian zhi*	Fujian	18.0	14.7
1530	*Tongzhou zhi*	Nanzhili	22.1	13.7
1530	*Youxi xian zhi*	Fujian	18.8	14.0
1531	*Mianyang zhi*	Huguang	19.0	13.3
1535	*Changde fu zhi*	Huguang	21.3	14.5
1536	*Ganzhou fu zhi*	Jiangxi	20.3	15.7
1536	*Haimen xian zhi*	Nanzhili	20.3	14.4
1536	*Shixing xian zhi*	Guangdong	20.6	14.1
1537	*Hengzhou fu zhi*	Huguang	23.0	15.5
1537	*Neihuang xian zhi*	Beizhili	21.0	15.8
1537	*Sinan fu zhi*	Guizhou	20.9	14.1
1539	*Qinzhou zhi*	Guangdong	20.9	14.6
1540	*Yingshan xian zhi*	Huguang	20.8	14.8
1541	*Jianning fu zhi*	Fujian	19.8	14.0
1541	*Yunyang xian zhi*	Sichuan	20.7	13.6
1542	*Nanxiong fu zhi*	Guangdong	19.2	14.5
1543	*Ruijin xian zhi*	Jiangxi	22.0	15.8
1543	*Shaowu fu zhi*	Fujian	22.0	14.2
1546	*Hanyang fu zhi*	Huguang	18.3	13.8
1547	*Qishui xian zhi*	Huguang	22.6	15.2
1548	*Laiwu xian zhi*	Shandong	22.5	14.4
1549	*Pu'an zhou zhi*	Guizhou	20.5	14.5
1549	*Wucheng xian zhi*	Shandong	21.5	16.0
1550	*Guangping fu zhi*	Beizhili	25.0	18.0
1550	*Xundian fu zhi*	Yunnan	21.0	14.8
1551	*Badong xian zhi*	Huguang	19.7	13.8
1551	*Quwo xian zhi*	Shanxi	21.5	14.1

(*continued*)

Table 5.2
(continued)

Date	Title	Province	Height	Width
1552	*Anxi xian zhi*	Fujian	18.5	13.5
1552	*Linqu xian zhi*	Shandong	21.9	13.9
1552	*Xingning xian zhi*	Guangdong	19.5	16.0
1553	*Jianyang xian zhi*	Fujian	21.0	13.7
1553	*Luhe xian zhi*	Nanzhili	21.6	14.1
1554	*Yancheng xian zhi*	Henan	21.1	15.5
1555	*Mahu fu zhi*	Sichuan	28.8	17.5
1557	*Anji zhou zhi*	Zhejiang	19.7	13.8
1562	*Gaochun xian zhi*	Nanzhili	20.5	14.5
1567	*Yizhen xian zhi*	Nanzhili	20.5	14.2
1570	*Ruichang xian zhi*	Jiangxi	20.6	14.5
1572	*Haizhou zhi*	Nanzhili	20.0	14.0
1572	*Linjiang fu zhi*	Jiangxi	22.3	15.5
1573	*Cili xian zhi*	Huguang	22.4	15.0
1575	*Luzhou fu zhi*	Nanzhili	27.1	15.0
1576	*Chenzhou zhi*	Huguang	20.5	14.0
1579	*Xinchang xian zhi*	Zhejiang	19.2	14.4
1588	*Nanchang fu zhi*	Jiangxi	22.8	13.4
1621	*Chengdu fu zhi*	Sichuan	24.3	15.0
1640	*Jiangyin xian zhi*	Nanzhili	22.0	14.2
	n = 59	Average	21.1	14.6
	~Paper size/folio page, with margins		25.2	33.2

twenty from a sheet 133 cm by 129 cm, and twelve from a sheet 150 cm by 76 cm.

The average length of ten local gazetteers in table 5.1 is 663 folio pages, thus one copy would require 22.1 sheets of paper 172 cm by 151 cm, 27.6 sheets 158 cm by 153 cm, 33.2 sheets 133 cm by 129 cm, or 55.25 sheets 150 cm by 76 cm. If the paper, like that of Ye Mengzhu's youth, cost 0.02 taels per 75 sheets, it would mean a per-copy paper cost of 0.006 taels, 0.0074 taels, 0.0089 taels, or 0.015 taels. The paper for one hundred copies would have cost 0.6 taels, 0.74 taels, 0.89 taels, or 1.5 taels. The average production cost of the ten titles used to calculate average length was 120 taels, and thus, cheap paper for one hundred copies would have been less than 1.25 percent of the total cost.

If more expensive paper were used, or if Ye Mengzhu's figure refers to a smaller-sized paper, these figures would have to be adjusted accordingly. For example, according to Shen Bang's 沈榜 1593 *Wan shu za ji* 宛署雜記 (Miscellaneous records of the Wanping yamen), when the Ministry of Rites published a new edition of the *Da Ming hui dian* (1587), it used 11,600 sheets of a high-quality printing paper (連七紙),[79] at a cost of 9.28 taels, or 0.08 taels per 100 sheets, about triple the cost of Ye Mengzhu's paper.[80] We can assume that the paper for the *Da Ming hui dian* came in large sheets because Shen's entry on the expenses of the *Taipusi* (Court of the Imperial Stud) includes *lianqi zhi* at the same price, but specifies that it was "large" (*da*).[81] From Zeng Shengwu's 1580 memorial, we know that sheet dimensions described as "large" were either 158 cm by 153 cm, or 172 cm by 151 cm, while the one described as "large/medium" was 133 cm by 129 cm. If we use the smaller "large" sheet, the 158 cm by 153 cm sheet, then at 0.08 taels per 100 sheets the average-sized local gazetteer would require 27.6 sheets at a cost of 0.022 taels per copy, or 2.2 taels for 100 copies. This is less than 2 percent of the average total production cost of 120 taels.

The above calculations were done for the titles as a group, but they can also be done for individual titles. For example, the 1530 *Qizhou zhi* is 214 folio pages long, each folio page is 24.7 cm high by 34.2 cm wide (including margins), and the gazetteer lists costs of 38.56 taels for "wood for blocks, craftsmen's wages and board, printing paper, etc." If we assume a 158 cm by 153 cm sheet-size costing 0.08 taels per 100 sheets, then printing one copy would require 8.9 sheets at a cost of 0.0071 taels. Paper for one hundred copies would be 0.71 taels, or 1.8 percent of the total cost. In sum, if in fact the figures in table 5.1 include paper for not more than one hundred copies, then the margin of error introduced by the unknown paper costs was likely under 10 percent. See table 5.3 for projected paper costs assuming various numbers of copies printed.

This analysis is not inconsistent with Martin Heijdra's analysis of xylographic printing costs in the nineteenth century. His figures are based on an 1834 article from the *Chinese Repository*, a missionary publication, which compares the costs of printing Chinese Bibles by various

79. *Kaopan yushi* describes *lianqi zhi* as thick, large, and high-quality. Tu, *Kaopan yushi*, 2.10a–b.
80. Shen Bang, *Wan shu za ji*, 145.
81. Ibid., 150.

Table 5.3

Paper costs of three local gazetteers, assuming the use of papers of four different sizes and per-sheet costs

Size A: 0.02 taels per 75 sheets, each sheet 150cm by 76cm
Size B: 0.08 taels per 100 sheets, each sheet 172cm by 151cm
Size C: 0.08 taels per 100 sheets, each sheet 150cm by 136cm
Size D: 0.08 taels per 100 sheets, each sheet 150cm by 76cm

Date, Title, (Province)	Total listed cost	Items included in the total cost	Folio pages	Folio-page size with margins (cm)	Paper sheet size	Folio pages per sheet	Sheets per copy	Paper cost for n copies (taels)			Paper as % of total cost for n copies		
								50	100	200	50	100	200
1530 Qizhou zhi Huguang	38.56 taels	"wood for blocks; craftsmen's wages; and board, printing, paper, etc."	214	24.7×34.2	A	12	17.8	0.24	0.48	0.95	0.6	1.2	2.5
					B	30	7.1	0.28	0.57	1.14	0.7	1.5	2.9
					C	24	8.9	00.36	0.71	1.42	0.9	1.8	3.7
					D	12	17.8	0.71	1.42	2.85	1.8	3.7	7.4
1552 Xingning xian zhi Guangdong	10 taels	pear woodblocks, "cutters' wages, food, printing paper"	110	23.2×36.5	A	12	9.2	0.12	0.25	0.49	1.2	2.5	4.9
					B	28	3.9	0.16	0.31	0.63	1.6	3.1	6.3
					C	20	5.5	0.22	0.44	0.88	2.2	4.4	8.8
					D	12	9.2	0.37	0.74	1.47	3.7	7.4	14.7
1588 Nanchang fu zhi Jiangxi	150 "and some" taels	total compilation costs and supplies, including paper	1,251	27.1×30.6	A	10	125.1	1.67	3.33	6.67	1.1	2.2	4.4
					B	35	50.0	2.00	4.00	8.01	1.3	2.7	5.3
					C	20	62.55	2.5	5.0	10.0	1.7	3.3	6.7
					D	10	125.1	5.01	10/02	20.03	3.3	6.7	13.3

methods, most likely in Batavia, Dutch East Indies. Heijdra lists paper as constituting 4.0 percent of the total cost of blocks, tools, transcription, cutting, printing, binding, and paper, assuming the printing of 100 copies of a 500-page book.[82] He goes on to calculate costs of these items assuming print runs of 2,000, 5,000, and 7,000 copies, and shows that as the number of copies increases, the percentage of the total cost made up by paper also increases. This occurs because block cutting is a one-time cost, unless the blocks wear out, whereas paper costs increase with every copy made. For a 5,000-copy edition, paper would be the largest single cost and would constitute 41.5 percent of the total.

Although paper costs loomed large in economic calculations for printing Chinese Bibles, they were less important in publishing local gazetteers because for magistrates the definition of success differed from that for missionaries. Missionaries wanted to print and distribute the maximum number of Bibles at the lowest unit cost; magistrates mainly wanted the blocks cut. In fact, the act of cutting the blocks was considered the essential indicator of completion. This is clear from prefaces, which routinely praise magistrates for getting the blocks cut but never praise them for distributing a large number of copies. Although magistrates did present copies to their superiors and a small number of other individuals, they were not funding large-scale printing and distribution. Cutting blocks for a local gazetteer was more akin to repairing a bridge or a school; it was a worthy infrastructure project for which the magistrate would be praised, even though much of the actual use would come later. Most local gazetteers were finished late in a magistrate's term of office, and he would move on to another post soon after publication, leaving behind a record of his successful administration. Paper costs for future government-paid copies, such as copies provided to visiting officials, would come out of a different magistrate's budget and not be part of the publishing magistrate's original calculations.

In addition to the potential error created by unknown paper costs, three of the figures in table 5.1 have a second problem: they may have included editorial costs, which as we have already seen were often monetized, at least in part. When the *Yong'an xian zhi* compilation began, the magistrate gave 90 strings of cash to the assistant magistrate and

82. Heijdra, "Technology, Culture, and Economics," 230.

clerk "to manage the project's expenses," but the text does not describe the expenses. The *Jiangyin xian zhi* lists the amounts of donations but not the expenses. The per-page costs of these two titles were substantially higher than the others. A third figure that may have included editorial costs is for the 1588 *Nanchang fu zhi*. One hundred and fifty "and some" taels were approved for the "local gazetteer compilation costs," but the costs were not itemized.[83]

A final difficulty in using these figures is that none record printing and binding costs separately. Some include wages and board for "crafts-men"; others list only "cutters." For example, the 1530 *Qizhou zhi* lists both "craftsmen's wages and food" and "printing paper" among the costs, sug-gesting that the total figure included printing and binding of the initial copies. The labor costs for the 1552 *Xingning xian zhi* are phrased more narrowly as, "cutter wages and food" 刻字工食. Nevertheless, the text also mentions printing paper, implying that printing costs were included. Heijdra lists printing and binding as being approximately the same as the cost of paper in a 100-copy print run, about 4 percent of the total.

Even though most of these figures contain ambiguities, the set as a whole is nonetheless useful in assessing book production costs between 1510 and 1642. Of the eleven figures, ten are for books of known length and cost. The per-page costs of cutting, without adjusting for editorial, paper, printing, and binding costs, ranged from 0.091 to 0.437 taels per page, and averaged 0.201 taels per page. Throwing out the three figures that may include editorial costs, the per-page cost ranged from 0.091 to 0.232 taels per page, and averaged 0.16 taels per page. If we assume that the cost of paper, printing, and binding one hundred copies was included in the figures given, and subtract 10 percent to reflect those costs, the average cutting cost would be about 0.14 taels per folio page.

The local gazetteers in table 5.1 reveal additional information that makes possible rough calculations of the relative proportions of wages, board, woodblocks, and paper. The 1536 *Yingzhou zhi* records that the craftsmen's daily necessities, food, and drink 工人日用飲食 were double the craftsmen's wages 工銀.[84] From the 1552 *Xingning xian zhi* we know that its pear woodblocks were 5.5 percent of the 10 taels it cost for blocks,

83. *Nanchang fu zhi*, 20.
84. *Yingzhou zhi*, 1110.

cutter wages, food, and printing paper. If paper was 4.4 percent (assuming 100 copies printed from 150 cm by 136 cm sheets costing 0.08 taels per hundred) and we split the remaining 90.1 percent along the lines of the *Yingzhou zhi*, then a rough breakdown of costs for the *Xingning xian zhi* would be: 60 percent craftsmen's food, drink, and daily necessities; 30 percent craftsmen's wages; 6 percent woodblocks; 4 percent paper.

Another way to determine relative proportions of total costs would be to use the 42-tael figure from the 1536 *Yingzhou zhi* to calculate a per-page cost for craftsmen's food, drink, and daily necessities, and apply that to the two titles closest in time, the 1530 *Qizhou zhi* and the 1542 *Gushi xian zhi*. The Yingzhou board cost was 42 taels divided by 302 pages, or 0.14 taels per page. Applying that to the *Qizhou zhi*, which was 214 pages, would mean that 29.76 taels out of 38.56 taels total, or 77 percent, went to the craftsmen's board. Assuming 10 percent for woodblocks and paper would mean that only 13 percent went to wages. Applying the 0.14 taels per-page board figure to the 207-page 1542 *Gushi xian zhi*, which lists costs of 34 taels for "only the craftsmen's wages, wood for blocks," would mean 29 taels out of 63 total (for blocks, wages, and board), or 46 percent, went to board.[85] If the blocks cost about 2 taels, 32 taels out of 63, or 51 percent, would have been for wages. These calculations suggest substantial variation in the ratio of wages to board costs, but do show that board costs made up a large part of the total.

The variability of costs also applies to woodblocks. The *Xingning xian zhi* price for pear woodblocks, 0.01 taels per block, is much lower than previously known late-Ming prices, which range from 0.03 to 0.4 taels per block. *Wan shu za ji* lists prices from 0.1 taels to 0.4 taels, figures that represent the expenses of various government offices in Beijing and the nearby Wanping in the 1580s.[86] Chow argues that those prices would have been for more expensive woods, such as jujube, and that because all of the prices came from a single text, the price differences reflected differences in block size and quality.[87] One other source is the Wanli-era (1572–1620) edition of *Fangce zang* 方冊藏 (Rectangular-folio Tripitaka), printed in Zhejiang, which records a price of 0.03 taels per block for pear

85. 1542 *Gushi xian zhi*, prefaces, 8a–b; postface.
86. Shen Bang, *Wan shu za ji*, 138–42.
87. Chow, *Publishing, Culture, and Power*, 34.

wood.[88] The *Xingning xian zhi* price of 0.01 taels is noteworthy because it is just one-third of the previously known lowest price, is three decades earlier than Shen Bang's prices, and comes from eastern Guangdong. The fact that the 1552 Xingning price was only one-fortieth of the high-end 1580s Beijing price shows that we still need to find many more prices from different times and regions to be confident that we understand Ming woodblock costs.

We also should not assume that magistrates publishing local gazetteers always tried to use the cheapest blocks. The blocks of the Zhengtong-era (1436–50) gazetteer of Xincheng 新城, Jiangxi, were made from red jujube 華棗, a high-quality wood.[89] Just as a magistrate who wanted a high-quality book could retain skilled editors, calligraphers, and block cutters, he could also use high-quality materials, both blocks and paper.

For magistrates who wished to reduce costs, cutting blocks on both sides was an option. The *Xingning xian zhi* reveals how much could be saved. If the blocks were cut on one side only, fifty-five additional blocks would have been needed at a cost of 0.55 taels. This would have meant a 5.5 percent increase in the total cost (listed as blocks, cutters' wages, board, and printing paper). Despite the higher cost of cutting on one side only, the publishers of the 1530 *Qizhou zhi* and 1642 *Wuxian zhi* chose this option. This probably was done to maintain quality. A block cut on both sides would have worn more quickly than a block cut on one side, because pressure would be applied twice for each imprint. According to Lucille Chia, pear woodblocks could be expected to print approximately 2,000 to 3,000 copies before needing repairs.[90] I have found nothing to suggest that initial print runs were anything near that size, so even if the blocks wore twice as fast as those cut on one side, hundreds of crisp prints could be had at lower cost during the tenure of the magistrate who sponsored the project. The repair or recutting of cheaply cut blocks would be a later magistrate's problem.

Another way to save money was to reuse surviving blocks from previous editions. When the gazetteer of Wuwei 無為, Nanzhili, was

88.   Zhang Xiumin, *Zhongguo yinshua shi*, 534.

89.   *Xincheng xian zhi*, 831.

90.   Chia, *Printing for Profit*, 31 n. 37. Chia's figure comes from modern woodblock printers. Tsien, *Paper and Printing*, 201, states that fifteen thousand imprints can be made before repairs are necessary, but he did not specify the type of wood.

recompiled and printed in 1528, about 50 to 60 percent of the blocks for the previous edition were already lost. The magistrate reused the surviving blocks without alteration to save money and honor the original compilers' effort.[91]

One of the local gazetteers listed in table 5.1, the 1510 *Guiji zhi*, sheds light on both the pace of cutting and block cutters' earnings for high-quality work. Fifteen block cutters worked over a period of seven and a half months, putting in 1,600 workdays 工. The text was 1,030 folio pages. Thus, on average, each folio page took 1.55 workdays to cut; in other words, one cutter could complete about two-thirds of a block per day.[92] The total of "labor, board, and other costs" was 110 taels of silver. If 30 percent was for the block cutters' wages, that cost would be thirty-three taels, and the daily wage would be 33 taels/1,600 workdays, or 0.02 taels. If 45 percent was for the block cutters' wages, the daily wage would have been 0.03 taels. The fifteen block cutters each worked an average of 106.7 days during the 225-day period. If the block cutters were all paid the same rate, each would have received about 2 to 3 taels for the project. This figure seems reasonable in light of the 6-tael annual salary of the staff printer in the Pu'an, Guizhou, provincial administration commission branch office as of 1565, discussed in chapter 4.

The wage rate could also be expressed in terms of amount paid per number of characters cut. Yang Shengxin estimates that block cutters could cut 100 to 150 characters per day and were paid 0.02 to 0.05 taels per 100 characters.[93] To convert the 0.02 taels per-day wage for the *Guiji zhi* to a piece rate requires a count of characters per page. Each folio page of the 1510 *Guiji zhi* has twenty columns with space for twenty large characters or forty small characters per column. Thus, a full page would have four hundred large characters, plus about seven to nine small characters along the page crease for the title, *juan*, and page number. Few pages, however, are full. Based on character counts of sample pages, approximately 70 percent of each page was filled, 90 percent by large characters and 10 percent by small, which would mean about 316 characters, large and small, per page. At 1.55 days per block, the block cutters cut the

91. *Wuwei zhou zhi.*
92. *Guiji zhi* (1510 imprint held in National Central Library, Taibei), postface.
93. Yang Shengxin, "Lidai kegong gongjia," 553–67.

equivalent of about 204 characters per day. Calculated as a piece rate, their wage was about 0.0135 taels per one hundred characters. That is one-third below the low end found by Yang.

The above data is predominantly from the sixteenth and early seventeenth centuries. Data on the costs of producing pre-1400 gazetteers is extremely limited. Joseph McDermott has argued that the cost of book publishing dropped substantially in the fifteenth and sixteenth centuries due to falling labor, paper, and binding costs.[94] Timothy Brook, in his important 1997 article on Yuan gazetteers, argued that producing a gazetteer was a "rather expensive project" in the Yuan because woodblock cutting was labor-intensive and the skill was not widely practiced. In Brook's view, xylographic printing became a cheap technology only "about the turn of the sixteenth century, with the rise of a relatively free labour market"[95] and after "the cost of engraving woodblocks had fallen dramatically, as illiterate laborers mastered the necessary skills."[96] To set a Yuan baseline for comparison, Brook relied on Ye Dehui's discussion of the most detailed description of pre-1400 gazetteer printing, a compilation order from the 1344 *Jinling xin zhi*.[97] In Brook's words, "The total cost for engraving and printing copies came to over 143 *ding* (one *ding* was nominally valued at ten ounces of silver), a considerable sum, which the circuit chose not to absorb."[98] Instead, the circuit placed the burden of printing on four schools within its jurisdiction: one subprefectural school was ordered to print five *juan*, and another subprefectural school, an academy, and the circuit school were each required to print three. Ye Dehui used the above figure to compare Yuan cutting costs to those of the late Ming, and found them to be seven times as expensive on a per-block basis.

Evidence suggests, however, that one should not overestimate the expense of publishing a gazetteer in Song and Yuan China. At first glance it does seem that printing the *Jinling xin zhi* was far more expensive than printing late-Ming gazetteers, but on closer inspection this

94. McDermott, *A Social History*, 25–31.

95. Brook, "Native Identity," 239–40.

96. Brook, "Censorship in Eighteenth-Century China," 181.

97. Brook, "Native Identity," 239 n. 11, citing Brook, "Censorship in Eighteenth-Century China," 181 n. 10, which cites Ye Dehui, *Shulin qing hua*, 7.7b, 14b.

98. Brook, "Native Identity," 239–40.

sum is less than it seems. The problem is that the cost was given in paper currency, the *zhongtong chao* 中統鈔, not silver. When originally issued in 1260, the currency was convertible to silver at the rate of 50 *liang* 兩 per *ding* 錠, but it was devalued in 1287 to 10 *liang* per *ding*. Thus, 143 *ding* of paper currency was nominally 1,430 *liang*, or more than 57 kilograms of silver.[99] The gazetteer has 1,164 folios, so at the nominal rate, the per folio cost would have been 1.23 *liang* of silver, or more than six times the average calculated above for the late Ming. However, by 1344 the actual value in silver of paper currency was much less than its nominal value. According to Richard Von Glahn, the *zhongtong chao* steadily depreciated after 1311 and it reached "catastrophic levels" by the late 1340s.[100]

How far the currency had fallen in 1344 Jinling and what 143 *ding* of paper meant to the schools is a difficult question to answer. The year 1344 brought major flooding and plague outbreaks to the north, and chaos was spreading, so it seems likely that inflation was high. The fact that the block cutting was divided between schools also does not necessarily mean that the printing was expensive. To cut 1,164 blocks at a single site would entail either a long, but modest, disruption by a small number of cutters, or a large disruption by many. Distributing the chapters to multiple schools may have been done for reasons of space and speed, not cost. Brook himself notes that almost all of the 173 Yuan dynasty gazetteers to which he has found a reference were produced in printed rather than manuscript form, suggesting that they were not overly expensive to print.[101]

Because the 1344 gazetteer appears to be an unreliable basis for comparing Yuan and late-Ming printing costs, we need other approaches. One possibility is to compare the number and type of donors and how they characterized their donations. If printing a gazetteer took many donors at one point in time but few in another, or if only high-ranking officials could pay in one period while low-ranking officials could pay in another, that would suggest either changes in cost or changes in donors' relative wealth. What is striking from the above cases of donations is

99. Von Glahn, *Fountain of Fortune*, 57, 63. *Hanyu da cidian*, index, 19, contains a list of historical weights based on excavations. In the Song, one *liang* was approximately 40 grams.

100. Von Glahn, *Fountain of Fortune*, 68.

101. Brook, "Native Identity," 239.

that in the thirteenth and fourteenth centuries, publishing a substantial book was not unduly burdensome for one or a small group of officials making donations from their salaries. Many of these local officials were not highly paid, yet none of the prefaces that discussed financing characterized the donations as large or the printing as expensive. In the late Ming, one or several officials or local gentry financed the printing of a gazetteer. From this perspective, there is remarkable continuity in the number and type of donors needed to print a gazetteer from the start of the thirteenth century until the end of the Ming.

Although officials did not consider printing a gazetteer to be overly expensive, one does get the impression that it was not something done with petty change. When Huating County funds were depleted, the magistrate was unwilling to use government money to print the 1193 gazetteer. Payment for the 1201 *Wuxing zhi* was spread over the terms of two prefects. A fundraising drive was needed to print the 1307 *Pingyang zhou zhi*, and a Wuzhou, Guangxi, registry office official was unable to self-publish his 1368 *Cangwu jun zhi*, although the assistant prefect was able to pay for it out of his salary.

A second issue related to the cost of gazetteers is the cost of printing a single copy. McDermott, citing Inoue, argues that paper was expensive in the Song but cheap by the mid Ming. Unfortunately there is only one known figure from before 1400, that for an imprint of the *Guiji zhi* 會稽志 (Guiji Gazetteer) made in 1202, six months after the book was completed. A note appended to *juan* 20 says: "Shaoxing Prefecture today prints one copy of the *Guiji zhi* in twenty *juan* using 800 sheets of book printing paper 印書紙, ten sheets of ancient sutra paper 古經紙, twenty sheets of insert paper 副葉紙, and ten backing sheets for the ancient sutra paper 背古經紙平表. The printing cost is 800 *wen* 文."[102]

How much was 800 *wen*? One way to get a rough idea is to compare that figure to other figures found in the *Guiji zhi*. For example, the summer tax on the 273,343 registered households of Shaoxing Prefecture's eight subordinate counties amounted to 53,582,668 *wen*. Thus, an average household's share would be about 196 *wen*. The cost of one copy of the gazetteer was thus equivalent to the summer tax on four households. The summer tax was only one of several taxes and not the largest. Shaoxing's

102.   *Guiji zhi* (HYM), postface; *Guiji zhi* (SYFZ), 7090.

juan 絹 silk tax was 99,809 bolts, or an average of 0.365 bolts per household. The price of *juan* silk in 1202 was about 4,000 *wen* per bolt, so the *juan* silk tax per household was equivalent to about 1,460 *wen*, or enough to print almost two copies of the gazetteer.[103] The labor tax came to 614 *wen* per household. This suggests not many common farm families could easily afford a copy, but someone on the next step up the economic ladder, such as a modestly successful landlord, merchant, or artisan, probably could. This conclusion is supported by references to officials getting copies of gazetteers from commoners.

Conclusion

This chapter has provided new information on the economics of book production, primarily in the Ming, and illustrated a method for further research. Data presented in this chapter makes possible cost estimates for craftsmen's wages, living expenses, and production materials. Data on funding shows that local gazetteers were financed locally by donations, levies, and government funds, most of which came from named sources, especially money collected in magistrates' courts. Although this project has uncovered substantial new information, it also reveals that we are still at an early stage of research on the economics of book publishing in imperial China. For example, the fact that pear woodblocks used to print a 1552 gazetteer in Guangdong cost only 0.01 taels per block suggests that woodblocks could be very cheap. But we also know that 0.01 taels was only one-fortieth the price of high-quality blocks used by the Beijing government in the 1580s. This suggests significant cost variation by time, place, and type of book. We need more data before we can confidently make broad conclusions about how to characterize publishing expenses. Ascertaining the affordability of books to readers is an even greater challenge because if we wish to make informed conclusions, we need not only price and wage data across time and space, but also ways to get at the disposable income of people in various occupations.

103. Guo Dongxu, "Song chao de wujia."

Nonetheless, and despite these challenges, this study shows that much can be learned about the economics of book publishing in imperial China by casting a wide net for scattered pieces of information contained in local gazetteers. Previous scholarship did not consider local gazetteers to be important sources for the study of the book industry. However, through careful analysis of the minutiae contained therein—by poring over the comments and complaints of the compilers and preface writers, by scrutinizing the work of craftsmen, by mapping out movements of compilers, materials, and manuscripts, by examining administrators' petitions concerning publication—a fascinating portrait emerges of how officials, scholars, and even common people worked to compile, finance, and publish local gazetteers. While a single local gazetteer may reveal little, in the accumulated data from numerous local gazetteers patterns begin to emerge. In terms of listed production costs, we have seen here that mid- to late-Ming local gazetteers ranged in cost from as little as 10 taels to over 370 taels, which on a per-page basis would be 0.091 to 0.437 taels. Although most of these figures contain ambiguities regarding the exact costs covered, especially the amount of paper included in the listed cost, we can get a rough idea of costs from this set of figures.

There is still much more to be found in local gazetteers. Material for this project was drawn from a review of only half of the approximately one thousand extant Ming local gazetteers. Compare that to the more than six thousand surviving Qing and Republican local gazetteers, and it is clear that useful information can still be gleaned from these sources, especially because later local gazetteers are even richer in economic information related to publishing. It is possible to construct a set of data stretching from the origin of the genre to the early twentieth century, and although it would be much thinner for the earlier period, it would nevertheless be an important contribution to both publishing history and economic history as a whole.

PART III

Reading and Using Gazetteers

CHAPTER 6

Target Audiences and Distribution

To understand the significance of local gazetteers, we must first understand who read them and the meanings readers derived and created from them. As we saw in chapter 5, some scholars of imperial China have argued that books were too expensive for most people to afford, while others have argued that by the late sixteenth century, books were affordable to a broader reading public that included skilled workers as well as officials and merchants. This question matters because it affects our conception of social stratification and social mobility in premodern China. If few people had access to books, literacy would have been limited and the knowledge transmitted through books would have been largely confined to a self-reproducing elite. If, on the other hand, a greater range of people had access to books, then a more literate and socially mobile Chinese society becomes plausible. A study of gazetteer readership and reading can contribute to this debate.

Evidence presented in this chapter and in chapter 7 will show that officials and literati were the main readers of local gazetteers, but references to readers include people of many backgrounds. This lends support to those who argue that by the late Ming there was an expanding reading public and that people besides officials and literati had access to books and read them. Up to this point we have seen numerous examples of officials, teachers, and students working on gazetteers, and these groups were also core gazetteers readers. But readership went further and included a wide range of readers who had various motivations and ways of reading: some used local gazetteers in genealogical research, while others gathered evidence in support of lawsuits, pondered issues of local policy, or read for pleasure about local scenic and historic sites and persons. Other readers included book collectors, travelers, and authors on various topics.

Gazetteer readership was both local and nonlocal. The term "local reader" could be construed in various ways: It could refer only to a person native to, and resident in, a gazetteer's subject locale, but could also include a native living elsewhere, and an out-of-town visitor reading a gazetteer on-site. In this section of the book I draw no precise distinction between "local" and "nonlocal." The point is that a variety of people read gazetteers both inside and outside of the subject locale, and some were natives and some were not. Explanations of gazetteer reading must take account of these various types of readers.

Statements of Target Audiences

Two initial steps in reconstructing gazetteer reception are creating a typology of people compilers expected would read their works, and documenting who had access to gazetteers. Target audiences and actual distribution can be partially reconstructed from gazetteer prefaces and administrative orders that mention target readers, statements that a particular title was sent to a certain person or institution, catalogs of books owned by institutions and individuals, and records of book acquisitions. These can be found in collected writings of officials, catalogs of private book collections, and local gazetteers themselves.

Throughout late imperial times elite males were the key target audience of most gazetteer compilers, but substantial evidence shows that some compilers imagined, or at least claimed they imagined, a broader audience. These compilers asserted that women as well as men, ordinary people as well as elites, could read their gazetteers. A preface to the 1550 gazetteer of Tianchang, Nanzhili, a county seat about 70 kilometers north of Nanjing, states:

> When worthy scholar gentry obtain the gazetteer, they will be forever able to observe and investigate the ordinary people; when the ordinary people

obtain it, they will be able to strictly encourage and admonish women; when daughters obtain it, they will be able to discuss virtue and duty. For later generations there will be a source for those who wish to follow our customs to know virtue, or open the maps and illustrations to investigate that which is hidden.[1]

The 1542 gazetteer of nearby Yangzhou, also describes females as part of the intended audience:

> This gazetteer is important in a greater way in that imperial historians can use it to compile the exalted canon. It is important in a lesser way in that scholars can use it to investigate profound knowledge, officeholders can use it to invigorate their feelings and cultivate their deportment as a governor, subject, and son, and women can use it to fully contemplate loyalty, fully contemplate filiality, and fully contemplate virtue.[2]

Both of these examples explicitly including women in the intended audience came from the Jiangnan region, which as Wilt Idema, Beata Grant, Grace Fong, and others have noted, was the major center of women's writing and education in the late Ming. Women there read a variety of literary genres, including poetry and biographies of exemplary women.[3] These two categories of writing are found in most late imperial gazetteers, long before the Ming and not only in Jiangnan. Some Song and Yuan dynasty gazetteers have "virtuous women" biographies as distinct sections, and most others contained them mixed in with other types of biography.[4] Along the northern frontier, the 1514 gazetteer of the Xuanfu Garrison includes an entire *juan* of poetry and a section on virtuous women, while the 1608 gazetteer of the Gansu 甘肅 Garrison, in the extreme west, has biographies of exemplary women. So if, as Idema and Grant argue, women were the main audience for biographies of exemplary women, it is likely that women were part of gazetteer compilers'

1. *Tianchang xian zhi*, prefaces, 3b.
2. *Weiyang zhi*, Cui Tong preface, 8a.
3. Idema and Grant, *The Red Brush*, 347–48; Fong and Widmer, eds., *The Inner Quarters*, 4; Fong, *Herself an Author*, 2.
4. *Wujun zhi*, 897; *Shan lu*, 7218; *Siming zhi* (1227), 5107; *Lin'an zhi*, 3974; *Jinling xin zhi*, 5878.

target audiences, either as readers or as listeners, much earlier than the sixteenth century and in more geographic regions than Jiangnan. It is also possible that some compilers did not expect women to read gazetteers but merely claimed a female audience as a way of covering for their strategic use of gazetteers to publicize their female relatives' virtues and lay the foundation for their imperial recognition.

Compilers used various terms to describe ordinary people as part of their intended audiences. In the Tianchang gazetteer preface cited above, the author used *lüyan* 閭閻 and *lixiang* 里巷 to describe potential readers who were distinct from, and lower in the social hierarchy than, "worthy scholar gentry" 賢士大夫, but who were cultured enough to promote female virtue. Both terms originated from words for village gates, villages, neighborhoods, streets, and alleys, but by the Ming, used together they meant "ordinary people" who were not part of the literati or official classes. In the preface to the 1456 gazetteer of Jingzhou 荊州, Huguang, the prefect wrote that he had the blocks cut in the prefectural yamen so that "ordinary people could obtain and thoroughly read it" 庶人得而徧觀 之.[5] The term *shuren*, like the terms *lüyan* and *lixiang*, is a broad term for the great mass of people outside of the literati and official classes.

In the above examples, the claimed intended audiences went beyond the emperor, officials, and male gentry. Of course, intended audiences are not necessarily the same as actual audiences, and we should not take claims of having ordinary readers too far. After all, the majority of the population was poor and illiterate. But records of possession and reading do document cases in which people who were neither scholars nor officials acquired gazetteers. Such evidence supports the idea of an expanding book readership. Gazetteer prefaces written after the main texts had already begun to circulate sometimes characterized initial readership. For example, a 1348 preface to the gazetteer of Shangyu, Zhejiang, stated that the county's "officials, functionaries, scholars, ordinary people, and Buddhist and Daoist monastics praised [the gazetteer] to each other."[6] The mention of clerical readers should not be surprising, because in late imperial China many monasteries compiled institutional gazetteers. "Functionaries" refers to unranked government office personnel, such as clerks.

5. *Jingzhou fu zhi*, 1456 preface.
6. *Shangyu xian zhi jiao xu*, 3808.

One of the best sources for identifying what types of people had gazetteers is compilers' statements about where they found earlier editions. Such notes provide examples of non-elite people who owned gazetteers. As discussed in chapter 3, gazetteer compilers looking for previous editions first checked the local yamens and Confucian schools, then asked locals with official status.[7] But if they were unsuccessful, they would ask "commoners" (*min* 民) and often found ones who had what they wanted. As a term of art, *min* is a household registration category that could also be translated as "general population." In the Ming, it was one of the three largest categories (commoner, military, and artisan) and covered the majority of people, including farmers, merchants, doctors, scholars who were not officials, and others.[8] In addition to the three main categories, there were registers for officials, saltern families, and various other occupations.

Standing alone, *min* tells us relatively little about social and economic status. In context, however, we can see that sometimes it refers to people who were not considered members of the elite. In a preface to the 1572 gazetteer of Linjiang, Jiangxi, the prefect wrote, "I happened to obtain the Hongwu-era (1368–98) gazetteer from among the commoners 偶得于民間, but it was missing more than half. Many great families 世家 have the Hongzhi era (1488–1506) edition."[9] Here, "commoners" is contrasted with "great families," a term used to denote lineages that had produced ranked officials over multiple generations. Similarly, the preface to the 1565 gazetteer of Taizhou, Zhejiang, noted that two earlier editions were extant but many of the woodblocks were damaged, and copies in gentry homes 搢紳家 were rarely complete. The author then "searched among the commoners and obtained high-quality imprints" 尋於民間得善本.[10] Here again, the contrast is between families that had produced officials and were part of a local elite, and those that had not and were of lower status.[11] There are many references to *min* having gaz-

---

7. For example, Lü Nan, the compiler of the 1527 gazetteer of Yangwu, Henan, got the old edition from a local *jinshi*, Wang Guang. *Yangwu xian zhi*, 827, 912, 926.

8. Wei, *Mingdai huangce*, 21.

9. *Linjiang fu zhi* (1572), preface.

10. *Chicheng xin zhi*, 202.

11. For more on debates about the status of the "gentry," see Martin Heijdra, "Socio-Economic Development" (1998), 552–54.

etteers that do not explain the term further: A postface to the 1516 gazetteer of Changyuan 長垣, Beizhili, noted that there was an older printed edition, and "among the commoners, some have copies," and a 1553 preface to the gazetteer of Jianyang, Fujian, stated that the 1544 edition was "still kept among the commoners."[12] In such cases the officials writing the prefaces implicitly contrasted *min* with elite families. In most cases such commoners were likely educated merchants or landlords who aspired to higher status for themselves or their families.

One case that strongly suggests that people of modest status could acquire gazetteers comes from Guangchang 廣昌, Jiangxi, in the hill country near the Fujian border. Mr. He Wenyuan 何文淵, the compiler of the 1440 edition, wrote that a local man named Lian Zhongmo 連仲默 (fl. late 1200s) had compiled a two-volume gazetteer early in the Yuan dynasty but it had been almost completely destroyed in war, presumably the overthrow of the Mongols in the 1360s. Mr. He's son asked for it all around the local area and got the first volume from the home of a farmer and the second volume from the home of a lacquer artisan named Liu Wenxing 劉文興. He put the volumes together to make a complete text.[13] Although the farmer or artisan, or their ancestors who first acquired the gazetteers, could have been members of the elite, it seems unlikely, especially because the Yuan and Ming had hereditary occupation regimes and Guangchang was relatively poor and isolated. Lian Zhongmo himself came from a humble background. He worked as a tailor and at the age of thirty was still uneducated. One day while he was making clothes in the home of a wealthy family, a Confucian student arrived. The master set out a splendid feast and wine in the reception hall, while Lian ate and drank meager fare in a side room. He sighed and said, "Trades and scholarship are separated so!" Lian then gave up tailoring and took up scholarship. In ten years he mastered all of the classics and histories and eventually compiled two editions of the county gazetteer, one before the Mongol conquest and another after.[14] Such evidence lends support to Kai-wing Chow's, Joseph McDermott's, and Cynthia Brokaw's arguments that by the late Ming (or earlier), the reading public

12. *Changyuan xian zhi*, postface, 1a; *Jianyang xian zhi* (1553), 223.
13. *Guangchang xian zhi* (1683), old prefaces, 1–2.
14. Ibid., 419–20.

had expanded beyond elite men.[15] Additional evidence of commoners reading gazetteers will be presented in chapter 7.

Compilers discussed their intended audiences not only in terms of status, occupational group, and gender, but also in terms of place. Some claimed their texts were distributed widely, such as a contributor to the 1450 gazetteer of Linying 臨潁, Henan, who wrote that it "was distributed to the four corners of the realm."[16] Although this vague statement does not detail precisely where the gazetteer was sent, it was an assertion that imprints left the locale that was the subject of the gazetteer. Similarly, in a preface to the 1562 gazetteer of Wuning 武寧, Jiangxi, Lu Shen 陸深, an official who had visited Wuning in 1533, wrote that he was happy about the publication and that "even those who do not come to this land will have Wuning before their eyes as soon as they open this book."[17] In this case, Lu assumed that people outside of Wuning, such as himself, would read the gazetteer.

Some compilers focused on the local audience. Xie Zhaozhe's postface to the 1612 gazetteer of Yongfu, Fujian, claimed that the new high-quality gazetteer would have a large audience of "locals" 邑之人, explaining that although Yongfu had produced multiple gazetteers over the years, they were poorly written and unpublished and few people read them. He argued that because of this, local people had been ignorant about important local issues. In his view, the newly published gazetteer would give locals a source for understanding "recent and past affairs."[18]

In fact, most compilers anticipated both local and nonlocal readers, and some explicitly said so. A preface to the 1499 gazetteer of Suzhou 宿州, Nanzhili (not to be confused with the better-known Suzhou 蘇州), stated that upon reading the gazetteer, "Those born in Suzhou will feel admiration and be moved to action; those serving in Suzhou will feel invigorated and improve their administration; those investigating the customs of Suzhou will have selections to present to the Son of Heaven."[19]

15.   Chow, *Publishing, Culture, and Power*, chap. 1, 302; McDermott, *A Social History*, 25–31; Brokaw, *Commerce in Culture*, 552.

16.   *Linying xian zhi*, old prefaces, 3b.

17.   *Wuning xian zhi*, 361–65.

18.   *Yongfu xian zhi*, 379–80.

19.   *Suzhou zhi*, 225.

Distribution

Commercial publishers sold books in a variety of ways: in bookstores and stalls, at periodic book markets, and through itinerant peddlers.[20] Gazetteers, however, were noncommercial books and their distribution channels were more limited. There is no evidence of new local gazetteers being sold in bookstores during the period of this study, although older ones were. There also is no evidence of gazetteers being sold by itinerant booksellers. Instead, upon completion, printed gazetteers were distributed to government offices and individuals associated with the compilation, and thereafter published on demand. Distribution through official channels meant that most readers had government connections, either through government service or as members of local elites. Manuscript gazetteers were placed in only a few locations. We will first consider these two categories, manuscript and print, separately, and then examine gazetteers that appeared in lists of books owned by schools, yamens, and collectors.

DISTRIBUTION OF MANUSCRIPT GAZETTEERS

Thousands of local gazetteers done in response to imperial compilation edicts, such as the Yongle Emperor's 1418 edict and the Jingtai Emperor's 1454 edict, were submitted to the court as handwritten copies, while the originals and other handwritten copies were retained locally.[21] Additional manuscript gazetteers were done in response to provincial and prefectural compilation orders.[22]

In the case of the gazetteer of Yanzhou 嚴州, Zhejiang, compiled in response to the 1454 imperial edict, a handwritten copy was sent to the Hanlin Academy, and another copy was placed in the prefectural school. In this record, the use of terms meaning "copies from originals" (*lu ben* 錄本 and *fu ben* 副本) implies that there was also an original manuscript (*zhengben* 正本 or *diben* 底本).[23] Because the Yanzhou prefect received

20.   McDermott, *A Social History*, 94–103.
21.   *Jingzhou fu zhi*, He Xing'an preface.
22.   He Qiaoxin, *Jiaoqiu wenji*, 9.17a.
23.   *Xincai xian zhi* (1579), preface, 1a.

the initial order to compile the gazetteer, the original was presumably kept in the yamen.[24] Placement of manuscripts in the local yamens and schools was standard. The 1557 gazetteer of Wengyuan 翁源, Guangdong, was a manuscript edition made in two copies, one of which was placed in the yamen and the other in the Confucian school.[25] In 1434, when Song Ji arrived in Xuzhou, Nanzhili, to take office as an instructor in the Confucian school, he asked students for the gazetteer done in response to the 1418 imperial compilation edict but was unable to get a copy at the school. He eventually found the hastily compiled work in the yamen.[26] This suggests that one might expect to find gazetteers in schools, but they did not always have them. One reason is that local officials often planned to improve and print gazetteers after sending the handwritten copies to court, and thus did not make handwritten copies for the schools.[27] Of course, many were not printed and soon lost. Late fifteenth- and sixteenth-century gazetteer compilers frequently noted that earlier editions were no longer extant.[28] Some compilers in this period did not even know of Hongwu- and Yongle-era editions that appear in bibliographies.

As a result of repeated submissions of gazetteers, the court had large collections. The collection sizes are indicated by their catalogs. The 1441 *Wenyuange shumu*, discussed in chapter 3, divides local gazetteers into "old gazetteers" and "new gazetteers," and lists 600 of the former and 568 of the latter.[29] The Wenyuange collection was destroyed by fire in 1449.[30] The Wanli-era *Neige cang shu mu lu* 內閣藏書目錄 (Catalog of books held by the Grand Secretariat) lists approximately 880 local gazetteers.[31] One might expect even larger collections based on the number of administrative units in the empire, but gazetteers compiled on local initiative were not routinely submitted to the court, the library probably lost many others to pilfering officials, and manuscript gazetteers submitted

24. *Yanzhou fu zhi*, 12.
25. *Wengyuan xian zhi*, last page.
26. *Pengcheng zhi*, Song Ji preface.
27. *Chaoyang xian zhi*, 1419 preface, old prefaces, 7b.
28. *Weishi xian zhi*, 4.3b.
29. Yang Shiqi, *Wenyuange shumu*, 183–216.
30. Shen Defu, *Wanli Yehuobian*, 1.4.
31. Zhang Xuan, *Neige cangshu mulu*, chap. 7.

for use in national projects may not have been kept in these collections because officials from the Ministry of Revenue and the Ministry of Rites, as well as the Hanlin Academy, led the 1418 and 1454 projects.

At least one other central government bureau also collected local gazetteers. Officials of the Messenger Office 行人司 collected books as they traveled around the country, and their 1602 book catalog lists 270 works under the heading of "geographies" 地理類, most of which were county and prefectural gazetteers.[32] The Messenger Office was responsible for delivering nonroutine messages to important dignitaries and would have benefited from having access to detailed local information.

The intended audience for the gazetteers in the palace library was the emperor and officials. As discussed in chapter 1, the Zhengde Emperor wanted to read gazetteers on his trip to Nanjing. The Jingtai Emperor's compilation edict stemmed from his "desire to read the realm's local gazetteers in his spare time"; it was not designed to benefit local and general readers.[33] Many of the early-Ming manuscript gazetteers were copied into the *Yongle da dian*, the massive work commissioned in 1403 and completed in 1408, which was produced only in manuscript form.[34] As Frederick Mote and Chu Hung-lam have argued, the *Yongle da dian* was written by hand because of the nature of the compendium and its intended audience, not to avoid the cost of printing. It was initially conceived as a project neither of cultural dissemination nor of making knowledge available to the educated population, but was instead a reference library for the emperors and their intimate literary officials at court.[35]

There was a strong perception among gazetteer compilers that access to the palace library was difficult for most readers, and this led many to quickly print their gazetteers after submitting manuscripts.[36] In 1418 Zhu Hui printed his local gazetteer of Xincheng, Jiangxi, for "dissemination to people" because the manuscript he submitted to the palace library was "not easy for people to see."[37] After Hanlin academicians issued princi-

---

32. Xu Tu, *Xingrensi chongke shumu*, 627–29.

33. *Jingzhou fu zhi*, He Xing'an preface.

34. Mote and Chu, *Calligraphy*, 79. Some lost local gazetteers have been reconstructed from the *Yongle da dian*. See Wang and Liu, *Yongle dadian fangzhi jiyi*.

35. Mote and Chu, *Calligraphy*, 78.

36. Xue Xuan, *Jingxuan wenji*, 13.8b.

37. *Xincheng xian zhi*, 826–31.

ples of compilation in 1454, the prefect of Jingzhou, Huguang, compiled a gazetteer, made a handwritten copy, and submitted it to the court. But he soon thereafter had blocks cut in the prefectural yamen to expand the audience. He wanted people, even those from distant places, to be able to read it, and thought that it would be hard for them to see the court's copy.[38] The 1457 print edition of the gazetteer of Huizhou, Guangdong, was an expanded and edited version of the 1455 manuscript edition that had been sent to the court. The compilers did it because "few people saw it there."[39]

Select officials did have access to the court's local gazetteers. Most were Hanlin academicians or other high-ranking officials, but evidence suggests that lesser officials gained access, either directly or through intermediaries. Some officials used old, rare editions from court when compiling new editions; others used the court's gazetteers as references or even read them casually. In 1493 Hanlin academician and classics colloquium lecturer Li Dongyang wrote, "When I read in the palace library I see the realm's gazetteers with maps, books piled up like a mountain, and I sometimes pick one up and read it."[40] The early-Ming grand secretary Yang Shiqi 楊士奇 (1365–1444) consulted a gazetteer of Raozhou 饒州, Jiangxi, in the palace library to verify information in a genealogy for which he had been asked to write a preface.[41] In 1519 Grand Guardian of the Heir Apparent Li Sui 李鐩 (retired 1521), a native of Zhangde 彰德, Henan, obtained Song and Yuan dynasty editions of the local gazetteer from the palace library and sent them to the Zhangde gazetteer compilation office for use in a new edition.[42]

The officials discussed above had positions that allowed for direct access to the palace library collections. For lesser officials, the experience of Dai Min 戴敏, the magistrate of Yizhou 易州, Beizhili, 100 kilometers south of Beijing, was probably typical. When he compiled the 1502 Yizhou gazetteer, he first had a Yizhou native write a draft, then wrote a letter to his elder brother Dai Xian 戴銑, a supervising secretary in the Office of Scrutiny for the Ministry of War and Hanlin bachelor, asking

38. *Jingzhou fu zhi*, 1456 preface, 3a.
39. *Huizhou fu zhi* (1556), old prefaces, 1b–2a. Also see *Yunnan zhi*, 284.
40. *Xuzhou zhi* (1541), 6a.
41. Yang Shiqi, *Dongli ji, xu ji*, 30.26a.
42. *Zhangde fu zhi*, table of contents, 2a.

him to check the references and polish the draft.[43] Dai Xian accepted, read the draft, and compared entries to books in the palace collections. When Dai Xian finished, Dai Min went to Beijing to get the gazetteer from his brother.[44]

Manuscripts retained in the locales that were the subject of the gazetteer were read in the interim between completion and printing, either on-site in the place where stored, or off site through handwritten copies. For example, according to a 1084 preface to the *Wujun tu zhi*, the 1011 map guides were simple, and by the 1070s, out of date. In about 1078 the Suzhou prefect asked Zhu Changwen 朱長文 to supplement the old map guide, which he did. The prefect, however, was transferred and Zhu kept the expanded work in his home, unpublished. Three years later, at the request of a new prefect, Zhu polished his manuscript and had a handwritten copy made and placed in the yamen as a reference.[45] Zhu also kept a copy at home and let others read it.[46] In 1098 a new Suzhou vice prefect decided to print Zhu's work. He said that even with the yamen copy, few read it, and so he had woodblocks cut in the yamen storehouse in 1100.[47] Thus, for about twenty years the gazetteer was read, but only in manuscript form. A similar case from the Yuan dynasty is the *Qi sheng*, compiled by Yu Qin 于欽 (1284–1333), a Shandong native who once served as tax commissioner of Yidu Circuit 益都路, his native place. While there, he gathered materials for the gazetteer and completed the manuscript, which he kept in his home. On his deathbed in 1333, he said to his son, Yu Qian 于潛, "My body is like the morning dew, you must publish it." The son, who was an official, did not do so until 1351, claiming that until then he was too busy with his duties. In the eighteen years between the author's death and publication, the *Qi sheng* manuscript circulated. In a 1339 preface the famous official Su Tianjue 蘇天爵 told how he first read the gazetteer in Yangzhou and recommended it to officials serving in Shandong.[48] Such cases were not unusual throughout the Song, Yuan, and Ming.

43. *Yizhou zhi*, prefaces, 1b–6b.
44. Ibid.
45. *Wujun tujing xu ji*, Zhu Changwen preface.
46. Ibid., Lin Fu postface.
47. Ibid., Zhu Anshang postface.
48. *Qi Sheng*, Su Tianjue preface.

Scattered notes show that borrowing and hand copying were important ways of circulating gazetteers. The famous scholar Fang Xiaoru 方孝孺 (1357–1402) explained in a letter to a friend that he was writing a book on the unknown deeds of local historical figures to create role models for the local people.[49] So he went from his home in Ninghai, Zhejiang, to the Taizhou prefectural school, about 80 kilometers south, borrowed the local gazetteer, had it copied, and sent back the original.[50] In another case, the prefect of Kuizhou, Sichuan, wrote in 1511 that he obtained a handwritten copy of a prefectural gazetteer from a government student at the prefectural Confucian school.[51] Gui Youguang 歸有光 (1507–71) borrowed the late-fourteenth-century gazetteer of Nanjing from Wu Zhongying 吳中英 while he was in Nanjing to take the 1531 provincial examination. Twenty-nine years later, when Gui read a Yuan dynasty gazetteer of Nanjing, he thought about historical changes and once again borrowed the gazetteer from the Wu family, reread it, and wrote a colophon.[52] In the 1610s or 1620s a student in Renhe 仁和, Zhejiang, had a handwritten copy of a 1549 manuscript local gazetteer compiled by Renhe native Shen Chaoxuan 沈朝宣. The magistrate borrowed but did not return it. In 1657 Shen Qiu 沈蚪, possibly a relative of Shen Chaoxuan, borrowed the gazetteer from the magistrate's family, a Renhe townsman copied it by hand, and published it.[53]

DISTRIBUTION OF PRINTED GAZETTEERS

Once woodblocks were cut, an initial run of imprints was made and distributed. There were no formal rules for who was to receive imprints, but they were generally sent to the yamen, Confucian school, superior and inferior territorial yamens and other government offices, compilers, preface authors, donors to publication expenses, and various interested people. Multiple copies were probably printed for the yamen that published the gazetteer: some for the officials involved in compilation, some

49. Fang Xiaoru, *Xunzhizhai ji*, 11.
50. See McDermott, *A Social History*, 127–34, for more on access to government schoolbooks.
51. *Kuizhou fu zhi*, 12.59a.
52. Gui Youguang, *Zhenchuan ji*, 5.1a–2b.
53. Zhang Mingke, *Shanben shushi cangshu zhi*, 291.

to give away later to officials, and some for internal yamen offices and private secretaries.[54] Evidence of distribution comes from various types of sources, including statements by compilers, preface authors, and others; petitions and orders related to compilation; lists of books owned by Confucian schools, yamens, private academies, and book collectors; statements of where blocks were held; and seals on book covers and inside pages.

After the initial print run, the cut blocks were stored, usually in the yamen or school, for further printing on demand. Printed on the title page of the Shanghai Library's copy of the 1671 gazetteer of Xinchang, Zhejiang, are the words "Held by this county's yamen." Because this phrase was cut into the block, it refers to the blocks, not the extant imprint. By the nineteenth century it became common for the gazetteer title pages to specify the blocks' storage location.[55] Some extant imprints have yamen stamps on the covers. The Harvard-Yenching Library and Bibliothèque nationale de France copies of the mid-Qing reprint of the 1614 *Huayin xian zhi* 華陰縣志 both have red yamen seal impressions over the title block, indicating that the prints came from the yamen.

Petitions from local governments for permission to print their local gazetteers, and administrative orders in response, indicate that completed gazetteers were often submitted to superior offices beyond the immediately higher territorial unit. This was sometimes done for prepublication review, but other times only after the text was finalized. The magistrate of Fengrun, Beizhili, was ordered to send an imprint of the newly printed 1570 gazetteer to the Beizhili grand coordinator; the 1621 gazetteer of Chengdu, Sichuan, was sent to the provincial surveillance and administration commissions; and the 1552 gazetteer of Xingning, Guangdong, was sent to the provincial superintendent of schools.[56] The Shandong regional inspector's branch office in Laiwu 萊蕪, Shandong, received a copy of the 1533 provincial gazetteer immediately after its publication.[57] The woodblocks for this title were kept in the provincial

54. *Sinan fu zhi*, Zhang Lie postface, 2a.

55. *Jingyuan xian zhi*.

56. *Fengrun xian zhi*, 520; *Chengdu fu zhi*, postface; *Xingning xian zhi*, prefatory matter, 2a.

57. *Laiwu xian zhi*, Li Kaixian preface, 1b.

administration commission office in Jinan, the provincial capital, and were still there as of 1640.[58] Providing copies to superior offices happened long after the initial printing as well. In 1534 the Huguang grand coordinator's office ordered Changde Prefecture to recompile its gazetteer because the copy it had sent their office was "outdated and incomplete." This led to compilation of the 1538 edition.[59]

Copies of gazetteers were supplied to preface authors, some who were from superior offices and some who had no connection to the gazetteer project. The copy could be supplied before or after the initial print run.[60] Prefaces were solicited in both distant locales and the subject locale. A messenger took the completed 1498 gazetteer of Xuanfu Garrison to Beijing, 150 kilometers southeast of Xuanfu, and solicited a preface from an official.[61] Such out-of-town preface authors were not unusual, and giving them copies was one means of expanding the nonlocal audience. Soliciting prominent people in the locale was common. In 1555 Yang Yingqi 楊應奇, a native of Xiayi, Henan, was appointed Guizhou administration vice commissioner and stopped at his home on the way from Beijing to Guizhou. The magistrate showed him the newly completed gazetteer and asked Yang for a preface. Yang read the gazetteer, then wrote one.[62]

As discussed in chapters 4 and 5, the total number of imprints from the first run was probably less than one hundred in most cases, and subsequent publication on demand was the most important distribution method. Gazetteer publishers expected that imprints would continue to be made from the cut woodblocks for decades after the initial print run. As Magistrate Shi An 史安 explained in his preface to the 1215 *Shan lu* 剡錄 (Record of Shan), "There is nothing that this book fails to record. Examining these blocks we can tell that 100 years from now people will not cast them aside even though they be worn down."[63] This may appear to be mere bragging, but imprints of the 1494 gazetteer of Baoding were in fact still being made 114 years later from woodblocks stored in

58. *Licheng xian zhi*, 15.11a.
59. *Changde fu zhi*, 20.18a.
60. *Weishi xian zhi*, 5.63b; *Xinchang xian zhi* (1579), Jia Yingbi preface, 1b.
61. *Xuanfu zhen zhi*, preface, 2a–b.
62. *Xiayi xian zhi*, prefaces, 9a–b.
63. *Shan lu*, 7195. Some bibliographies use the pronunciation Yan rather than Shan.

the yamen.[64] Of course, many blocks did not last nearly that long. When a new magistrate arrived in Zhangzhou, Fujian, in 1243, he found that the blocks for the 1213 gazetteer were already old and the words unclear.[65] How long woodblocks lasted varied with climate, wood quality, and the number of impressions made. Some blocks may have worn out faster than others because particular *juan* or items were popular and readers requested partial printings. This may also help explain why there are many cases in which only particular *juan* are extant.

Notations contained in gazetteers show that the cut woodblocks were generally stored in the local yamen or school, but occasionally in a compiler's home, that people who were not officials in the yamen or school could print from the blocks under certain conditions, and that steps were taken to maintain the integrity of the texts. The printing supervisor for the 1637 gazetteer of Wucheng 烏程, Zhejiang, Fei Renbang 費仁邦 of the yamen document office 書東科, had the following statement included in the gazetteer: "The gazetteer blocks are kept in the storehouse and the storekeeper is responsible for them. If someone privately prints [new copies] and recklessly adds to or subtracts from the gazetteer, rigorously investigate."[66] A warning in the 1602 gazetteer of Chengtian, Huguang, made two officers responsible for the blocks: "The gazetteer blocks are kept in the prefecture's storehouse and the ritual affairs officer is in charge of them. Should anyone without authority add to or subtract from [the original] when privately printing, the warden shall be held responsible."[67] The 1608 gazetteer of Huanggang, Huguang, included an inspection requirement and a technique of documenting the blocks for incoming magistrates: "The local gazetteer's woodblocks are kept in the county yamen's storehouse and they have been recorded in the administrative affairs register 交盤册 that is presented to incoming magistrates. The blocks shall be managed by a functionary from the yamen's ritual affairs office. Whenever a print is made, the blocks shall be inspected. The blocks must not be lost so that [the text] may long endure."[68] Administrative affairs registers were

64. *Baoding fu zhi*, prefatory matter, *zuanxiu fu zhi xi wen*, 2a, 40.26a.
65. Zhang Guogan, *Zhongguo gu fangzhi kao*, 433–34.
66. *Wucheng xian zhi* (1637), 227.
67. *Chengtian fu zhi*, 12.
68. *Huanggang xian zhi*, prefatory matter.

presented to incoming magistrates as part of the procedure for transferring authority.

Administrators' need to balance access to the gazetteer with maintaining textual integrity is explained in a note appended to the 1536 gazetteer of Yingzhou, Nanzhili:

> As has been the practice in various places, I put the gazetteer books and blocks in the [local] school. If [the subject of the gazetteer had been either of the] two capitals, then [a copy] also would have been given to the national university and the prefectural school. According to public opinion, [in compiling a gazetteer] one not only must not subtract from or add to the facts, but one further must not allow the gazetteer to be lost. I have now installed a cabinet in the Confucian school library for storing the blocks. It is on the right side of the upper [floor], side by side with the cabinet for storing the dynastic histories, which is to its east.
>
> When worthy scholar gentry who travel through here or who live here want copies, the paper's [cost] should be calculated and craftsmen should be ordered to print it. Yet they must not use their status to carry away [the blocks] and the guardians of Confucian ideals, righteous teachers and students, must not be cowed into submission by scholar gentry status. They must not let [the blocks] one day leave the library; [their adherence to duty] will be the gazetteer's good fortune.[69]

Together these notes show that private printing was allowed from government-held gazetteer blocks, that compilers worried about unsanctioned changes and theft of the blocks, and that those who made prints for personal use paid for the paper.

Keeping woodblocks in yamens and schools made it convenient for new administrators, Confucian school instructors, and traveling officials to get imprints. In previous chapters we saw examples of administrators asking for the gazetteer upon arrival, and their citation of Zhu Xi doing the same. In a 1376 preface to the gazetteer of Chaozhou, Guangdong, the author claimed that "those who serve here regularly get the gazetteer and take it with them when they leave."[70] Many new administrators probably were given gazetteers without asking as part of the transfer of

69. *Yingzhou xian zhi,* 1110.
70. Wang and Liu, *Yongle dadian fangzhi jiyi,* 2775.

power. A record in the Wanli-era (1573–1628) *Gongxue shuyuan zhi* 共學
書院志 (Gongxue Academy gazetteer) states that a new imprint was to be
run off for each new academy administrator. The academy's rules stated,
"In the Academy, banquets are only permitted on assembly days. Liquor
must not be set out and there shall be no plays or music; they harm the
refined Way. Whenever there is a new administrator, print and deliver
one copy of the academy gazetteer for his review and to assist him in
strictly maintaining [these rules]."[71]

Gazetteers were also presented to touring inspectors. One magistrate even spoke of this practice as a requirement. In 1618 the magistrate
of Xinchang, Zhejiang, complained that according to precedent, whenever censorial or surveillance officials came to town he was expected to
present a copy of the local gazetteer, but because the woodblocks had
burned, the magistrate had to buy surviving imprints, which were becoming increasingly rare and more expensive with each purchase.[72] This
situation led him to recut the blocks. In the Qing Shunzhi era (1644–61),
two officers of the Ganzhou, Jiangxi provincial administration commission branch office had to buy a copy of the 1621 Ganzhou gazetteer for
the provincial commissioner because the blocks had been destroyed in
the Ming collapse.[73]

Not all gazetteer woodblocks were stored in government buildings;
some were kept in compilers' homes. After the original blocks for the
gazetteer of Qizhou, Huguang, were cut in 1530, the magistrate ordered
that they be stored in the home of compiler Gan Ze in order to "make it
convenient for commoners to print from them" 便民印行.[74] But this convenience came at a price. Seventeen blocks had disappeared by 1536, and
a new magistrate had to have them recut from an imprint.[75] Another
example of private block storage is the 1537 *Hengzhou fu zhi* (the compilation of which was discussed in chapter 3). They were kept by the
editor, Liu Fu, a retired official who ventured into publishing and
planned to make copies of the gazetteer for interested persons. He wrote:

71. *Gongxue shuyuan zhi*, 180, 183.
72. *Xinchang xian zhi* (1579, 1618), *Xin zhi xu xiaoyin* (A short introduction to the
continuation of the Xinchang gazetteer).
73. *Ganzhou fu zhi*, preface.
74. *Qizhou zhi*, 9.72a.
75. Ibid., postface, 8.72a.

"The Yueting Bookroom has published an edition of the prefectural gaz-etteer. The total number of blocks is two hundred. They should be shelved in the pavilion so that they will not rot. After the printing, their number shall be counted so none will be lost. Since this is not a canonical work that is to be transmitted across generations without [re]-printing, we may now respond to urgent requests [for copies]."[76] Recording the number of blocks was a technique that allowed easier identification of missing or added blocks. Some compilers specified not only the total number of blocks for the entire gazetteer, but a total for each *juan*.[77]

The above passages are important because they imply that private, yet authorized, publishers planned to make copies of local gazetteers on demand. While charging for the copies is not mentioned, it appears that both Liu Fu and Gan Ze were selling copies from their homes. Perhaps the magistrate allowed this in exchange for their taking charge of com-piling the gazetteer and cutting the woodblocks, thus saving him the trouble and cost.

Those who wanted a local gazetteer but could not make a face-to-face request of the block holder could send a letter asking for a copy. In 1404 Chen Lian 陳璉 (1379–1454), the prefect of Xuzhou, in Kaifeng 開封 Prefecture, Henan, compiled a manuscript gazetteer that served as the basis for an edition printed in 1414, after Chen had already left of-fice. Twenty-two years later, Chen, who was then serving as the vice minister of rites in Nanjing, decided he wanted a copy. So he wrote a letter to the Kaifeng prefect, who had the Xuzhou magistrate print it for Chen.[78] The ability for people with official connections to get gazetteers from long distances made possible large gazetteer collections, which will be discussed in chapter 7.

DISTRIBUTION AS SEEN IN BOOKLISTS

Lists of books and woodblocks owned by the local Confucian schools and yamens provide some of the best available evidence on gazetteer distribution. School book lists are found in gazetteer chapters on local

---

76. *Hengzhou fu zhi* (1537), 9.14b.
77. *Ninghai xian zhi, fanli*, 2a–b; *Wuliang kao zhi*, 1.104a.
78. *Yingchuan jun zhi*, preface and postfaces.

schools, in sections titled "Register of essential documentation" 典籍, "Register of books" 書籍, "Book catalog" 書目, or "Stored books" 藏書 or 貯書. They usually follow the lists of schools' ritual implements and musical instruments. Yamen lists appear with school book lists, or in the "literature" 藝文 or "miscellaneous" 雜 chapters. Private academies, book collectors, and government institutions, such as the palace library, discussed above, also compiled lists of their holdings. "Book accession records" 藏書記 or 貯書記 sometimes accompany book lists in library records. It is important to keep in mind that schools without separate library buildings might still have books. For example, as of 1609 the county school of Raoyang 饒陽, Beizhili, stored its books in a senior official's private residence, where they were managed by a clerk.[79]

Book lists provide concrete examples of gazetteer distribution, but they are inadequate for quantitative analysis due to compilers' disagreements over whether it was necessary to include such lists in gazetteers, and if so, what types of books should be recorded. The biggest problem is that many local gazetteers do not include any book list. One compiler explained, "We have not included a register of books issued to the school, its ritual implements, etc., because the Confucian school has a separate register."[80] A second problem is that lists undercount the number of local gazetteers, because most omit the new gazetteer that contains the list. It is often apparent from notations in a gazetteer's front matter that its woodblocks were kept in the school or yamen, but their booklists nevertheless fail to record either the blocks or imprints because compilers made the lists before the new blocks were cut and imprints made.[81] At the time of writing, the new local gazetteer did not yet exist, and most compilers did not add its title to the list before cutting the blocks.

A third problem is that many compilers only recorded books issued to the Confucian school by the court, doing only what was needed to show that their school had the orthodox works consisting of classics and commentaries, moral texts, law codes, and a few other titles.[82] Other compilers recorded nonimperial editions but still excluded titles not

79.   *Raoyang xian zhi*, 257.
80.   *Xihe xian xin zhi*, 2.35a–b.
81.   *Huanggang xian zhi*, prefatory matter, 2.7a, 9.66b–68a.
82.   Brook, *The Chinese State*, 101–7.

directly related to the core of *Daoxue* (Learning of the Way) and the civil service examination. This is explained in the introduction to the books section of the 1517 gazetteer of Jianchang 建昌, Fujian: "The books section records the writings of civilization. Recording major works makes possible the 'adequate documentation' [demanded by Confucius]. This is acceptable. But as for publications on the lesser arts 小技, these are not worth recording."[83] Gazetteers, although not classified as part of the "lesser arts," were not imperial editions, or core *Daoxue* texts, and were thus omitted by many gazetteer compilers.

Comparing lists of works cited by local gazetteer compilers to the lists of books in the school and yamen of the same locale shows that more gazetteers were available locally than is suggested by the latter. The 1573 gazetteer of Zhangzhou, Fujian, lists forty-six titles held by the prefectural school, and twelve sets of woodblocks for books published by the yamen, not one of which was a local gazetteer. But there are fifteen local gazetteers in the list of works used in compiling the *Zhangzhou fu zhi*: four earlier editions of the prefectural gazetteer, six gazetteers of subordinate counties, two of neighboring prefectures, plus provincial, circuit, and regional gazetteers.[84] Similarly, for the 1604 gazetteer of Huairou County, Beizhili, the Shuntian prefectural school instructor consulted the provincial gazetteer, those of Jichang 冀昌 and Miyuan 密雲 counties, and "the old gazetteers of Xunyi 順義 and other neighboring jurisdictions."[85] Local gazetteers clearly were available, even if it is not always clear where they were stored.

A fourth problem in using school booklists is that they are snapshots in time of library book collections and often skew our perception of the availability of particular titles. Some identify books known to have been lost, but most do not. The 1573 gazetteer of Zhangzhou, discussed above, divides the prefectural school's list into "currently held" and "lost," and one of the lost titles was the 1489 *Ba Min tong zhi* 八閩通志, the Fujian provincial gazetteer. The list does not record when this gazetteer was lost, and we have no idea whether it was available for one year or eighty-four years. The reverse of this problem is that some copies of old editions

83. *Jianchang fu zhi*, 8.1a.
84. *Zhangzhou fu zhi, xiu zhi yin yong shu mu*, 11.47–48.
85. *Huairou xian zhi*, 4a–b.

may have been newly acquired but no accession date is recorded. When local gazetteer blocks were held by a yamen, the magistrate could replace a school's lost imprint, but it may have been lost for years, thus giving a false appearance of long-term availability. For example, when the magistrate of Dingxiang 定襄, Shanxi, published a new county gazetteer in 1616, he gave the school a copy of the 1579 edition along with his new edition, likely replacing a lost copy. The book list documents this event, but it does not say when the earlier edition was lost. In most cases a replacement copy would not be identified as such.[86]

Nonetheless, even with these caveats, enough book lists do record gazetteers for us to learn a substantial amount about their distribution, and even though most contain no record of gazetteers in the local yamen or school, it is clear that most yamens and schools received copies. A list of books held in the yamen storeroom of Yongzhou Prefecture, Huguang, as of 1571 shows that in addition to the yamen that published or supervised publication of the local gazetteer, superior yamens also received imprints. The list records the title, publisher, and publication date of seven local gazetteers, all from Yongzhou and its subordinate territories.[87] Three were previous editions of the prefectural gazetteer published in 1494, 1541, and 1555. Three were from subordinate territories: the 1528 gazetteer of Dong'an 東安, the 1545 gazetteer of Daozhou 道州, and the 1555 gazetteer of Ningyuan 寧遠. They were published by their respective local magistrates, not the prefecture, but the prefecture nevertheless had copies. The seventh was a 1541 gazetteer of a local mountain.

These seven do not, however, represent a complete set of Yongzhou gazetteers. Missing were the gazetteers of Yongzhou's four other counties and the 1571 *Yongzhou fu zhi* itself, the book that contains the list.[88] Likely reasons for two of the county local gazetteers being missing are readily apparent: Lingling 零陵 had just become a county in 1567 and probably had not yet published one. Jianghua 江華 published a gazetteer in 1574, most likely based on the materials gathered for the 1571 prefectural gazetteer, and that is the first extant edition. The Yongzhou book list shows subordinate-unit gazetteers being provided to the superior

86. *Dingxiang xian zhi*, 375–76.
87. *Yongzhou fu zhi* (1571), 11.
88. Ibid., preface, 4b.

territorial unit, but the movement went in both directions; prefectural and provincial governments also provided their gazetteers to their counties and subprefectures. This could happen long after the blocks were cut. As the 1608 Baoding was being compiled, one imprint of the 1494 edition was made from stored woodblocks for each of Baoding's twenty subordinate administrative units.[89]

In addition to yamens, Confucian schools received imprints, even when they were not the production site and did not store the cut blocks. Confucian school teachers and students were important contributors to, and readers of, gazetteers and with the rise of local history writing in the Ming and evidential learning 考證學 in the Qing, local gazetteers became a genre collected by school libraries. In the Ming, Confucian schools were most likely to have the gazetteers of their own locales and the national gazetteer, the *Da Ming yitong zhi*, which was issued to schools and yamens by the central government after its publication in 1461. Some schools also had gazetteers of superior, subordinate, and neighboring territories. Many schools, however, only had the gazetteer of their own jurisdiction.[90] Some county schools also had their prefectural gazetteer.[91]

Provincial gazetteers were more likely to be found in higher-level Confucian schools, but some were provided to county schools.[92] In 1488, the Yuezhou Prefecture School 岳州府學, Huguang, had the provincial gazetteer. In 1543 the schools of Baoning Prefecture 保寧府, Sichuan, and its two subprefectures, Bazhou 巴州 and Jianzhou 劍州, each had a copy of the provincial gazetteer, while three subordinate county schools did not.[93] The Jianzhou copy was provided by magistrate Li Bi 李璧, who served from 1515–21.[94] In contrast to the above examples, as of 1590 the county school of Pingyuan 平原, Shandong, had the gazetteers of its immediate superior territorial unit, Dezhou, and its province, both of which were provided by a prefectural official.[95]

---

89. *Baoding fu zhi, zuanxiu fu zhi wen,* 2a, 40.26a.
90. *Yunyang fu zhi,* 450; *Lingshi xian zhi,* 4.3a–b.
91. *Shidai xian zhi,* 1547 preface. Shidai County school had the *Chizhou fu zhi,* probably the 1545 edition.
92. *Yunyang fu zhi,* 457.
93. *Yuezhou fu zhi,* 66; *Baoning fu zhi,* 19–26.
94. Ibid., 22a.
95. *Pingyuan zhi,* 2.26b–27a.

It was standard practice to give the school a copy of the local gazetteer when it was first completed, but schools got other gazetteers on an ad hoc basis. Book donations were often associated with new construction, major renovations, retiring officials, and local authors. In 1522 the magistrate of Bozhou, Nanzhili, gave eight titles to the newly constructed school, including the prefectural gazetteer and those of two neighboring jurisdictions, Guide Prefecture and Luxian County 鹿縣.[96] After the county school library of Pinghu, Zhejiang, was rebuilt following its collapse in a 1588 storm, Minister of Personnel Lu Guangzu 陸光祖, a Pinghu native, donated the Zhejiang provincial gazetteer and other books.[97] The Jiading 嘉定, Zhejiang, school library book collection expanded through multiple donations over seven decades, totaling 111 titles, including three gazetteers. In 1537 the magistrate donated forty-three titles, and in 1591 Minister of Rites Xu Xuemo 徐學謨 (1521–93), a local, donated seventeen from his private collection, but none were gazetteers.[98] In 1603, five people donated books, including three gazetteers: magistrate Han Jun 韓浚 donated eighteen titles, including the Shandong provincial gazetteer. Han was a native of Jinan, the Shandong provincial capital, where, as we saw above, the provincial gazetteer's blocks were stored, so he probably asked someone in his hometown to send him a copy or donated his own. National University student Xu Zhaoji 徐兆稷, Xu Xuemo's son, donated seven titles, including the 1591 Huguang provincial gazetteer compiled by his father; government student Li Shengzhi 李繩之 donated five titles, including the gazetteer of Qingzhou, Shandong; the instructor donated seventeen titles, and another student donated four.

Book donations also occurred when an official was disturbed by a particular school's lack of books. This often happened in remote areas where Chinese officials hoped to stimulate Chinese-style education and culture. Two of the largest Ming Confucian school book collections were in peripheral regions populated largely by non-Chinese people who resisted state authority. One was in Gansu Garrison, in the extreme

---

96. *Bozhou zhi* (1564), *fanli*; *Bozhou zhi* (1894), 232.
97. *Pinghu xian zhi*, 439–42.
98. *Jiading xian zhi*, 707–9.

northwest of the Ming state, and the other in Yunyang 鄖陽, Huguang, near the borders with Shaanxi and Henan. In the Ming, Gansu was part of Shaanxi Province and had large Tibetan, Mongol, and Muslim populations. The provincial capital was in distant Xi'an, but daily governance was carried out by the Regional Military Commission Branch 陝西行都司 headquartered at Ganzhou. The town, also known as Gansu Garrison, was located at the site of modern Zhangye 張掖, about 500 kilometers northwest of the current Gansu capital, Lanzhou 蘭州.

Ganzhou's school library was renovated in 1551, and a few years later it was stocked with books, including gazetteers. Gansu Grand Coordinator Chen Fei 陳斐 wrote in his *Shaanxi xingdusi ru xue zunjingge zhu shu ji* 陝西行都司儒學尊經閣貯書記 (Record of acquiring books for the Shaanxi Regional Military Commission school library) that the provincial examination was going to be held the year after he took office, 1558, but the students only had damaged copies of the classics and had never even heard of many other works. To fix this problem, he took money for book acquisition from collected fines and the surveillance commission's paper budget. Chen dispatched someone to buy books in Xi'an, approximately 1,000 kilometers southeast of Ganzhou, and to make imprints from woodblocks held by prefectural governments. Through this collecting trip, 147 new titles were added to the preexisting 31, for a total of 188 titles held by the school.[99]

The types of books Chen wanted were those of "each school of poetry and prose, collected works, astronomy, medicine and divination, and law," but the person dispatched also brought back five local gazetteers and the *Da Ming yitongzhi* to add to the four previously acquired gazetteers. Before the new acquisitions, the school had the Shaanxi provincial gazetteer, the *Yong da ji* 雍大記, a gazetteer of Shaanxi by He Jingming 何景明 (1483–1521); the Yan'an 延安 prefectural gazetteer, and Ningxia Garrison 寧夏鎮 gazetteer. The newly acquired local gazetteers were second copies of the Shaanxi provincial gazetteer and the *Yong da ji*; the provincial gazetteer of Henan; the *Chang'an zhi* 長安志, Song Minqiu's 宋敏求 eleventh-century work on Chang'an (Xi'an); and the *Yong lu* 雍錄, Cheng Dachang's 程大昌 twelfth-century work on the old

99. *Ganzhen zhi*, 38–41.

capitals of the Xi'an region. The booklist also contained the gazetteer of Gansu Garrison, the book in which the list was published.[100]

Chen Fei took multiple steps to document and protect the books. He ordered construction of four large cabinets to hold them, and had notices stamped in each book's front and back saying that the book had been recorded by his office. The surveillance office was ordered to maintain a record of each book. Chen ordered the school to cut a wooden plaque to be mounted behind the main lecture hall and inscribe a stone tablet with the name of each book and place it in the library. In addition, he wrote the record that was later incorporated into the gazetteer, thereby creating an external, circulating record of the books. He wrote further that titles of books acquired in the future should be added to the records. The extensive protective measures taken likely reflected the difficulty of acquiring books in such a remote place.

Chen proudly stated that Hexi 河西 (the Gansu Corridor) would now have a store of books and argued it was important to expand education in Gansu and bring culture to it. He noted that in the distant past the area was considered outside the realm of Chinese civilization, but that Confucian culture had been slowly spreading. Books, he argued, strengthened the culture, and gazetteers were part of his civilizing project.

Yunyang, a prefecture created in 1476 in an area that John Dardess called the "largest blank on the administrative map of interior China" in the early Ming, was the other site of a major sixteenth-century school book collection.[101] The area had an influx of settlers in the fifteenth century, and banditry was followed by suppression campaigns.[102] Yunyang continued to have serious problems with bandits and refugees through the next century until a regional defense command was established to control the mountainous region.[103] The prefectural school was founded contemporaneously with the prefecture in 1476, and over the next century became a focus of attempts to firmly establish Chinese culture and governance. The first extant record of the school's book collection was

100.   Ibid., 39.
101.   Dardess, *Ming China*, 116.
102.   Ibid., 117.
103.   *Yuntai zhi*, 292–300; Lai Jiadu, *Mingdai Yunyang*.

the receipt of twenty titles in 1547.[104] Then in the winter of 1573–74, regional military commissioner Sun Ying'ao 孫應鰲 issued 171 titles to the school, including eight local gazetteers: two from Yunyang, the prefectural and defense command gazetteers; six from neighboring jurisdictions, including three from Henan (the Henan provincial gazetteer and the Dengzhou 鄧州 and Nanyang 南陽 gazetteers); and three from Shaanxi (the *Shanglüe quan zhi* 商略全誌, and the Shangnan 商南 and Hanzhong 漢中 gazetteers). In 1575 the collection grew further when Yunyang's military superintendent Wang Shizhen purchased 93 titles. Fifty-eight more titles were added in 1590, for a total of 342 known titles.[105]

For school libraries in the Ming, the Gansu and Yunyang collections were large in terms of total numbers of books, but they were not the largest in terms of total number of gazetteers. In 1560 the prefectural school of Ningbo, Zhejiang, had twenty local gazetteers, all but one from Zhejiang,[106] and in 1622 the prefectural school of Quzhou, Zhejiang, had twenty-one local gazetteers, all from Zhejiang, including all five of Quzhou's subordinate counties (fig. 6.1).[107] These Confucian schools, however, had only one-third as many gazetteers as the private Meiguo Academy 梅國書院 in Dayu 大庾, Jiangxi. In 1536 it held 493 titles, including sixty-seven works categorized as "gazetteer." There were three national gazetteers, eight provincial gazetteers, thirty-six prefectural gazetteers, five subprefectural gazetteers, nine county gazetteers, three mountain gazetteers, one academy gazetteer, and two other local historical works.[108] Fifteen of the sixty-four local gazetteers came from Nanzhili, twelve from Zhejiang, eight from Jiangxi, six from Fujian, five from Huguang, four from Guangdong, two from Sichuan, and one each from Guizhou and Shandong. Almost all of the books were donated by the academy's co-founder, Liu Jie 劉節, who retired as vice minister of punishments in 1533 and soon thereafter opened the academy.[109] Liu had collected the books over the course of his life, and they included Liu's

104. *Yuntai zhi*, 303.
105. *Yunyang fu zhi*, 309–10, 319, 335–43, 812–19.
106. *Ningbo fu zhi* (1560), 7.23a–b.
107. *Quzhou fu zhi* (1622), 12.4b–5a.
108. *Nan'an fu zhi*, 1028–61.
109. Ibid., 17, 751–53.

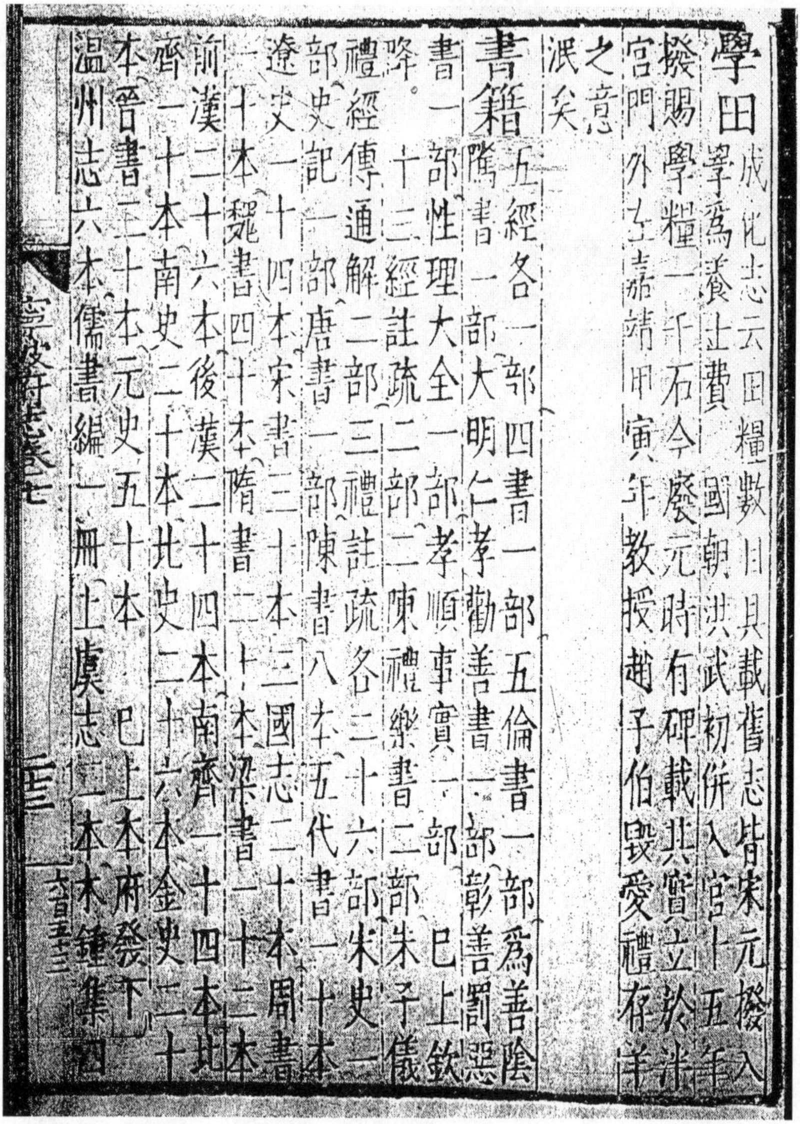

學田成化志云田糧數目具載舊志皆宋元撥入
學爲養士費 國朝洪武初併入官十五年
撥賜學糧一千石今廢元時有碑載其實立於泮
宮門外左嘉靖甲寅年教授趙子伯毀愛禮存羊
之意
泯矣
書籍五經各一部四書一部五倫書一部爲善陰
隲書一部大明仁孝勸善書一部彰善罰惡
書一部性理大全一部孝順事實一部已上欽
降。十三經註疏二部二陳禮樂書二部朱子儀
禮經傳通解二部三禮註疏各二十六部宋史一
部史記一部唐書一部陳書八本五代書一十本
遼史一十四本宋書三十本三國志二十本周書
一十本魏書四十本隋書二十本梁書一十二本
前漢二十六本後漢二十四本南齊一十四本北
齊一十本南史二十本北史二十六本金史二十
本晉書三十本元史五十本已上本府發下
溫州志六本儒書編一冊上虞志三本木鐘集四
寧波府志卷七 三 六百五十三

FIGURE 6.1. List of books held by the Ningbo prefectural school library as of 1560, including twenty gazetteers (Harvard-Yenching Library).

own works and works bestowed by the court. Donating books late in life to schools and other government institutions was probably common. In one case a capital education intendant had no heir, so in his old age sent his books, including a gazetteer of Xujiang, Jiangxi, to a "government storehouse."[110]

In the early Ming, local Confucian schools and the imperial universities in Beijing and Nanjing were the dominant educational institutions. In the sixteenth century, however, many students began to attend academies that were separate from the established Confucian school system. Most were founded and run by individuals, although often with official approval and sponsorship.[111] The number of academies rapidly expanded during the Jiajing (1522–66) and Longqing eras (1567–72) before temporarily contracting in the decades after Zhang Juzheng's 1579 suppression. But by the last decades of the Ming, the expansion resumed.[112]

Because academies were travel destinations for students and officials, teachers and literati, many of whom were not locals, gazetteers were especially important additions to their holdings. Although study and teaching were the focus, academies were often built at scenic sights, and many were also places for sightseeing and networking. The flourishing of local gazetteers coincided with the flourishing of academies, and by the sixteenth century gazetteers began to appear in academy book lists.

The expanding number of local gazetteers in academy libraries can be seen in a series of library catalogs from the White Deer Grotto Academy 白鹿洞書院 in Nankang 南康, Jiangxi. The academy had been famous since the Song dynasty due to its association with the famous Neo-Confucian scholar Zhu Xi. White Deer had a Ming revival and published four academy gazetteers. Each edition contains a list of books owned by the academy. The oldest extant list is found in the *Bailudong Shuyuan xin zhi* 白鹿洞書院新志 (New gazetteer of White Deer Grotto Academy), which was originally compiled in 1511 and supplemented and published in 1525. The only gazetteer on that list was the *Da Ming yitongzhi* and the woodblocks for the academy gazetteer.[113]

110. Cao Xuequan, *Da Ming yitong mingsheng*, 237.
111. Meskill, "Academies and Politics," 152–62.
112. Ibid., 169.
113. Li Chenguang, *Bailudong shuyuan gu zhi*, 144–45.

The next book list is found in the 1554 edition of the academy gazetteer. It added the Jiangxi provincial gazetteer, likely the 1525 edition; a gazetteer of Zengcheng County 增城縣, Guangdong, likely the 1538 edition; one of Xinquan Academy 新泉精舍 in Nanjing; and two White Deer Grotto Academy gazetteers, their supplement, and woodblocks.[114]

The third book list is found in the 1592 academy gazetteer.[115] This list contained all of the previously listed local gazetteers plus a new edition of the Jiangxi provincial gazetteer, three new prefectural gazetteers, four county gazetteers, and one regional gazetteer. The prefectural gazetteers were those of Nankang, the prefecture in which the White Deer Grotto Academy was located, and two from outside of Jiangxi.[116] The county gazetteers were those of Duchang 都昌, in Nankang Prefecture; two from southern Jiangxi; and one from Zhejiang.[117] The regional gazetteer covered the area around Ganzhou, in southern Jiangxi.

The fourth book list is found in the 1622 edition of the academy gazetteer, which was supplemented in the early Qing and contains materials up through 1657.[118] It contained all of the previous catalog's local gazetteers, but no new ones.[119] The number of gazetteers being produced temporarily slowed as the Ming collapsed, which might explain why no more were added.

Many Ming academy libraries, like most Confucian school libraries, had gazetteers only from their immediate surroundings.[120] Over the course of the Qing, local gazetteer collections in academies grew, and by the late Qing it was not uncommon for academies to have dozens of local gazetteers. For example, the 1846 *Yi shan shuyuan zhi* 嶧山書院志 (Mount Yi Academy Gazetteer) lists eighty-four Henan local gazetteers in the academy's collection.[121]

114.   Ibid., 430.

115.   Ibid., 4.

116.   There were two Taiping Prefectures in Ming China: one in Beizhili and one in Guangxi. The catalog does not indicate which Taiping Prefecture the local gazetteer came from.

117.   Li Chenguang, *Bailudong shuyuan gu zhi*, 510–11.

118.   It appears that part of the edition was printed in the Ming and the rest in the Qing Shunzhi era. Ibid., 4.

119.   Ibid., 998–99.

120.   *Yushan Shuyuan zhi*, 121.

121.   Mount Yi Academy was located in Kaifeng. The local gazetteers included three prefectural gazetteers, seven subprefectural gazetteers, and seventy-four county gazetteers.

After its publication in 1461 the *Da Ming yitongzhi* became one of the core titles in Confucian school libraries. It condensed information collected from local gazetteers from all Ming territories, and it certainly had the greatest circulation of any Ming work of this genre.[122] Many book lists note that it was issued 頒 to the school. Although originally published in 1461, it had multiple reprint editions, including those of the Palace Treasury 内府, the Fuzhou Prefecture Confucian School,[123] and commercial reprints in 1505, 1559, and 1588.[124] In the Hongzhi era (1488–1506) it was issued to schools.[125] Many scholarly families owned a copy of the *Da Ming yitongzhi*. A 1519 preface to the gazetteer of Cizhou, Beizhili, noted that it had already been in circulation for a long time, "all between the seas have it in their homes" 海内咸家藏, and people read it to learn about a place's old events, landscape, and philosophers without having to leave their homes or ask elders.[126] Its widespread distribution no doubt stimulated interest in local gazetteer compilation and reading, especially in schools. Its placement in Confucian schools may have contributed to teachers and students becoming involved in producing, collecting, and reading local gazetteers.

The *Da Ming yitongzhi* would not have been detailed enough for many readers. Its limited nature can be understood by comparing its coverage to that found in local gazetteers. In the *Da Ming yitongzhi*, Shaoxing Prefecture, Zhejiang, was covered by one chapter consisting of twenty-six folios, but the 1587 gazetteer of Shaoxing was fifty chapters with 1674 folios. Thus, the *Da Ming yitongzhi* was less than 2 percent as large as the prefectural gazetteer. It also did not cover key topics of interest to magistrates and local literati, such as population, taxes, and degree holders. Biographies were few. For example, in the "famous people" 人物 section for Shaoxing, there was not a single biography of a person from Shaoxing's Xinchang County (discussed in chapter 2), and only one biography of a Xinchang virtuous woman 列女. In contrast, the 1579 *Xinchang xian zhi* had entire chapters on local worthies and virtuous women. Because the *Da Ming yitongzhi* was so terse and by the mid sixteenth

122. For a discussion of works issued to school libraries, see Brook, "Edifying Knowledge," 103–5.

123. Zhou Hongzu, *Gujin shuke*, 28–30.

124. Ibid.; Xie Shuishun, *Fujian gudai keshu*, 314–15.

125. *Shouchang xian zhi*, 188.

126. *Cizhou zhi*, 775–76.

century so dated, it would have been only marginally useful except for some of its geographical sections.

The *Da Ming yitongzhi* was modeled on the *Huang Yuan da yitongzhi*, but this earlier work does not seem to have circulated widely. When completed in 1297, it was placed in the palace library, where according to the 1351 *Qi sheng* it was not accessible to society 書成藏之祕府世莫得而見焉.[127] There are few references to the *Huang Yuan da yitongzhi*, and compilers of the 1450 provincial gazetteer of Yunnan who wanted to use it could not because of its rarity.[128]

The Market for Used Gazetteers

Although there is no evidence of first-run gazetteers being sold in bookstores, used and antique ones were bought and sold in bookstores and directly. Cao Xuequan, in a preface to his 1623 *Da Ming yitong ming sheng zhi* 大明一統名勝志 (Comprehensive gazetteer of the famous sights of the Great Ming), explained how he gathered materials for the book over a number of years.[129] Cao collected local gazetteers and took notes on ones he did not have. He bought Nanzhili local gazetteers while stationed in Nanjing, and bought Hunan and Huguang local gazetteers from "heirs of local notables and gentry." Cao obtained Shandong, Zhejiang, and Jiangxi gazetteers from four provincial officials who had acquired them while serving in those provinces. He acquired more local gazetteers from the home of Zhang Mingfeng 張鳴鳳 of Guilin 桂林, Guangxi. Zhang had been demoted and transferred to Lizhou Garrison 利州衛, Sichuan, and collected local gazetteers from the places he passed through on the way to and from Sichuan. Like Zhang, Cao collected local gazetteers while traveling in the Southwest, and in this way got copies of Yunnan's provincial gazetteer and Guo Zizhang's 1604 *Qian ji* 黔記 (Record of Qian). On his way home to Houguan 侯官, Fujian in 1623, Cao passed through western Guangdong, where he met with two men, Yu Zifen 喻子奮 and Chen Youmei 陳有美, borrowed their local

---

127.   *Qi sheng*, 509.
128.   *Yunnan zhi*, 11.
129.   Cao Xuequan, *Da Ming yitong mingsheng*, 234–38.

gazetteers, and collected materials. At home in Fujian he was visited by Xie Zhaozhe, an official and gazetteer compiler, and from him obtained various local gazetteers, including Xie's *Dian lüe* 滇略 (Sketch of Yunnan).[130]

Some of Cao's gazetteers may have been purchased in bookstores. Although Cao wrote that he bought Nanzhili gazetteers while stationed in Nanjing, he did not say whether he bought them from individuals, institutions, or bookshops. There is, however, evidence of an antique gazetteer being sold in a Nanjing bookstore in the late Ming. In 1805 a Suzhou book collector, Qu Yong 瞿鏞, recorded the provenance of a 1365 edition of the *Qinchuan zhi*, a gazetteer of Suzhou:[131]

Townsman Yan had a copy of the Yuan dynasty printed edition and I traced it 影寫. In front it had five maps, which were missing in the two [reprint] editions published by the Jigu 及古 and Zhaokuang 照曠 [publishing houses].[132] The original edition had a handwritten postface by townsman Gong Liben 龔立本 (1572–1644), which said the following:[133]

This book was originally obtained by Shao Linwu 邵麟武 of the Ministry of War [Shao Mou 邵鰲, 1586 *jinshi*] from the Xingfu Temple 興福寺. One fascicle had been lost. I went to [Shao's home] to borrow and examine the [original], but Shao refused [to show it to me] and instead showed me a handwritten copy. People in town who were interested [in the gazetteer] copied the copy. After Shao died, the original edition came into the possession of the scholar Xu Taomei 許弢美. I again went to borrow and examine it and [found] that the incomplete edition was now complete. When I inquired, Xu [told me] he bought the missing fascicle when he chanced upon an incomplete copy in a Nanjing bookshop. Ahh! After three hundred years the separated swords of Yanping are reunited, it truly is not just chance.[134] Of old, Shao stored it like a jewel and today Xu gathered it up. Both deserve praise. I was moved and so record it.

130. For a biography of Xie Zhaozhe, see *DMB*, vol. 1, 546–50.

131. Qinchuan is another name from Changshu County, Jiangsu.

132. The Jiguge and Zhaokuangge were famous publishers in Changshu. *Suzhou fu zhi* (1883), 1345.

133. Gong Liben was a secretary in the Ministry of Punishments and a native of Changshu. Ibid., 1396.

134. The phrase "swords of Yanping" refers to the story from the *Jin shu* 晉書 (History of the Jin) about two great swords lost at Yanping Ford.

Qu Yong continued recounting the book's history:

> In the beginning of autumn of the Chongzhen *yisi* year (1629), Mr. Yan
> Chaoji 言朝楫 wrote a postface saying: "The *Qinchuan zhi* is kept in my
> home and all of the illustrations were complete. Suddenly, someone who
> had a need for it borrowed it, but when the day came that I asked for it
> back, several pages of illustrations were missing. I lamented this for a long
> time."[135]

Gong Liben and Yan Chaoji's postfaces show that in the late Ming, an
antique gazetteer was sold in a bookshop, found in a local temple, owned
by people in the county of publication, and circulated through borrowing and hand copying.

Conclusion

This chapter has shown that gazetteer compilers imagined their audiences
to include men and women, elite and common, local and nonlocal. Records of where gazetteers were kept and actual readings confirm the image
of an audience that was mostly officials and literati, but extended beyond
the elite, even prior to the sixteenth century and outside of the Jiangnan
core. Gazetteers compiled in response to orders of the court or superior
territorial administrations were often submitted as manuscripts while the
original was kept in the yamen. Another copy was often made for the
school. Manuscripts collected by the palace library and those held locally
were read by officials and copied by hand. Following submission of manuscripts, many compilers printed their gazetteers.

Newly printed gazetteers were distributed to government offices, local
schools, compilers, donors, and other interested people. Imprints were
provided to resident administrators, officials who passed through the locale, and others. After initial distribution, the blocks were stored, usually in the local yamen or Confucian school, but occasionally in private
homes, and published on demand. Steps were taken to protect the cut

---

135.   Qu Yong, *Tieqin tongjian*, 667–68.

blocks from loss. There is no evidence of newly published gazetteers being sold in bookstores or by itinerant book peddlers, but there was a market for old gazetteers. New gazetteers were noncommercial books acquired through official channels, mostly by officials and literati.

We now have an outline of the intended audience for gazetteers and actual distribution, but we do not yet know what people did with gazetteers. For this, we need to examine detailed records of actual readings, which we will do in chapter 7.

CHAPTER 7

Reading and Using Gazetteers

To understand the significance of local gazetteers as a genre, it is not enough to examine only the agendas in the compilers' minds and the signposts of their finished products. As Roger Chartier argues, we must look at "the way in which texts and printed works that convey them organize the prescribed reading" and " the collection of actual readings tracked down in individual confessions or reconstructed on the level of communities of readers—those 'interpretive communities' whose members share the same reading styles and the same strategies of interpretation."[1] This chapter explores questions of audience, going beyond authorial intent to examine who read gazetteers, what parts they read, and how they read them. Such reconstruction of gazetteer readings will allow further exploration of compilers' agendas and local gazetteers' significance in local and nonlocal societies.

Theorists look to various sources to understand how people create meaning in the act of reading. Gerard Genette analyzes a work's "paratext," including the prefaces, postfaces, layout, and commentaries that guide the reader's interpretation of the text.[2] Michel de Certeau emphasizes readers' creative responses to texts and their abilities to ignore authorial guidance and subvert intended meanings. Texts, he argues, have meaning only through their actualization by readers.[3] And thus, as

1. Chartier, "Texts, Printing, Readings," 157–58.
2. Genette, *Paratexts.*
3. de Certeau, *Practice of Everyday Life*, 170–71.

Roger Chartier said, we must look to "individual confessions" or to communities of readers. To reconstruct how contemporaries read gazetteers, we will examine paratext, readers' critiques of gazetteers, their comments on what they read, and other records of individual readings gathered from diaries, letters, legal records, gazetteer prefaces, literati writings, genealogies, and other sources.

Up to this point we have seen numerous examples of officials, teachers, students, and local literati working on gazetteers, and these were the core of gazetteer readership. But readership went further and included a wide range of local and nonlocal readers with various motivations and ways of reading. Some, as we saw in chapter 2, used local gazetteers in genealogical research. Others read them to gather evidence in support of lawsuits, ponder issues of local policy, or seek local information while traveling. Pleasure readers enjoyed records of and literature about local scenic and historic sites and persons, and authors on various topics collected gazetteers and used them as sources for their own writing. No doubt there were other types of readers as well. Explanations of authorial intent and compilation agendas must take account of these varied readers.

Anecdotes presented below will illustrate various ways in which particular individuals read and used gazetteers, but they cannot establish how frequently or widely they were read. However, as more texts from imperial China have been digitized in recent years, it has become easier to search for reading references and get some sense of the importance of particular texts in elite culture. Many, but not all, of the anecdotes discussed in this chapter were found by searching for gazetteer titles in two full-text, keyword-searchable databases, Scripta Sinica 漢籍電子文獻資料庫, a collection of approximately 688 important titles for sinological research, and the Siku quan shu 四庫全書, which contains 3,460 titles judged to be important by leaders of the late-eighteenth-century imperial project.[4] These databases contain key works of late imperial literati culture, but they omit many genres. Thus, although they are a good place to start reconstructing the significance of particular titles, they are only a beginning.

If one searches them for citations to the *Gusu zhi*, the 1506 gazetteer of Suzhou, Scripta Sinica yields 301 hits in thirty-five titles and Siku

4. New titles are being regularly added to Scripta Sinica as of 2013.

yields seventy-seven hits in thirty-eight titles, plus the full text of the *Gusu zhi*. Ming works that cited the *Gusu zhi* included gazetteers of mountains and higher administrative units, a medical text, a record of meritorious service to the state, biographical collections, collected works of authors, book catalogues, and historical works. Its inclusion in the Siku collection was a recognition of the gazetteer's significance as of the late eighteenth century.

But how do the seventy-seven citations of the *Gusu zhi* in the Siku database compare to those of other titles? Its citations were negligible compared to key classical works such as the *Lunyu* 論語 (Analects of Confucius), which appeared 18,061 times, and much fewer than commentaries on classical works, such as the *Daxue yanyi bu* 大學衍義補 (Supplement to the exposition on the great learning) (554 times). However, it did have nearly as many citations as the *Da Ming ling* (81); and more than some core titles held by Confucian school libraries, such as *Da Ming huidian* (62), *Wei shan yin zhi* 爲善陰騭 (The blessings of doing good secretly) (47), *Jiaomin bangwen* (36), and *Quan shan shu* 勸善書 (Exhortation to goodness) (27).[5] These figures suggest that the best-known Ming local gazetteers, although clearly not at the core of intellectual and literary activity that surrounded the classics and commentaries on them, nonetheless were read and cited by substantial numbers of literati. Most, however, had more limited readership of the types discussed below.

Sojourners' Readings of Gazetteers

In previous chapters we saw that resident administrators stationed outside their native places had access to gazetteers. But in order to characterize their level of interest in reading them, we must go deeper into how administrators used them. Peter Bol argued in his study of Song and Yuan gazetteers that officials had little interest in them. In support, Bol noted that it was often a century between gazetteer editions, there was little official impetus to keep them up-to-date, and in occasional

---

5.   For a list of core titles in Ming school libraries, see Brook, *The Chinese State*, 109.

comments that a gazetteer was lost, the loss was discovered only when the rare interested official asked for a copy.[6] By the mid Ming, however, gazetteers were of great interest to many officials, because more territories produced them and on the whole they were more up-to-date and had greater coverage than earlier gazetteers. An expectation grew that they would exist and be useful, and they became important vehicles for circulating local information. As discussed in chapter 1, the genre was universalized down to the county level only in the Ming; in the Song and Yuan, far fewer locales had gazetteers.[7] As the economy and literate population expanded over the course of the Ming, more gazetteers were printed and their circulation increased. Even in cases in which one hundred years passed between editions, gazetteers were, as we saw in chapter 3, living documents that were updated with supplemental blocks and handwritten additions between editions. Many lost Ming gazetteers were the hastily drafted early-Ming manuscripts produced in response to Hongwu, Yongle, and Jingtai-era edicts. Slapdash gazetteers summarizing yamen records would have had little appeal and were often ignored, but elaborate mid- and late-Ming gazetteers that were products of sustained efforts by knowledgeable officials and scholars were worth reading. As the length and scope of gazetteers expanded over the course of the Ming and Qing, they became more useful and interesting to readers. In the more decentralized regimes that followed the Southern Song localist turn, records of locales' participation in governance and Chinese culture took on added significance. Engaging with the locale was a major part of late imperial governance, and one way to do that was by reading gazetteers and using information found therein.

One way officials read local gazetteers was for background on the territories in which they were about to serve, or on arrival in a new post. Officials reported to the Ministry of Personnel for initial assignment and for reassignment after completing posts in the provinces, and this gave them opportunity to borrow gazetteers from friends and colleagues in the capital before leaving. Once informed of their next post, they could seek out officials who had been stationed there before, talk to them about their experiences, and ask for the gazetteer. Officials who began

6. Bol, "Rise of Local History," 47.
7. Huang Wei, *Fang zhi xue*, 176–84.

their careers in the provinces often took local gazetteers with them when promoted to capital posts. In 1258, when Hu Taichu was appointed prefect of Tingzhou, Fujian, his close friend warned him that it was distant, isolated, and hard to govern. Hu wanted to know more about Tingzhou and got the prefectural gazetteer from someone in the capital who had served there.[8] When Liu Zhu 劉鑄 was appointed magistrate of Zhangping, Fujian, in the spring of 1548, he was in his hometown of Xuancheng 宣城, Nanzhili, and said he "had no way of knowing in advance the affairs of Zhangping." But as he was packing and preparing to leave, a compiler of the newly published Zhangping gazetteer sent him a copy. He immediately read it, found it to be well organized and on point, but thought it needed an illustration of the county yamen. So soon after he arrived he ordered craftsmen to draw the yamen and cut a block for the illustration, which was added to the gazetteer in the fall of 1548.[9] The sharing of gazetteers was one way that information about locales circulated among officials and a way for officials to meet and bond with local elites.

In gazetteer prefaces, officials routinely claimed that the first thing they did after "getting down from their carriage" upon arriving in their new post was to ask for the local gazetteer. As discussed earlier, this claim evoked Zhu Xi's reading of the local gazetteer upon arriving in Nankang, Jiangxi, and highlighted the importance of gazetteers by tying them to this key figure of Confucian learning and governance.[10] Magistrate's manuals, a genre widely read among officials, reinforced this norm by advising newly arrived officials to read the locale's gazetteers. Huang Liuhong's 1694 *Fu hui quan shu* 福惠全書 (A complete book concerning happiness and benevolence) has a section, "reviewing the gazetteer" 覽志書, which states:

> A county's mountains, rivers, noted inhabitants, tribute, local products, large and small communities, shrines and temples, bridges, and so on, are all fully recorded in the local gazetteer. When first taking office in a locale, if you read the local gazetteer you will be able to know all of its

8.   Wang and Liu, *Yongle dadian fangzhi jiyi*, 1467.

9.   *Zhangping xian zhi*, 939–40.

10.   *Pengcheng zhi*, Song Ji preface; *Linying xian zhi*, preface to the 1448 edition; Zhu Xi, *Hui'an ji*, 7.1b; *Anxi xian zhi*, prefaces, 1b.

lands' elevations and critical passes, the amounts and rates of taxation, and the increase or decrease of its population and prosperity, and use this information to make correct decisions in administration.[11]

Many officials described reading the gazetteer upon arrival as their regular practice. Prefect Li Yi's preface to the 1300 *Nanfeng jun zhi* 南豐 郡志 (Jiangxi), states, "Wherever I have traveled as an official I have always obtained the gazetteer and read it."[12] A Fujian assistant surveillance commissioner noted in his preface to the 1351 *Xian xi zhi* 仙溪志 (Fujian) that whenever he traveled the first thing he did upon arriving in a prefectural or county seat was to look for the gazetteer to help him understand the locale. Although one may suspect hyperbole in gazetteer prefaces, there are clear cases of magistrates who were excited to read high-quality local gazetteers upon arrival in a new locale. When Zhang Lie 張烈 first heard in the winter of 1538–39 that he would become prefect of Sinan, Guizhou, on the southwestern border, he was alarmed. He worried about how he would govern an isolated region, full of non-Chinese people, far from other scholar officials. In the three months between hearing of his assignment and leaving for Sinan, he researched border governance and looked for, but did not find, a Sinan gazetteer. In the spring of 1539 he reluctantly set out for Guizhou. After a long journey Prefect Zhang assumed office on July 3, 1539, and as he was receiving visitors in the yamen's reception hall noticed wooden crates along the wall, which held the 1537 Sinan gazetteer edited by Tian Rucheng 田汝成, a prominent scholar official. He quickly got an imprint from the private secretaries' office 幕廳. When he picked it up and looked at it, he "could not put it down nor control his happiness and satisfaction." His first few days in office were extremely busy, so he read the gazetteer quickly, but he did not have enough free time to delve deeply. After visiting the Confucian school on the third day, he set out for the provincial capital, a journey of approximately 250 kilometers. He took the gazetteer with him in the sedan chair, where he "thoroughly read and deeply savored it" along the way.[13]

11. Huang Liuhong, *Fuhui quanshu*, 3.12b–13a.
12. Zhang Guoggan, *Zhongguo gu fangzhi kao*, 561.
13. *Sinan fu zhi*, Zhang Lie postface, 2a–3a.

Many magistrates wrote that gazetteers were meant as reference books for future officials.[14] The kinds of things that officials read can be seen in the 1518 gazetteer of Ruizhou, Jiangxi. The prefect wrote that when he arrived he knew nothing about Ruizhou's "territory, distances between places, lands, etc." and so looked for the local gazetteer, which he obtained from a commoner's home.[15] In the 1530 gazetteer of Tongzhou 通州, Nanzhili, the vice magistrate complained that when he first arrived, he wanted to learn about the region's past, but there was no local gazetteer.[16] When a gazetteer was available, it could give a new arrival a quick overview of the locale's topography, history, transportation, institutions, products, water system, villages, elite families, and other topics that, unlike the tax and population records, were not available or readily accessible in yamen files.

Effective governance required attaining a basic knowledge of the territory in which an official served, and gazetteers were linguistic bridges in a polyglot state. Due to the law of avoidance, resident administrators were nonlocal people, many of whom could not speak the local Chinese dialect, much less any non-Chinese languages in their jurisdiction. When a magistrate or Confucian school instructor first arrived, his ability to learn about the area would be constrained by differences in spoken language. Most could converse easily and in depth with only a limited number of yamen functionaries, merchants, retired officials, teachers, and students who had learned Mandarin, the spoken language of officials. Among those who knew Mandarin, facility with it was likely limited, except for those who traveled regularly or had served in government for an extended period. There was no television, Internet, or radio to reinforce official pronunciation; only rhyme dictionaries, such as the *Hongwu zhengyun* 洪武正韻 (Correct rhymes of the Hongwu Era), rhyme tables, and conversations with other speakers.[17] The written language of gazetteers, in contrast, was understood by literate people throughout the empire, and it would have been easier for a magistrate to converse with locals once he had seen in written form the names of prominent local

---

14. *Longqing zhi*, postface, 1b.
15. *Ruizhou fu zhi*, 571.
16. *Tongzhou zhi*, 683.
17. Wilkinson, *Chinese History: A New Manual*, 28.

families, places, and things. It gave him direct access to local information unmediated by interpreters and local staff with unknown agendas. As the magistrate of Yizhou, Beizhili, explained in 1502, "When scholar-gentry first arrive, they necessarily rely on the gazetteer."[18]

Once familiar with the territory, a magistrate might consult a gazetteer before taking certain types of administrative actions. Hanlin academician Liu Duan 劉端 stressed the importance of local gazetteers to administration, saying that from them one could know what to maintain and what to discard.[19] Managing the ritual landscape was one of the magistrate's many duties and he looked to the gazetteer for documentation of the official sacrifices, usually in sections titled "sacrificial canon" 祀典 or "record of sacrifices" 祀志. Gazetteers also documented approved Buddhist and Daoist institutions in separate sections, and sometimes described heterodox shrines as well.[20] If a magistrate wanted to add to the official sacrifices, he could petition for permission to build a new shrine or change an existing shrine's status.[21] For a new shrine to a local worthy, he would need to do historical research on the person to be venerated and gazetteers were important sources. In the mid-sixteenth century, the magistrate of Yingshan 應山, Huguang, wanted to build a shrine to six famous local officials. In his petition to the provincial government, the magistrate wrote that the officials were documented in the *Da Ming yitong zhi* and the gazetteers of Yingshan County's superior territories, Suizhou 隨州 and De'an 德安.[22] The magistrate's gazetteer research formed the basis of his argument that a shrine was appropriate and his superiors credited his argument and granted permission.

In a 1600 petition to the military defense circuit vice commissioner, the magistrate of Dacheng 大成, Beizhili, used the county gazetteer to support his argument that a local temple to Lü Shang 呂尚, the *Taigong miao* 太公廟, should be rebuilt and included in the official sacrifices.

18. *Yizhou zhi*, postface, 1a.

19. Ibid., prefaces, 3a.

20. For more on the categorization of religious institutions in Ming China, see Taylor, "Official Altars," 93–125.

21. *Dacheng xian zhi*, 543.

22. The magistrate also consulted one official's biography in the Song dynastic history, and the record of another from a Yuan dynasty stele. *Yingshan xian zhi* (1540), *juan xia*, 40b–45a.

Magistrate Ren Yanfen 任彥棻 explained that in Ziya Village 子牙鎮 there was a structure called "Taigong's Fishing Platform" and "Ziya" was the style name of Lü Shang, who became famous when King Wen of Zhou (b. twelfth-century BCE) recognized him as a great man by watching him fish. Magistrate Ren asked villagers about Lü Shang's connection to Ziya Village, and they all said he had once lived there. The magistrate then checked the story of Lü Shang in *Mengzi*, the canonical Confucian text, which said that Lü hid from the evil King Zhou 紂 of Shang by living on the eastern seacoast. Ren did further research in the county gazetteer and found two shrines associated with Lü. Based on this evidence, Ren's petition was approved.[23]

Memorials to the court also cited gazetteers. Around 1262–64, Wang Su 王橚, the magistrate of Chenzhou 郴州 (modern Hunan), used the local gazetteer and a Tang dynasty geographical text, the *Shi dao zhi* 十道志 (Record of the ten circuits), to support his memorial arguing for the closure of iron mines and smelters in the Chenzhou region. Wang drew from the texts to recount centuries of problems caused by local mining. He argued that Chenzhou's lands were infertile and people could barely find enough to eat without the mining, but every time the mines and smelters were opened, thousands of migrant laborers came to Chenzhou and drove up the price of food. Furthermore, the mine openings and shafts destroyed graves, and polluted runoff from the smelting process damaged fields. All of this led to banditry and lawsuits. He further noted that the amount of iron and tin obtained was small, and when weighed against the problems caused, it was not worth the trouble.[24]

Benjamin Elman argued that there was a link between military needs and gazetteers in the Ming-Qing period, but he did not develop the point in detail.[25] Analysis of memorials regarding military affairs shows that local gazetteers were used in drafting, even in the Song dynasty. In 1257 Li Zengbo 李曾伯 was sent to Jingjiang Prefecture 靜江府 (modern Guilin, Guangxi) to investigate defensive preparations for the anticipated Mongol invasion. In a memorial written circa 1259 Li told

---

23. *Dacheng xian zhi*, 552–55.

24. Wang Su, "Feng tie ye shu" 封鐵冶疏 (memorial to close iron smelters), in *Chenzhou zhi*, 11.16b–18a.

25. Elman, "Geographical Research."

how he was trying to get his spies into the Dali Kingdom to determine the number of Mongol troops facing them. Li then quoted from the Jingjiang gazetteer for distances between Chinese towns and the Dali capital, making the point that while many of those dispatched could make it to Temo 特磨 near the border with Dali, few could make it to the capital. Li submitted the gazetteer volume on geography with his memorial.[26]

Limited use of gazetteers in military planning likely continued throughout the late imperial period. In a preface to the 1549 gazetteer of Guanping 廣平, Beizhili, the local commander praised the gazetteer's usefulness for the military, while also acknowledging that gazetteers were thought of as serving the civilian government: "Although I am foolish, when I examine the prefectural gazetteer's lands and territories section, I see the firmness of the prefecture's walls and moats. When I examine its mountains and rivers section, I see the defensibility of its passes. It has details on the military fields and horse administration. Although this compilation is considered a civil project, its strength is that it does not forget the military. Indeed it is fortunate that the gazetteer's completion has some benefit for military preparation."[27]

Because administrators read gazetteers when arriving at a new post, they became vehicles for both current administrators and locals to transmit policy ideas to future administrators. An administrator usually served in one location for only three or six years before transferring to another post, and gazetteers were one of the only ways for him to influence his successor's views on local issues. After Di Sibin 狄斯彬 (1547 *jinshi*) retired, he compiled an unofficial gazetteer of Liyang 溧陽 County, Yingtian Prefecture, Nanzhili, in which he criticized the "unequal and multiple taxation" of Liyang. In 1575 Yingtian prefect Wang Zongyi 汪宗伊 read Di's gazetteer and submitted a memorial to the court requesting a reduction in Liyang's annual tax quota, and the elimination of one entire category of monetary tax along with excess labor taxes. He further asked that these changes be printed in the tax registers to inform all government offices, and recorded in the prefectural gazetteer.[28] Wang's memorial led to a

---

26. Li Zengbo, *Kezhai zagao*, 9.2b–6b.
27. *Guangping fu zhi*, prefaces, last page (unpaginated).
28. Gu Qiyuan, *Kezuo zhui yu*, 290.

6,300-silver-tael reduction in the county's tax quota, and as a result a shrine was built to venerate Di Sibin as a "local worthy."[29] In a preface to the 1570 gazetteer of Ruichang 瑞昌, Jiangxi, the prefect of Ruichang's superior prefecture, Jiujiang, tried to influence opinion on local tax policy, or at least express sympathy for locals:

> The county's cultivatable lands are not extensive, yet the three garrisons of Jiujiang, Nanchang, and Qizhou have concentrated their military fields therein. The military has abundance while the civilians have scarcity. One cannot but indignantly think, is anyone taking care of them? The county has not gotten any bigger than before, yet the taxes and labor service are rapidly multiplying; I do not know how in the future the people will be able to bear the burden. One cannot but sadly think, is anyone true to them? Although the county's lands are remote, the silver sent annually to Jiujiang is counted in the thousands. This is Ruichang feeding Jiujiang. How can we call a place remote and then punish it without end?[30]

Local elites' use of gazetteers as sites for advocacy can be seen in a letter written circa 1514 from one native of Yingtian Prefecture, Gu Lin, to another, Chen Yi 陳沂 (1469–1538). Gu wrote that he had heard that Yingtian prefect Bai Qi had asked Chen to compile the prefectural gazetteer. After first discussing various issues related to gazetteer compilation, Gu argued that the Mingdao Academy and Liyang Dikes had been "important to human livelihood and morality," and said, "You must investigate their traces and ask Master Bai to rebuild them."[31] Although, as discussed in chapter 1, Chen Yi's Yingtian gazetteer was not finished until the Zhengde Emperor's southern tour in 1519–20 and is no longer extant, his 1535 gazetteer of Nanzhili, Yingtian's superior territorial unit, survives. From it we can tell that Chen Yi agreed to Gu Lin's request. Chen's gazetteer recorded the Mingdao Academy's association with the great Confucian philosopher Cheng Hao 程灝, that it went to ruin in the Yuan, and that it was rebuilt early in the Jiajing era (1522–66), shortly

29. *Liyang xian zhi, huanji* section.
30. *Ruichang xian zhi*, 1b–2a.
31. Gu Lin, "Fu Chen Lunan" 復陳魯南 (Response to Chen Lunan), in *Gu Huayu ji*, 9.1a–2b.

after the gazetteer for the Zhengde Emperor was completed.[32] The gazetteer entry on the Liyang Dikes cited a memorial by the renowned Su
Shi (1037–1101), which said that there had been five dikes since ancient
times regulating the area's rivers, and then explained that, "later, a merchant who sold wood from Zhejiang tricked an official into removing
the dikes because they blocked his route. Now, when the waters rise,
the Jing Stream from Xuanxing flows into the region. Disastrous flooding has occurred ever since."[33] Chen used the gazetteer to frame Lower
Yangzi water control as a clash between the merchant's special interest
and society's general good. Although it is unclear whether Chen's record influenced subsequent water control policy, Gu and Chen at least
hoped that it would. In this case, one local wrote to another to ask him
to document a water control problem in the gazetteer. The recipient
succinctly described in the gazetteer the cause of the area's flooding,
creating a "historical fact" that both hoped would lead to action on the
part of future officials. The correspondents saw the gazetteer as a strategic tool by which locals could lay groundwork for persuading officials
to change policies. Local elites who participated in gazetteer compilations had opportunities to express their own and others' views on local
policy to the administrator and to get their ideas into the text. After the
original administrator rotated out and a new administrator took office,
the old gazetteer could serve as a point of departure and framing of
discussions between the new administrator and members of the local
elite. Gazetteers were not the primary vehicles of elite influence on
magistrates—retired officials and others tried to shape policy by writing letters to magistrates and meeting with them—but when an issue
could not be favorably resolved immediately, raising the issue in a gazetteer enhanced the likelihood of future consideration. A gazetteer was
most useful when an issue had an important historical component.
From the above examples we can see that gazetteers were important
vehicles for transmitting certain types of local knowledge to the central
government and its officials, and disseminating information within
local societies.

32. *Nanji zhi*, 5.8b.
33. Ibid., 4.19a. For more on the Five Dikes of Liyang, see Gui Youguang, *Sanwu shuili lu, juan* 2.

The Liyang Dikes case, along with a water rights case from Shangyu, Zhejiang, discussed later in this chapter, show that there were dual record-keeping systems for local governments. The tax rate change in Liyang and the water rights decision in Shangyu were recorded in both the ya-men files and the gazetteer. The tax registers and case files in the yamen were for internal use, while the gazetteer that circulated among the local people, sojourning officials, in provincial offices, and around the country, was public. Gazetteers provided a means for local people and provincial officials to know basic tax, land, and other local information at a glance, and in some situations this could act as a restraint on corrupt officials and local bullies. Putting such records in the gazetteer provided future magistrates with both a way to cross-check internal records if they suspected tampering, and a backup for records that could be lost to war, corruption, or natural disaster.

In a case from 1600, the magistrate of Gutian, Fujian, discovered encroachment on school lands when he read the gazetteer's record of a land swap between the county government and a landowner a century earlier.[34] In 1489, after Lu Rong 陸容 was appointed Zhejiang provincial administration vice commissioner, he consulted gazetteers while investigating suspected corruption.[35] He noticed that the surveillance commission and administration commission branch offices in each local administrative seat were usually the same size, but in some locales the surveillance commission offices were spacious and ornate, while the administration commission offices were cramped and spare. He was suspicious but upon reading the local gazetteers discovered a valid reason for the variation: the grand surveillance commission yamens had been built in the Hongwu era, the founding period of the Ming dynasty, with the assumption that imperial censors would be staying in them while on inspection trips. This required appropriate grandeur. Most of the branch administration commission offices, in contrast, were built a half-century later on lands cut from the preexisting compounds, which meant the new buildings had to be smaller.[36] In the above cases, gazetteers were sources of records used in investigating cases with historical elements.

34. *Gutian xian zhi*, 8.6b.
35. *Ming Shilu, Xiaozong shilu*, 487.
36. Lu Rong, *Shuyuan za ji*, 10.126.

In addition to resident and provincial administrators, touring inspection officials used gazetteers in their work. In chapter 6 we noted one magistrate's statement that according to precedent, he was expected to present a copy of the local gazetteer whenever a surveillance official came to town, but he did not explain what the officials did with the presented gazetteers. Regional inspectors did annual on-site evaluations of magistrates, and gazetteers could affect their images. Reputation was especially important in making assessments that could change a magistrate's career.[37] A gazetteer documenting major accomplishments could make a good first impression, and one showing the intractability of a local problem could help deflect blame for failure to resolve it. When Xiang Tingji 項廷吉, the regional inspector of four prefectures in the capital region, arrived in Guangping, Beizhili, on an inspection trip in 1549, the prefect presented the gazetteer. Subsequently Xiang wrote a preface to it explaining that everywhere he went, the first thing he did was ask for the gazetteer, because he valued them. He continued on to argue that gazetteers documented benevolent government in a particular locale.[38] Thus, for magistrates and prefects the gazetteer had the potential to reveal their benevolence to inspectors before they began their careful examinations of tax records, court files, and other daily business. Similarly, the gazetteer could bolster an administrator's personnel file used in evaluating him for new a post.

The resident administrators discussed above were sojourners, long-term travelers who spent several years in a given location and needed a detailed understanding of it. Late imperial China also had other types of sojourners, domestic and foreign, such as monks, merchants, and envoys from foreign lands, some of whom read or collected Chinese local gazetteers. We have already seen records of gazetteers found in Buddhist monasteries. There also is evidence that Jesuit missionaries read them, most likely to familiarize themselves with the local areas and to make maps. A 1617 inventory of items in the Jesuit residence in Nanjing included the 1598 gazetteer of Jiangning, one of Nanjing's two urban counties.[39] Ma Yong argues that the Jesuit Martino Martini's famous atlas of

37. Nimick, *Local Administration*, 111–13; Hucker, *The Censorial System*, 66–107.
38. *Guangping fu zhi*, prefaces, 4a.
39. Dudink, "Inventories," 144–45.

China, *Novus atlas Sinensis*, published in 1655, was "undoubtedly" based on local gazetteers.[40] The Jesuits were not the only foreigners to acquire gazetteers. In 1539 the Japanese monk Sakugen was given the gazetteer of Mount Jiuhua 九華, a major Buddhist mountain approximately 350 kilometers west of Ningbo, while leading a two-year trade mission to China on behalf of Lord Ōuchi, and hundreds of gazetteers were shipped to Japan in the late 1600s and early 1700s.[41] Koreans published their own gazetteers, such as the 1608 Yŏngga chi 永嘉誌, a gazetteer of Andong Prefecture, as did Vietnamese, turning the gazetteer genre into an East Asia-wide phenomenon.[42]

Local Gazetteers and Travelers

Up to this point we have been examining only sojourners, but have left out travelers on the road. Local gazetteers were in important respects a form of travel writing. Examining how travelers used gazetteers reveals them as key nodes for acquiring local information. Travelers were interested in many topics covered in local gazetteers, such as maps, distances between towns, descriptions of scenic and historic sites, and collected writings related to those sites. Travel in late imperial China was considered a form of self-cultivation, and many literati did at least some travel writing. Sightseeing for scholars included the writing of poems, making diary entries, and writing records of their trips for exchange with friends or for publication. Sometimes literati writings were cut directly into rocks or stelae at scenic sites. Richard Strassberg has argued that such "textualizing of the landscape" was one way a place became significant and was mapped onto an itinerary for other travelers and served to bring the sites within the Chinese world order.[43] A significant portion of most gazetteers consisted of poems and records of scenic sites composed by both locals and nonlocals. Local gazetteers condensed these writings as

40. Ma Yong, "Martino Martini's Activity," 258.
41. Makita Tairyō, *Sakugen nyūminki no kenkyū*, vol. 2, 75, 166; Ba Zhaoxiang, *Zhongguo difangzhi liubo Riben*.
42. See, e.g., *Yŏngga chi*; *Thành chương huyện chí*.
43. Strassberg, *Inscribed Landscapes*, 6.

well as transcriptions of the "textualized landscape" into a single book, thereby allowing even those who could not physically travel to a site to participate in cultural processes connected to it. For those who could make the journey, reading the local gazetteer and perhaps adding to the writings associated with the site enhanced their experience and knowledge of the empire.

Travel and travel writing were not new in the late imperial period; officials, monks, pilgrims, merchants, soldiers, and others had been making their way across China for centuries, and many wrote accounts of their travels. Travel diaries have existed at least since Ma Dibo's *Fengshan ji* 封禪記 (A record of feng and shan sacrifices), written in 56 CE.[44] The Six Dynasties period (222–589) saw the rise of geographical accounts written by Buddhist monks who journeyed to Central Asia and India. Fa Xian's 法顯 *Fo guo ji* 佛國記 (Record of Buddhist states), written in 416, is one of the earliest examples. Strassberg argues that such accounts were intended as intelligence for the ruler and guidebooks for later travelers, but travel writing was not a central part of Chinese literature until it emerged as an independent genre in the thirteenth and fourteenth centuries.[45]

A surge of interest in geography and tourism in the mid Ming provided a stimulus to gazetteer production and led to the creation of many records of how explorers, travelers, and readers of travel writing responded to gazetteers. One area where tourism blossomed in the late sixteenth and early seventeenth centuries was Zhejiang. Liping Wang argued that Hangzhou sightseeing grew after the threat of pirate raids lessened in the mid-1560s and that there was a change in the nature of sightseeing. In earlier times officials and students saw the sights when they came to Hangzhou on official business or to take examinations, but late-Ming literati took trips solely for sightseeing.[46] Hangzhou was only one of many late-Ming Zhejiang tourist destinations. In eastern Zhejiang, travelers such as Xu Xiake 徐霞客 and Wang Shixing 王士性 toured and wrote about their trips to Mount Tiantai and Xinchang County.[47]

---

44. Ibid., 23.
45. Ibid., 9, 32–33.
46. Wang Liping, "Paradise for Sale," 33, 42.
47. Wang Shixing, *Wu yue you cao*, 84.

The ways in which literati toured is important to understanding the connection between tourism and gazetteer production. According to Wang, for late-Ming literati "the act of sightseeing had always been much more than a physical movement and momentary aesthetic experience. Writing was a crucial part of sightseeing and made this kind of activity an important element of their participation in, and production of, elite culture."[48] In the words of Richard Strassberg, "By applying the patterns of the classical language, writers symbolically claimed unknown or marginal places, transforming their 'otherness' and bringing them within the Chinese world order."[49] Literati travel stimulated gazetteer compilation because gazetteers were key sources of geographical knowledge and tied national cultural processes to individual locales.

Travel diaries show that many travelers consulted local gazetteers while on the road and provide details on how they were used. Travelers could borrow a copy, buy one while traveling, or bring one from home. An education official in Xuzhou, Nanzhili, wrote in 1441 that "everyone who enters Xuzhou asks to see the gazetteer."[50] Educated travelers approached officials for this purpose. The magistrate of Nankang, Jiangxi, wrote in a preface to the 1555 gazetteer, "Person after person who passes through [Nankang], coming from or going to the Nanjing National University for study or to take the exams, sees the surrounding beauty of Nankang's mountains and rivers and the flourishing of its population, asks for the local gazetteer, and reads it."[51]

Borrowing could be for on-site reading, to take notes, copy sections, or take on a sightseeing trip, or even to prepare a lecture. While traveling in the lower Yangzi Delta in the mid-1500s, renowned scholar Zhan Ruoshui 湛若水 stopped at the Yangzhou Confucian school. There he lectured to local teachers and students on the significance of Confucius' saying "A gentleman who lacks gravity does not inspire awe" 君子不重則不威.[52] He introduced his concluding point by quoting the following characterization of Yangzhou from the prefectural gazetteer: "Light and

48. Wang Liping, "Paradise for Sale," 45.
49. Strassberg, *Inscribed Landscapes*, 6.
50. *Pengcheng zhi*, Song Ji preface.
51. *Nankang xian zhi*, 1229.
52. The translation is that of D. C. Lau, *Confucius: The Analects*, 60 (bk. 1: 8).

frivolous are its local customs, thus it is named 'Gossamer Region'—Yangzhou." Zhan then stressed that "gravitas" was the treatment for the disease of frivolity.[53]

Some travelers bought gazetteers while traveling. Ming China's most famous traveler, Xu Xiake, did this while in Xundian Prefecture, Yunnan, in 1638 and recorded it in his diary:

> I first wanted to take a walk and went into to the prefectural yamen to look at the area's maps. To the left of the gate as I exited was a shop with two Confucian scholars inside. I asked them whether there were woodblocks from which I could print maps and gazetteers. They responded that it was not possible. I did not leave and eventually they said, "There is an unbound imprint in a home outside the city walls." They asked for money in the amount of 400 *qian*. Once I had given them more than half the money they said, "You must wait until tomorrow morning to get it." And so I had to wait.[54]

When Xu got the gazetteer the next day, he was unhappy because it had mostly the same materials on the locale as the *Da Ming yitong zhi* and was incomplete. Even though some parts were newly added, he decided to return it to the sellers.

In 1513 Du Mu 都穆 (1459–1527), a director in the Ministry of Rites, traveled on official business from Beijing to the Princely Establishment of Qing 慶蕃 in Ningxia. His travel diary reveals that he got local gazetteers in government offices and from local officials and students as he traveled, and used them to learn about the history, geography, and culture of the places through which he passed. After returning to Beijing, he used notes he took on local gazetteers during his trip in writing his book, *You mingshan ji* 遊名山記 (Records of travels to famous mountains).[55] By examining Du Mu and how he used local gazetteers both during and after the trip, we can see local gazetteers as critical nodes in Chinese cultural production.

53. Zhan Ruoshui, *Quanweng da quan ji*, 12.17a–b.
54. Xu Hongzu, *Xu Xiake youji*, 6.42b.
55. Du Mu, *You mingshan ji*.

Du Mu left Beijing for Ningxia in May 1513, traveling overland southwest toward the Yellow River (map 7.1).[56] When he arrived in Neiqiu 內丘, about 300 kilometers southwest of Beijing, the county school's assistant instructor, Chi Lin 池鱗, came to visit him and said that he had compiled the local gazetteer.[57] Du asked Chi about the county's ancient sites, and Chi used what he had learned from the project to inform Du about famous natives and a shrine on top of Que Mountain 鵲山, about 60 *li* west of town, where thousands of locals gathered annually to pray and donate money to maintain the shrine (collected by a county official at the end of the event). From this meeting we can see that compiling the local gazetteer was a way for Chi to learn about the local society, history, religion, and governance of a place he was temporarily posted. Sharing it provided Chi a way to bond with a traveling official. For Du Mu, discussing the local gazetteer was a way to learn about this particular locale, incorporate it into his imagination of the Ming state, and make a personal connection.

Du left Neiqiu and traveled on to Huojia 獲嘉 in northern Henan. There he took a midday rest in the censor's office, which happened to be close to the ruins of a structure called the Comb and Makeup Tower 梳粧臺.[58] Someone told Du that it had been built by the last king of the Shang dynasty, King Zhou, to use while traveling. The informant also said it was where King Zhou's beloved consort Da Yi 妲己 combed her hair and made up her face, hence the name. Du Mu wrote in his diary that he initially did not believe the story but confirmed it by obtaining and reading the county gazetteer. For Du, the gazetteer was a place to look for an authoritative presentation of local history.

Further on, Du arrived in Xiazhou 陝州, Henan, where he met with assistant censor Yin Wenji 殷文濟.[59] They had lunch together and in the evening went to look at two iron statues beneath the city wall's lookout tower. Xiazhou magistrate Yan Ruhuan 顏如環 accompanied them on their walk and said, "The departmental gazetteer has an inscription regarding the iron men. It tells the story thus. . . ." Yan knew what the

56.   Du Mu, *Shi xi ri ji*, 7.
57.   Ibid., 17.
58.   Ibid., 27.
59.   Ibid., 36–37.

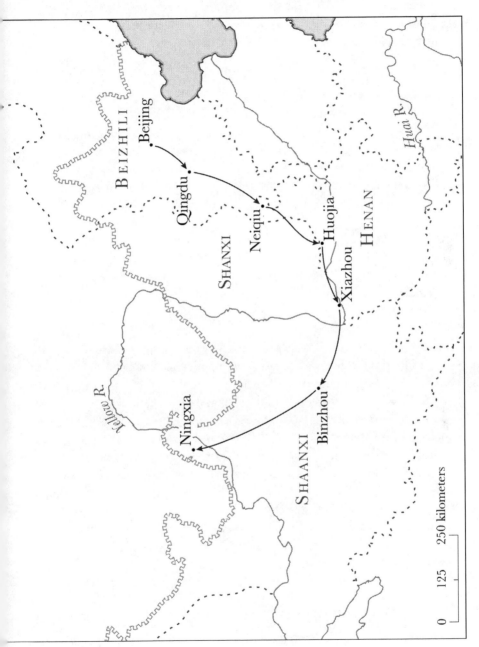

MAP 7.1 Du Mu's trip to Ningxia

local gazetteer said because he had compiled it, and gave Du a copy.[60] Du did not have time to go to other Xiazhou sites on the outbound leg of his trip, but on the way back from Ningxia, he visited Whetstone Pillar 砥柱, a famous rock outcropping in the Yellow River, and consulted the gazetteer for information on it.[61] Later Du wrote a colophon on his copy, praising the quality of the local gazetteer and of Magistrate Yan's administration.[62]

Continuing on from Xiazhou toward Ningxia, Du came to Binzhou 邠州, Shaanxi, northwest of Xi'an.[63] The next day Binzhou magistrate Qi Ning 齊寧 invited Du to travel to the Stone Dragon Whirlpool 石龍 渦. They ate breakfast and left with two local students, Liu Cheng 劉澄 and Liu Rudao 劉儒道. The four men drank together below the Five Dragon Spirits Shrine 五龍神祠. Du Mu dug through piles of broken stones and found one inscribed in the year 1213 with two poems written by Zhang Wei 張瑋, an assistant to a Jin dynasty military commissioner. The travelers checked the gazetteer to see if the poems were recorded therein, but they were not.

Although Du Mu traveled along a narrow road from one government office, school, and postal station to the next, the local gazetteers in conjunction with side trips helped him flesh out his knowledge of the surrounding areas. Soon after returning to Beijing, Du published his Ningxia travel diary, and two years later he published *You mingshan ji*, which consists of short pieces describing mountains he visited on trips to Ningxia and other places. Du's records drew heavily from the local gazetteers he consulted and collected while traveling and show how local information was taken into works that became national in scope.

Du Mu's encounters with local gazetteers were not unusual, especially for traveling officials. When Tan Xisi 譚希思, assistant prefect of Shuntian in the late-sixteenth century, climbed Mount Langya in neighboring Chuzhou, he drank wine at the Old Drunkard's Pavilion 醉翁亭, made famous by Ouyang Xiu's essay, then read the Chuzhou gazetteer for more on the famous literati who had also visited.[64] Another regular reader

60. Du Mu, *Nanhao jushi wen ba*, 2020.
61. Du Mu, *You mingshan ji*, 1.7.
62. Du Mu, *Nanhao jushi wen ba*, 2020.
63. Du Mu, *You mingshan ji*, 56–58.
64. *Shuntian fu zhi*, 4.

of local gazetteers was Xu Xiake, mentioned above, who was not an official. On a journey around Lake Dian 滇池, Yunnan, in 1638, Xu lodged in
the yamen of Jinning Subprefecture while waiting for the weather to
clear.[65] There he spent parts of several days reading the Jinning gazetteer
and taking notes on Jinning's historical territory, the names and location
of rivers, and various aspects of local history.[66] While traveling again in
Jinning the following year, Xu recorded that "the assistant regional commander ordered the doorman to bring the subprefectural gazetteer."[67]
Xu's experience shows that in some cases a person who was not in government service could nevertheless enjoy a yamen's hospitality. Although Xu
Xiake was not an official, he was well known and presumably could get
letters of introduction from official friends to help him gain entrance.
Perhaps not just any person could knock on the yamen door and ask for
the local gazetteer, but some certainly could.

Xu Xiake's diary also records that he carried at least some volumes
of the *Da Ming yitongzhi* with him as he traveled. That would be appropriate for a person traveling long distances because it covered more
territory, although in much less depth, than local gazetteers, and came
in separate volumes, not all which would have been necessary to carry
on a given trip.

Xu's diary not only reveals how he got access to gazetteers, it also
shows how he used them. As Xu traveled, he compared gazetteer accounts
to his direct impressions of mountains, rivers, and structures; used gazetteers as guidebooks to historic and scenic sights; and used entries on
local sites as the basis for discussions with people residing in the area.
For example, while traveling in Jinning in 1638, Xu consulted the *Da
Ming yitongzhi* about a site he was visiting.[68] Xu wrote:

> After eating I went out the west gate with Huang Yishui 黄沂水. . . . To
> the northwest is the Lady Minghui Temple 明惠夫人廟. The temple is for
> worshipping the daughter of Jinning Subprefecture Magistrate Li Yi 李毅.
> The Lady's merit can be seen in the *Da Ming yitongzhi*, which records a

65. Entry for the tenth month of the Chongzhen *wuyin* year.
66. Xu Hongzu, *Xu Xiake youji*, vol. 4, 4–9.
67. Ibid., vol. 5, 70.
68. *Da Ming yitongzhi*, 5270.

Yuan dynasty stele inscription. The first section of the stele says: "The Lady was named Yang Xiuniang 楊秀娘. She was Li Yi's daughter, and thus she was called Girl Li. But she was surnamed Yang; wasn't this a serious error? Could it be that the Lady's husband was surnamed Yang?"

Xu Xiake commented, saying: "But the *Da Ming yitongzhi* does not explain further. People say that the flesh of her body is still inside and that it has been lacquered, and thus, [the corpse] is twice as big as a person. I did not believe it. Yishui explained that in earlier years rats damaged her foot, exposing the bone [and that was why she was lacquered]. This is not an unreasonable [explanation]."

Xu's diary entry shows that he used the *Da Ming yitongzhi* as a basis for discussing the temple and its history with his traveling companion. He obtained background information from it, and then discussed the site in light of local knowledge. Xu then extended the dialogue between the *Da Ming yitongzhi*, himself, and Huang by writing about it in his diary. This was a common way for literati to use gazetteers.

Some travelers both read and responded in writing to gazetteers as they traveled. In the Ming Hongwu era (1368–98), Cheng Liben 程立本 was an official sent to pacify the "100 barbarian tribes" of the Southwest. When he stopped in Lijiang 麗江, Vice Prefect Zhang Zhu 張矞 showed him Fan Chuo's 樊綽 *Yunnan zhi* 雲南志 (Record of Yunnan). Although Cheng criticized the ninth-century book's quality, he nevertheless read it and even wrote a poem mentioning it:

Lancang (Mekong) River
Fan's *Yunnan zhi* I once did see,
Now into the Lancang my boat does go.
Mountains from the Ailao stretching north
Waters like the Ruoshui flowing south
A country of dullards—most are scoundrels
Barbarians, livestock in human clothes
Order obtained, I look back from on high
Range upon range, where is civilization?[69]

69.   Cheng Liben, *Xunyin ji*, 1.21b, 3.1a–3b. Writing poetry in response to reading a gazetteer was not unusual in late imperial China. For another example, see Wang Yi, *Du Chang'an zhi shu shi shier shou* 讀長安志書事十二首, in *Yibin ji*, 11.3b–5a.

One item of particular interest to Cheng was the gazetteer's history of Zhuge Liang's "barbarian suppression" in the Yongchang 永昌 area. After noting this history he pointed out that there was still a Zhuge Village in Yongchang.

Gazetteer records read by literati travelers often led to new writings that were included in the later gazetteers. In "Yuzhang Liu Xijue you Zuiyuan Banmutang ji" 豫章劉錫爵游醉園半畝塘記 (Record of visiting the Drunken Garden's half-acre pond), published in the 1671 gazetteer of Xinchang, Zhejiang, Liu Xijue 劉錫爵 tells that he read in an earlier edition about the garden's connection to Song dynasty scholars Zhu Xi and Shi Zizhong 石子重. Liu was from Jiangxi, but was visiting the garden with a local person, Mr. Lü. Liu described how he felt as he viewed the garden and recorded his conversation with Lü about its history.[70] So in this case, a gazetteer provided background on a historic site to a traveler, informed his on-site discussion with a local man, and aided him in composing a new piece related to the site, which was included in the next edition of the gazetteer. From these cases, we can see local gazetteers as important nexuses in literati cultural production.

Carrying a local gazetteer with you as you traveled was a good idea, according to sixteenth-century official Li Kaixian 李開先, a ministerial-level official from Zhangqiu 章丘, Shandong. In a 1548 preface to the gazetteer of Zhangqiu's neighboring county, Laiwu, Li wrote that he had always enjoyed the study of landforms, so everywhere he traveled he asked about the local soil fertility and the people's customs. Fifteen years earlier Li had traveled through Laiwu on assignment and even though the county seat was only 75 kilometers from Zhangqiu, Li knew little about Laiwu. Thus, he asked people about the local economy and defense as he traveled and when the Laiwu magistrate met him at the border, Li asked for the county gazetteer. The magistrate instead gave Li the Shandong provincial gazetteer (published fifteen years earlier), which Li read. He then declared, "If a traveler carries this book with him, there is no need to consult the *Qi sheng*, the *Huanyu ji* 寰宇記 (Record of the realm), the *Yitong zhi*, the *Yudi san qi* 輿地三齊 (Lands of the Three Qi), and so on," earlier works that were in whole or in part about Shandong.[71]

---

70. *Xinchang xian zhi* (1671), 18.27a.
71. "Three Qi" refers to eastern Shandong. *Laiwu xian zhi*, preface, 1a–b.

Reading Gazetteers for Evidence in Lawsuits

In chapter 2 we saw how the 1477 and 1579 editions of the *Xinchang xian zhi* were read as documenting intangible social status. But gazetteers also documented various types of tangible property, which led some people involved in disputes having an historical element to carefully scrutinize local gazetteers for materials supporting their positions. The following section examines roles gazetteers played in water rights litigation. In the first case, the history of a reservoir was falsified in the 1606 gazetteer of Shangyu, Zhejiang, to bolster an individual claim to water. In the second, neighboring counties used their respective gazetteers to advocate their claims to disputed water.

THE LAKE ZAOLI DISPUTE: BRINGING CHAOS TO THE GAZETTEER

The story of the Shangyu gazetteer spans several centuries and illustrates not only the politics of gazetteer compilation, but also how local gazetteers were used in legal disputes. The battle over water rights at the center of the story resulted in two separate lawsuits brought more than sixty years apart. An excerpt from the 1587 gazetteer of Shaoxing Prefecture, Shangyu County's superior territorial administration, provides an entry point to the story:

> The Shangyu gazetteer was written [in 1441] in twelve chapters by townsman Guo Nan 郭南. Nan lived next to Lake Caoli 曹黎 and wanted the lake to be his personal property. He pretended to be a descendant of Guo Ziyi 郭子儀 and revised the gazetteer, thoroughly changing the old edition.[72] He changed "Caoli" to "Zaoli 皂李" and falsely recorded himself as Guo Ziyi's descendant (fig. 7.1).
>
> When later he served as an assistant prefect he became rich through corruption. He then bought up copies of the old gazetteers at a high price, burned them, and destroyed the woodblocks. Now, the only extant

---

72.   Guo Ziyi was a Tang dynasty noble, the Prince of Fenyang. Szonyi, *Practicing Kinship*, 1.

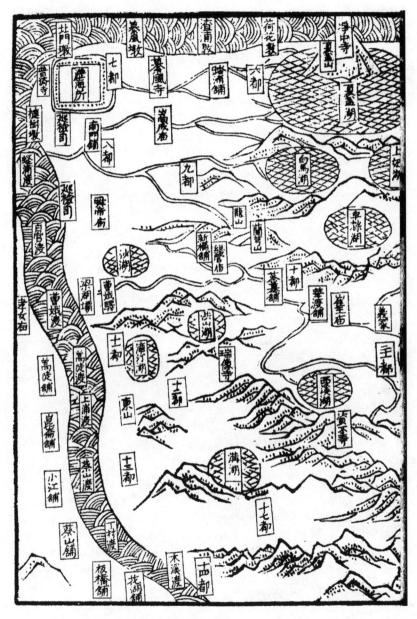

FIGURE 7.1. Gazetteer map of Lake Zaoli and Shangyu County in the 1606 *Shangyu xian zhi* (Tianjin Public Library).

gazetteer is Nan's edition. Much time has passed, and the woodblocks for Nan's gazetteer have also been destroyed by fire. His descendants' fortunes have declined and they now ask for loans against their copies of Nan's gazetteer. It is thus said that "Nan's rise began in the county personnel office" (this puns with "Nan was born of a county pheasant"). Recently, magistrate Zhu Weifan 朱維藩 has substantially added to the manuscript for a new gazetteer but almost all past matters were taken from Guo and it is not yet a "finished book."[73]

The above anecdote was written in the 1580s as the Shaoxing prefectural gazetteer was being compiled. To aid in its compilation, each subordinate county was ordered to update its gazetteer and in Shangyu, Ge Xiao 葛曉 (also known as Ge Jue 葛橺) did the work. He used Guo Nan's 1441 edition, completed a manuscript in 1583, and submitted it to the compilers in the Shaoxing prefectural seat, where some of his materials, including the passage above, were incorporated into the prefectural gazetteer. Ge's work was not immediately published locally as a county gazetteer.

Guo Nan's 1441 Shangyu gazetteer is no longer extant, so it impossible to compare it directly to the 1606 edition, however, Guo's preface does survive, and it gives no hint of the alleged subterfuge. Guo stated that he compiled parts of the new gazetteer, that there were two gazetteers compiled during the Yuan dynasty, and one in the Ming Yongle era (1403–25), but he did not mention Lake Caoli/Zaoli or the burning of earlier gazetteers. In 1441 Guo Nan collated and updated the Yongle-era manuscript and used his own money to have the woodblocks cut and imprints made.[74]

When the new Shangyu gazetteer was finally published in 1606 after updating and additional editing, the Shangyu magistrate read Ge Xiao's allegation of fraud and expressed his anger at the long-dead Guo Nan, saying, "The prefectural historical documentation has been tainted by Guo Nan and his burning of the old gazetteer. For two hundred years no reliable history has been transmitted."[75] Within eight months of pub-

73.   *Shaoxing fu zhi* (1587), 3338.

74.   *Shangyu xian zhi jiao xu*, 3810–11; *Shangyu xian zhi* (1606, HYM), *juan* 18 (page number illegible), biography of Guo Nan.

75.   The 1990 *Shangyu xian zhi* says that an edition was published in 1583 by Magistrate Zhu Weifan, but this contradicts the 1587 *Shaoxing fu zhi*, which says that Zhu

lication, however, people living near the lake filed a lawsuit, alleging that in fact, it was not Guo Nan's 1441 edition, but rather Ge Xiao's 1606 edition, that had been falsified. The 1671 edition contains records of the lawsuit and summarized the case as follows:

> When Ge Xiao recompiled the county gazetteer in the thirty-fourth year of the Wanli era, the powerful commoner Zheng Yongjiu 鄭用九 took the opportunity to bribe Ge to create seven false records [relating to Lake Zaoli's history] and destroy the old gazetteers. People of the lake region, Huang Wen 黃文 and others, prepared an account of the Seven Records' errors and brought suit in the prefectural yamen. Prefect Zhu Qin 朱芹 and assistant prefect Ye went to the lake for an on-site investigation and all the facts were clear. Grand coordinator Gan corrected the Seven Records and ordered a stele be inscribed to forever prohibit draining the lake. County magistrate Wang Tongqian 王同謙 followed the order and erected a stele.[76]

The 1671 *Shangyu xian zhi* also contains a transcript of the stele erected at Lake Zaoli.[77] It describes the case in much greater detail and traces its path through the Ming bureaucracy. A closer examination of the stele's inscription sheds additional light on gazetteers' roles in local societies, how the government used them, and the degree to which gazetteer integrity mattered to the late Ming and early Qing governments.

Following is a summary of the stele's rendition of the case. The case title was "In the matter of investigating and restoring water rights in order to settle a dispute that arose among the people in Shaoxing Prefecture, Shangyu County."[78] According to the stele record, on April 24, 1607, the county magistrate received a dispatch from an administration circuit vice commissioner regarding a complaint by Huang Wen and a group of people who lived near Lake Zaoli. The complaining parties alleged that Zheng Yongjiu and his friends had seized control of the lake, thereby causing disaster for the people, and that they had altered

---

Weifan's gazetteer was not printed. *Shangyu xian zhi* (1990), 869; *Shaoxing fu zhi* (1587), 3338; *Shangyu xian zhi jiao xu*, 3816.

76. Zhu Qin served as Shaoxing prefect from 1606 to 1608. *Shaoxing fu zhi* (1792), 603; *Shangyu xian zhi* (1671), 189–90.

77. Ibid., 192–95.

78. Ibid., 190.

the gazetteer to support Zheng's claim. The dispatch said that the provincial grand coordinator had ordered an on-site investigation of every sluice gate to see whether Zheng had in fact seized control of the lake's water.

Assistant Prefect for Irrigation Ye Mengxiong 葉夢熊 investigated.[79] Meanwhile, as prefect Zhu Qin traveled through the affected area, he was approached by several thousand local people: "They crowded the road calling out accusations; the ring of 'Injustice!' filled the road. He almost could not bear to hear it. When the prefect asked them what had happened, they all said, 'Lake Zaoli's [history] was altered in the gazetteer for the private benefit of Zheng Yongjiu.'" The people further explained that Zheng had opened a channel from the lake to fill a canal.

Prefect Zhu and assistant prefect Ye learned that next to the lake were thousands of acres of cultivated fields that relied on the lake for irrigation and that this system had been in place since the Tang dynasty (618–906 CE). The two officials noted that in old records the lake was called Caoli, but in Guo Nan's gazetteer the name appeared as Zaoli. They pointed out that although the lake's name had changed, the way that it stored and released water had not. The prefect and assistant prefect concluded that Zheng Yongjiu took advantage of Ge Xiao's gazetteer's recompilation to alter the lake's history in a way that would support his right to use lake water to raise the water level in a canal, thereby enhancing transport and allowing him to irrigate dry areas outside of the lake's long-standing irrigation zone. Thus, their conclusion was that Ge Xiao, not Guo Nan, had falsified the gazetteer. The officials further found that Zheng Yongjiu's scheme would completely drain the lake, shift water to people who were not entitled to it, threaten the locals' ability to survive, and "bring chaos to a one thousand-year old system of water regulation."

The prefect reported the facts to the provincial surveillance commission and requested a decree ordering erection of a stele on the lakeshore to ensure future compliance. The report was sent on to the branch circuit office, which further found that Zheng Yongjiu and his friends, including Ge Xiao, the gazetteer compiler, "advocated deviant records and

---

79. Ye served as assistant prefect from 1606 to 1607. *Shaoxing fu zhi* (1792), 610.

plotted to drain the water to fill the channel," that it was an "evil conspiracy," and that violators of the order would be punished to the full extent of the law.

> The grand coordinator, the top provincial official, then issued his final order: Zheng Yongjiu feigned a public interest to attain his private interest and moreover was able to add to and alter the county gazetteer. He also caused an incident that severely harmed the people. The lake's water shall gather as in the past and benefit the nearby fields. The new gazetteer shall be corrected in order to prevent disputes.

Upon receiving the order, the prefect had the stele inscribed and placed on the lakeshore in 1609. The case was closed two and a half years after the initial complaint was made, and three years after the falsified gazetteer was published.

The 1609 decision did not, however, end litigation over Lake Zaoli's water. A second lawsuit was brought sixty-two years later during the compilation of a new edition of the Shangyu gazetteer. A summary of the second lawsuit was included when the new edition was published in 1671. It again referred to Ge Xiao's disputed "Seven Records" that were used to justify draining lake water:

> At the time [of the 1609 decision] the Seven Records had already been published [in the gazetteer] and they were not immediately corrected. Now in the tenth year of the Great Qing dynasty's Kangxi era [1671], Prefect Zhang Sanyi 張三異 has ordered counties to recompile their gazetteers. The scholars and commoners living by the lake, Zhang Jun 張俊 and others, brought suit based on the prior case.

Shangyu County Magistrate Zheng Qiao 鄭僑 explained the background to the new lawsuit:

> Now the county gazetteer is being recompiled and the scholar Zhang Jun and others want the Seven Records excised, the earlier [1441] gazetteer followed, and the release of water banned. Thus they gathered a mob and

brought suit before the censor, struggling as if it were a matter of life and death. Because it was a critical matter that cut their flesh, how could they not cry out loudly and fiercely?

The 1671 gazetteer summary explained further:

> Provincial Governor Fan instructed the prefect to carefully investigate. Prefect Zhang ordered county magistrate Zheng Qiao to investigate. Upon investigation, the facts were clear and were reported back to the governor with a request for permission to excise the false and restore the old. The provincial governor then dispatched Mr. Yuan of the provincial administration commission to investigate. Mr. Yuan verified the facts and reported back to the governor, who granted permission for the case to be inscribed in stone.[80]

A transcript of the inscribed text was also published in the new gazetteer and provides additional information on the investigation. It said that in the spring of 1671 Governor Fan ordered prefect Zhang to have the complaining parties submit a description of the incident, to quickly investigate their claims, and submit a report along with "the four editions of the gazetteer."[81] Magistrate Zheng reported that Lake Zaoli had been constructed by resident commoners 居民 in the Tang dynasty (618–906 CE), had been maintained by the people living by the lake 湖民 ever since without spending government money, and that the locals carefully protected their water. He noted that the lake is elevated above the surrounding lands and that it could drain away extremely rapidly, causing the fields it normally irrigated to "become parched and cracked like tortoise shells." After reviewing extant Ming dynasty records and receiving reports from subordinates sent to the lake, the magistrate confirmed the facts, and suggested that, "it is best to follow the old principle of 'those who build the dikes use the water.'"

80. *Shangyu xian zhi* (1671), 192.
81. This suggests that at least one pre-1583 edition survived the attempt to destroy it and was still extant in 1671. According to the 1990 *Shangyu xian zhi*, prior to 1583 there were editions in 1348, 1354, 1418, and 1441. The stele does not identify which four editions were requested. Records of the next case discussed below suggest that the 1418 gazetteer was still extant in 1606.

Shaoxing Prefect Zhang observed that the facts of the earlier conspiracy were clear from the old gazetteer and stele inscription and that it was Ge Xiao, not Guo Nan, who conspired to destroy the old gazetteers. Prefect Zhang's report recommended that the false records be deleted, and "the old [1441] gazetteer be restored in order to pass on forever [the prohibition on improperly draining lake water]." The report was sent up to commissioner Yuan, who determined that Lake Caoli was built by local people surnamed Cao and Li, and reiterated that it had been maintained without government money. Yuan "reviewed the lake's maps, the stelae, gazetteers, and documents from the case file," confirmed the Ming case findings, and determined that the new lawsuit had merit. The provincial governor ordered the magistrate to correct the gazetteer and erect a second stele. Magistrate Zheng then "sent his report to the gazetteer compilation office and ordered the compilers to publicly record the matter" 送志局秉公載. He further ordered that no one was to gather kinsmen to seize control of the water.[82]

This case is a rich source for exploring the politics of compiling gazetteers, their readership, authority, and uses in local society and governance. Whereas the *Xinchang xian zhi* case discussed in chapter 2 exposed struggles over the portrayal of prominent families in local gazetteers, the *Shangyu xian zhi* case shows that disputes over gazetteer content could be about more than relative social status. In Shangyu, immediate, tangible interests were at stake, and the dispute over local history was intense, involving bribery, fraud, burning of old gazetteers, and lawsuits.

The case also shows that local residents had access to the content of county gazetteers. Shortly after publication, several thousand locals protested the gazetteer's forgery and some filed a lawsuit. While that does not mean that all protesters had read the gazetteer, it does reveal that they had some way to learn of the gazetteer's contents soon after publication and that the contents mattered to them. Presumably, many of those "several thousand" were illiterate, so in describing audiences for local gazetteers we must include people who learned of gazetteer contents through oral transmission. The grand coordinator's 1609 order stated that the gazetteer was to be corrected in order to prevent disputes. He assumed that local people would view the gazetteer as an authoritative

82. *Shangyu xian zhi* (1671), 192–95.

public record. Unlike government case files kept in the yamen or lakeside stelae, gazetteers circulated in the local society and acted as public documentation of important decisions, policies, and cases. This point is made explicitly in the 1671 case, which says the magistrate sent his case report to the gazetteer compilation office to be "publicly recorded."

The case also reveals the persistence of local historical memory and a willingness to take action based on it. In 1671 it had already been sixty-two years and a change of dynasty since the earlier lawsuit was decided, but locals still remembered and took legal action to correct Lake Zaoli's history upon learning that a new gazetteer was being compiled. While it is impossible to know the exact mechanism by which the memory was maintained; it was probably reinforced by the stelae erected on the lakeshore, and surviving copies of old gazetteers. Local residents also likely transmitted the story orally. Battles over water rights sometimes led to long-running feuds, a possibility suggested by the prohibition on "gathering kinsmen," and it would not be surprising if residents maintained their own written records to document their claims.[83] The conspirators had been unable to completely erase the lake's history.[84] Guo Nan's descendants' use of imprints as loan collateral and the conspirators' attempts to buy up old gazetteers to eliminate the history embodied therein demonstrates the potential value of local gazetteers.

Clearly gazetteers could be used as evidence in lawsuits. Gazetteers were critical to the outcome of both the 1607 and 1671 cases. Zheng Yongjiu believed that the gazetteer's portrayal of Lake Zaoli's history affected his ability to control the water, and thus he went to the trouble of bribing Ge Xiao, the compiler. The weight a magistrate would give a record found in a gazetteer may have varied with the quality of the gazetteer and the specific facts, but this case shows that gazetteers could be significant. Rules of evidence were not codified in the Ming, but documents created or approved by government bodies would have had greater probative value than private records. County gazetteers were almost always compiled under official auspices and paratextual elements portrayed gazetteers as official texts. Thus, gazetteers had an official air about them

83.   For a discussion of feuds in Shaoxing, see Cole, *Shaohsing*.

84.   One work on Shangyu County's water resources that was extant at the time of the dispute was Chen Tian's 1362 *Shangyu xian wu xiang shuili benmo* 上虞縣五鄉水利本末 (The water resources of Shangyu County's five districts, from beginning to end). Gu Zhixing, *Zhejiang chubanshi yanjiu*, 100.

even if most of the actual compilation work was typically done by locals who were not currently serving ranked officials. Magistrates gave gazetteers—and written documents more generally—added weight because, due to the law of avoidance, they had to serve outside their native places and often could not understand the local spoken dialect. In such cases, they could not question witnesses without assistance from an interpreter. This likely caused magistrates to give more weight to written evidence, which they could understand without mediation. If a gazetteer was printed, as was the norm, it would have carried even more weight because, as discussed in chapter 4, in the eyes of officials, printing enhanced the fixity and reliability of the text.

Magistrates, in fact, often looked to local gazetteers for materials related to local lawsuits. Lü Nan, in his preface to the 1524 gazetteer of Jizhou 薊州, Beizhili, explained that when he first arrived in Jizhou, he learned of various matters related to the "lawsuits of officials and commoners" that should have been contained in the 1478 gazetteer compiled by a former magistrate. Lü then "picked it up, read it completely, and found that some items had private purposes, some were false, and some were exaggerated and weird."[85] Lü clearly understood that not all gazetteers were authoritative sources, but he believed that they should be. He expected to be able to get a quick historical overview of major local cases from the gazetteer.

If people in late imperial China believed that gazetteers could be used as evidence in court, then they had a powerful incentive to influence content. Even though materials published in the 1606 *Shangyu xian zhi* were gathered pursuant to the Shaoxing prefect's order and the history of Lake Zaoli was critically important to water rights, a powerful local and his co-conspirators were nonetheless able to temporarily alter that history through bribery and destruction of old gazetteers. Zheng Yongjiu and Ge Xiao even fooled the compilers of the 1587 *Shaoxing fu zhi* (or perhaps conspired with them).

It is interesting that in the 1607 case, despite an order from the top provincial official to correct the gazetteer—a simple proposition—the local magistrate did not immediately cut corrected woodblocks. Perhaps he considered the stele erected at the lake and the case files kept in the government offices to be sufficient documentation of the decision and order. Or perhaps he expected that the next magistrate would soon update

85. *Jizhou zhi*, preface.

the gazetteer to reflect his service, and at that time he could remove the woodblocks containing the Seven Records and cut corrected woodblocks. The case title given by Ming officials, "In the matter of investigating and restoring water rights in order to settle a dispute that arose among the people in Shaoxing Prefecture, Shangyu County," suggests that the gazetteer fraud was of secondary importance to resolving the underlying water dispute. However, the early-Qing case title, "In the matter of bringing chaos to the gazetteer, seizing the lake, dodging taxes, and causing death in Shaoxing Prefecture, Shangyu County, calling to the utmost for Heaven's Law to excise the false records and benevolently restore the old gazetteer to make whole the water resources for 10,000 years," suggests greater weight was given to correcting the gazetteer.[86] This might be explained by the fact that in 1671 the new Qing government was still consolidating its rule in Zhejiang, so restoring the documentary record of rights in local society was critical to laying the foundation for future stability, especially when records were tied up with violent feuds.

The case also raises the question of how the people living near the lake learned of the gazetteer's contents so quickly. It is important to note that even before a gazetteer compilation began, many local people would know of the project. If a proclamation announcing the gazetteer project and soliciting sources was posted on the yamen gate, as discussed in chapter 3, knowledge of it would have spread widely. Thus, it should not be surprising that rural Shangyu County residents knew what was recorded in the local gazetteer soon after it was published. From this case, we can see that gazetteers were not only for an occasional curious reader, rather, gazetteers could be important texts for legitimating rights in local society.

GAZETTEERS IN INTER-JURISDICTIONAL DISPUTES

Although local gazetteers focused on matters internal to the subject jurisdiction, they also could be used to advocate the interests of one locale over those of its neighbor. This is illustrated by gazetteer writings about a multicentury dispute between Shangyu and Yuyao counties over the rights to the water of Lake Xiagai 夏蓋 (fig. 7.2). This lake was on the border between the two counties, and access to it had been the cause of

---

86. *Shangyu xian zhi* (1671), 192. It is not clear who was killed.

FIGURE 7.2. Gazetteer map of Lake Xiagai in the 1606 *Shangyu xian zhi* (Tianjin Public Library).

repeated litigation since the Song dynasty. The 1606 *Shangyu xian zhi*, discussed in the previous section, not only contained a false history of Lake Zaoli, it also asserted that Yuyao County had distorted its gazetteer's records of water resources to support the right of Yuyao residents to tap into Shangyu County's water supply.

The comments in the 1671 *Shangyu xian zhi* are translated below:

According to the Yuyao gazetteer, there are three lakes on its border with Shangyu to which Yuyao has partial rights: Lakes Baima 白馬, Xiagai, and Xiaocha 小查. It asserts that Lake Baima irrigates three Yuyao districts: Dongshan 東山, Lanfeng 蘭風, and Kaiyuan 開原, and five wards of Shangyu's Xiqian 西漖 District. It says that Lake Xiagai has always irrigated Xinxing 新興 and four other Shangyu districts and Yuyao's Lanfeng 蘭風 district.

The Yuyao gazetteer further asserts that the Yongle-era (1403–25) edition of the Shangyu gazetteer says, "on the third day of autumn the Chen Storehouse Sluice releases water for eight hours," and that various people in the Shangyu dike control organization point to this as an excuse for not releasing water at the appropriate times, causing most of Lanfeng District's fields to become parched.

An order from prefect Chen Yun 陳耘 [who was Shaoxing prefect from 1429–31], set forth his judgment that Shangyu people had been malevolent. He sentenced and punished the wrongdoers and in addition split the water evenly with Yuyao.

The Yuyao gazetteer says that Lake Xiaocha irrigates Yuyao's Yunlou 雲樓 District. According to what Yuyao people record in their gazetteer, every locale that borders on Shangyu has rights in common with Shangyu. Although Yuyao areas bordering on Shangyu might have some rights, how is it that we have never heard of Shangyu receiving rights from Yuyao?

Now, people are divided into jurisdictions and land is divided into territories. If one crosses the border and takes possession of another person's property, is it legal? According to the local gazetteer of Xiahou Zengxian 夏候曾先, Baima's old name was Yupu 漁浦 and it was originally in Lanfeng District in Yuyao. In the second year of the Tang dynasty's Zhenyuan era (786 CE), four or five *li* were cut from Lanfeng District and placed in Yongfeng 永豐 District, which was added to Shangyu County. The lake is now within the boundaries of Yongfeng District. Lanfeng's people had since olden days irrigated with lake water and it was considered to be a normal practice. There is nothing strange about that.

But now the irrigated area has been extended to Yuyao's Dongshan and Kaiyuan districts while in Shangyu it is limited to the five wards of Xiqian. This is as if the Tang redistricting had never happened, and although territory is entered into the land registers as lying in Shangyu, the rights are transferred to Yuyao. So what was the point of redistricting! It is as if there were property that at first belonged to the East and an East family owned it, but now it belonged to the West, yet the East still occupied it.

Lake Xiagai has very broad flatlands surrounding it. They are lowest to the northeast of the lake and highest to the west, and the difference is more than one *zhang*.[87] This causes the water to drain like an overturned bottle straight to Lanfeng District in Yuyao. Those Yuyao people who desire more water are always drooling over Lake Xiagai. Some take opportunities to steal water from new district dams, some call out from the nearby irrigation ditches to release water. They have done this for a long time and see it as appropriate. Therefore they fight for the water and draw it off.

Higher officials consider them all to be our people, thinking, how can we bear to just sit and watch their difficulties? It is like when one brother is about to starve to death, one who fulfills his responsibility as a father gives him grain from another brothers' storehouse even though it is not his.

Yet if we turn this around to call Shangyu people malevolent and split the water rights evenly, how can we not look upon this as a change in jurisdiction? Moreover, Yuyao's Lanfeng District is already irrigated by Lake Baima. Lanfeng being further irrigated by Lake Xiagai destroys what is appropriate; Lanfeng's crops will all ripen while Shangyu people cannot enjoy their own resource. All they can do is give it to Yuyao with their eyes wide open and hands in the air.

The land cut from Yuyao long ago was only the five *li* in the west of the district, and so only the lands of this area should be allowed irrigation from Lake Xiagai. But the water flows into one district and then continues on to water East Mountain and Kaiyuan. Prefect Chen Yun's order makes it possible for all of Lake Xiagai's water to be released and transported to those districts, but they are still not satisfied. A scholar from Yuyao, named Cen岑, even said, "if we could seize complete control of Lake Baima and Lake Xiagai and have their waters return to Yuyao, then the northern districts could avoid disasters brought on by drought." Yuyao people's state of mind is thoroughly revealed therein. Moreover, Cen used the word "seize," so obviously it is not something that belongs to Yuyao.

Now if we examine the case of Lake Xiaocha's irrigating Yuyao's Yunlou District, we see that Yuyao has opened up many fields on the border of

---

87. One *zhang* 丈 was equal to about 3.1 meters.

Shangyu's First District. Its fields depend on this lake's water, but they also let it flow on into the rest of their district. Its boundary is close and its topography well suited for this, yet it is not appropriate that they let it flow beyond Yunlou.

Yuyao people say that Shangyu people want to use their gazetteer compilation to monopolize the water. Or is it actually the case that Yuyao people are using their gazetteer compilation as an opportunity to seize the water! The fact is that the Shangyu people's gazetteer records their own lands and that is all. But Yuyao people take other people's lands and record them as their own!

In sum, Yuyao is located downstream and it is most easy for water to drain into it. In times of drought we would work hard to save them and forgive the emotions of desperate people in need of rescue, manifesting the duty to save one's neighbor. Would not Yuyao people still enjoy the benefit?

This matter has already been decided, yet what led the people of the past to decide the matter in this way was basically that people who live in close contact with each other cannot vigorously fight one another. Thus, I argue a little for the Shangyu farmers to clarify that the situation is as I have stated herein.[88]

Like the passages on Lake Zaoli, this text sheds light on how people used gazetteers to legitimate rights in local society. It also reveals one way that some read gazetteers of neighboring counties. People in both Shangyu and Yuyao used their gazetteers to advance arguments about the proper criteria for determining water rights when a reservoir was located on or near a county border. Each county's respective gazetteer advocated a position that would benefit its own people. People in Shangyu, who had the reservoir within their borders but were upstream from Yuyao, argued that borders mattered, even though water naturally flows downhill and crosses borders; whereas Yuyao people argued that their fields needed water just as much as the Shangyu people's fields, and that some Shangyu lands that were once part of Yuyao had been irrigated with lake water prior to redistricting. People in both counties knew of the early-fifteenth-century gazetteer record that said, "on the third day of autumn the Chen Storehouse Sluice releases water for eight hours" and

88. *Shangyu xian zhi* (1671), 176–81.

Shangyu members of the Lake Xiagai dike control unit used it as justification for not releasing water to Yuyao at other times. As with the genealogies discussed by David Faure, the *Xinchang xian zhi* discussed in chapter 2, and the battle over Lake Zaoli, the Shangyu and Yuyao gazetteers attempted to legitimate rights in local society.[89] In this case, however, "local" crossed county borders.

The use of the local gazetteers to assert water rights reflects a salient issue in Eastern Zhejiang, an area with extensive and complicated water systems that served both agriculture and commerce. By understanding gazetteers as strategic texts and examining how they were compiled and read, in both this region and others, new insights can be gained into how local societies worked.

Collectors of Local Gazetteers

Geographical works, the precursors to local gazetteers, began to appear in private book collections in the Tang dynasty. The earliest known example is the *Liang jing ji* 兩京記 (Record of the Two Capitals), collected by Wei Shu 韋述 in the eighth century.[90] In the fifteenth century, Ye Sheng 葉盛 (1420–74), an official known for his book collection, had dozens of comprehensive gazetteers and a few local gazetteers.[91] But by the sixteenth and seventeenth centuries many literati began to collect them. In fact, they constituted a substantial portion of several of the best-known Ming book collections, with titles numbering in the hundreds. Major collectors included the imperial clansman Zhu Mujie 朱睦㮮 (1516–85), whose *Wanjuantang shumu* 萬卷堂書目 (Ten-Thousand-Volume Hall catalog) lists 177 titles under the category "local gazetteers" 地志, and more under "various gazetteers" 雜志.[92] The collection of Fan Qin 范欽 (1506–85), founder of the Tianyige Library 天一閣 in Ningbo, is probably the best-known today because over 200 of the approximately 435 gazetteers in the Tianyige collection at its peak are extant and are widely

89. Faure, "Lineage as Cultural Invention," 6–8, 28.
90. Huang Wei, *Fang zhi xue*, 43.
91. Ye Sheng, *Luzhutang shumu*, 127.
92. Zhu Mujie, *Wanjuantang shumu*, 1077–82.

available in reprints.[93] An even larger collection was that of Zhao Qimei 趙琦美 (1563–1624) of Changshu, Nanzhili, who had nearly 800 gazetteers.[94] Other collectors included Chao Li 晁瑮 (1506–76) of Kaizhou 開州, Henan, who had over 400 "maps and gazetteers"; Xu Bo 徐㶿, of Minxian 閩縣, Fujian, who had over 300 gazetteers; and Chen Di 陳第 (1541–1617) and Huang Juzhong 黃居中 (1562–1644), also from Fujian, who each had over 100 titles.[95]

Most of the above gazetteer collectors were officials or literati who used their local gazetteers as sources when writing on various topics. Zhao Qimei copied biographical materials from gazetteers in his work on calligraphers and painters, *Zhao shi tie wang shan hu* 趙氏鐵網珊瑚.[96] Xu Bo was a poet, calligrapher, and book collector who traveled extensively, and read and took notes on gazetteers for use in his writings.[97] Xu's notebook, *Xu shi bi jing* 徐氏筆精, is full of citations to gazetteers, especially biographical materials on poets, authors, calligraphers, literary works, and stelae, from Fujian and other regions, from the Ming and earlier states.[98] Xu's *Rongyin xin jian* 榕陰新檢, a collection of classified biographical sketches of Fujianese, draws from gazetteers and notes biographies that were left out of local gazetteers.[99] Zhu Mujie was particularly interested in local history and helped compile gazetteers.[100]

One of the best-documented gazetteer collectors was Qi Chengye 祁承㸁 (1563–1628), owner of the *Danshengtang* 澹生堂 library in Shanyin, Zhejiang.[101] The following pages will examine Qi's collection and use of

---

93.   Yan Yifan, *Qi Chengye*, 105, citing Luo Zhaoping, "Tan Tianyige cang Ming-dai difangzhi," 190–99. For studies of the Tianyige collection, see the bibliography in Cai Peiling, *Fan shi Tianyige yanjiu*.

94.   Miao, *Mingdai chuban shi*, 31; Zhao Qimei, *Mowangguan shumu*.

95.   Chao Li, *Chao shi baowentang shumu*; Huang Wei, *Fang zhi xue*, 44; Chen Di, *Shishantang shu mulu*; Huang Yuji, *Qianqingtang shumu*; Xu Bo, *Hongyulou shumu*.

96.   Zhao Qimei, *Zhao shi tiewang shanhu*, 10.76b; *Wujiang zhi*, 373.

97.   *DMB*, 597.

98.   *Xu shi bi jing*, 5.14a, 5.16a, 5.31a, 5.33b, 6.8b, 6.10a, 7.1a, 7.28a, etc.

99.   *Rongyin xin jian*, 1.3a, 1.4a, 2.4a, 2.5a, 3.2a, 6.6a, 6.7a, 7.6b, etc.

100.   Zhu helped compile the *Henan tong zhi* and *Kaifeng fu zhi*.

101.   Scholars disagree on whether his name should be pronounced "Chengye" or "Chenghan," but he is better known in English-language scholarship as Chengye. For discussion of this issue, see Wang Yanrong and Zhu Yuangui, "Danshengtang zhu." For more on the Qi family, see Handlin Smith, "Ch'i Piao-chia's Social World."

gazetteers from around the Ming state, using his travel diary and letters from his collected works, the *Danshengtang ji*. Doing so will reveal ways in which local gazetteers circulated local information on a national stage and helped situate localities in national cultural, social, and political processes. It will also help explain why literati began collecting gazetteers.

Qi grew up in eastern Zhejiang, a region known for its bookstores and book collectors, and he began collecting books as a youth. He had built a substantial collection by 1597, when it was destroyed by fire.[102] After the fire, he started over and built a collection with over 6,700 titles at the time of his death in 1628.[103] He cataloged 715 gazetteers, including eight comprehensive works, thirty-seven provincial gazetteers, sixty-four subprefectural gazetteers, 325 county gazetteers, and an assortment of others.[104]

Qi used various means to acquire books. He shopped the bookstores in Shanyin, and took short trips to nearby book centers, such as Hangzhou, Yuyao, and Ningbo. When Qi passed the *jinshi* exam in 1604, as had his grandfather and great-great grandfather before him, he embarked on an official career that made possible the rapid expansion of his gazetteer collection.[105] When he traveled to take the examinations, he scouted for books on the road and after he arrived in the capital. As inspecting censor of the Jiangnan horse administration beginning in 1613, he carried duplicate books while traveling on business and traded along the way. While serving as assistant surveillance commissioner in Fuyang 滏陽, Henan, in 1621–22, Qi obtained a complete set of the province's local gazetteers 全省志書 and shipped them back to Shaoxing in two crates. The initial source of the local gazetteers is unclear, but Qi most likely wrote to an official in each administrative subdivision asking for a copy. Several of Qi's postings were in major book centers: in 1607, he was stationed in Changzhou 長州, Nanzhili, and in 1610 he was transferred to Nanjing. This was the start of Qi's most active period of book collecting. He met many other collectors and started a book collecting club that

---

102. Yan Yifan, *Qi Chengye*, 87.
103. Ibid., 97.
104. Ibid., 99.
105. Ibid., 84, table 2.

required members to collect a certain number of unusual and old books each month or be fined.[106]

Qi also got gazetteers through friends and acquaintances who were officials serving in, or natives of, the subject locale. In 1618 Zhejiang Provincial Administration Commissioner Xiao Jingao 蕭近高 sent Qi the Zhejiang provincial gazetteer and that of Jinhua Prefecture.[107] The provincial gazetteer had been published fifty-seven years earlier by the provincial administration commission, and Xiao might have taken a spare imprint from the yamen or printed a new one from the blocks.

Qi also had special printings done for his collection.[108] In 1621–22, his younger brother, Qi Chengxun, was an official in Shaanxi and had a crate of books printed for him.[109] When woodblocks were no longer available, he had books hand copied.[110] In the 1610s and early 1620s Qi Chengye had about two thousand books copied by hand.[111]

Why did Qi collect so many gazetteers? Cai Peiling 蔡佩玲 has argued that Qi did not value his local gazetteers, citing a letter Qi sent home regarding the Henan gazetteers mentioned above.[112] It said, "I sent back a total of eight boxes. Among them, two boxes are a set of Henan local gazetteers from the entire province, which are not very precious 不甚 貴重. Other than those, they are all good books 此外皆好書也." This passage could be understood as saying that local gazetteers, as a category of books, were not important to Qi, but it is better understood to mean that the local gazetteers he bought in Henan were not rare, antique, or finely printed editions. Other evidence demonstrates that Qi greatly valued his local gazetteer collection. Not only was more than one-tenth of his entire book collection local gazetteers, he actively promoted local gazetteer compilation, read local gazetteers, carried on correspondence about them, discussed them with friends, and used them as key sources for writing studies of regional literature and unofficial local gazetteers.

106.   Ibid., 88–89.
107.   Qi Chengye, *Danshengtang ji*, 13.36a; Zhu and Xie, *Ming-Qing jinshi*, 1444.
108.   Huang Chang, "Qi Chengye jia shu," 261, 266.
109.   Yan Yifan, *Qi Chengye*, 93.
110.   Ibid.
111.   Huang Chang, "Qi Chengye jia shu," 266, Qi Chengye letter number 24.
112.   Cai Peiling, *Fan shi Tianyige yanjiu*, 97. The letter was written ca. 1621–23 and is reproduced in Huang Chang, "Qi Chengye jia shu," 266.

Qi was interested in how the local fit into the national, and to understand that, he needed to read local writings. In a society in which the local had become critical to national governance and culture, local gazetteers brought the local onto a national stage.

Qi's deep interest in gazetteers can be seen in the time he spent in Jiangxi after being appointed prefect of Ji'an in 1615. There, he carried on correspondence about local gazetteers, discussed them with those who shared his interest, and contributed to their compilation. He developed a friendship with Guo Zizhang 郭子章 (1542–1618) of Taihe 太和, one of Ji'an's subordinate counties, who had served as governor of Guizhou and compiled the 1604 Guizhou provincial gazetteer, *Qian ji*.[113] In a diary entry, Qi noted that he wrote a letter to Guo to tell him about a worthy person who should have been included, but was not.[114] Eight days later, Qi shared a meal with Guo, and as they ate, Guo told Qi about Guizhou.[115] The gazetteer brought them together. Also while in Ji'an, Qi wrote a letter to his superior, Wang Huyun 王岵雲, noting that Jiangxi's historical documentation was the best in the realm, yet the provincial gazetteer had not been revised in over one hundred years.[116] Qi urged Wang to attend to this, saying, "It should not be done in a hurry; if it is done properly using an author whose fame shall last 1,000 autumns, then it will become one province's great canon. Is it not, sir, something for you to do today?"[117] Qi also noted that Ji'an already had a local gazetteer, but asked Wang to allow him to produce a treatise on the prefecture's literary accomplishments.

The roles played by local gazetteers in Qi's literary activities can be seen in his letters, diary entries, and other writings. A 1618 entry states:

> The sun was high at the *shen* hour [3–5 p.m.] and as I was lying down I received a letter and the [1602] *Guangdong tong zhi* sent by my classmate Master Lin 林公 of Guangzhou. It was the one compiled by Grand Master Guo Fei 郭棐 in the Wanli era. Upon partial examination and reading I

113. Yan Yifan, *Qi Chengye*, 353. For more on Guo Zizhang, see his biography in the *DMB* and Dardess, *A Ming Society*.

114. Qi Chengye, *Danshengtang ji*, 13.8b.

115. Ibid., 41a.

116. Qi was wrong about the date of the last provincial gazetteer.

117. Qi Chengye, *Danshengtang ji*, 17.61a.

consider it superior to the *Huanyu tong zhi*.[118] The [1561] *Guangdong tong zhi* was [originally] written by the Supervisor of the Household of the Heir Apparent Huang Caibo 黄才伯 (Huang Zuo 黄佐). I have entered it [into my study of Guangdong historical sources]. It is well organized, each prefecture having its own section, which is especially convenient for reference and reading. As for our Zhejiang provincial gazetteer, it was compiled by Education Intendant Xue Fangshan 薛方山 (Xue Yingqi 薛應旂), but its fault is that it is overly concise. When I read it I feel a rather hollow exasperation. In addition, it has already been over sixty years since his gazetteer was compiled yet the officeholders have not discussed [recompiling] it. Does this locale's historical record reflect its true circumstances?[119]

In this passage we see Qi reading, critiquing, and comparing gazetteers' styles, readability, and ease of use. He also stressed the importance of keeping local gazetteers current. Accurate, thorough, and up-to-date local gazetteers were important to Qi because without them he would lack sources for his compilations of local literature.

While in Fuyang, a town close to the Henan/Hebei border, Qi worked on a cross-border gazetteer. He wrote about it in a letter to "Zongzheng, who lives among the bamboo" 竹居宗正. Here we see Qi wanting to use someone else's book collection and home to allow a third person to research an unofficial regional gazetteer:

The exalted scholar from Zhongzhou 中州, Ruan Dingbo 阮定博, [also called] Taichong 太沖, is a refined gentleman. I, this untalented one, am going to do a combined local gazetteer for three Hebei prefectures, to be called *Heshuo wai shi* 河朔外史 (Unofficial gazetteer of Heshuo). Its format will not be the same as prefectural gazetteers. I am thinking I want to trouble this gentleman's great hand to write it and that we could polish it together. However, this place is isolated and backward; there are no old documents, essays, and biographies to consult. I would provide something for the costs of writing supplies and a salary and invite this gentleman. If he could use a room in your honorable home, he could make selections from your 10,000 volumes and consult the writings of the past. Once his

118. See chapter 1 for discussion of the *Huanyu tong zhi*.
119. Qi Chengye, *Danshengtang ji*, 13.41a–b. The entry is for the twelfth day of the fourth month of the *wuwu* year (May 6, 1618).

research met with success, I would invite him to Fuyang to borrow the summer's fragrance from a small area to complete a generation's new history. It seems it is a happy affair. I hope you will discuss it with this gentleman and favor me with a reply.[120]

Qi also compiled a series of studies on regional and local literature that drew heavily on local gazetteers. In his essay, *Zhuzuo kao gai* 著作考概 (Outline of the studies on writings), Qi explained how he gathered materials:

It is hard to exhaust the written record. I endured hardships traveling to and fro collecting materials. The sources for these works were gathered first from biographies in the dynastic histories, next from prefectural gazetteers, after that from county gazetteers, and next again from genealogies. After that, I collected everywhere from what was in the Four Classifications, broadly investigating the explications of the hundred schools. All can provide evidence. Thus the work is extremely detailed and comprehensive.[121]

This passage shows that local gazetteers were key sources for his works and that he looked to them before most types of other sources. There are many records of Qi receiving gazetteers for use in his studies on local literature. The following three notes from his diary show that Qi used local gazetteers in two ways in his studies of local writings: he looked for relevant materials contained therein, and cataloged local gazetteers as parts of local literatures:

1. Received the *Jinhua zhi* and the *Zhejiang tong zhi* from the Honorable Provincial Administration Commissioner Xiao Jiusheng.[122] I am just now editing my *Liang Zhe zhuzuo kao* 兩浙著作考 (Study of the writings of Zhejiang) and so must examine and read them. I am very happy to have received them.[123]

120.   Qi Chengye, *Danshengtang ji*, 18.53b.
121.   Ibid., 14.85b–86a.
122.   Jiusheng is the style name of Xiao Jingao.
123.   Qi Chengye, *Danshengtang ji*, 13.36.

2. Reviewed [my] *Hangzhou fu zhuzuo kao* 杭州府著作考 (Study of the writings of Hangzhou Prefecture), added nine items. Obtained local gazetteers of Xincheng and Qiantang 錢塘 and entered them.[124]

3. Reviewed [my] *Jinhua zhuzuo kao* 金華著作考 (Study of the writings of Jinhua Prefecture) and added eleven items. Finally, I obtained the *Yiwu xin zhi* 義烏新志 (New Yiwu gazetteer) and entered it.[125]

Like many late-Ming literati, Qi Chengye also used local gazetteers to document claims he was making about his relatives in family histories. In Qi's biography of his parents, he said of his great-great grandfather Qi Siyuan 祁司員, "He lifted up his family by obtaining the *jinshi* degree and gained fame as a censor . . . his administrative accomplishments in the prefecture are all recorded in the local gazetteers."[126]

As Qi traveled he recorded bits of information that he hoped would eventually make it into local gazetteers. A 1618 travel diary entry illustrates this:

After finishing the grave visit we gathered near the gravesite. As all of the elders ate, I asked why this place was called "Four Divining Diagrams." It was said that in olden days, before Luo Yin 羅隱 became successful, he had someone conduct divinations in this area.[127] Every day [the diviner] used only four trigrams [instead of the normal eight]. When he passed this place he did not divine further. At the base of the mountain there is a spring with pure, drinkable water. To this day it is still called "Luo Yin Spring." The [name] is an artifact of the [divination]. Whether there is proof of the event I cannot ascertain. For now, I will be aware of it and will wait for it to be collected by the compiler of the county's local gazetteer.[128]

This passage shows one way that local oral history became written history. Someone would hear something and report it to local gazetteer

124.   Ibid., 13.54a.
125.   Ibid., 13.54b.
126.   Ibid., 15.46b.
127.   Luo Yin was a native of Qiantang, Zhejiang, who lived from 833 to 909. He was a great poet but was said to be so ugly that a woman who had been fascinated by his poems could no longer read them once she saw him. Giles, *A Chinese Biographical Dictionary*, 536.
128.   Qi Chengye, *Danshengtang ji*, 13.38b.

compilers, who might include it, with or without further research. Qi was especially interested in the history of his native place and his collection's catalog lists all of the late-sixteenth century official local gazetteers of Shaoxing Prefecture and its eight subordinate counties.[129]

Like many late-Ming literati, Qi Chengye liked to travel, and he used gazetteers to read and write about the places he visited. Qi's *Xinchang dao zhong you Tianmu su Guanling ji* 新昌道中遊天姥宿關嶺記 (Record of Visiting Tianmu and Resting at Guanling on the Road to Xinchang) reveals that he used the writings of eastern Zhejiang traveler Wang Shixing to discuss Mount Tianmu's relationship to the Tiantai Mountains, and looked up Mount Tianmu's height in a gazetteer:

> Past Banzhu 斑竹 [Village] is Huishu Ridge. On the left side of the ridge is Taiping Shrine 太平庵. It is very secluded. 10,000 stalks of huge bamboo obscure the clouds. As I entered, it was as if green snow was falling along the path; it stained the front of my robe. Inside there was one monk in seclusion chanting the Diamond Sutra. Someone called out that guests had arrived but he nonetheless did not answer. At first I was apprehensive about approaching him and did not move. But when we arrived at the gate I talked with him. He was just a wandering beggar monk engaged in ascetic practice. Below the ridge is Mt. Tianmu. We saw what Wang Hengshu 王恆叔 [Wang Shixing] described as, "All of the mountains of Tiantai are Mt. Tianmu's grandchildren, and thus the mountain is called 'Tianmu' (Heaven's Grandmother)." According to the illustrated gazetteer it is 3,500 *zhang* high and [the ridges] mutually intersect for several hundred *li*. But looking at it, it does not appear especially high.[130]

In this passage, the gazetteer to which Qi referred was likely the 1579 *Xinchang xian zhi*, the book studied in chapter 2. Qi owned a copy, and it listed Mount Tianmu's height as 3,500 *zhang*, whereas the national and provincial gazetteers did not provide Mount Tianmu's height. Qi Chengye's ways of using local gazetteers were unusual only in that they are well documented. Using local gazetteers as travel guides, literary reference works, and proof of family history was not uncommon for late-Ming officials.

129. Qi Chengye, *Danshengtang cang shumu*, 976, 979.
130. Qi Chengye, *Danshengtang ji*, 11.38b.

Other Literati Uses of Gazetteers
in Cultural Production

In the pages above we saw gazetteers used as sources for works on literature of particular provinces and famous mountains. They were used in other literary and artistic genres as well. By the mid Ming, gazetteers were the most important vehicle for gathering and funneling information on distant locales to elite cultural producers around the empire. They became building blocks for works distributed nationally. There were other sources, such as authors' collected works, but these were not generally confined to particular locales and unlike gazetteers, not arranged in ways that enabled easy topical research. Once literati had, to use the words of Bol, "begun to reconceptualize the nation as something less imperial, less derivative of court culture, and less centralized," gazetteers became both expressions of local participation in national culture and governance, and tools for producing new cultural products.[131] As the number and quality of gazetteers increased, their value increased even more. With a critical mass of local gazetteers, authors could produce many new works. In the sixteenth and seventeenth centuries, the number of literati who failed the examinations or chose careers outside of office increased and the commercial book market expanded. Literati, officials, and former officials became deeply involved in writing and publishing, and many used local gazetteers.

Various types of late imperial literature were largely excerpts from other works, and gazetteers were widely quoted. Other common uses of gazetteers include research for writing commemorative records, especially those of schools, temples, shrines, yamens, and other buildings.[132] *Leishu* 類書 (books arranged by categories) drew heavily on gazetteers. For example, the "fish" section of Peng Dayi's 彭大翼 1595 encyclopedia *Shan tang si kao* 山堂肆考 contains the following entry citing the gazetteer of Ningbo:

131.   Bol, "Rise of Local History," 76.

132.   See, e.g., Wu Kuan, *Taikang xian xiu xue ji* 太康縣修學記 (Record of reconstructing the Taikang County school), *Jia cang ji*, 31.18b.

Lu 鱸 Fish Slices

Ningbo Gazetteer: "The *lu* fish has a huge mouth and fine scales. The body has black dots. It is best for salting or pickling. The Sui dynasty and Tang dynasty courts praised the Songjiang *lu* fish slices sent in tribute by Wu Commandery. Emperor Yang [reigned 605–17] said 'Golden chopped jade fish slices are an excellent taste of the southeast.' There also is a four-gill variety that has crisp skin [when cooked] and thick [pieces of] meat. It is called crisp *lu* fish. There is a river *lu* fish that is smaller and has two gills. Its flavor is light. There is a pond *lu* fish that is huge, yet [its skin does] not [become] crisp." [133]

Li Shizhen 李時珍, in his famous materia medica, *Bencao gangmu* (published in 1500), cited the local products section of the gazetteer of Kuizhou, Sichuan, about a fish type, *jiayu* 嘉魚.[134]

Gazetteers were an important source for many *biji* 筆記 (notebooks), a widely read genre in which authors published their reading notes, sometimes with further polishing, commentary, and arrangement. The writing of *biji* became widespread in the Tang and Song dynasties, and continued throughout the late imperial period.[135] One of the most famous fifteenth-century *biji*, the *Shuyuan za ji* 菽園雜記 (Miscellaneous records from the bean garden), by Lu Rong, who was discussed above as an official who read gazetteers when investigating suspected corruption, reveals extensive engagement with gazetteers. Lu was from Taicang 太倉, Nanzhili, and in the *Shuyuan za ji* Lu makes clear citations to the gazetteers of Yangzhou, Songjiang, Zhenjiang, Suzhou, Kunshan, Ningbo, Shaoxing, Longquan 龍泉 (Jiangxi), Minxian 閩縣 (Fujian), Liaodong 遼東, and Sichuan. He also cited unnamed gazetteers in regard to ruins in Huanxian 環縣, Shaanxi.[136] Many additional notes and stories appear to draw on gazetteers and it is clear that he read them widely.

One of his favorite gazetteers was the 1468 *Ningbo fu zhi*. Lu probably got it while serving as Zhejiang provincial administration vice commissioner, beginning in 1489, and read it prior to his death in

---

133. Peng Dayi, *Shantang si kao*, 5b.
134. Li Shizhen, *Bencao gangmu*, 2437.
135. De Weerdt, "Production and Circulation."
136. Lu Rong, *Shuyuan za ji*, 1.4.

1494.[137] Lu seemed to have read it for pleasure and to resolve specific questions. For example, in one entry Lu noted that in Ningbo's Fenghua County there was a place called Jie 鮚, and he did not understand the meaning of its name. He looked in the gazetteer, which cited an explanation from the *Han shu*.

In another entry Lu wrote that since he was a child he had heard the story of Liang Shanbo 梁山伯 and Zhu Yingtai 祝英臺 but had never seen any reference to it. Then he found the story while reading the *Ningbo fu zhi*. He copied the story from the gazetteer into his notes:

> Liang and Zhu lived in the Eastern Jin. Mr. Liang wanted to marry Miss Zhu, but she was already betrothed to Mr. Ma. Mr. Liang soon died of illness and was buried in Ningbo. The following year, Zhu married Ma, but when her boat came close to Liang's gravesite, it could not go forward due to strong wind and waves. When Zhu mourned at his grave, the earth suddenly split open and she threw herself in and died. . . . It is said that in Wu there is a colorful butterfly that is transformed from a tangerine bug. Women call them Liang Shanbo and Zhu Yingtai.[138]

Lu also used gazetteers in writing colophons for paintings. In the late fifteenth century he copied biographies of Mo Yueding 莫月鼎 from the Huzhou and Suzhou gazetteers onto a portrait of him painted by Shen Wenming 沈文明. Mo was a thirteenth-century Daoist who was born in Huzhou and died in Suzhou. Mo's disciple, Zeng Keshan 曾可山, took the portrait to the Zhangsheng Daoist Monastery 長生道院 in Taicang, his hometown. Zeng died there and Lu Rong got the portrait. He kept it in his home and when he mounted it on a scroll he added the biographies.[139]

Because biographies constituted a large percentage of the content of most gazetteers, they were a ready source for other types of biographical works. Liao Daonan 廖道南 used gazetteers in his 1545 collection of biographies of court officials, *Diange cilin ji* 殿閣詞林記.[140] Jiao Hong 焦竑 (1541–1620) used them in his 1618 collection of biographies of Hanlin

137. *Ming Shilu, Xiaozong shilu*, 487.
138. Lu Rong, *Shuyuan za ji*, 135.
139. Ibid., 128.
140. Liao Daonan, *Diange cilin ji*, 6.13a.

scholars, *Yutang cong yu* 玉堂叢語.[141] In writing a virtuous woman biography of his friend Cheng Daonan's 程道南 grandmother, Ai Mu used a record of her contained in the gazetteer of her native place, Huizhou.[142]

Many authors collected anecdotes from gazetteers, often from a specific region, as with the *Jiang han cong tan* 江漢叢談 (Collected chatter from the Jiang Han region), by Chen Shiyuan 陳士元 (*jinshi* 1544), which is about the area near the confluence of the Jiang and Han Rivers, in Huguang Province. In a section titled "random treasures," which consists of interesting or surprising stories, Chen cites the gazetteer of Changde for a story about a magistrate who saved a sparrow in the Yongle era (1403–24) and was later saved by a sparrow when he was gravely ill.[143]

The Use of Gazetteers in Genealogical Research and Lineage Construction

As lineage formation intensified in the fifteenth century, gazetteers became an important source for genealogical research. People who came from modest or obscure backgrounds and rose to high positions wanted to stretch their known family lines to include illustrious ancestors, but the migration and destruction that accompanied the Mongol conquest and later collapse left many people with only a vague understanding of their heritage.

In the mid-fifteenth century, the high-ranking official Ye Sheng wrote about his genealogical research. He explained that he could only trace his ancestry back to Ye Xiushi 葉秀實, who during the Mongol Yuan dynasty (1279–1368) moved in with his father-in-law in Kunshan, Nanzhili. But Ye Sheng did not know where Ye Xiushi came from or the names of his immediate family members. Thus, he searched in genealogies of families surnamed Ye and books on the distribution of people of various surnames. He noted that previous Ye genealogy compilers had

141. Jiao Hong, *Yutang cong yu*, vol. 5, 165; Wang Shizhen, *Yanzhou sibugao xugao*, 63.18b.

142. Ai Mu, *Ai Xiting xiansheng wenji*, 734.

143. Chen Shiyuan, *Jiang han cong tan*, 1.24a.

used the gazetteer of Suzhou prefecture to research family origins and concluded that the Ye came from Huzhou to Changzhou (a subordinate territory of Suzhou). Ye Sheng, however, argued their conclusion was not necessarily correct because surname books recorded people named Ye in the Kingdom of Wu (222–80 CE) and thus it was possible that the Kunshan group predated the Huzhou migrants.[144]

In another piece, "Feng Wenqing fu Qingmin gu yuan" 豐文慶復清 敏故園 (Feng Wenqing recovers the old Qingmin Garden), Ye recorded how his colleague used a local gazetteer to find his ancestral home for the purpose of burying his father. Feng's ancestors had lived for generations in Yin, a county in Ningbo Prefecture, and he was the descendant of an eleventh-century official, Feng Qingmin. Feng Wenqing's great-great grandfather, however, had moved to the neighboring county of Fenghua, and his great-grandfather moved on to Dinghai, another Ningbo county. When Feng's father died in the Zhengtong era (1436–50) he took the coffin back to Yin County, hoping to bury his father with his ancestors. Unfortunately, Feng did not know the gravesite, and inquiries initially led nowhere. He was dejected until someone suggested he try the ruins of Ziqing Abbey 紫清觀 and drew him a map of how to get there. On the road he met a diviner who cast the *feng* 豐 and *ge* 革 hexagrams, the first means "abundance" and happens to be Feng's surname, and the second means "change." Feng was happy and said, "Must not this divination of my surname mean that this is my land?" Soon thereafter, Feng got a copy of the 1320 prefectural gazetteer, which said, "Ziqing Abbey is three *li* west of the city, it is Feng Qingmin's old garden." According to Ye Sheng, Feng Wenqing was overjoyed and set his mind to restoring the garden. First he obtained the abbey's land registration documents from a local person. These recorded more than thirty *mu* of attached lands, but neighbors had encroached on them, so Feng bought the land back, carefully restored the stone funerary statues in front of his ancestor's 300-year-old grave, and made the spot his home.[145] In this case, Feng Wenqing used the local gazetteer to confirm his interpretation of a divination and someone's memory of a connection between an abbey

144.   Ye Sheng, *Shuidong riji*, 186–87.
145.   Ibid., 81.

and his family. He then was able to recover his ancestral home and bury his father with his ancestors.

Conclusion

The cases discussed in this chapter reveal ways in which readers gave meaning to gazetteers and used them as sites for expressing and contesting local issues, for legitimating tangible interests in local societies, and for advocating policy positions. The examples of gazetteers' use in genealogical research show how people could read gazetteer entries as points of light illuminating obscure family pasts and points of connection in building or recovering family ties. Gazetteers contained public genealogical information that could either bolster or undermine a desired family agenda and therefore had to be engaged.

In the case of Lake Zaoli's falsified history, we can see gazetteers as sites for contesting economic rights and explaining government rationales for decisions on local issues. The author of the 1606 *Shangyu xian zhi* tried to present the lake's history in a way that would support taking water from those having customary rights to it. The lake residents were an "interpretive community" who read the new gazetteer as an attack on them, and successfully challenged in court the history embodied therein.

The author of the passage on the Shangyu-Yuyao water dispute advocated a method of allocating water rights in an inter-jurisdictional water system that was contrary to the established prefectural policy. If we consider gazetteers to be official documents, we might have expected the author to have taken the broader view of benefiting the prefecture as a whole, yet the position taken was decidedly that of the Shangyu County residents. The author criticized the fifteenth-century prefect's order to split the water evenly and argued that it was wrongly decided. He even alleged that a Yuyao scholar recognized that the water did not belong to Yuyao and that the Yuyao people were using their gazetteer to make improper claims to Shangyu's water.

Thus, in conceptualizing Ming local gazetteers, we should not think of them as dry compendia of statistics and miscellaneous writings akin to encyclopedias. In fact, as we have seen, they were living and evolving documents. Gazetteers were important sites in struggles for status, power, and wealth in Ming local societies, and a medium for transmitting and reifying successes. They were also important sites for communicating and debating ideas of local concern and were key nodes for disseminating local information to a broader audience. Chapter 2 showed how one kinship group controlled the compilation of a gazetteer. This chapter has shown why it could be worth the effort.

From what we have seen above, it is clear that gazetteers had an intimate connection to travel. Ming travelers used them as guidebooks, doing background reading before trips or upon arrival. Sometimes they even carried local gazetteers with them on the road. In addition to serving as guidebooks, local gazetteers brought together travelers and locals, or two or more travelers. They were objects around which educated men finding themselves in out-of-the-way places could bond with other such men and reaffirm and enhance their ties to the national elite culture. By gathering in one book writings connected to a given locale and making possible their transmission to travelers, local gazetteers helped put those sites on the greater Chinese cultural map.

Local gazetteers also were one of the basic sources for various types of writing that were empire-wide in scope. In addition to other forms of travel writing, such as Du Mu's *You mingshan ji*, local gazetteers were a key source for biographical works, histories, books arranged by category, etc. Thus, in thinking of local gazetteers and their relation to cultural production in Ming China, one might imagine them as cells in a honeycomb that covered the empire. Local gazetteers were the vessel in which materials gathered by dozens of contributors were, like honey from bees, distilled and deposited. Local gazetteer contents then became available for consumption and transformation into new cultural products by locals, travelers, and those residing in other places. In the Ming, local gazetteers were an important genre for literati and cultural production, and they deserve our careful attention.

EPILOGUE

Local gazetteers persisted as an important genre throughout the imperial and Republican periods. After two decades of neglect in the People's Republic of China during the 1960s and 1970s, in 1980 the PRC government began reviving the genre. The government organized local compilation committees, issued regulations, held conferences about gazetteers, and created journals devoted to their study, most prominently *Zhongguo difangzhi* 中國地方志 (Chinese gazetteers). As in late imperial China, new compilation committees were organized in a hierarchy through territorial units, and are now led by a central government organ in Beijing, the Chinese Gazetteer Leadership Small Group. Most compilation committee members are local bureaucrats, but local scholars also participate. The revival has led to publication of thousands of new gazetteers since 1982.

In China today, gazetteer studies is a major field. There has been a steady stream of publications about the best ways to organize new gazetteers, studies of old gazetteers and important compilers, and extended analysis of theoretical issues in gazetteer compilation. Academics and bureaucrats meet and exchange ideas in national and provincial conferences on gazetteers. Some conferences, such as the 2011 International Conference on Chinese Local Gazetteers sponsored by the Leadership Small Group and the city government of Ningbo, Zhejiang, involved hundreds of participants meeting for several days. Old gazetteers have become widely available through reprinting and digitization projects.

Most major Chinese libraries have reprinted gazetteers in their collections, and the National Library of China has put nearly seven thousand pre-1949 gazetteers online. Printed gazetteers, old and new, are sold in bookstores.

As we have seen in this study, gazetteers from the Song, Yuan, Ming, and early-Qing dynasties were produced by people with varying agendas, and read and used in many ways. Studying their production, circulation, and audience provides windows into the societies in which they were published. Similarly, new gazetteers are complex texts that can reveal much about contemporary society. The revival of the local gazetteer genre is part of a wider interest in, and desire to recover, local history lost during the Cultural Revolution. But many more agendas are expressed in new gazetteers, such as the promotion of industry, tourism, and Communist Party successes. Although the topics covered in gazetteers, underlying agendas, and significance in the information order may have changed since the imperial period, the gazetteer genre lives on.

Bibliography

References are listed in the following order: (1) gazetteers, (2) other primary sources, and (3) secondary sources. Gazetteers are listed alphabetically by title. Successive editions of the same title are listed chronologically within the alphabetized list. Because most gazetteers had multiple compilers and were supplemented after the original block cutting, it is often impossible to identify a primary compiler. Thus, entries follow common attribution in major catalogs to assist readers in locating the sources. Because this study cites numerous gazetteers, to limit the size of the bibliography only one compiler is listed and titles for gazetteers are not translated when they follow the standard title pattern (place name, administrative unit, gazetteer). Dating gazetteers is complex and listed dates are approximate. Listed dates are the dates when either the manuscript was completed, the blocks were cut, or the first preface was written, followed by dates of known supplements. Readers needing detailed author and date information should consult the gazetteer itself or an annotated gazetteer catalog. Gazetteers that have a prefix to their title, such as "recompiled," or a reign period, are listed twice: once under the prefix and once under the place name. In the footnotes, years are given only when multiple editions are cited. Page numbers in gazetteers are listed by the reprint numbering in widely available reprints, and in the original numbering in others, using "a" and "b" to indicate recto and verso.

Gazetteers

Anji zhou zhi 安吉州志. 1557. Jiang Yilin 江一麟. In *TYG*.
Anqing fu zhi 安慶府志. Li Xun 李遜. 1554. In *ZFC*.
Anxi xian zhi 安溪縣志. 1552. Lin Younian 林有年. In *TYG*.

Badong xian zhi 巴東縣志. 1551. Yang Peizhi 楊培之. In *TYG*.
Bailudong shuyuan gu zhi wu zhong 白鹿洞書院古志五種. Li Chenguang 李晨光 et al., eds. Beijing: Zhonghua shuju, 1995.
Baoding fu zhi 保定府志. 1608. Feng Weimin 馮惟敏. In *RBC*.
Baoding jun zhi 保定郡志. 1494. Zhang Cai 張才. In *TYG*.

Baoning fu zhi 保寧府志. 1543. Yang Sizhen 楊思震. HYM.
[*Baoqing*] *Siming zhi* [寶慶] 四明志. 1227. Fang Wanli 方萬里. In *SYFZ*.
Bozhou zhi 亳州志. 1564. Li Xianfang 李先芳. HYM.
Bozhou zhi 亳州志. 1894. Zhong Tai 鍾泰. In *ZDJ*.

Cangzhou zhi 滄州志. 1603. Li Mengxiong 李夢熊. HYM.
Chaling zhou zhi 茶陵州志. 1525. Zhang Zhi 張治. In *TYG*.
Changde fu zhi 常德府志. 1535, 1538, 1547. Chen Hongmo 陳洪謨. In *TYG*.
Changguo zhou tuzhi 昌國州圖志. 1298. Feng Fujing 馮福京. In *SYFZ*.
Changle xian zhi 昌樂縣志. 1546. Zhu Mu 朱木. In *TYG*.
Changshan xian zhi 常山縣志. 1585, 1660. Zhan Lai 詹萊. HYM.
Changshu xian zhi 常熟縣志. 1539. Deng Fu 鄧韍. In *ZSX*.
Changyuan xian zhi 長垣縣志. 1541. Liu Fang 劉芳. In *TYG*.
Changzhou fu zhi 常州府志. 1618. Tang Hezheng 唐鶴徵. In *NTGB*.
Chaoyang xian zhi 潮陽縣志. 1572. Lin Dachun 林大春. In *TYG*.
Cheng'an yi sheng 成安邑乘. 1618, 1646. Jia Sance 賈三策. In *MDGB*.
Chengdu fu zhi [新修] 成都府志. 1621. Zhang Shiyong 張世雍. LCM.
Chengtian fu zhi 承天府志. 1602. Sun Wenlong 孫文龍. In *RBC*.
Chenzhou zhi 郴州志. 1576. Hu Han 胡漢. In *TYG*.
Chicheng xin zhi 赤城新志. 1497. Xie Duo 謝鐸. In *SKCM*.
Chizhou fu zhi 池州府志. 1545. Wang Chong 王崇. In *TYG*.
[*Chong xiu*] *Qishan xian zhi* 重修岐山縣. 1657. Wang Gu 王穀. BNF.
[*Chongxiu*] *Hezhou zhi* 重修合州志. 1579. Liu Fangsheng 劉芳聲. In *RBC*.
Chongyi xian zhi 崇義縣志. 1552. Zheng Qiao 鄭喬. HYM.
Chun'an xian zhi 淳安縣志. 1524. Yao Mingluan 姚鳴鸞. In *TYG*.
Chuxiong fu zhi 楚雄府志. 1568. Xu Shi 徐栻. In *RBC*.
Cili xian zhi 慈利縣志. 1573. Chen Guangqian 陳光前. In *TYG*.
Cizhou zhi 磁州志. 1553. In *TYG*.

Da Ming yitongzhi 大明一統志. 1461. Li Xian 李賢. Taibei: Wenhai chubanshe, 1965.
Dacheng xian zhi 大成縣志. 1583, 1620s. Di Tonggui 狄同奎. In *MDGB*.
Dangshan xian zhi 碭山縣志. 1639. Liu Fang 劉芳. In *MDGB*.
Dantu xian zhi 丹徒縣志. 1515. Li Dong 李東. HYM.
Dengfeng xian zhi 登封縣志. 1529. Hou Tai 侯泰. In *NTGB*.
Dezhou zhi 德州志. 1528. He Hong 何洪. In *TYG*.
Dezhou zhi 德州志. 1570s, 1620s. Tang Wenhua 唐文華. HYM.
Dingxiang xian zhi 定襄縣志. 1616. An Jiashi 安嘉士. In *MDGB*.
Dongguang xian zhi 東光縣志. 1693. Bai Weiji 白煒璣. NLCD.
Dongxiang xian zhi 東鄉縣志. 1524. Rao Wenbi 饒文璧. In *TYG*.

Fengrun xian zhi 豐潤縣志. 1570. Shi Bangzheng 石邦政. In *SKCM*.
Fengyang xian zhi 鳳陽縣志. 1578. Zhang Yunxiang 張雲翔. HYM.
Fu'an xian zhi 福安縣志. 1597. Lu Yizai 陸以載. In *RBC*.
Fushi zhi 浮石志. 1995. Zhao Enpu 趙恩普. Taishan, Guangdong: Fushan yuebao she 浮山月报社.
Fuzhou fu zhi 撫州府志. 1503. Yang Yuan 楊淵. In *TYG*.

Ganshui zhi 澉水志. 1230. Chang Tang 常棠. In *SYFZ*.

Ganzhen zhi 甘鎮志. 1608, 1657. Yang Chunmao 楊春茂. In *ZDJ*.

Ganzhou fu zhi 贛州府志. 1536. Dong Tianxi 董天錫. In *TYG*.

Ganzhou fu zhi 贛州府志. 1621, 1660. Yu Wenlong 余文龍. In *BTGJ*.

Ganzhou fu zhi 甘州府志. 1779. Zhong Gengqi 鐘賡起. HY.

Gaochun xian zhi 高淳縣志. 1562. Li Qidong 劉啓東. In *TYG*.

Gong'an xian zhi 公安縣志. 1543. Wei Qi 魏奇. HYM.

Gong'an xian zhi 公安縣志. 1874, 1937. Wang Wei 王慰. In *ZFC*.

Gongxian zhi 鞏縣志. 1555. Kang Shaodi 康紹第. In *TYG*.

Gongxue shuyuan zhi 共學書院志. Wanli era (1573–1620). Yue Hesheng 岳和聲. In *Zhongguo lidai shuyuan zhi*.

Guangchang xian zhi 廣昌縣志. 1683. Wang Jingsheng 王景升. In *ZFC*.

Guangdong tong zhi 廣東通志. 1561. Huang Zuo 黃佐. Hong Kong: Dadong tushu gongsi, 1977.

Guanghua xian zhi 光化縣志. 1515. Cao Lin 曹璘. In *TYG*.

Guangping fu zhi 廣平府志. 1550. Chen Fei 陳棐. In *TYG*.

Guangshan xian zhi 光山縣志. 1556. Wang Jiashi 王家士. In *TYG*.

Guiji xian zhi 會稽縣志. 1575. Yang Weixin 楊維新. In *TYG*.

Guiji zhi 會稽志. 1201, 1510. Shi Su 施宿. HYM.

Guiji zhi 會稽志. 1201, 1510. Shi Su 施宿. In *Siku quanshu zhenben* 四庫全書珍本. Taibei: Taiwan shangwu yinshuguan, 1977.

Guiji zhi 會稽志. 1201, 1510. Shi Su 施宿. In *SYFZ*.

Gushi xian zhi 固始縣志. 1659. Bao Ying 包㦤. In *RBC*.

Gushi xian zhi 固始縣志. 1542. Ge Chen 葛臣. In *TYG*.

Gusu zhi 姑蘇志. 1506. Wang Ao 王鏊. In *ZSX*.

Gutian xian zhi 古田縣志. 1600, 1606. Liu Riyi 劉日暘. HYM.

Haimen xian zhi 海門縣志. 1536. Cui Tong 崔桐. In *TYG*.

Haizhou zhi 海州志. 1572. Zhang Feng 張峰. In *TYG*.

Hangzhou fu zhi 杭州府志. 1474. Chen Rang 陳讓. HYM.

Hanyang fu zhi 漢陽府志. 1546. Zhu Yi 朱衣. In *TYG*.

Henan tong zhi 河南通志. 1670. Jia Hanfu 賈漢復. NLCD.

Hengzhou fu zhi 衡州府志. 1537. Liu Fu 劉黻. In *TYG*.

Hengzhou fu zhi 衡州府志. 1671, 1682. Zhang Qixun 張奇勛. In *BTGJ*.

Hezhou zhi [*Chongxiu*] [重修] 合州志. 1579. Liu Fangsheng 劉芳聲. In *RBC*.

Hezhou zhi 河州志. 1546. Wu Zhen 吳禎. In *Zhongguo Xizang ji Gan Qing Chuan Dian Zang qu fangzhi huibian* 中國西藏及甘青川滇藏区方志彙編 (Collected reprints of China's Tibet, Gansu, Qinghai, Sichuan, and Yunnan, Tibetan region gazetteers). Zhang Yuxin 張羽新, ed. Beijing: Xueyuan *chubanshe*, 2003.

Hongdong xian zhi 洪洞縣志. 1591. Qiao Yinyu 喬因羽. NLCD.

Huaiqing fu zhi 懷慶府志. 1566. Liu Jing 劉淐. HYM.

Huairen xian zhi 懷仁縣誌. 1601. Yang Shoujie 楊守介. HYM.

Huairou xian zhi 懷柔縣志. 1604. Zhou Zhongshi 周仲士. HYM.

Huanggang xian zhi 黃岡縣誌. 1608. Wang Tonggui 王同軌. HYM.

Huangzhou fu zhi 黃州府志. 1500. Lu Xizhe 盧希哲. In *TYG*.

Huating xian zhi 華亭縣志. 1521. Shen Xi 沈錫. LCM.

Huguang zong zhi 湖廣總志. 1578. Xu Xuemo 徐學謨. In *SKCM*.

Hui'an xian zhi 惠安縣志. 1530. Zhang Yue 張岳. In *TYG*.

Hui da ji 惠大記. 1528. Zheng Weixin 鄭維新. In *TYG*.

Huixian zhi 輝縣志. 1528. Zhang Tianzhen 張天眞. In *TYG*.

Huizhou fu zhi 徽州府志. 1502. Wang Shunmin 汪舜民. In *TYG*.

Huizhou fu zhi 惠州府志. 1542. Liu Wu 劉梧. In *RBC*.

Huizhou fu zhi 惠州府志. 1556. Yang Zaiming 楊載鳴. In *TYG*.

Jiading xian zhi 嘉定縣志. 1605. Han Jun 韓浚. In *SKCM*.

Jiahe zhi 嘉禾志. 1288. Xu Shuo 徐碩. In *SYFZ*.

Jianchang fu zhi 建昌府志. 1517. Xia Liangsheng 夏良勝. In *TYG*.

Jiangle xian zhi 將樂縣志. 1505. Li Min 李敏. In *TYG*.

Jiangning xian zhi 江寧縣志. 1521. Wang Gao 王誥. In *BTGJ*.

Jiangxi sheng da zhi 江西省大志. 1597. Wang Zongmu 王宗沐. In *NTGB*.

Jiangyin xian zhi 江陰縣志. 1640. Feng Shiren 馮士仁. In *MGHY*.

Jianning xian zhi 建寧縣志. 1541. He Menglun 何孟倫. In *TYG*.

Jianping xian zhi 建平縣志. 1531. Yao Wenye 姚文燁. In *TYG*, HYM.

Jianyang xian zhi 建陽縣志. 1553. Tian Juzhong 田居中. In *RBC*.

[*Jiatai*] *Wuxing zhi* 嘉泰吳興志. 1201. Tan Yao 談鑰. In *SYFZ*.

Jiayu xian zhi 嘉魚縣誌. 1449. Mo Zhen 莫震. HYM.

[*Jingding*] *Jiankang zhi* [景定] 建康志. 1261. Zhou Yinghe 周應合. In *SYFZ*.

Jingxian zhi 涇縣志. 1552. Wang Tinggan 王廷榦. In *TYG*.

Jingyuan xian zhi 靖遠縣志. 1833. Chen Zhiji 陳之驥. BNF.

Jingzhou fu zhi 荆州府志. 1532. Sun Cun 孫存. HYM.

Jinhua fu zhi 金華府志. 1578. Wang Maode 王懋德. In *SKCM*.

Jinhua fu zhi 金華府志. 1578. Wang Maode 王懋德. In *ZSX*.

Jinling xin zhi 金陵新志. 1344. Zhang Xuan 張鉉. In *SYFZ*.

Jinxian xian zhi 進賢縣志. 1563. Wang Ji 汪集. HYM.

Jixi xian zhi 績溪縣志. 1581. He Tang 何棠. HYM.

Jizhou zhi 薊州志. 1524. Xiong Xiang 熊相. HYM.

Kaifeng fu zhi 開封府志. 1585. Zhu Mujie 朱睦㮮. HYM.

Kuizhou fu zhi 夔州府志. 1513. Wu Qian 吳潛. In *TYG*.

Laiwu xian zhi 萊蕪縣志. 1548. Chen Ganyu 陳甘雨. In *TYG*.

Liangzhou fu zhi bei kao 涼州府志備考. Zhang Shu 張澍 (ca. 1776–1847). *n.d.* BNF.

Lianzhou fu zhi 廉州府志. 1637. Zhang Guojing 張國經. In *RBC*.

Licheng xian zhi 歷城縣志. 1640. Ye Chengzong 葉承宗. LCM.

Lin'an zhi 臨安志. 1265–74. Qian Shuoyou 潛說友. In *SYFZ*.

Lingshi xian zhi 靈石縣志. 1601. Lu Yilin 路一麟. HYM.

Linjiang fu zhi 臨江府志. 1572. Liu Song 劉松. In *TYG*.

Linqu xian zhi 臨朐縣志. 1552. Wang Jiashi 王家士. In *TYG*.

Linying xian zhi 臨穎縣志. 1529. Lu Tang 盧鏜. HYM.

Linzhang xian zhi 臨漳縣志. 1506. Jing Fang 景芳. In *TYG*.

Lixian zhi 蠡縣志. 1534. Li Fuchu 李復初. In *TYG*.

Liyang xian zhi 溧陽縣志. 1813. Li Jingyi 李景嶧. In *ZDJ*.

Longqing zhi 隆慶志. 1549. Xie Tinggui 謝庭桂. In *TYG*.
Lucheng xian zhi 潞城縣志. 1591, 1625. Feng Weixian 馮惟賢. In *MGHY*.
Lüeyang xian zhi 略陽縣志. 1552. Li Yuchun 李遇春. In *TYG*.
Luhe xian zhi 六合縣志. 1553. Dong Bangzheng 董邦政. In *TYG*.
Luzhou fu zhi 盧州府志. 1575. Wu Daoming 吳道明. LCM.

Mahu fu zhi 馬湖府志. 1555. Yu Chengxun 余承勳. In *TYG*.
Mianyang zhi 沔陽志. 1531. Tong Chengxu 童承敘. In *TYG*.

Nan'an fu zhi 南安府志. 1536. Liu Jie 劉節. In *TYG*.
Nanchang fu zhi 南昌府志. 1588. Zhang Huang 章潢. In *RBC*.
Nanji zhi 南畿志. 1535. Chen Yi 陳沂. In *BTGJ*.
Nankang fu zhi 南康府志. 1519. Chen Lin 陳林. In *TYG*.
Nankang xian zhi 南康縣志. 1555. Liu Zhaowen 劉昭文. In *TYG*.
Nanxiong fu zhi 南雄府志. 1542. Tan Dachu 譚大初. In *TYG*.
Neihuang xian zhi 內黃縣志. 1537. Dong Xian 董弦. In *TYG*.
Neixiang xian zhi 內鄉縣誌. 1485. Hu Kuang 胡匡. HYM.
Ningbo fu zhi 寧波府志. 1560. Zhang Shiche 張時徹. HYM.
Ningbo jun zhi 寧波郡志. 1468. Yang Shi 楊寔. HYM.
Ningguo xian zhi 寧國縣志. 1531. Fan Gao 范鎬. In *TYG*.
Ninghai xian zhi 寧海縣志. 1632. Song Kuiguang 宋奎光. HYM.
Ninghai zhou zhi 寧海州志. 1548. Li Guangxian 李光先. In *TYG*.
Ningxia xin zhi 寧夏新志. 1501. Hu Ruli 胡汝礪. In *TYG*.
Ningzhou zhi 寧州志. 1543. Gong Xian 龔暹. In *TYG*.

Pengcheng zhi 彭城志. 1438, 1441. Song Ji 宋驥. HYM.
Pinghu xian zhi 平湖縣志. 1627. Sun Hongqi 孫弘祺. In *TYG*.
Pingliang fu zhi 平涼府志. 1560. Zhao Shichun 趙時春. In *SKCM*.
Pingyuan zhi 平原縣志. 1590. Gao Zhizhi 高知止. HYM.
Pu'an zhou zhi 普安州志. 1549. Shen Xu 沈勗. In *TYG*.
Pujiang zhi lüe 浦江志略. 1526. Mao Fengshao 毛鳳韶. In *TYG*.
Putai zhi 蒲臺志. 1591. Wang Eryan 王爾彥. HYM.
Puzhou zhi 濮州志. 1527. Deng Fu 鄧黻. In *TYG*.
Puzhou zhi 蒲州志. 1559. Bian Xiang 邊像. HYM.

Qi sheng 齊乘. 1351. Yu Qian 于欽. In *SYFZ*.
[*Qiandao*] *Siming tu jing* 乾道四明圖經. 1169. Zhang Jin 張津. In *SYFZ*.
Qinchuan zhi 琴川志. 1363. Sun Yingshi 孫應時. In *SYFZ*.
Qingyun xian zhi 慶雲縣志. 1585. Ke Yiquan 柯一泉. HYM.
Qingzhou fu zhi 青州府志. 1565. Chen Ganyu 陳甘雨. In *TYG*.
Qinzhou zhi 欽州志. 1539. Lin Xiyuan 林希元. In *TYG*.
Qishui xian zhi 蘄水縣志. 1547. Xiao Pu 蕭璞. NLCD.
Qizhou zhi 蘄州誌. 1529, 1536. Gan Ze 甘澤. In *TYG*.
Queli zhi 闕里志. 1505. Chen Gao 陳鎬. HYM.
Quwo xian zhi 曲沃縣志. 1551. Liu Lusheng 劉魯生. In *TYG*.
Quzhou fu zhi 衢州府志. 1622. Ye Bingjing 葉秉敬. In *ZFC*.

Raoyang xian zhi 饒陽縣志. 1601, 1609. Shi Jingshi 石徑世. In *MDGB*.
Rugao xian zhi 如皋縣志. 1560. Xie Shaozu 謝紹祖. In *TYG*.
Ruichang xian zhi 瑞昌縣志. 1570. Liu Chu 劉儲. In *TYG*.
Ruijin xian zhi 瑞金縣志. 1543. Zhao Dong 趙動. In *TYG*.
Ruizhou fu zhi 瑞州府志. 1518. Xiong Xiang 熊相. In *TYG*.
Ruzhou zhi 汝州志. 1506, 1510. Cheng Tiangui 承天貴. In *TYG*.

Shaanxi tong zhi 陝西通志. 1667. Jia Hanfu 價漢復. NCLD.
Shan lu 剡錄. Gao Sisun 高似孫. 1214. In *SYFZ*.
Shandong tong zhi 山東通志. 1533, 1616. Lu Yi 陸釴. BNF.
Shangcheng xian zhi 商城縣志. 1551. Wan Jiong 萬炯. In *TYG*.
Shangyu xian zhi 上虞縣志. 1606. Xu Daiping 徐待聘. HYM.
Shangyu xian zhi 上虞縣志. 1606. Xu Daiping 徐待聘. Tianjin Public Library.
Shangyu xian zhi 上虞縣志. 1671. Zheng Qiao 鄭僑. In *ZFC*.
Shangyu xian zhi 上虞縣志. 1891. Tang Xuchun 唐煦春. In *ZFC*.
Shangyu xian zhi 上虞縣志. Shangyu xian zhi bianzuan weiyuanhui. Hangzhou: Zhejiang renmin chubanshe, 1990.
Shangyu xian zhi jiao xu 上虞縣誌校續. Chu Jiazao 儲家藻. 1889. In *ZFC*.
Shangyuan xian zhi 上元縣志. 1593. Cheng Sanxing 程三省. HYM.
Shaowu fu zhi 邵武府志. 1543. Chen Rang 陳讓. In *TYG*.
Shaoxing fu zhi 紹興府志. 1587. Zhang Yuanbian 張元忭. In *ZFC*.
Shaoxing fu zhi 紹興府志. 1792. Li Hengte 李亨特. In *ZFC*.
Shenxian zhi 莘縣志. 1515. Wu Zongqi 吳宗器. In *TYG*.
Shidai xian zhi 石埭縣志. 1547. Huang Ying 黄鎣. HYM.
Shihu zhi 石湖志. Mo Dan 莫旦. In *XXSK*.
Shixing xian zhi 始興縣志. 1536. Wang Qingzhou 汪慶舟. In *TYG*.
Shouchang xian zhi 壽昌縣志. 1586, 1650. Li Siyue 李思悦. In *MDGB*.
Shouning daizhi 壽寧待志. 1637. Feng Menglong 馮夢龍. Fuzhou: Fujian renmin chubanshe, 1983.
Shuntian fu zhi 順天府志. Xie Jie 謝杰. 1593. In *SKCM*.
Sichuan zong zhi 四川總志. 1542. Liu Damo 劉大謨. In *BTGJ*.
Siming tu jing 四明圖經. 1169. Zhang Jin 張津. In *SYFZ*.
Siming xu zhi 四明續志. 1342. Wang Yuangong 王元恭. In *SYFZ*.
Siming zhi 四明志. 1227. Fang Wanli 方萬里. In *SYFZ*.
Siming zhi 四明志. 1320. Yuan Jue 袁桷. In *SYFZ*.
Sinan fu zhi 思南府志. Tian Rucheng 田汝成. 1537, 1539. In *TYG*.
Songjiang fu zhi 松江府志. 1512. Gu Qing 顧清. In *TYG*.
Suqian xian zhi 宿遷縣志. 1577. Yu Wenwei 喻文偉. In *TYG*.
Suzhou fu zhi 蘇州府志. 1379. Lu Xiong 盧熊. HYM.
Suzhou zhi 宿州志. 1499. Zeng Xian 曾顯. In *TYG*.

Taicang zhou zhi 太倉州志. 1548, 1629. Zhang Yin 張寅. In *TYG*.
Taikang xian zhi 太康縣志. 1524. An Du 安都. In *TYG*.
Taiping fu zhi 太平府誌. 1575. Cai Ying'en 蔡迎恩. In *RBC*.
Tangyin xian zhi 湯陰縣志. 1637. Sha Yunjin 沙蘊金. In *MDGB*.

Taoyuan xian zhi 桃源縣志. 1576. Zheng Tianzuo 鄭天佐. In *RBC*.

Tengxian zhi 滕縣志. 1585. Yang Chengfu 楊承父. In *RBC*.

Thành chương huyện chí 清漳縣志. 1800. Diễn Nguyễn.

Tianchang xian zhi 天長縣志. 1550. Wang Xin 王心. In *TYG*.

Tiantai xian zhi 天台縣志. 1684. Li Deyao 李德耀. NLCD.

Tingzhou fu zhi 汀州府志. 1527. Shao Youdao 邵有道. In *TYG*.

Tongling xian zhi 銅陵縣志. 1563. Li Shiyuan 李士元. In *TYG*.

Tongzhou zhi 通州志. 1530. Lin Ying 林穎. In *TYG*.

Weinan xian zhi 渭南縣志. 1541. Nan Daji 南大吉. HYM.

Weishi xian zhi 尉氏縣志. 1549. Wang Xin 汪心. In *TYG*.

Weiyang zhi 惟揚志. 1542. Sheng Yi 盛儀. In *TYG*.

Wengyuan xian zhi 翁源縣誌. 1557. Li Kongming 李孔明. In *TYG*.

Wenxian zhi 溫縣志. 1577. Zhang Di 張第. HYM.

Wenxian zhi 文縣志. 1702. Jiang Jingrui 江景瑞. BNF.

Wucheng xian zhi 武城縣志. 1549. You Qi 尤麒. In *TYG*.

Wucheng xian zhi 烏程縣志. 1637. Liu Yichun 劉沂春. In *RBC*.

Wuding zhou zhi 武定州志. 1548. Liu Dian 劉佃. In *TYG*.

Wuding zhou zhi 武定州志. 1588. Xing Tong 邢侗. In *MGHY*.

Wujiang xian zhi 吳江縣志. 1561. Xu Shizeng 徐師曾. In *ZSX*.

Wujiang zhi 吳江志. 1488. Mo Dan 莫旦. In *ZSX*.

Wujun tujing xu ji 吳郡圖經續記. 1100. Zhu Changwen 朱長文. In *SYFZ*.

Wujun zhi 吳郡志. 1229. Fan Chengda 范成大. In *ZFC*.

Wukang xian zhi 武康縣志. 1550. Luo Wensheng 駱文盛. In *TYG*.

Wuliang kao zhi 五涼考治. 1749. Zhang Shaomei 張玿美. BNF.

Wuning xian zhi 武寧縣志. 1543, 1562. In *TYG*.

Wuwei zhou zhi 無爲州志. 1520, 1528. Wu Zhen 吳臻. HYM.

Wuxi xian zhi 無錫縣志. 1496. Li Shu 李庶. In *NTGB*.

Wuxi xian zhi 無錫縣志. 1574. Qin Liang 秦梁. HYM.

Wuxian zhi 吳縣志. 1642. Niu Ruolin 牛若麟. In *TYG*.

Wuxing zhi 吳興志. 1201. Tan Yao 談鑰. In *SYFZ*.

Xiajin xian zhi 夏津縣志. 1540. Yi Shizhong 易時中. In *TYG*.

[*Xianchun*] *Lin'an zhi* 咸淳臨安志. 1265–74. Qian Shuoyou 潛説友. In *SYFZ*.

Xianghe xian zhi 香河縣志. 1620. Shen Weibin 沈惟炳. HYM.

Xiangshan xian zhi 象山縣志. 1556. Mao Dejing 毛德京. In *TYG*.

Xianxi zhi 仙溪志. 1351. Zhao Yumi 趙與泌. In *SYFZ*.

Xiayi xian zhi 夏邑縣志. 1545. Zheng Xiang 鄭相. In *TYG*.

Xihe xian xin zhi 西和縣新志. 1775. Qiu Daying 邱大英. BNF.

[*Xin xiu*] *Chengdu fu zhi* 新修成都府志. 1621. Zhang Shiyong 張世雍. LCM.

Xincai xian zhi 新蔡縣志. 1579. Liu Da'en 劉大恩. HYM.

Xincai xian zhi 新蔡縣志. 1795. Mo Xizhang 莫璵章. In *ZFC*.

Xinchang xian zhi 新昌縣志. 1477, 1521. Mo Dan 莫旦. LCM.

Xinchang xian zhi 新昌縣志. 1477. Mo Dan 莫旦. Manuscript copy held in Nanjing zhongguo kexueyuan dili yanjiusuo.

Xinchang xian zhi 新昌縣志. 1579. Lü Guangxun 呂光洵. In *TYG*.

Xinchang xian zhi 新昌縣志. 1579, 1618. Zheng Dongbi 鄭東璧. Facsimile copy held in the Toyo Bunko, Tokyo, Japan (original in the National Diet Library).

Xinchang xian zhi 新昌縣志. 1671. Liu Zuoliang 劉作樑. Shanghai Library.

Xinchang xian zhi 新昌縣志. 1919. Jin Cheng 金城. In *ZFC*.

Xinchang xian zhi 新昌縣志. Xinchang xian zhi bianzuan weiyuanhui 新昌縣志編纂委員會, eds. Shanghai: Shanghai Shudian, 1994.

Xincheng xian zhi 新城縣志. 1516. Huang Wenyue 黃文鷟. In *TYG*.

Xinding xu zhi 新定續志. 1260–65. Fan Renrong 方仁榮. HYM.

Xingguo zhou zhi 興國州志. 1554. Lin Aimin 林愛民. HYM.

Xinghua fu zhi 興化府志. 1503, 1871. Zhou Ying 周瑛. NLCD.

Xingning xian zhi 興寧縣志. 1552. Sheng Ji 盛繼. In *TYG*.

Xingxian zhi 興縣志. 1577. Gou Chun 緱純. HYM.

Xinzhou zhi 忻州志. 1608. Yang Weiyue 楊維嶽. HYM.

Xiong sheng 雄乘. 1533. Wang Qi 王齊. In *TYG*.

Xuanfu zhen zhi 宣府鎮志. 1514. Wang Chongxian 王崇獻. In *NTGB*.

Xuanping xian zhi 宣平縣志. 1546. Xiao Yan 蕭彥. HYM.

Xundian fu zhi 尋甸府志. 1550. Wang Shangyong 王尚用. In *TYG*.

[*Xuxiu*] *Yanzhou fu zhi* 續修嚴州府志. 1578, 1613. Lü Changqi 呂昌期. In *RBC*.

Xuzhou zhi 徐州志. 1494. Ma Tingzhen 馬廷震. HYM.

Xuzhou zhi 許州志. 1541. Zhang Liangzhi 張良知. In *TYG*.

Yancheng xian zhi 郾城縣志. 1554. Zhao Yingshi 趙應式. In *TYG*.

Yangwu xian zhi 陽武縣志. 1527. Lü Nan 呂柟. In *TYG*.

Yanling zhi 鄢陵志. 1537. Liu Ren 劉訒. In *TYG*.

Yanping fu zhi 延平府志. 1525. Zheng Qingyun 鄭慶雲. In *TYG*.

Yanshi xian zhi, 偃師縣志. 1504. Wei Jin 魏津. In *TYG*.

Yanting xian zhi 鹽亭縣志. 1786. Lei Maode 雷懋德. HY.

[*Yanyou*] *Siming zhi* 延祐四明志. 1320. Yuan Jue 袁桷. In *SYFZ*.

Yanzhou fu zhi 嚴州府志. 1578, 1613. Lü Changqi 呂昌期. In *RBC*.

Yanzhou tujing 嚴州圖經. 1186. Chen Gongliang 陳公亮. In *SYFZ*.

Yanzhou xu zhi 嚴州續志. 1272. Zheng Yao 鄭瑤. In *SYFZ*.

Yaozhou zhi 耀州志. 1541. Zhang Lian 張璉. In *TYG*.

Yexian zhi 葉縣志. 1542. Niu Feng 牛鳳. HYM.

Yicheng xian zhi 翼城縣志. 1548. Yan Guizhi 鄢桂枝. In *TYG*.

Yingchuan jun zhi 穎川郡志. 1404, 1414, 1429. Chen Lian 陳璉. HYM.

Yingshan xian zhi 應山縣志. 1540. Yan Mu 顏木. In *TYG*.

Yingshan xian zhi 營山縣志. 1576. In *TYG*.

Yingtian fu zhi 應天府志. 1577. Cheng Sigong 程嗣功. In *SKCM*.

Yingzhou xian zhi 穎州縣志. 1536. Lü Jingmeng 呂景蒙. In *TYG*.

Yingzhou zhi 穎州志. 1511. Liu Jie 劉節. In *TYG*.

Yizhen xian zhi 儀眞縣志. 1567. Shen Jiarui 申嘉瑞. In *TYG*.

Yizhou zhi 易州志. 1502. Dai Xian 戴銑. In *TYG*.

Yong'an xian zhi 永安縣志. 1594. Su Minwang 蘇民望. In *RBC*.

Yongfeng xian zhi 永豐縣志. 1544. Guan Jing 管景. In *TYG*.

Yongfu xian zhi 永福縣志. 1612. Xie Zhaozhe 謝肇淛. In *ZSX*.

Yŏngga chi 永嘉誌. Ki Kwŏn (1546–1624). Andong: Kwŏn Sang-hak, 1889.
Yongnian xian zhi 永年縣志. 1641. Shen Jiayin 申佳胤. In *MDGB*.
Yongping fu zhi 永平府志. 1501. Wu Jie 吳傑. In *TYG*.
Yongzhou fu zhi 永州府志. 1383. Hu Lian 胡璉. HYM.
Yongzhou fu zhi 永州府志. 1571. Shi Zhaofu 史朝富. LCM.
Youxi xian zhi 尤溪縣志. 1530. Tian Xu 田頊. In *TYG*.
Yuanshi xian zhi 元氏縣志. 1642. Zhang Shenxue 張慎學. In *MDGB*.
Yuanzhou fu zhi 袁州府志. 1514. Yan Song 嚴嵩. In *TYG*.
Yuanzhou fu zhi 袁州府志. 1543. Chen Dewen 陳德文. In *TYG*.
Yuezhou fu zhi 岳州府志. 1488. Liu Ji 劉璣. In *TYG*.
Yufeng zhi 玉峰志. 1252. Ling Wanqing 凌萬頃. In *XXSK*.
Yuncheng xian zhi 鄆城縣志. 1634. Sun Jing 孫鯨. In *MDGB*.
Yunjian zhi 雲間志. 1193. Yang Qian 楊潛. In *SYFZ*.
Yunnan zhi 雲南志. 1510. Zhou Jifeng 周季鳳. In *TYG*.
Yuntai zhi 鄆臺志. 1590. Pei Yingzhang 裴應章. In *ZSX*.
Yunyang fu zhi 鄆陽府志. 1578. Zhou Shaoji 周紹稷. In *ZSX*.
Yunyang xian zhi 雲陽縣志. 1541. Qin Jue 秦覺. In *TYG*.
Yushan Shuyuan zhi 虞山書院志. Wanli era (1573–1620). Zhang Nai 張鼐. In *Zhongguo lidai shuyuan zhi*.

Zengcheng xian zhi 曾城縣志. 1538. Zhang Yuandao 張原道. In *TYG*.
Zhangde fu zhi 彰德府志. 1522. Cui Xian 崔銑. In *TYG*.
Zhangping xian zhi 漳平縣志. 1549. Zeng Rutan 曾汝檀. In *TYG*.
Zhangzhou fu zhi 漳州府志. 1573. Xie Bin 謝彬. In *ZSX*.
Zhaozhou zhi 趙州志. 1567. Cai Maozhao 蔡懋昭. In *TYG*.
Zhejiang tongzhi 浙江通志. 1561. Xue Yingqi 薛應旂. In *TYG*.
Zhending xian zhi 真定縣志. 1576, 1582. Yang Fang 楊芳. HYM.
Zhenjiang zhi 鎮江志. 1333. Yu Xilu 俞希魯. In *SYFZ*.
[*Zhiyuan*] *Jiahe zhi* 至元嘉禾志. 1288. Xu Shuo 徐碩. In *SYFZ*.
[*Zhizheng*] *Siming xu zhi* 至正四明續志. 1342. Wang Yuangong 王元恭. In *SYFZ*.
Zhongdu zhi 中都志. Chenghua era (1465–87), 1569. Liu Ying 柳瑛. In *TYG*.
Zichuan xian zhi 淄川縣志. 1546. In *TYG*.

Other Primary Sources

Ai Mu 艾穆. *Ai Xiting xiansheng wenji* 艾熙亭先生文集 (Collected works of Ai Xiting). Beijing: Beijing chubanshe, 1997.
Anonymous. "Estimate of the Proportionate Expense of Xylography, Lithography, and Typography, as Applied to Chinese Printing: View of the Advantages and Disadvantages of Each." *Chinese Repository* 3, no. 6 (1834): 246–52.

Bai Gui 白圭 (1442 *jinshi*). 1456. "Shu zhuzhai xiansheng shi ji juan hou" 書竹齋先生詩集卷後 (Afterword to Mr. Zhuzhai's poetry collection). In Wang Mian 王冕, *Zhuzhai ji* 竹齋集. In *SKQS*.

Beijing tushuguan guji zhenben congkan 北京圖書館古籍珍本叢刊 (Collectanea of rare editions from the Beijing Library). Beijing: Shumu wenxian chubanshe, 1988.

Cao Xuequan 曹學佺. 1623. *Da Ming yitong mingsheng zhi* 大明一統名勝志 (Comprehensive gazetteer of the famous sights of the Great Ming). In *SKCM*.

Chao Li 晁㻛. Jiajing era (1522–67). *Chao shi baowentang shumu* 晁氏寶文堂書目 (Catalog of the Chao family's Baowentang). Shanghai: Gudian wenxue chubanshe, 1957.

Chen Di 陳第. Wanli era (1573–1620). *Shishantang shu mulu* 世善堂書目錄 (Catalog of the Shishantang). Taibei: Guangwen shuju, 1969.

Chen Shiyuan 陳士元 (1544 *jinshi*). *Jiang Han cong tan* 江漢叢談 (Collected anecdotes from the Jiang-Han region). In *Baibu congshu jicheng* 百部叢書集成, 63. Taibei: Yiwen, 1968.

Chen Zhensun 陳振孫 (-1183–1262). ca. 1238. *Zhizhai shulu jieti* 直齋書錄解題 (Annotated catalog of the Zhizhai studio). Taibei: Xin wenfeng, 1985.

Cheng Liben 程立本 (d. 1402). *Xunyin ji* 巽隱集篁墩文集 (Collected works of Xunyin). In *SKQS*.

Cheng Minzheng 程敏政. (-1445–1500). *Huangdun wenji* 篁墩文集 (Collected works of Huangdun). In *SKQS*.

Confucius. *Analects*. In *The Chinese Classics*, translated by James Legge. Hong Kong: Hong Kong University Press, 1960.

———. *Confucius: The Analects*. Translated by D. C. Lau. London: Penguin Books, 1979.

Du Mu 都穆 (1459–1525). *Nanhao jushi wen ba* 南濠居士文跋 (Writings of Nanhao Jushi). In *XXSK*.

———. *Shi xi ri ji* 使西日記 (Daily record of a mission to the West). 1513. *Xibei shi di wenxian* 西北史地文獻. Lanzhou: Guji shudian, 1990.

———. *You mingshan ji* 遊名山記 (Record of travels to famous mountains). 1515. *Congshu jicheng chubian* 叢書集成初編. Taibei: Zhonghua shuju, 1991.

Fang Xiaoru 方孝孺 (1357–1402). *Xunzhizhai ji* 遜志齋集 (Xunzhi studio collection). In *SKQS*.

Feng Fujing 馮復京 (1573–1622). *Ming Changshu xian xian shi lüe* 明常熟先賢事略 (Sketch of the affairs of past worthies of Ming dynasty Changshu). In *Mingdai zhuan ji cong kan* 明代傳記叢刊. Taibei: Mingwen shuju, 1991.

Gallagher, Louis, trans. *China in the Sixteenth Century: The Journals of Matthew Ricci, 1583–1610*. New York: Random House, 1953.

Gao Nuo 高懦. *Baichuan shuzhi, Gujin shuke* 百川書志, 古今書刻 (Record of the books of Baichuan, published books old and new). Shanghai: Gudian wenxue chubanshe, 1957.

Gao Tai 高臺. "Zeng Xinchang Haohe Ding gong rong shou xu" 贈新昌好和丁公榮壽序 (Birthday essay for Ding Haohe of Xinchang), 1519. In *Caiyan Ding shi zongpu, juan* 1.

Gu Lin 顧璘 (1476–1545). *Gu Huayu ji* 顧華玉集 (Collected works of Gu Huayu). In *SKQS*.

Gu Qiyuan 顧起元 (1565–1628). *Kezuo zhui yu* 客座贅語 (Rambling talks of a guest). 1617. In *XXSK*.

Gui Youguang 歸有光 (1507–71). *Sanwu shuili lu* 三吳水利錄. (Record of water resources of the Three Wu). In *Baibu congshu jicheng* 百部叢書集成, vol. 63. Taibei: Yiwen, 1966.

———. *Zhenchuan ji* 震川集 (Collected works of Zhenchuan). In *SKQS*.

Guo Zhengyu 郭正域 (1554–1612). *Wanli sanshiyi nian guimao Chu shi yao shu shi mo* 萬曆三十一年癸卯楚事妖書始末 (The complete story of the heterodox writings of the Chu affair in the 31ˢᵗ year of the Wanli era, *guimao* year). 1611. In *Zhongguo yeshi jicheng xubian* 中國野史集成續編. Chengdu: Bashu shushe, 2000.

He Qiaoxin 何喬新 (1427–1502). *Jiaoqiu wenji* 椒邱文集 (Collected works of Jiaoqu). In *SKQS*.

He Shi zongpu 何氏宗譜 (He lineage genealogy). 1935. Qingyuantang 慶原堂. Xinchang County Archives.

He Tang 何瑭 (1474–1543). *Bozhai ji* 栢齋集 (Collected works of Bozhai). In *SKQS*.

Huang Liuhong 黃六鴻 (1613–1717). *Fuhui quanshu* 福惠全書 (A complete book concerning happiness and benevolence). 1694. Shizando 詩山堂, 1850. Waseda University Library.

Huang Yuji 黃虞稷 (1629–91). *Qianqingtang shumu* 千頃堂書目 (Qianqingtang catalog). Mid-seventeenth century. Shanghai: Shanghai guji chubanshe, 1990.

Jiao Hong 焦竑 (1541–1620). *Guochao xianzheng lu* 國朝獻徵錄 (Record of our dynasty's worthies). In *Mingdai zhuanji congkan* 明代傳記叢刊. Taibei: Minwen shuju, 1991.

———. *Yutang cong yu* 玉堂叢語 (Collected words of Yutang). Beijing: Zhonghua shuju, 1981.

Li Dongyang 李東陽 (1447–1516) and Shen Shixing 申時行 (1535–1614). *Da Ming huidian* 大明會典 (Collected statutes of the Great Ming). 1587. Taibei: Dongnan shubaoshe, 1963.

Li Panlong 李攀龍 (1514–70). *Cangming ji* 滄溟集 (Collected works of Cangming). In *SKQS*.

Li Rihua 李日華 (1565–1635). *Liuyanzhai biji* 六研齋筆記 (Liuyan Studio notebook). In *Siku quanshu zhe ben qiji* 四庫全書珍本七集. Taibei: Shangwu yinshuguan, 1977.

Li Shizhen 李時珍 (1518–93). *Bencao gangmu* 本草綱目 (Great pharmacopeia). Beijing: Renmin weisheng chubanshe, 1985.

Li Zengbo 李曾伯 (b. 1198). *Kezhai zagao, xugao* 可齋雜藁, 續藁 (Collected writings of Kezhai, and supplement). In *SKQS*.

Liao Daonan 廖道南 (d. 1547). *Diange cilin ji* 殿閣詞林記. Taibei: Shangwu yinshuguan, 1979.

Lin Zhaoen 林兆恩 (1517–98). *Linzi quanji* 林子全集 (Complete works of Master Lin). 1631. In *BTGJ*.

Lin Zhisheng 林之盛. Wanli era (1573–1620). *Huang Ming ying shi ming chen bei kao lu* 皇明應謚名臣備考錄. *Ming dai zhuan ji cong kan* 明代傳記叢刊. Taibei: Mingwen shuju, 1991.

Lü Ben 呂本 (1504–87). "Guanglusi shucheng Tangzhou Gong ji pei Ruren Pan Shi hezang muzhiming" 光祿寺署丞崇洲公暨配孺人潘氏合葬墓志銘 (Grave epitaph for the jointly buried Court of Imperial Entertainments Assistant Office Director Mr. Tangzhou and his wife, child nurturess Pan). In *LSZP-YM*, 4.17a.

Lu Rong 陸容 (1436–94). *Shuyuan za ji* 菽園雜記 (Miscellaneous notes from the bean field). Taibei: Guangwen shuju, 1970.

Lü Shi zongpu, Xiao 呂氏宗譜, 孝 (Lü lineage genealogy, Xiao branch). Mingyantang 明煙堂, 1930. Xinchang County Archives.

Lü Shi zongpu, You Mu 呂氏宗譜, 友睦 (Lü lineage genealogy, You and Mu branches). Mingyantang 明煙堂, 1930. Xinchang County Archives.

Ma Duanlin 馬端臨 (ca.1254–ca.1323). *Wenxian tongkao* 文獻通考 (Comprehensive study of documents). Taibei: Shangwu yinshuguan, 1987.

Makita Tairyō 牧田諦亮. *Sakugen nyūminki no kenkyū* 策彥入明記の研究 (Research on Sakugen's journey to Ming). Kyoto: Hōzōkan, 1955.

Mao Jin 毛晉. *Jiguge jiaoke shumu* 汲古閣校刻書目 (Catalog of books published by the Jiguge). In *Xiaoshi shanfang congshu* 小石山房叢書. Taibei: Yiwen yinshuguan, 1971.

Meidu Huang shi zongpu 梅渡黃氏宗譜 (Meidu Huang lineage genealogy). Compiled by Huang Xining 黃錫寧. Yongsitang 永思堂, 1799. Shanghai Library.

Meiguo Hafo daxue Hafo Yanjing tushuguan cang Zhongwen shanben huikan 美國哈佛大學哈佛燕京圖書館藏中文善本彙刊 (Collected reprints of Chinese rare books in America's Harvard-Yenching Library). Guilin: Guangxi shifan daxue chubanshe, 2003.

Mingdai guben fangzhi xuan 明代孤本方志選 (Selected sole exemplar Ming dynasty gazetteers). Edited by Ma Xiaolin 馬小林 and Meng Fanyu 孟繁裕. 12 vols. Beijing: Zhonghua quanguo tushuguan wenxian suowei fuzhi zhongxin, 2000.

Mingdai shumu tiba congkan 明代書目題跋叢刊 (Collected reprints of Ming dynasty book catalog prefaces and postfaces). Edited by Feng Huimin 馮惠民 et al. Beijing: Shumu Wenxian chubanshe, 1992.

Ming shilu 明實錄. 183 vols. Nangang, Taiwan: Zhongyang yanjiuyuan lishi yuyan yanjiusuo, 1961–66.

Nanjing tushuguan guben shanben congkan: Mingdai guben fangzhi zhuanji 南京圖書館孤本善本叢刊: 明代孤本方志專輯 (Nanjing Library reprints of sole exemplars and fine editions: Ming dynasty sole exemplar gazetteers). Edited by Gong Aidong 宮愛東. Beijing: Xianzhuang shuju, 2003.

Nanming Zhang Shi chongxiu zongpu 南明張氏重修宗譜 (Nanming Zhang lineage genealogy, recompiled). 1946. Shanghai Library.

Pan Sheng 潘晟. "Chongxiu Xinchang Caiyan Zhao Shi zongpu xu" 重修新昌彩煙趙氏宗譜序 (Preface to the recompilation of the Xinchang County Caiyan Village Zhao family genealogy). 1581. In *Xinchang Caiyan Zhao Shi*, juan 1.

———. "Zheng shi kao" 正始考 (Study of true origins), 1582. In *Shicheng Pan Shi zongpu* 石城潘氏宗譜 (Shicheng Pan lineage genealogy), cited in Pan Biaohui, *Xinchang xiangcun wenhua yanjiu*, 144.

Peng Dayi 彭大翼 (fl. sixteenth century). *Shantang si kao* 山堂肆考 (Four studies from Shantang). 1595. In *SKQS*.

Qi Chengye 祁承爍 (1563–1628). *Danshengtang cang shumu* 澹生堂藏書目 (Catalog of books held by the Danshengtang). In *MDSM*.

———. *Danshengtang ji* 澹生堂集 (Collected works of Danshengtang). LCM.

———. 1621–23. Family letters. In Huang Chang 黃裳, "Qi Chengye jia shu ba" 祁承爍家書跋. *Zhonghua wenshi luncong* 中華文史論叢 4 (1984): 233–84.

Qu Yong 瞿鏞. *Tieqintong jianlou cangshu mulu* 鐵琴銅劍樓藏書目錄 (Catalog of books held by the Tieqintongjianlou). Mid-nineteenth century. Taibei: Guangwen shuju, 1967.

Riben cang zhongguo hanjian difangzhi congkan 日本藏中國罕見地方志叢刊 (Collected reprints of rarely seen Chinese local gazetteers held in Japan). Beijing: Shumu wenxian chubanshe, 1990–92.

Ricci, Matteo. *China in the Sixteenth Century: The Journals of Matthew Ricci, 1583–1610*. Translated by Louis J. Gallagher. New York: Random House, 1953.

Shang Qiweng 商企翁. *Mishu jian zhi* 秘書監志 (Palace Library gazetteer). Taibei: Shangwu yinshuguan, 1974.

Shanyin Baiyutan Zhang Shi zupu 山陰白漁潭張氏宗譜 (Shanyin Baiyutan Zhang lineage genealogy). Edited by Zhang Yuanshu 張元淑. 1628. LCM.

Shen Bang 沈榜 (fl. 1590s). *Wan shu za ji* 宛署雜記 (Miscellaneous records from the Wanping office). 1593. Beijing: Beijing Guji chubanshe, 1980.

Shen Chi 沈敕. *Jingxi wai ji* 荊溪外紀 (Unofficial record of Jingxi). 1545. LCM.

Shen Defu 沈德符 (1578–1642). *Wanli yehuobian* 萬曆野獲編 (Unofficial gleanings from the Wanli reign). Beijing: Zhonghua shuju, 1997.

Shicheng Pan Shi zongpu, hou fang 石城潘氏宗譜, 後房 (Shicheng Pan lineage genealogy, rear branch). 1919. Privately held in Xia Pan Cun 下潘村, Xinchang County, Zhejiang.

Sikuquanshu cunmu congshu 四庫全書存目叢書. 1200 vols. Tainan, Taiwan: Zhuangyan wenhua shiye youxian gongsi, 1996.

Song Yingxing 宋應星, E-tu Zen Sun, and Shiou-chuan Sun, trans. *Chinese Technology in the Seventeenth Century: T'ien-kung k'ai-wu*. Mineola: Dover, 1966, 1997.

Song Yuan fangzhi congkan 宋元方志叢刊 (Collected reprints of Song and Yuan gazetteers). 8 vols. Beijing: Zhonghua shuju, 1990.

Sun Cheng'en 孫承恩 (1485–1565). *Wenjian ji* 文簡集 (Collected works of Wenjian). In *Siku quanshu zhenben er ji* 四庫全書珍本二集. Taibei: Taiwan shangwu yinshuguan, 1971.

Tang Shunzhi 唐順之 (1507–60). *Jingchuan Xiansheng wen ji* 荊川先生文集 (Collected works of Mr. Jingchuan). 1573. Shanghai: Shangwu yinshuguan, 1922.

Tu Long 屠隆 (1542–1605). *Kaopan yushi* 考槃餘事 (Matters extraneous to examination circles). In *Baibu congshu jicheng* 百部叢書集成, series 32. Taibei: Yiwen, 1968.

Wang Duanlai 王端來 and Liu Xian 柳憲, eds. *Yongle dadian fangzhi jiyi* 永樂大典方志輯佚 (Gazetteers reconstructed from the Yongle Encyclopedia). Beijing: Zhonghua shuju, 2004.

Wang Mian 王冕 (1287–1359). *Zhuzhai ji* 竹齋集 (Collected works of Zhuzhai). In *SKQS*.

Wang Shenzhong 王慎中 (1509–59). *Zunyan ji* 遵巖集 (Collected works of Zunyan). In *SKQS*.

Wang Shixing 王士性 (1547–98). *Wu yue you cao* 五嶽游草 (Notes on travels to the Five Marchmounts). In *Wang Shixing dili shu san zhong*. Shanghai: Shanghai guji chubanshe, 1993.

Wang Shizhen 王世貞 (1526–90). *Yanzhou sibugao xugao* 弇州四部稿續稿 (Draft and supplement of Yanzhou Shanren's works in four categories). In *SKQS*.

Wang Shu 王恕 (1416–1508). *Wang Duanyi zou yi* 王端毅奏議 (Wang Duanyi's memorials and petitions). In *Siku quanshu zhenben* 四庫全書珍本五集. Taibei: Taiwan shangwu yinshuguan, 1974.

Wang Tingchen 王廷陳 (1517 *jinshi*). *Mengze ji* 夢澤集 (Collected works of Mengze). In *SKQS*.

Wang Yi 王沂 (1314 *jinshi*). *Yibin ji* 伊濱集 (Collected works of Yibin). In *SKQS*.

Wang Yinglin 王應麟 (1223–96). *Yu Hai* 玉海 (Jade sea). In *SKQS*.

Wang Zhen 王貞. (1333). *Nong shu* 農書 (Book of agriculture). Beijing: Zhonghua shuju, 1956.

Wang Zhi 王直 (1379–1462). *Yi'an wen ji* 抑菴文集 (Collected works of Yi'an). In *SKQS*.

Wu Kuan 吳寬 (1472 *jinshi*). *Jia cang ji* 家藏集 (Collection kept in my home). In *SKQS*.

Xie Yingfang 謝應芳. (1377). *Guichao gao* 龜巢稿. (Writings of Guichao). In *SKQS*.

Xinchang Banzhu Zhang Shi zongpu 新昌班竹章氏宗譜 (Xinchang Banzhu Zhang lineage genealogy). Last materials recorded in the Guangxu era (1875–1909). Shanghai Library.

Xinchang Caiyan Zhao Shi zongpu 新昌彩煙趙氏宗譜 (Xinchang Caiyan Zhao lineage genealogy). Zhao Taibin 趙太琳. 1845. Shanghai Library.

Xinchang Caiyan Ding Shi zongpu 新昌彩煙丁氏宗譜 (Caiyan Ding lineage genealogy). Compiled by Ding Zhixian 丁志賢. Yongsitang 永思堂, 1924. Xinchang County Archives.

Xu Bo 徐㶇 (1570–1642). *Hongyulou shumu* 紅雨樓書目 (Catalog of the Hongyulou). Wanli era (1573–1620). Shanghai: Gudian wenxue chubanshe, 1957.

———. *Rongyin xin jian* 榕陰新檢 (New inspections from the shade of a banyan tree). 1606. In *SKCM*.

———. *Xu shi bi jing* 徐氏筆精 (Essential works of Mr. Xu). 1632. In *SKQS*.

Xu Hongzu 徐宏祖 (1586–1641). *Xu Xiake youji* 徐霞客游記 (Travel diary of Xu Xiake). In *SKQS*.

Xu Mingshan 徐明善 (1250–?). *Fangu ji* 芳谷集 (Collected works of Fanggu). In *SKQS*.

Xu Tu 徐圖 (1583 *jinshi*). *Xingrensi chongke shumu* 行人司重刻書目 (Recompiled catalog of books held by the Messenger Office). 1602. In *MDSM*.

Xuxiu siku quanshu 續修四庫全書. 1800 vols. Shanghai: Shanghai Guji chubanshe, 2002.

Xue Xuan 薛瑄 (1392–1464). *Jingxuan wenji* 敬軒文集 (Collected works of Jingxuan). In *SKQS*.

Yang Shen 楊慎 (1488–1559). *Shen'an ji* 升菴集 (Collected works of Shen'an). In *SKQS*.

Yang Shiqi 楊士奇 (1365–1444). *Dongli ji, xu ji* 東里集續集 (Collected works of Dongli, and supplement). In *SKQS*.

———. *Wenyuange shumu* 文淵閣書目 (Catalog of the Wenyuange). In *MDSM*.

Ye Mengzhu 葉夢珠 (seventeenth century). *Yueshi bian* 閱世編 (Essays examining the world). In *Qingdai shiliao biji congkan* 清代史料筆記叢刊. Beijing: Zhonghua shuju, 2007.

Ye Sheng 葉盛. *Luzhutang shumu* 菉竹堂書目 (Catalog of the Luzhutang). In *Congshu jicheng chubian* 叢書集成初編. Shanghai: Shanghai yinshuguan, 1935.

———. *Shuidong riji* 水東日記 (Shuidong diary). Beijing: Zhonghua shuju, 1980.

Yingyin Wenyuange Siku quanshu 影印文淵閣四庫全書. 1500 vols. Taibei: Shangwu, 1983–86. Reprint. 1800 vols. Shanghai: Shanghai guji chubanshe, 1987.

Yu Shi Jing'an Fang Dong Zhai Cuihe Ci zongpu 俞氏靜安坊東宅萃和祠宗譜 (Yu lineage genealogy, Jing'an Arch, Eastern Residence, Cuihe Shrine branch). 1889. Family History Library.

Yu shi Xizhai Shide Ci zongpu 俞氏西宅世德祠宗譜 (Yu lineage genealogy, Western Residence, Shide Shrine branch). 1886. Xinchang County Archives.

Yuan shi zongpu 袁氏宗譜 (Yuan family genealogy). 1874. Family History Library.

Yuan Shuoyou 袁説友 (1140–1204), *Dongtang ji* 東塘集 (Collected works of Dongtang). In *SKQS*.

Zhan Ruoshui 湛若水 (1466–1560). *Quanweng da quan ji* 泉翁大全集 (Grand compendium of the works of Quanweng). 1540. HYM.

Zhang Mingke 張鳴珂 (1829–1908). *Shanben shushi cangshu zhi* 善本書室藏書志 (Record of books held by the Shanben Shushi). 1901. In *XXSK*.

Zhang Tingyu 張廷玉. *Ming shi* 明史. 1739. Taibei: Dingwen shuju, 1980.

Zhang Xuan 張萱 (1582 *juren*). *Neige cangshu mulu* 內閣藏書目錄 (Catalog of books held by the Grand Secretariat). Wanli era (1573–1620). Taibei: Guangwen shuju, 1968.

Zhang Yuanbian 張元忭 (1538–88). "Wozhou Lü Gong xingzhuang" 沃洲呂公行狀 (Record of the deeds of Lü Wozhou). Ghostwritten by Xu Wei 徐渭. Ca. 1584. In *LSZP-YM*, 4.5a.

Zhao Qimei 趙琦美 (1563–1624). *Mowangguan shumu* 脈望館書目 (Catalog of the Mowangguan). Wanli era (1573–1620). In *MDSM*.

———. *Zhao shi tiewang shanhu* 趙氏鐵網珊瑚 (Zhao's coral in the iron net). In *SKQS*.

Zheng Xingyi 鄭興裔 (1126–99). *Zheng Zhongsu zou yi yi ji* 鄭忠肅奏議遺集 (Collected memorials and petitions of Zheng Zhongsu). In *SKQS*.

Zhongguo difangzhi jicheng 中國方志集成 (Collected Chinese gazetteers). Nanjing: Jiangsu chubanshe, 1998–2008.

Zhongguo fangzhi congshu 中國方志叢書 (Collectanea of Chinese gazetteers). Taibei: Chengwen chubanshe, 1966–85.

Zhongguo lidai shuyuan zhi 中國歷代書院志 (Academy gazetteers from China's former dynasties). Edited by Zhao Suosheng 趙所生 et al. Nanjing: Jiangsu jiaoyu chubanshe, 1995.

Zhongguo shixue congshu 中國史學叢書 (Collectanea of Chinese historical studies). Taibei: Taiwan xuesheng shuju, 1965–87.

Zhou Bida 周必大 (1126–1204). *Erlaotang shi hua* 二老堂詩話 (Poems of Erlaotang). *Keisetsuken sōsho* 螢雪軒叢書. Ōsaka: Aoki sūzandō, 1892.

Zhou Fujun 周復俊 (1496–1574). *Quan Shu yiwenzhi* 全蜀藝文志 (Record of literature from all of Sichuan). In *SKQS*.

Zhou Hongzu 周弘祖 (1559 *jinshi*). *Gujin shuke* 古今書刻 (Published books old and new). Wanli era (1573–1620). Changsha: Yeshi guangetang, 1906.

Zhu Mujie 朱睦㮮 (1517–86). *Wanjuantang shumu* 萬卷堂書目 (Catalog of the Wanjuanlou). In *MDSM*.

Zhu Baojiong 朱保炯 and Xie Peilin 謝沛霖, eds. *Ming-Qing jinshi timingbeilu suoyin* 明清進士題名碑錄索引 (Index to names recorded on Ming and Qing *jinshi* stelae). Shanghai: Shanghai guji chubanshe, 1980.

Zhu Xi 朱熹 (1130–1200). *Hui'an ji* 晦菴集 (Collected works of Hui'an). In *SKQS*.

Secondary Sources

Adams, Thomas R., and Nicolas Barker. "A New Model for the Study of the Book." In *The Book History Reader*, 2nd ed., edited by David Finkelstein and Alistair McCleery, 47–65. London: Routledge, 2006.

Anderson, Benedict. *Imagined Communities: Reflections on the Origins and Spread of Nationalism*. London: Verso, 1991.

Aoyama, Sadao 青山定雄. *Tō Sō chihōshi mokuroku oyobi shiryō kōshō* 唐宋地方誌目錄及び資料考証. Yokohama: Yokohama Shiritsu Daigaku, 1958.

Ba Zhaoxiang 巴兆祥. "Lun Mingdai fangzhi de shuliang yu xiu zhi zhidu" 论明代方志的数量与修志制度 (Discussion of the number of Ming dynasty gazetteers and the compilation system). *Zhongguo difangzhi* 中国地方志 4 (2004): 45–51.

———. "Mingdai fangzhi zuanxiu shulüe" 明代方志纂修述略 (Sketch of the compilation of Ming dynasty gazetteers). *Wenxian* 文獻 3 (1988): 152–62.

———. *Zhongguo difangzhi liubo Riben yanjiu* 中國地方志流播日本研究 (Research on the transmission of Chinese gazetteers to Japan). Shanghai: Remin chubanshe, 2008.

Bao Guoqiang 鲍国强. "Ming ke Huizhou Songtang Huang shi zuxing ditu ji xiangguan wenti kaolue" 明刻徽州竦塘黄氏族姓地图及相关问题考略 (Brief study of Ming lineage and surname maps of the Huangs of Huizhou, Songtang village, and related questions). In *Livres et imprimés des gens de Huizhou* (Books and imprints by Huizhou people), edited by Michela Bussotti and Zhu Wanshu. Sinologie française, 13:299–301. Beijing: École française d'Extrême-Orient and Zhonghua shuju, 2008.

Blair, Ann. "Afterword." In Chia and De Weerdt, *Knowledge and Text Production in an Age of Print*, 349–60.

Bol, Peter. "The Rise of Local History: History, Geography, and Culture in Southern Song and Yuan Wuzhou." *Harvard Journal of Asiatic Studies* 61, no. 1 (2001): 37–76.

Brokaw, Cynthia. *Commerce in Culture: The Sibao Book Trade in Qing and Republican Periods*. Cambridge, MA: Harvard University Asia Center, 2007.

Brokaw, Cynthia J., and Kai-wing Chow. *Printing and Book Culture in Late Imperial China*. Berkeley: University of California Press, 2005.

Brook, Timothy. "Censorship in Eighteenth-Century China: A View from the Book Trade." *Canadian Journal of History* (August 1988): 177–96.

———. *The Chinese State in Ming Society*. London: RoutledgeCurzon, 2005.

———. "Edifying Knowledge: The Building of School Libraries in Ming China." *Late Imperial China* 17, no. 1 (1996): 93–119.

———. *Geographical Sources of Ming Qing History*. Ann Arbor, MI: Center for Chinese Studies, 2002.

———. "Guides for Vexed Travelers: Route Books in the Ming and Qing." *Ch'ing-shih wen t'i* 4 (June 1981): 32–76.

———. "Native Identity under Alien Rule: Local Gazetteers of the Yuan Dynasty." In *Pragmatic Literacy East and West, 1200–1330*, edited by Richard Brutnell, 236–47. Woodbridge, Suffolk, UK: Boydell Press, 1997.

Bussotti, Michela. *Gravures de Hui: Étude du livre illustré chinois de la fin du XVI᷄ siècle à la première moitié du VVII᷄ siècle*. Mémoires Archéologiques, vol. 26. Paris: École française d'Extrême-Orient, 2001.

Cai, Peiling 蔡佩玲. *Fan shi Tianyige yanjiu* 范氏天一閣研究. Taibei: Hanmei tushu youxian gongsi, 1991.

Carlitz, Katherine. "Shrines, Governing-Class Identity, and the Cult of Widow Fidelity in Mid-Ming Jiangnan." *Journal of Asian Studies* 56, no. 3 (1997): 612–40.

Chang, Michael. A Court on Horseback: Imperial Touring and the Construction of Qing Rule, 1680–1785. Cambridge, MA: Harvard University Asia Center, 2007.

Chartier, Roger. "Gutenberg Revisited from the East." *Late Imperial China* 17.1 (1996): 1–9.

———. "Texts, Printing, Readings." In *The New Cultural History*, edited by Lynn Hunt, 154–75. Berkeley: University of California Press, 1989.

Chen Baigang 陳百剛 and Pan Biaohui 潘表惠. *Xinchang xiangcun wenhua yanjiu: Baixing xun gen lu* 新昌鄉村文化研究：百姓尋根錄 (Xinchang village culture studies: Record of common people searching for their roots). Beijing: Minzhu yu jianshe chubanshe, 1997.

Chen Guangyi 陳光貽. *Zhongguo fangzhi xue* 中國方志學 (Chinese gazetteer studies). Fuzhou: Fujian renmin chubanshe, 1989.

Chen Shiqi 陳詩啓. *Mingdai shougongye de yanjiu* 明代手工業的研究 (Ming dynasty handicrafts research). Wuhan: Hubei renmin chubanshe, 1958.

Chia, Lucille. *Printing for Profit: The Commercial Publishers of Jianyang, Fujian (11th–17th Centuries)*. Cambridge, MA: Harvard University Asia Center, 2002.

———. "Of Three Mountains Street: The Commercial Publishers of Ming Nanjing." In Brokaw and Chow, *Printing and Book Culture*, 107–51.

Chia, Lucille, and Hilde De Weerdt, eds. *Knowledge and Text Production in an Age of Print: China, 900–1400*. Leiden: Brill, 2011.

Chow Kai-wing. *Publishing, Culture, and Power in Early Modern China*. Stanford: Stanford University Press, 2004.

———. "Writing for Success: Printing, Examinations, and Intellectual Change in Late Ming China." *Late Imperial China* 17, no. 1 (1996): 120–57.

Clunas, Craig. *Fruitful Sites: Garden Culture in Ming Dynasty China*. Durham, NC: Duke University Press, 1996.

Cole, James H. Shaohsing: Competition and Cooperation in Nineteenth-Century China. Tucson: University of Arizona Press, 1986.

Cui Wenyin 崔文印. "Gujin shuke qian shuo" 古今書刻淺說 (Brief comments on published books old and new). Zhongguo dianji yu wenhua 中國典籍與文化1 (2007): 4–10.

Dardess, John W. *Ming China, 1368–1644: A Concise History of a Resilient Empire*. Plymouth, UK: Rowman and Littlefield, 2012.

———. *A Ming Society: T'ai-ho County, Kiangsi, Fourteenth to Seventeenth Centuries*. Berkeley: University of California Press, 1996.

Darnton, Robert. "What Is the History of Books?" *Daedalus* 111 (Summer 1982): 65–83.

de Certeau, Michel. *The Practice of Everyday Life*. Translated by Steven Rendall. Berkeley: University of California Press, 1984.

De Weerdt, Hilde. "Byways in the Imperial Chinese Information Order: The Dissemination and Commercial Publication of State Documents." *Harvard Journal of Asiatic Studies* 66, no. 1 (2006): 145–88.

———. "Production and Circulation of Written Notes (*biji*). In *Imprimer autrement: Le livre non commercial dans la Chine impériale*. Edited by Michela Bussotti and Jean-Pierre Drège. Ecole pratique des hautes études. Geneva: Librairie Droz, 2013.

———. "Regional Descriptions: Administrative and Scholarly Traditions." In *Treasures of the Yenching: Seventy-Fifth Anniversary of the Harvard-Yenching Library: Exhibition Catalog*, edited by Patrick Hanan and Mikael Adolphson, 121–53. Cambridge, MA: Harvard-Yenching Library, Harvard University, 2003.

Dennis, Joseph. "Between Lineage and State: Extended Family and Gazetteer Compilation in Xinchang County." *Ming Studies* 45, no. 6 (2002): 69–113.

———. "Early Printing in China Viewed from the Perspective of Local Gazetteers." In Chia and Hilde De Weerdt, *Knowledge and Text Production*, 105–34.

———. "Financial Aspects of Publishing Local Histories in the Ming Dynasty." *East Asian Library Journal* 14, nos. 1–2 (2010): 158–244.

———. "Mingdai daxueshi Li Ben wei shenme tuixiu hou gai xing Lü?" 明代大学士李本为什么退休后改姓吕? (Why did Ming dynasty grand secretary Li Ben change his surname to Lü after he retired?). *Zhongguo shehuishi ping lun* 中国社会史评论 (Chinese social history critique) 10 (2010): 57–64.

Des Forges, Roger. *Cultural Centrality and Political Change in Chinese History: Northeast Henan in the Fall of the Ming*. Stanford: Stanford University Press, 2003.

Du Xinfu 杜信孚. *Mingdai banke zonglu* 明代版刻综録 (Comprehensive record of Ming dynasty imprints). Yangzhou: Jiangsu guangling guji keyinshe, 1983.

Dudink, Adrian. "The Inventories of the Jesuit House at Nanking Made Up during the Persecution of 1616–1617 (Shen Que, *Nangong shudu*, 1620)." In *Western Humanistic Culture Presented to China by Jesuit Missionaries (XVII–XVIII centuries): Proceedings of the Conference Held in Rome, October 25–27, 1993*, edited by Federico Masini, 119–58. Rome: In sititum Historicum S.I., 1996.

Ebrey, Patricia Buckley. *Chu Hsi's Family Rituals: A Twelfth-Century Chinese Manual for the Performance of Cappings, Weddings, Funerals and Ancestral Rites*. Princeton: Princeton University Press, 1991.

Ebrey, Patricia Buckley, and James L. Watson, eds. *Kinship Organization in Late Imperial China, 1000–1940*. Berkeley: University of California Press, 1986.

Edgren, Sören. "Southern Song Printing at Hangzhou." *Bulletin of the Museum of Far Eastern Antiquities* 61 (1989): 1–212.

Eisenstein, Elizabeth. *The Printing Press as an Agent of Change: Communications and Cultural Transformation in Early-Modern Europe*. Cambridge: Cambridge University Press, 1979.

Elman, Benjamin. *A Cultural History of Civil Examinations in Late Imperial China*. Berkeley: University of California Press, 2000.

———. "Geographical Research in the Ming-Ch'ing Period." *Monumenta Serica* 35 (1981–83): 1–18.

Elvin, Mark. *The Retreat of the Elephants: An Environmental History of China*. New Haven, CT: Yale University Press, 2004.

Fang, Jun. "A Bibliography of Extant Yuan Gazetteers." *Journal of Sung-Yuan Studies* 23 (1993): 123–38.

Farmer, Edward. *Early Ming Government: The Evolution of Dual Capitals*. Cambridge, MA: Harvard University Press, 1976.

Faure, David. "The Lineage as Cultural Invention: The Case of the Pearl River Delta." *Modern China* 15, no. 1 (1989): 4–36.

Febvre, Lucien, and Henri-Jean Martin. *The Coming of the Book: The Impact of Printing, 1450–1800.* London: N.L.B., 1976.

Fisher, Carney. "Center and Periphery: Shih-tsung's Southern Journey, 1539." *Ming Studies* 18 (1984): 15–34.

———. *The Chosen One: Succession and Adoption in the Court of Ming Shizong.* Sydney, Australia: Allen and Unwin, 1990.

———. "The Great Ritual Controversy in the Age of Ming Shih-tsung." *Society for the Study of Chinese Religions Bulletin* 7 (Fall 1979): 71–87.

Fong, Grace. *Herself an Author: Gender, Agency, and Writing in Late Imperial China.* Honolulu: University of Hawai'i Press, 2008.

Fong, Grace, and Ellen Widmer, eds. *The Inner Quarters and Beyond: Women Writers from Ming through Qing.* Leiden: Brill, 2010.

Fu Zhenlun 傅振倫. "You yi jian Ming chu zhongyao xiu zhi wenxian" 又一件明初重要修志文獻 (One more important early-Ming document on gazetteer compilation). In *Zhongguo shizhi luncong* 中國史志論叢 (Collected essays on China's historical gazetteers), edited by Fu Zhenlun, 144–45. Hangzhou: Zhejiang renmin chubanshe, 1986.

Genette, Gerard. *Paratexts: Thresholds of Interpretation.* Translated by Jane E. Lewin. Cambridge: Cambridge University Press, 1997.

Gerritsen, Anne. *Ji'an Literati and the Local in Song-Yuan-Ming China.* Leiden: Brill, 2007.

Giersch, C. Patterson. *Asian Borderlands.* Cambridge, MA: Harvard University Asia Center, 2006.

Giles, Herbert. *A Chinese Biographical Dictionary.* 1898. Taibei: Chengwen, 1975.

Goodrich, L. Carrington, and Chaoying Fang, eds. *Dictionary of Ming Biography, 1368–1644.* New York: Columbia University Press, 1976.

Gu Zhixing 顧志興. *Zhejiang chubanshi yanjiu* 浙江出版史研究 (Research in the history of Zhejiang publishing). Hangzhou: Zhejiang renmin chubanshe, 1991.

Guo Dongxu 郭東旭. "Song chao de wujia biandong yu ji zang lun zui" 宋朝的物價變動與計贓論罪 (Changes in Song dynasty commodity prices and the calculation of fines and punishments). *Zhongguo jingjishi yanjiu* 中國經濟史研究 1 (2004): 69–75.

Han Zhangxun 韓章訓. "Fanli zong lun" 凡例綜論 (Comprehensive theory of *fanli*). *Zhongguo difangzhi* 中國地方志 3 (2006): 23–26.

Handlin Smith, Joanna. "Ch'i Piao-chia's Social World: Wealth and Values in Late-Ming Kiangnan." *Journal of Asian Studies* 51, no. 1 (1992): 55–81.

Hargett, James M. "Historiography in Southern Sung Dynasty Local Gazetteers." In *The New and the Multiple: Sung Senses of the Past*, edited by Thomas H. C. Lee, 287–306. Hong Kong: Chinese University Press, 2004.

———. "Song Dynasty Local Gazetteers and Their Place in the History of Difangzhi Writing." *Harvard Journal of Asiatic Studies* 56, no. 2 (1996): 405–42.

Hazelton, Keith. "Patrilines and the Development of Localized Lineages: The Wu of Hsiu-ning City, Hui-chou, to 1528." In Ebrey and Watson, *Kinship Organization in Late Imperial China*, 137–69.

Heijdra, Martin. "Socio-Economic Development of Ming Rural China." In *The Cambridge History of China*, vol. 8, *The Ming Dynasty, 1368–1644*, part 2, edited by

Denis Twitchett and Frederick W. Mote, 417–578. Cambridge: Cambridge University Press, 1998.

———. "Socio-Economic Development of Ming Rural China (1368–1644): An Interpretation." Ph.D. diss., Princeton University, 1994.

———. "Technology, Culture, and Economics: Movable Type versus Woodblock Printing in East Asia." In Isobe, *Higashi Ajia shuppan bunka*, 223–40.

———. "Town Gazetteers and Local Society in the Jiangnan Region during the Qing Period." Translated by Mori Masao 森正夫 as "Shindai Kōnan deruta no kyōchinshi to chiiki shakai" 清代江南デルタの郷鎮志と地域社会. *Tōyōshi kenkyū* 62, no. 4 (2004): 1–53.

Herman, John E. "The Cant of Conquest: Tusi Offices and China's Political Incorporation of the Southwest Frontier." In *Empire at the Margins: Culture, Ethnicity, and Frontier in Early Modern China*, edited by Pamela Kyle Crossley, Helen F. Siu, and Donald S. Sutton, 135–70. Berkeley: University of California Press, 2006.

Hoshi Ayao 星斌夫. *Chūgoku shakai keizaishi goi* 中國社會經濟史語彙 (Vocabulary of Chinese social and economic history). Tokyo: Kindai Chūgoku kenkyū sentā, 1966.

Hostetler, Laura. *Qing Colonial Enterprise: Ethnography and Cartography in Early Modern China*. Chicago: University of Chicago Press, 2001.

Hou Zhenping 侯眞平. "Ming mo Fujian banke shuji kegong lingshi" 明末福建版刻書籍刻工零拾 (Miscellaneous items on late-Ming Fujian woodblock book blockcutters). In *Chuban shi yanjiu* 出版史研究: 第四輯, edited by Ye Zaisheng 葉再生, 217–38. Beijing: Zhongguo shuji chubanshe, 1996.

Huang Chang 黃裳. "Qi Chengye jia shu ba" 祁承爜家書跋 (Qi Chengye's family letters and colophons). *Zhonghua wenshi luncong* 中華文史論叢 4 (1984): 233–84.

Huang, Ray. "The Ming Fiscal Administration." In *The Cambridge History of China*, vol. 8, *The Ming Dynasty, 1368–1644*, part 2, edited by Denis Twitchett and Frederick W. Mote, 106–71. Cambridge: Cambridge University Press, 1998.

———. *Taxation and Governmental Finance in Sixteenth-Century Ming China*. London: Cambridge University Press, 1974.

Huang Wei 黃葦. *Fang zhi xue* 方志學 (Gazetteer studies). Shanghai: Fudan daxue chubanshe, 1993.

Hucker, Charles. *The Censorial System of Ming China*. Stanford: Stanford University Press, 1966.

———. *A Dictionary of Official Titles in Imperial China*. Stanford: Stanford University Press, 1985.

Hymes, Robert P. "Marriage, Descent Groups, and the Localist Strategy in Sung and Yuan Fu-chou." In Ebrey and Watson, *Kinship Organization in Late Imperial China*, 95–136.

Idema, Wilt. *Chinese Vernacular Fiction: The Formative Period*. Leiden: Brill, 1974.

———. "Review of Evelyn Sakakida Rawski, *Education and Popular Literacy in Ch'ing China*." *T'oung Pao* 66, nos. 4–5 (1980): 314–24.

Idema, Wilt, and Beata Grant. *The Red Brush: Writing Women of Imperial China*. Cambridge, MA: Harvard University Asia Center, 2004.

Inoue Susumu 井上進. "Zōsho to dokusho" 蔵書と読書 (Book collecting and reading). *Tōhō gakuhō* 東方学報 62 (1990): 409–45.

Isobe Akira 磯部彰, ed. *Higashi Ajia shuppan bunka kenkyū: Niwatazumi* 東アジア出版文化研究：にわたずみ (Studies in publishing culture in East Asia: Niwatazumi). Tokyo: Nigensha, 2004.

Johns, Adrian. *The Nature of the Book: Print and Knowledge in the Making.* Chicago: University of Chicago Press, 1998.

Katsuyama Minoru 勝山稔. "Mindai ni okeru bōkaku bon no shuppan jōkyō ni tsuite: Mindai zenpan no shuppanshū kara miru Kenyō bōkaku bon ni tsuite" 明代における坊刻本の出版状況について: 明代全般の出版数から見る建陽坊刻本につい (Regarding the circumstances of Ming dynasty commercial publishers: Jianyang commercial editions from the perspective of the number of books published in the entire Ming dynasty). In Isobe, *Higashi Ajia shuppan bunka*, 83–100.

Lai Jiadu 賴家度. *Mingdai Yunyang nongmin qiyi* 明代鄖陽農民起義 (Peasant uprising in Ming dynasty Yunyang). Wuhan: Hubei renmin chubanshe, 1956.

Leslie, Donald, Colin Mackerras, and Gungwu Wang, eds. *Essays on the Sources for Chinese History.* Canberra: Australian National University Press, 1973.

Li Guoqing 李國慶. *Mingdai kangong xingming suoyin* 明代刊工姓名索引 (Ming dynasty print craftsmen name index). Shanghai: Shanghai guji chubanshe, 1998.

Li Ruiliang 李瑞良. *Zhongguo chuban biannian shi* 中国出版编年史 (Chronicle of Chinese publishing history). Fuzhou: Fuzhou renmin chubanshe, 2004.

Li Xiaorong. "Gender and Textual Politics during the Qing Dynasty: The Case of the *Zhengshi ji*." *Harvard Journal of Asiatic Studies* 69, no. 1 (2009): 75–107.

Li Yanqiu 李艳秋. "Mingdai Wenyuange difangzhi shoucang kaoshu" 明代文渊阁地方志收藏考述 (Study of gazetteers collected by the Wenyuange in the Ming dynasty). *Tushu yu qingbao* 图书与情报 2 (1998): 28–30.

Liang Hongsheng 梁洪生. "Pudie yu xinzhi de duijie" 新譜與新志的對接 (Comparison of new genealogies and new gazetteers). In *Zhongguo pudie yanjiu* 中國譜牒研究, edited by Wang Heming 王鶴鳴, 339–57. Shanghai: Shanghai guji chubanshe, 1999.

Lin Ping 林平 and Zhang Jiliang 張紀亮. *Mingdai fangzhi kao* 明代方志考 (Study of Ming dynasty gazetteers). Chengdu: Sichuan daxue chubanshe, 2001.

Littrup, Leif. *Subbureaucratic Government in China in Ming Times: A Study of Shandong Province in the Sixteenth Century.* Oslo: In stituttet for sammenlignende kulturforskning, 1981.

Liu Weiyi 劉緯毅. "Song dai fangzhi shu lüe" 宋代方志述略 (Sketch of Song dynasty gazetteers). *Wenxian* 文獻 4 (1986): 129–39.

Luo Zhaoping 骆兆平. "Tan Tianyige cang Mingdai difangzhi" 談天一閣藏明代地方志 (Discussion of Tianyige's Ming dynasty gazetteers). *Wenxian* 文獻 3 (1980): 190–99.

Luo Zhufeng 羅竹風, ed. *Hanyu da cidian* 漢語大詞典 (Big Chinese dictionary). Shanghai: Hanyu da cidian chubanshe, 2001.

Ma Lihui. "Spatial Distribution of Roots in a Dense Jujube Plantation in the Semi-arid Hilly Region of the Chinese Loess Plateau." *Plant Soil* 354, nos. 1–2 (2012): 57–68.

Ma Yong. "Martino Martini's Activity in China and His Works on Chinese History and Geography." In *Martino Martini: Geografo cartografo storico teologo*, edited by Giorgio Melis, 248–63. Trento: Museo Tridentino di Scienze Naturali, 1983.

McDermott, Joseph P. *A Social History of the Chinese Book*. Hong Kong: Hong Kong University Press, 2006.

Meskill, Johanna M. "The Chinese Genealogy as a Research Source." In *Family and Kinship in Chinese Society*, edited by Maurice Freedman, 139–61. Stanford: Stanford University Press, 1970.

Meskill, John. "Academies and Politics in the Ming Dynasty." In *Chinese Government in Ming Times: Seven Studies*, edited by Tilemann Grimm and Charles Hucker, 149–74. New York: Columbia University Press, 1969.

Meyer-Fong, Tobie. "Packaging the Men of Our Times: Literary Anthologies, Friendship Networks, and Political Accommodation in the Early Qing." *Harvard Journal of Asiatic Studies* 64, no. 1 (2004): 5–56.

Miao Yonghe. *Mingdai chuban shi gao* 明代出版史稿 (Draft history of Ming dynasty publishing). Nanjing: Jiangsu renmin chubanshe, 2000.

Miyazaki, Ichisada. *China's Examination Hell: The Civil Service Examinations of Imperial China*. New York: Weatherhill, 1976.

Moll-Murata, Christine. "Local Gazetteers." In *Brill's Encyclopedia of China*, edited by Daniel Leese, 601–3. Leiden: Brill, 2009.

Mote, Frederick W., and Hung-lam Chu. *Calligraphy and the East Asian Book*. Boston: Shambhala, 1989.

Nimick, Thomas G. *Local Administration in Ming China: The Changing Roles of Magistrates, Prefects, and Provincial Officials*. Minneapolis: Society for Ming Studies, 2008.

Nivison, David. *The Life and Thought of Chang Hsüeh-ch'eng (1738–1801)*. Stanford: Stanford University Press, 1966.

Pan Biaohui 潘表惠. Unpublished notes on the *Shicheng Pan Shi zongpu* 石城潘氏宗譜 (Shicheng Pan lineage genealogy).

Pan Guangdan 潘光旦. *Ming-Qing liangdai Jiaxing di wangzu* 明清兩代嘉興的望族 (Great families of Jiaxing in the Ming and Qing dynasties). 1947. Shanghai: Shanghai Shudian, 1991.

Schneewind, Sarah. "Competing Institutions: Community Schools and 'Improper Shrines' in Sixteenth Century China." *Late Imperial China* 20, no. 1 (1999): 85–106.

Sedo, Timothy R. "Linzhang County and the Culturally Central Periphery in Mid-Ming China." Ph.D. diss., University of British Columbia, 2010.

Shen Jin 沈津. "Mingdai fangke tushu zhi liutong yu jiage" 明代坊刻圖書流通與價格 (Circulation and price of Ming dynasty commercial books). *Guojia tushuguan guankan* 國家圖書館刊 1 (June 1996): 101–18.

Shin, Leo. *The Making of the Chinese State: Ethnicity and Expansion on the Ming Borderlands*. Cambridge: Cambridge University Press, 2006.

Skinner, G. William. *Marketing and Social Structure in Rural China*. Tucson: University of Arizona Press, 1965.

Strassberg, Richard E. *Inscribed Landscapes: Travel Writing from Imperial China*. Berkeley: University of California Press, 1994.

Szonyi, Michael. *Practicing Kinship: Lineage and Descent in Late Imperial China*. Stanford: Stanford University Press, 2002.

Taylor, Romeyn. "Official Altars, Temples, and Shrines Mandated for All Counties in the Ming and Qing." *T'oung Pao* 83, nos. 1–3 (1997): 93–125.

Teng, Emma Jinhua. *Taiwan's Imagined Geography: Chinese Colonial Travel Writing and Pictures, 1683–1895*. Cambridge, MA: Harvard University Asia Center, 2004.

Thatcher, Melvin. "Local Historical Sources for China at the Genealogical Society of Utah." *Hanxue yanjiu* 3, no. 2 (1985): 419–58.

Tianyige cang Mingdai fangzhi xuankan 天一閣藏明代方志選刊 (Selected reprints of Ming dynasty gazetteers held in the Tianyige). Shanghai: Shanghai guji shudian, 1964, 1981–82, 1990.

Tsien, Tsuen-hsuin. "Paper and Printing." In *Science and Civilisation in China,* ed. Joseph Needham and Dieter Kuhn. Cambridge: Cambridge University Press, 1987.

Twitchett, Denis, and Frederick W. Mote, eds. *The Cambridge History of China: The Ming Dynasty, 1368–1644*, vol. 8, part 2. Cambridge: Cambridge University Press, 1998.

Ueda Makoto. "Chūgoku no chiiki shakai to riniji: Jūyon-jūkyu seiji no Chūgoku tonanbu no ziturei" 中国の地域社会と宗族：十四―十九世紀の中国東南部の事例 (Chinese local society and lineage: The case of China's southeast region in the fourteenth to nineteenth centuries). In *Sekai shi e no mondai* 世界史への問い, vol. 4, *Shakaiteki ketugō* 社会的結合, edited by Shibata Michio 柴田三千雄, 47–73. Tokyo: Iwanami Shoten, 1989.

van der Sprenkel, Otto B. "Genealogical Registers." In Leslie, Mackerras, and Wang, *Essays on the Sources*, 83–98.

———. "Population Statistics of Ming China." *Bulletin of the School of Oriental and African Studies, University of London* 15, no. 2 (1953): 289–326.

van der Sprenkel, Sybille. *Legal Institutions in Manchu China*. 1962. London: Athlone Press, 1977.

Von Glahn, Richard. *Fountain of Fortune: Money and Monetary Policy in China, 1000–1700*. Berkeley: University of California Press, 1996.

Waltner, Ann. *Getting an Heir: Adoption and the Construction of Kinship in Late Imperial China*. Honolulu: University of Hawai'i Press, 1990.

Wang Liping. "Paradise for Sale: Urban Space and Tourism in the Social Transformation of Hangzhou, 1589–1937." Ph.D. diss., University of California, San Diego, 1997.

Wang Yanrong 王延榮 and Zhu Yuangui 朱元桂. "Danshengtang zhu ren Qi Cheng "" zi yin yi kaobian" 澹生堂主人祁承""字音議考辯 (A study of the pronunciation and meaning of the character in the master of Danshengtang, Qi Cheng "X"). *Shaoxing wenli-yuan bao (shekeban)* 紹興文理學院報 (社科版) 28, no. 5 (2008): 77–81.

Wei, Qingyuan 韋慶元. *Mingdai huangce zhidu* 明代黃冊制度. Beijing: Zhonghua shuju, 1961.

Wilkinson, Endymion. *Chinese History: A Manual.* Revised and enlarged edition. Cambridge, MA: Harvard University Asia Center, 2000.

———. *Chinese History: A New Manual.* Cambridge, MA: Harvard University Asia Center, 2012.

Will, Pierre-Etienne. *Chinese Local Gazetteers: An Historical and Practical Introduction.* Paris: Centre de recherches et de documentation sur la Chine contemporaine, 1992.

Xie Shuishun 謝水順. *Fujian gudai keshu* (Books published in Fujian in ancient times). Fuzhou: Fujian renmin chubanshe, 1997.

Xu Xiaoman. "Preserving the Bonds of Kin: Genealogy Masters and Genealogy Production in the Jiangsu-Zhejiang Area in the Qing and Republican Periods." In Brokaw and Chow, *Printing and Book Culture*, 332–67.

Yan Yifan 嚴倚帆. *Qi Chengye ji Danshengtang cangshu yanjiu* 祁承爍及澹生堂藏書研究 (Research on book collecting of Qi Chengye and the Danshengtang). Taibei: Hanmei Tushu, 1991.

Yang Shengxin 楊繩信. "Lidai kegong gongjia chu tan" 歷代刻工工價初談 (An initial discussion of block cutters' wages in historical times). In *Lidai keshu gaikuang* 歷代刻書概況 (An overview of book publishing in historical times), edited by Shanghai xinsijun lishi yanjiuhui, 553–67. Beijing: Yinshua gongye chubanshe, 1991.

Ye Dehui 葉德輝 (1864–1927). *Shulin qinghua* 書林清話 (Clear talk on the forest of books). Taibei: Shijie shuju, 1960.

Yee, Cordell. "Chinese Maps in Political Culture." In *The History of Cartography*, vol. 2, bk. 2, edited by J. B. Harley and D. Woodward, 71–95. Chicago: University of Chicago Press, 1987.

Yu Jingming 俞景明. "Wufeng Yu Shi" 五峰俞氏 (The Yu of Wufeng). In Chen and Pan, *Xinchang xiangcun wenhua yanjiu*, 86–106.

Zhang Guogan 張國淦. *Zhongguo gu fangzhi kao* 中國古方志考 (Studies of China's ancient gazetteers). Shanghai: Zhonghua shuju, 1962.

Zhang Sheng 張升. "Mingdai fangzhi suzhiyi" 明代方志數质疑 (Doubts about the number of Ming gazetteers). *Zhongguo difangzhi* 中國地方志 3 (2000): 64–67.

Zhang Xiumin 張秀民. *Zhongguo yinshua shi* 中國印刷史 (History of Chinese printing). Hangzhou: Zhejiang guji chubanshe, 2006.

Zhang Yingping 張英聘. *Mingdai Nanzhili fangzhi yenjiu* 明代南直隸方志研究 (Research on the gazetteers of Ming dynasty Jiangnan). Beijing: Shehui kexue wenxian chubanshe, 2005.

Zhuang Weifeng 莊威鳳, Zhu Shijia 朱士嘉, Feng Baolin 馮寶琳, and Wang Shuping 王素萍. *Zhongguo difangzhi lianhe mulu* 中國地方志聯合目錄 (Union catalog of Chinese gazetteers). Beijing: Zhonghua shuju, 1985.

Zurndorfer, Harriet T. "The *Hsin-an ta-tsu chih* and the Development of Chinese Gentry Society 800–1600." *T'oung Pao* 67, nos. 3–5 (1981): 154–215.

Index

Academies, private, 144, 268, 277, 296; booklists of, 270, 279–80. *See also* Hanlin Academy; Schools

Adams, Thomas R., 5

Ai Mu, 152, 337

Alaowading ('Alā-al-Dīn), 220

An Ao, 59, 61, 62

An family, 58–59, 61, 62

An Guo, 178

An Ji, 58

An Quan, 54

An Shixian, 123

An Yu, 131

Anhui gazetteers, 137, 178, 232. *See also* Nanzhili

Anji, Zhejiang, gazetteer, 236

Anqing, Nanzhili, gazetteers, 193, 194, 195

Anxi, Fujian, gazetteers, 180, 236, 290n10

Anzhou, Beizhili, gazetteer, 186

Aoyama Sadao, 30, 117

Ba Min tong zhi (Fujian gazetteer), 271

Ba Zhaoxiang, 9–10, 118–21, 125, 136, 164

Badong, Huguang, gazetteers, 183, 235

Bai Qi, 18, 296

Bai Shibian, 131

Bai Siqi, 222

Ban Gu, 23

Baoding, Beizhili, 198, 205; gazetteers of, 171, 186, 199, 200, 273

Barker, Nicolas, 5

Beijing, 137, 305; craftsmen from, 201–4, 212; publishing in, 165, 167

Beizhili, 138, 305; gazetteers of, 178, 193, 198–205, 210–11, 227, 256, 293–94, 295, 299, 319. *See also* Baoding; Beijing; Fengrun; Handan; Huairou; Xincheng; Yizhou; Yongping

Bencao gangmu (Great pharmacopeia; Li Shizhen), 197, 335

Biji (notebooks) genre, 335

Binzhou, Shaanxi, 305, 306

Biographies: in annals format, 32, 153; in *Da Ming yitong zhi*, 281; in gazetteers, 38, 42, 43, 46–47, 64, 65, 69, 326, 336; gazetteers as sources for, 13, 336–37, 340; from genealogies, 75, 112; increase in, 29, 31–32; in northern gazetteers, 136; as sources, 83, 160, 331; of virtuous women, 9, 31, 32, 47, 75, 253, 337; in *Xinchang xian zhi*, 72, 73, 75, 78, 80, 87, 93–96, 100, 114

Blair, Ann, 6

Bol, Peter, 2, 4, 23, 29, 30, 288–89, 334

Book of Documents (*Shangshu*), 22, 106, 158

Book of Odes (*Shijing*), 106

Book trade, 190, 191. *See also* Publishing

Books: affordability of, 213, 229, 247, 251;
  collectors of, 273, 325–33; donations of,
  274–75, 277, 279; history of, 5, 157, 213;
  lending of, 147, 263, 282–83, 284, 289,
  302; listed in gazetteers, 270–71; lists
  of, 269–82
Bookstores, 258, 282–84, 285, 327
Borderlands: assimilation of, 8,
  51–54, 57; biographies in gazetteers
  of, 32; book donations in, 274–75;
  and Chinese culture, 4, 8, 51–58,
  276–77, 289; compilation in,
  51–62, 130, 134–35; government in,
  61–62, 138
Bossler, Beverly, 29
Boyanchaer, 220
Bozhou, Nanzhili, gazetteers, 140, 146
Brokaw, Cynthia, 165, 190, 205, 206,
  213, 234, 256
Brook, Timothy, 2, 35, 66–67, 117–18,
  154, 171, 177; on costs, 244, 245
Buddhists, 30, 31, 32, 42, 227, 254, 301
Bussotti, Michaela, 190

Cai Peiling, 328
Calligraphers, 154, 162, 183, 191–96, 199,
  242; costs of, 230–31; literati, 32, 326;
  unskilled, 193, 196
Cangwu jun zhi, 222n34, 246
Cangzhou, Beizhili, 198; gazetteers of,
  199, 200
Cao Xuequan, 150, 282
Carlitz, Katherine, 65, 85
Catalogs, 110, 119, 126, 136, 252, 325;
  manuscripts *vs.* imprints in, 176,
  259–60. *See also* Books, lists of
Categories: books arranged by (*leishu*),
  334–35; and formats, 152–56; in
  gazetteers, 30–32, 36, 38–47, 73, 159
Ceng Yijing, 130
Chaling, Huguang, 198; gazetteers of,
  112, 129, 179, 191, 200
Chang Tai, 219
Chang Tang, 223
Chang'an zhi (Song Minqiu), 275

Changde, Huguang, gazetteers, 216,
  235, 337
Changguo zhou tu zhi (Illustrated
  gazetteer of Changguo Prefecture), 150
Changle, Shandong, gazetteer, 172
Changshan, Zhejiang, gazetteer, 227
Changshu, Nanzhili gazetteers, 76, 170,
  189, 283–84
Changyuan, Beizhili, gazetteers, 256
Changzhou, Nanzhili, 327; gazetteers of,
  170, 186
Chao Li, 110, 326
Chao shi baowentang shumu (Catalog of
  the Chao family Baowentang; Chao
  Li), 110
Chaoyang, Guangdong, gazetteers,
  126, 218
Chaozhou, Guangdong, gazetteers, 173
Chartier, Roger, 6, 12, 286, 287
Chen Ce, 131
Chen Di, 326
Chen Fei, 275–76
Chen Guangqian, 57
Chen Luan, 200
Chen Mo, 131
Chen Qi, 159
Chen Shiyuan, 337
Chen Shizhang, 82n83
Chen Yan, 106
Chen Yang, 200
Chen Yi, 296, 297
Chen Youmei, 282
Chen Yun, 322, 323
Chen Zhensun, 176
Chen Zhizhai, 106
Chen Zice, 82n83
Cheng Dachang, 275–76
Cheng Daonan, 337
Cheng Hao, 296
Cheng Liben, 308–9
Cheng Minzheng, 203
Chengdu, Sichuan, 24; gazetteers of,
  172–73, 236
Chengtian, Huguang gazetteers,
  20–21, 266

Chenzhou, Huguang, gazetteers, 236, 294

Chi Liangxin, 221–22

Chi Lin, 304

Chia, Lucille, 11, 167, 182, 209, 233, 242

Chicheng zhi, 144n91, 176, 181n65, 255n10

Chinese culture: in borderlands, 4, 8, 51–58, 276–77, 289; literati, 22, 29, 31, 35, 52, 63, 177, 197, 201, 212, 340; local, 22, 29, 31, 35, 63; and travel writing, 300–301, 302; written, 4, 8, 51–58, 63. *See also* Oral culture; Print culture

Chinese Gazetteer Leadership Small Group, 341

Chinese Repository (journal), 156, 237

Chinese Vernacular Fiction (Idema), 11

Chongjian dachengdian ji (Record of the reconstruction of the Hall of Great Accomplishment; Huang Xiang), 101

Chongyi, Jiangxi, gazetteer, 187

Chow Kai-wing, 10, 142, 165, 213, 228–29, 233, 241, 256

Chu Hung-lam, 260

Chu ji (Record of Chu), 22

Chun Shum (Shen Jin), 213

Chun'an, Zhejiang, gazetteers, 145

Chuxiong, Yunnan, gazetteers, 130–31, 134

Chuzhou, Nanzhili, gazetteers, 169, 306

Cili, Huguang, gazetteers, 57, 236

Civil service examinations, 4, 29, 34, 133, 141, 271; halls for, 143, 187; quota system in, 135; and social status, 65, 79, 83; in *Xinchang xian zhi*, 73, 74, 95, 99–100

Cizhou, Hebei, gazetteers, 111, 281

Clunas, Craig, 65

Cole, James, 88n102, 91, 109

Collectors, book, 273, 325–33

Commoners: and compilation, 73, 133, 145, 150, 152, 224; and financing, 193, 217, 219, 225, 226, 227, 248; and old editions, 255–56; as readers, 12, 173, 247, 254–57, 284, 292; as sources, 145–46

Compilation, 10, 17–114; and book collectors, 328; in borderlands, 51–62, 130, 134–35; and central government, 35–48, 62–63, 164; and commoners, 73, 133, 145, 150, 152, 224; edicts requiring, 12, 35–37, 117, 118, 124, 126, 149, 164, 173, 224, 232, 258–59, 284, 289; and extended families, 64–67, 69, 81, 86, 88, 114, 340; government initiatives for, 17–63; government permission for, 154–55; and local elites, 22, 63, 66, 86, 127, 130, 163, 164; local initiatives for, 64–114; local knowledge of, 320; and local policy, 287, 295–96, 297, 339; and local rights, 12, 150, 310–25; and lower-level governments, 24, 48–51, 63, 66, 127, 163; motivations for, 17–22, 50–51, 66, 108–9; and native officials, 58; and officials, 22, 24, 49–51, 66, 127, 129–30, 163, 187; participants in, 163, 215, 223, 224, 248, 254, 255, 257, 284, 286; politics of, 22, 70–75, 107, 310, 317, 324; private *vs.* public interests in, 110, 159; and readers, 254, 255, 257, 284, 286; and ritual, 155–56. See also *Fanli* (rules of compilation)

Complete books (*quan shu*), gazetteers as, 121–22, 125

Confucianism, 29, 52, 66, 90, 101. *See also* Schools

Confucius, 25, 76

Cong Pan, 149

Contributors, 78–86, 130–33, 135; lists of, 130–31

Corvée labor, 88, 180–81, 201

Costs: of calligraphers, 230–31; of craftsmen, 214, 216, 218, 224, 226, 230–31, 240, 241, 243–44, 247, 248; and currency, 244–45; and donations, 233, 240, 245–46; of editorial personnel, 214, 233, 239–40; in Ming, 244, 245, 246; in Nanzhili, 230–33, 240, 241, 242–43; of paper, 213, 229–39, 240, 241, 246, 248; per print run, 232; of printing, 177–78, 240–41; of

Costs (*continued*)
publishing, 228–47; in Song, 244, 246; types of, 215; of woodblock-cutting, 230–31, 239, 241, 243–44, 245; of woodblocks, 241–42, 247. *See also* Financing

Craftsmen: Beijing, 201–4, 212; business zones of, 167, 190–211, 212; costs of, 214, 216, 218, 224, 226, 230–31, 240, 241, 243–44, 247, 248; for genealogies, 190, 210; Jiangxi, 197–201, 212; lists of, 180–81; mobility of, 166, 182, 190, 207, 210; networks of, 166–67, 201, 209; and woodblock printing, 179–81

Cui Wenyin, 166

Cultural Revolution, 342

Customs (*fengsu*): in gazetteers, 30, 33, 36, 40, 44, 46, 50, 93, 153; local, 24, 173, 222, 253, 257, 303, 309; and map guides, 23; non-Chinese *vs.* Chinese, 32, 52, 54; and social cohesion, 88–89, 91–92; in *Xinchang xian zhi*, 91–92, 96. *See also* Chinese culture

Da Gao (Grand Pronouncement), 34

Da Ming huidian (Collected statutes of the Great Ming), 136, 221, 234, 237, 288

Da Ming ling (Great Ming Commandment), 34, 288

Da Ming lü (Ming Code), 34

Da Ming yitong ming sheng zhi (Comprehensive gazetteer of the famous sights of the Great Ming; Cao Xuequan), 282

Da Ming yitongzhi (Comprehensive gazetteer of the Great Ming), 48, 189, 273, 275, 279, 293, 309; *vs.* local gazetteers, 281–82; sources for, 18, 37; and travel writing, 303, 307–8

Da Ming zhi shu (Gazetteer of the Great Ming), 36, 125

Dacheng, Beizhili, gazetteers, 293–94

Dai Min, 261, 262

Dai Xian, 261–62

Dali Kingdom, 295

Dang Zhao, 50

Dangshan xian zhi, 218n20

Danshengtang ji (Qi Chengye), 327

Danshengtang library (Shanyin, Zhejiang), 326

Dantu, Nanzhili, gazetteers, 225

Daoists, 31, 32, 42, 151, 227, 254, 336; temples of, 143, 144, 293

Daolasha, 149

Dardess, John, 276

Darnton, Robert, 4

De Certeau, Michel, 286

De Weerdt, Hilde, 23, 176

De'an, Huguang, gazetteers, 293

Deng Fu, 76, 141–42

Deng Ji, 204

Deng Lian, 224

Deng Xiaoping, 17

Dengzhou, Henan, gazetteers, 277

Dengzhou, Shandong, gazetteers, 149

Deqing, Jiangnan, gazetteer, 25

Des Forges, Roger, 135

Dezhou, Shandong, gazetteers, 155, 273

Di Sibin, 295, 296

Dian lüe (Sketch of Yunnan; Xie Zhaozhe), 283

Diange cilin ji (Liao Daonan), 336

Dili zhi (Geographical treatise; Ban Gu; Han shu), 23

Ding Chuan, 107n151

Ding Haohe, 108

Ding Ming, 49

Dingxiang, Shanxi, gazetteers, 272

Distribution, 11, 12, 51, 252, 257, 258–84; and booklists, 269–82; by borrowing, 147, 263, 282–83, 284, 289, 302; by copying, 283, 284, 328; local *vs.* nonlocal, 284; of manuscripts, 258–63; market, 303; of printed copies, 263–69; regional, 135–39; of used gazetteers, 282–84

Donations, 219–24; of books to schools, 274–75, 277, 279; and financing, 215, 219–21, 233, 240, 245–46; and readers, 284; sizes of, 227–28; sources of, 78,

221, 222; for wood blocks, 226; in *Xinchang xian zhi*, 95

Dong'an, Huguang, gazetteers, 272

Dongguang, Beizhili, gazetteers, 178

Dong'ou zhi (gazetteer of Wenzhou), 142

Dongxiang, Jiangxi, gazetteer, 235

Dongyang, Zhejiang, gazetteer, 187

Du Mu, 303–4, 306, 340

Du Si, 155

Du Xinfu, 229n67

Duan Hui, 206

Duchang, Jiangxi, gazetteer, 280

Edgren, Soren, 190

Editions: old, 146, 255–56, 259, 261, 271–72, 285; ongoing production of, 121–26; private, 128, 142, 149, 150, 163–64; private *vs.* official, 127–29; reprinted, 122–23, 173, 174, 186, 189, 191, 206, 215, 264, 281, 283, 326, 341–42; of *Xinchang xian zhi*, 77–86, 87, 88, 92–98, 101, 104n146, 106, 217

Editorial personnel, 129–42; costs of, 139–42, 214, 233, 239–40; native *vs.* nonnative, 131

Editorial process, 10, 117–64; formats in, 152–56; official *vs.* private, 127–29; and printing process, 156–57, 162–63; sources for, 145–52, 158–61; spaces for, 142–45

Eisenstein, Elizabeth, 5, 6

Elites, 302, 334, 340. *See also* Literati; Officials

Elites, local: and compilation, 22, 63, 66, 86, 127, 130, 163, 164; as contributors, 78–86, 131–32, 133; endogamy among, 82–83, 85; genealogies of, 60, 110; and literati culture, 31; and morality, 91–92; in north *vs.* south, 135; and officials, 290, 292; and policy, 3, 4, 287, 295–96, 297, 339; and private gazetteers, 128–29; as readers, 11, 12, 258, 284, 287. *See also* Literati, local

Elman, Benjamin, 216, 294

Epitaph inscriptions, 160

Evidential learning (*kaozheng xue*), 164, 273

Fa Xian, 301

Families: extended, 8–9; and compilation, 64–67, 69, 81, 86, 88; at county level, 66, 95; endogamy among, 66, 82–83, 85, 109; and lineages, 109; and *Xinchang xian zhi*, 92–100

Fan Chuo, 308

Fan Qin, 325

Fan Wenli, 222

Fang Jun, 118, 171, 177

Fang Xiaoru, 144, 263

Fangce zang (Rectangular-folio Tripitaka), 241

Fangyan Academy (Zhejiang), 144

Fangzhi xue (Gazetteer studies), 118

Fanli (rules of compilation), 7, 37–47, 62–63; and formats, 152; on genealogies, 110–13; from Hanlin Academy, 260–61; on literature, 159; and lower-level gazetteers, 49–50; and orders for compilation, 126; on public *vs.* private, 159–60

Faure, David, 9, 68, 86, 88, 325

Feng Bo, 141

Feng Fujing, 150, 168

Feng Qingmin, 338–39

Feng Weixian, 133–34

Feng Wenqing, 338–39

"Feng Wenqing fu Qingmin gu yuan" (Feng Wenqing recovers the old Qingmin Garden; Ye Sheng), 338–39

Fenghua, Zhejiang, gazetteers, 178

Fengrun, Beizhili, gazetteers, 218, 230–31

Fengshan ji (A record of feng and shan sacrifices; Ma Dibo), 301

Fengxin, Jiangxi, 197–99, 198

Fengyang, Nanzhili, 198; gazetteers of, 199, 200

Financing, 213–48; and approval of gazetteers, 155; and commoners, 193, 217, 219, 225, 226, 227, 248; and craftsmen, 180; and donations, 215,

Financing (*continued*)
219–21, 233, 240, 245–46; with fines,
215, 218–19, 220, 247, 275; from *lijia*,
215–18; and local government, 215, 216,
219–20, 223; and local literati, 223–24,
228; methods of, 214, 215–28;
numerical data on, 215, 228–47; and
officials, 215–17, 219, 226, 228;
responsibility for, 215–17; and schools,
219, 244; and taxation, 217, 218, 219,
223, 246–47
Fish, Stanley, 12
Fo guo ji (Record of Buddhist states;
Fa Xian), 301
Fong, Grace, 253
Fu hui quan shu (A complete book
concerning happiness and benevolence; Huang Liuhong), 290–91
Fu Sizheng, 222
Fu Yongji, 162
Fu Yucheng, 149
Fu'an, Fujian, gazetteers, 155, 172, 218–19
Fujian, 7, 137, 138; financing of gazetteers
in, 217, 218–19, 226; lower-level
gazetteers of, 13, 51, 122, 144, 149, 173,
257, 291, 298, 335; provincial gazetteers
of, 182, 207, 271; publishing in, 165,
167, 211, 212. *See also* Anxi; Fu'an;
Guangze; Jiangle; Jianyang; Sibao;
Tingzhou; Yong'an; Zhangping;
Zhangzhou
Fuzai xinjian Dachengdian ji fu lu
(Addenda to the attached "Record of
the New Construction of the Hall of
Great Accomplishment"), 102–5
Fuzhou, Fujian, gazetteers, 189, 223

Gan Ze, 187, 188
Ganshui, Zhejiang, gazetteers, 183, 223
Gansu, 137; gazetteers of, 145–46, 151–52,
154, 197, 198, 275. *See also* Shaanxi
Gansu Garrison gazetteers, 253,
274–75, 276
Ganzhou, Gansu, gazetteers, 145–46, 154,
197, 198, 235, 275

Ganzhou, Jiangxi, gazetteers, 189, 198, 227
Gao Tai, 108
Gaochun xian zhi, 236
Gazetteers, local (*difangzhi*): administrative hierarchy of, 1, 153–54, 341;
advocacy in, 296–97; circuit, 35, 38,
49, 117, 142, 164, 232; conferences
on, 341; contents of, 1, 3, 37–47, 93;
county, 1, 69, 77, 86; critiques of, 287,
330; definitions of, 9–10, 119–20, 127;
destruction of, 150, 171–72; digitization
of, 341–42; extant, 137–39, 171, 173–74,
179n56, 248, 325; formats of, 152–56,
159; history of, 22–48; influences on,
77–86; market for, 150; modern, 69,
341–42; national, 1, 18, 35, 37, 38, 47,
48, 63, 125, 189, 273, 275, 279, 281–82,
293, 303, 307–8, 309, 330; numbers
produced, 117–21, 125–26, 232; official,
127–29, 168; as official texts, 318–19,
339; ongoing supplements to, 121–26;
paratextual elements of, 6, 174, 286,
287, 318; periodization of, 9–10, 117–21;
private, 127–29, 142, 149, 150, 163–64;
purposes of, 32–35, 38, 65, 87, 296–97;
scholarship on, 2–3, 6; titles of, 127–28;
updating of, 48, 122–23, 215, 312, 330;
use of, 286–340
Ge Chen, 225
Ge Jin, 199, 200
Ge Jingchang, 200
Ge Xiao (Ge Jue), 312–13, 314–15, 317, 318
Genealogies, 64–70, 107–14; biographies
from, 75, 112; compilers of, 133;
craftsmen for, 190, 210; endogamy
in, 85; as family histories, 25, 67–68,
113–14; *fanli* on, 110–13; in gazetteers,
31, 68; gazetteers as sources for, 287,
337–39; and histories, 109–10; and
lineages, 8–9, 64, 66, 75, 90; and local
rights, 9, 68; in Mahu, 59–61; in
modern gazetteers, 69; motivations
for, 67–68, 87, 91; and native officials,
59–61; ongoing additions to, 123;
public, 65, 67, 101; and readers, 252;

and security issues, 87, 88–92; as separate genre, 111–12; and social status, 65–66, 83, 92, 107–8; as sources, 3, 7, 83, 93, 109–10, 146, 147, 160, 331; *Xinchang xian zhi* as, 8–9, 92–100

Genette, Gerard, 286

Geography: in gazetteers, 39, 43–44, 56; of publishing, 165–67; and travel writing, 301; in *Xinchang xian zhi*, 73. *See also* Map guides

Gerritsen, Anne, 143–44

Giersch, C. Patterson, 59

Gong Jiang, 74

Gong Liben, 283, 284

Gong Long, 200

Gong'an, Huguang, gazetteers, 128, 169

Gongxian, Henan, gazetteers, 196

Government: in borderlands, 61–62, 138; and compilation of gazetteers, 17–63, 154–55; edicts from, 12, 35–37, 117, 118, 124, 126, 149, 164, 173, 224, 232, 258–59, 284, 289; and law, 33–34; permission from, 154–55; records of, 145, 146, 147, 298

Government, central: in borderlands, 61–62; censorship by, 154, 155; and compilation, 35–48, 62–63, 164; and craftsmen, 181; and formats, 153; and genealogies, 69; and local society, 3, 4, 10, 29–30, 297; and northern gazetteers, 136; and precursors to gazetteers, 22–23

Government, lower-level: booklists of, 269–70; and compilation, 24, 48–51, 63, 66, 127, 163; costs of, 247; and editorial process, 75, 132, 140–41, 143, 145, 146, 157–58, 169; and financing, 215, 216, 219–20, 223; and gazetteer integrity, 313; in gazetteers, 41, 65, 159; and higher-level, 272–73; levels of, 1, 7, 11, 48–49, 223; and printing, 10, 162, 183–84, 187, 189; and publishing, 166–69, 180, 182, 186–87, 193, 211, 214; and readers, 252; records of, 147, 159, 298; and regional distribution, 138–39;

storage of gazetteers with, 12, 126, 166, 169–72, 177, 259, 262, 284

Grant, Beata, 253

Grave epitaphs (*muzhiming*), 111

Great Ritual Controversy, 19–20

Gu Lin, 20, 296, 297

Guan Daxun, 33

Guangchang, Jiangxi, gazetteers, 256

Guangdong, 7; costs of gazetteers in, 230–31; financing of gazetteers in, 217, 218, 222, 224; gazetteers of, 126, 137, 138, 173, 179, 259, 261, 280, 329, 330; publishing in, 165. *See also* Xingning

Guanghua, Huguang, gazetteer, 235

Guangling zhi, 24

Guangping, Beizhili, gazetteers, 235, 299

Guangshan, Henan, gazetteer, 110

Guangxi: gazetteers of, 57, 137, 138, 180, 221–22, 294–95; native succession in, 60

Guangxin, Jiangxi, gazetteers, 218, 219

Guangze, Fujian, gazetteer, 124–25

Guanping, Beizhili, gazetteers, 295

Gui Youguang, 263

Guide, Nanzhili, gazetteers, 274

Guidebooks, 301, 307, 340

Guiji, Zhejiang gazetteers, 230–31, 243, 246

Guizhou gazetteers, 56–58, 137, 138, 180, 186, 291, 329

Guji, Shaoxing, 70

Gujin shuke (Published books old and new; Zhou Hongzu), 166–67, 206, 211

Guo Fei, 329

Guo Hongde, 159

Guo Nan, 150, 224, 310, 312–14, 317, 318

Guo Tingfeng, 199, 200

Guo Zhengyu, 21–22

Guo Ziyi, 310

Guo Zizhang, 282, 329

Gushi, Henan, gazetteers, 49, 180, 205, 207; costs of, 230–31, 233, 241; financing of, 224, 225–26

Gusu zhi (Suzhou gazetteer), 287–88

Gutenberg, Johann, 5, 6
Gutian, Fujian, gazetteers, 219, 298

Haimen, Nanzhili, gazetteer, 235
Haizhou, Nanzhili, gazetteer, 236
Han dynasty, 22–23
Han Jun, 274
Han shu (History of the Han), 23, 336
Handan, Beizhili, 202; block cutters
  from, 210–11
Hangzhou, Zhejiang, 165, 301; gazetteers
  of, 147
Hangzhou fu zhuzuo kao (Study of the
  writings of Hangzhou Prefecture; Qi
  Chengye), 332
Hanlin Academy, 126, 258; biographies of
  scholars from, 336–37; *fanli* from,
  260–61
Hanyang, Huguang, gazetteer, 235
Hanzhong, Shaanxi, gazetteers, 277
Hargett, James, 23, 24, 29
Hartwell, Robert, 29
Hazelton, Keith, 67
He Bangzhi, 203
He Chang, 80
He Cheng, 124–25
He Jian, 79, 81n75, 83
He Jingming, 275
He Jiong, 80, 80n70
He Jiugong, 81n75
He Jiuwan, 81n75
He Shilin, 226
He Tang, 140n70
He Wenyuan, 256
He Xun, 157n142, 158
Hebei, 137. *See also* Beizhili
Heijdra, Martin, 228, 237, 239, 240
Henan, 6, 137, 138; lower-level gazetteers
  of, 110, 111, 141, 143, 183, 191, 193, 196,
  198–203, 257, 277, 281; provincial
  gazetteer of, 275. *See also* Gushi;
  Huojia; Linzhang; Neixiang; Puzhou;
  Ruzhou; Tangyin; Weishi; Xiayi;
  Xiazhou; Xincai; Xuzhou
Hengshan, Huguang, gazetteers, 145

Hengzhou, Huguang, gazetteers, 10, 149,
  156–63, 186, 187, 235
Herman, John, 57
Heshuo wai shi (Unofficial gazetteer of
  Heshuo; Qi Chengye), 330
Hezhou, Shaanxi, 52, 202; gazetteers of,
  123, 204
Histories: of books, 5, 157, 213; of
  buildings, 334; dynastic, 20, 32, 35,
  77, 86, 93, 113–14, 153, 331; family,
  25, 67–68, 108, 113–14, 332, 333; *vs.*
  gazetteers, 1–2; gazetteers as, 25, 76,
  77; gazetteers as sources for, 13, 86,
  340; and genealogies, 68–69, 109–10;
  lineage, 77, 86, 93–94, 337–39; of
  minorities, 57–58
History, local, 29–30, 76, 298; and
  collectors, 326; in gazetteers, 304; and
  lawsuits, 310–25; modern, 342; oral, 57,
  151–52, 332–33
Hongdong, Shanxi, gazetteers, 144
Hongwu zhengyun (Correct rhymes of the
  Hongwu Era), 292
Hongwu zhi shu (Gazetteer of the
  Hongwu region), 36
Hongyulou shumu (Catalog of the
  Hongyulou; Xu Bo), 110
Hongzhi Emperor, 19
Hostetler, Laura, 57
Hou Zhenping, 182, 207
Hu Rui, 100
Hu Taichu, 122, 290
Hu Wenjing, 181
Hu Xian, 162
Hu Ziming, 181
Huai'an, Nanzhili, 205
Huaiqing fu zhi (Henan), 26
Huairen, Shanxi, 50, 202; gazetteers
  of, 179
Huairou, Beizhili, 198, 271; gazetteers of,
  199, 200, 216n8
Huang Chen, 105
Huang Du, 106
Huang Family Genealogy, 106
Huang Fan, 105

Huang Gun, 105
Huang Guokui, 141
Huang Juzhong, 326
Huang lineage, 9, 101–9
Huang Liuhong, 290
Huang Lu, 204
Huang Ming, 204
Huang Mouqing, 105–7
Huang Rui, 102, 105
Huang Ruqing, 207
Huang Wei, 32, 33, 118
Huang Wen, 313
Huang Xiang, 101, 105
Huang Xuanxian, 104n145
Huang Yan, 105
Huang Ying, 104
Huang Yishui, 307–8
Huang Yuan da yitongzhi (Comprehensive gazetteer of the august Yuan), 35, 282
Huang Yudong, 104, 105
Huang Zhan, 104
Huang Zhenzhi, 102–5, 107
Huang Zhongshao, 33
Huang Zhongwen, 207
Huanggang, Huguang, 205; gazetteers of, 193, 206
Huangzhou fu zhi (Huguang), 235
Huanyu ji (Record of the realm), 309
Huanyu tong zhi (Comprehensive gazetteer of the realm), 47, 330
Huating, Nanzhili, 19, 223; gazetteers of, 235, 246
Hubei, 137. *See also* Huguang
Huguang, 6, 137, 138; lower-level gazetteers of, 36, 49, 57, 126, 128, 145, 151, 159, 169, 183, 188–89, 272, 282, 293; native succession in, 60; provincial gazetteers of, 22, 274. *See also* Chaling; Changde; Chengtian; Chenzhou; Hengzhou; Huanggang; Jingzhou; Qizhou; Yongzhou; Yunyang
Hui da ji (Guangdong), 235
Hui'an xian zhi (Fujian), 235
Huixian, Henan, gazetteers, 191

Huizhou, Guangdong, 67, 165, 198; gazetteers of, 33, 222, 224, 261; woodblock cutting in, 190, 207, 210
Hunan, 137, 139; gazetteers of, 282. *See also* Huguang
Huojia, Henan, gazetteers, 304, 305
Huzhou, Zhejiang, 165, 207, 338; gazetteers of, 222, 336
Hymes, Robert, 29, 67

Idema, Wilt, 11, 213, 253
Illustrations, 24, 26–28, 95, 103, 152, 184
Inoue Susumu, 175, 176, 246
Inscriptions, 146, 151–52, 161, 313, 316–17

Japan, 3, 300
Jesuits, 3, 299–300
Ji Hao, 204
Ji Jin, 204
Ji qian jia zhu Du Gongbu shi ji (One thousand schools' collected commentaries on Du Fu's collected poetry), 209
Jia Hanfu, 49–50
Jia Ji, 28
Jia Jinxiao, 211
Jia Shouzong, 211
Jia Yingbi, 72, 74
Jiajing Emperor (Zhu Houcong), 19–20, 36
Ji'an, Jiangxi, 197, 198, 199
Jianchang, Fujian, gazetteers, 235, 271
Jiang Chang, 161
Jiang han cong tan (Collected chatter from the Jiang Han region; Chen Shiyuan), 337
Jiangle, Fujian, gazetteers, 226
Jiangnan region, 253, 284; block cutters from, 204–9; publishing in, 211–12
Jiangning, Nanzhili, 17, 19; gazetteers of, 222, 299
Jiangsu, 6, 137. *See also* Nanzhili
Jiangxi, 6, 137, 138; academies in, 277, 279, 280; compilation in, 49; craftsmen from, 197–201, 212; financing of gazetteers in, 219, 227; lower-level

Jiangxi (*continued*)
gazetteers of, 24, 171, 183, 187, 189, 256, 261, 296, 302; provincial gazetteers of, 280, 329; publishing in, 165; readers in, 255, 257. *See also* Fengxin; Linjiang; Nanchang; Nanfeng; Ruizhou; Xincheng

Jiangxia, Huguang, 206; gazetteers of, 21–22

Jiangyin, Nanzhili, 173; gazetteers of, 177, 227–28, 230–31, 236, 240

Jiankang (Nanjing) gazetteers, 121, 122, 153, 169

Jiankang shilu (True record of Jiankang), 121

Jianning, Fujian, 189; gazetteer of, 235

Jianping, Nanzhili, gazetteers, 151

Jianyang, Fujian, 198, 256; block cutters from, 209; gazetteers of, 112, 236; publishing in, 165, 167, 211

Jiao Hong, 336

Jiao Xicheng, 149

Jiaomin bangwen (Placard of People's Instructions), 34, 288

Jiaxing, Zhejiang, gazetteers, 113, 168

Jiguge (publisher), 283

Jin dynasty, 35, 139, 171–72

Jinan, Shandong, 166

Jing Fang, 135–36

Jingde, Anhui gazetteers, 178, 232

Jingding Jiankang zhi (Jinding-era Jiankang gazetteer), 153

Jingjiang, Guilin, Guangxi gazetteers, 294–95

Jingtai Emperor, 260

Jingzhou, Huguang, gazetteers, 254, 261

Jinhua, Zhejiang, 205; gazetteers of, 207

Jinhua, Zhejiang, gazetteers, 328, 331

Jinhua zhuzuo kao (Study of the writings of Jinhua Prefecture; Qi Chengye), 332

Jinling, Nanzhili, gazetteers, 18, 155, 187, 244–45

Jinning, Yunnan, gazetteers, 307

Jintai, Beizhili, 203

Jinxian, Jiangxi, 197, 198, 199; gazetteer of, 132

Jinyu ji (Collected works of Jinyu), 151

Jiujiang, Jiangxi, gazetteers, 171

Jiuyu tuzhi (Map guides of the nine regions), 23

Jixi gazetteer, 19

Jizhou, Beizhili, gazetteers, 319

Jizhou (Luling), Jiangxi gazetteer, 24

Ju Fu, 131

Ju Yiren, 131

Ju Yizheng, 131

Kangxi Emperor, 17, 37

Katsuyama Minoru, 175, 176

Khubilai Khan, 35

Korea, 6, 300

Kuizhou, Sichuan, gazetteers, 58, 235, 335

Kunshan, Jiangsu gazetteers, 37, 38, 335

Laiwu, Shandong, 309; gazetteer of, 235

Lake Xiagai dispute, 320–25

Lake Zaoli dispute, 310–20, 339

Lanzhou, Shaanxi, 202

Laws, 33–34; and fines, 215, 218–19, 220, 247, 275; on native succession, 59–60

Lawsuits, 12, 252, 287, 339; gazetteers as evidence in, 310–25; inter-jurisdictional, 320–25

Leishu (books arranged by categories), 334–35

Leiyang gazetteers, 161

Leslie, Donald, 69

Li Bi, 273

Li Cheng, 162

Li Dongyang, 191–92, 261

Li Guoqing, 190

Li Kaixian, 309

Li Langzhong, 222

Li Panlong, 155–56

Li Sanying, 104

Li Shengzhi, 274

Li Shihua, 162

Li Shiwei, 162

Li Shizhen, 335

Li Sui, 261
Li Xingjian, 62
Li Yangdong, 131
Li Yi, 219, 291, 307, 308
Li Zengbo, 294–95
Li Zheng, 189
Li Zicheng, 119
Lian Zhongmo, 256
Liang Benshi, 200
Liang Hongsheng, 69
Liang jing ji (Record of the Two
    Capitals), 325
Liang Shanbo, 336
Liang Xiyi, 104n146
Liang Zhe zhuzuo kao (Study of the
    writings of Zhejiang; Qi Chengye), 331
Liangzhou, Shaanxi, gazetteers, 128,
    151–52
Liangzhou fu zhi bei kao (Preparatory
    studies for the Liangzhou Prefecture
    gazetteer), 128
Lianzhou, Guangdong, gazetteers, 179
Liao Benxiang, 129
Liao Can, 187
Liao Daonan, 336
Liao dynasty, 35
Liao Ji, 178
Liaodong gazetteers, 335
Liaoning, 137, 138. *See also* Shandong
Licheng, Shandong, gazetteers, 151
Lichuan zhi (Li River gazetteer), 124
Lijia (administrative community), 215–18
Lijiang, Yunnan, 308
Lin Cai, 189
Lin Han, 203
Lin Shiyou, 173
Lin Zhaoen, 229
Linding, Fujian, gazetteers, 122
Lineages: and donations, 78; and
    extended families, 109; and family
    histories, 67–68; and genealogies, 8–9,
    64, 66, 75, 90; histories of, 77, 86,
    93–94, 337–39; Huang, 9, 101–9; Lü,
    78, 96–97; Nanming Zhang, 75; in
    north *vs.* south, 135; power of, 77–78,

88, 92; and social status, 65, 67, 79; in
    Xinchang xian zhi, 93–100
Linjiang, Jiangxi, 198, 255; gazetteers of,
    151, 180, 199, 236
Linqu, Shandong, gazetteer, 236
Linting, Fujian, gazetteers, 51
Linwu, Huguang, gazetteers, 159
Linying, Henan, gazetteers, 257
Linzhang, Henan, gazetteers, 135–36
Linzi quanji (Complete works of Master
    Lin; Lin Zhaoen), 229
Literacy, 4, 54, 163, 254, 289, 292, 317
Literati: as book collectors, 325–33;
    cultural centers of, 177, 197, 201, 212; as
    editors, 139–42; gazetteers as sources
    for, 340; non-local, 141–42; as readers,
    251, 254, 284, 285, 288; surplus of, 142;
    travel writing by, 300–309; use of
    gazetteers by, 334–37. *See also* Elites;
    Officials
Literati, local: biographies of, 32, 35; and
    compilation, 66, 163, 164; and costs,
    245–46; donations from, 222; and
    financing, 223–24, 228; and local
    history, 29–30; and printing, 184, 186;
    as readers, 287
Literature: and Chinese *vs.* barbarians,
    52, 54, 56, 63; in gazetteers, 42, 46,
    159–60, 287, 340; gazetteers as sources
    for, 287, 334; public *vs.* private, 159–60;
    and social status, 65
Liu chao shi ji (Traces of matters of the
    Six Dynasties), 121
Liu Cheng, 306
Liu Chengqing, 209
Liu Da'en, 187, 188
Liu Duan, 58, 293
Liu Fu, 10, 157–59, 160, 163, 186, 188
Liu Hongyi, 189
Liu Hongzai, 207
Liu Jie, 277
Liu Ren, 203
Liu Riyi, 219
Liu Rudao, 306
Liu Sumin, 131

Liu Weiyi, 117, 138–39
Liu Wenxing, 256
Liu Xian, 118
Liu Xijue, 309
Liu Xing, 200
Liu Yu, 19
Liu Zhen, 204
Liu Zhengjing, 160–61
Liu Zhongqi, 100
Liu Zhounan, 187
Liu Zhu, 290
Lixian, Beizhili, 202; gazetteers of, 204
Liyang, Nanzhili, gazetteers, 295
Liyang Dikes, 296, 297, 298
Local rights: and family history, 100; and gazetteers, 12, 150, 310–25; and genealogies, 9, 68; to water, 298, 313, 316–17
Local society: and central government, 3, 4, 10, 29–30, 297; and Chinese culture, 22, 29, 31, 35, 63; customs in, 24, 173, 222, 253, 257, 303, 309; information on, 13, 36–37, 289–99; and map guides, 23; and national society, 329, 334, 340; policy in, 287, 295–96, 339; products of, 39, 44, 73. *See also* Elites, local; History, local; Literati, local; Officials, local
Localist turn, 29, 63, 135, 164, 289
Long Sheng, 191, 200
Longqing, Beizhili, 202; gazetteers of, 193, 204
Longquan, Jiangxi, gazetteers, 335
Longyou, Zhejiang, 198; gazetteers of, 199, 200
Lü Ben (Li Ben), 79n63
Lü Buyong, 98
Lü Chenglin, 81n75
Lü Feng, 107n151
Lü Guangbi, 80, 97
Lü Guanghua, 74, 75, 80, 81
Lü Guangjin, 80n70
Lü Guanglong, 81, 81n72
Lü Guangqian, 99
Lü Guangxin, 99

Lü Guangxun, 64, 65, 70, 72–75, 79–83, 85–92, 96–98; garden of, 100; and genealogies, 87, 89–90, 91; lineage of, 96–97; and ritual reform, 92; on security, 88, 89–90
Lü Guangyan, 80, 81
Lu Guangzu, 274
Lü Ji, 96
Lü Jingmeng, 216
Lü Jipian, 81n75, 82
Lü Jiqiao, 82
Lü Jiru, 75, 82
Lü Jiucheng, 98
Lu Kecheng, 200
Lü Lian, 98
Lü Mengyan, 80n70
Lü Mingtai, 81n75
Lü Nai, 81
Lü Nan, 255n7, 319
Lü Pei, 98
Lu Rong, 298, 335–36
Lü Ruoyu, 70, 72, 75, 80, 100
Lü Shang, 293–94
Lu Shen, 257
Lü Sheng, 27, 97–98, 106
Lü Shi zongpu (Lü lineage genealogy), 78
Lü Shiliang, 87, 92, 96, 97
Lü Ting'an, 97, 98, 99
Lü Tinggui, 97
Lü Xian, 82
Lü Yi, 96
Lü Yingkui, 80n70
Lu Yizai, 218
Lü Yizong, 100
Lü Yunjin, 81n72
Lu'an, Shanxi, 202; gazetteers of, 203
Lucheng, Shanxi, 202, 203; gazetteers of, 133–34, 204, 210
Lüeyang, Shaanxi, gazetteers, 69, 150
Luhe, Nanzhili, gazetteers, 149, 172, 236
Luling, Jiangxi, 198
Lunyu (Analects), 288
Luo Congyan, 229
Luo Danian, 224
Luo Qi, 174

Luo Xiangxian, 224
Luo Yin, 332
Luxian, Nanzhili, gazetteers, 274
Luzhou, Nanzhili, gazetteer, 236

Ma Chengde, 178
Ma Dibo, 301
Ma Guangzu, 121
Ma Tao, 151
Ma Tun, 203
Ma Wenbiao, 131
Ma Yong, 299
Ma Yongcheng, 162
Ma Yongzhang, 162
Mahu, Sichuan, 52, 63, 68; gazetteers of,
  26, 58–62, 236
Manuscripts, 12, 125, 126, 284; of
  Chengtian gazetteer, 20; hand copying
  of, 169, 170, 263; mobility of, 210; *vs.*
  printed gazetteers, 10–11, 168–77, 172,
  211; publishing of, 167; as sources, 147,
  149, 150, 164
Mao Family Jiguge, 189
Map guides (*tujing, tuji, tuzhi*), 23–24,
  29, 62, 168, 171, 262
Martini, Martino, 299–300
McDermott, Joseph, 147, 175, 177, 213,
  244, 246, 256
Medhurst, William, 156, 157
Meiguo Academy (Dayu, Jiangxi), 277
Mencius (*Mengzi*), 153, 294
Merchants: as readers, 12, 256; travel
  writing by, 301; use of gazetteers by,
  3, 299
Meskill, Johanna, 67
Messenger Office, 157, 260
Metropolitan Regions, 6, 7, 47, 143
Mianyang, Huguang, gazetteers,
  32, 35, 235
Military: and gazetteer production, 135,
  216; in gazetteers, 41, 45, 47; and
  information from gazetteers, 294–95
Min Shu (Fujian gazetteer), 182, 207
Ming dynasty: administrative structure
  of, 48–49, 137–38; affordability of

books in, 213, 251; biographies in, 47;
  book collectors in, 273, 325; and
  borderlands, 51, 57; capitals of, 201; and
  compilation, 62, 63; costs in, 244, 245,
  246; craftsmen in, 179, 180; expansion
  of gazetteers in, 36, 289; as family-state,
  113–14; gazetteers produced in, 2, 7, 10,
  13, 38, 117, 118, 121, 164, 182, 232;
  gazetteers surviving from, 137–39,
  179n56, 248, 325; genealogies in, 67;
  laws of, 33, 34, 136, 221, 234, 237, 288;
  local government in, 11; and Mahu,
  58–59; manuscript copies in, 262; and
  Nanjing, 17; official gazetteers of, 127;
  printing in, 177, 183; publishing
  industry in, 211; readers in, 101–9, 232,
  256–57; regional distribution of
  gazetteers in, 136–38, 139; women in,
  253. See also *Da Ming yitongzhi*
Ming shilu (Ming Veritable Records),
  51, 58
Mingdao Academy, 296
Minorities, 32, 35, 134, 275, 291; *vs.* Han
  Chinese, 52–58
Minxian, Fujian, gazetteers, 335
Mo Dan, 76, 77, 93–94, 95, 112; and
  Huang lineage, 101–9
Mo Yueding, 336
Mo Zhen, 94
Monasteries. *See* Religious institutions
Monks, 3, 299, 300, 301
Mote, Frederick, 260
Mount Yi Academy (Kaifeng), 280n121
Mount Yi Academy Gazetteer (*Yi shan
  shuyuan zhi*), 280

Nanchang, Jiangxi, 197, 198, 199;
  gazetteers of, 230–31, 236, 238, 240
Nanfeng, Jiangxi, gazetteers, 183, 219, 291
Nanji zhi (Southern Capital Region
  gazetteer), 143
Nanjing, Nanzhili: block cutters from,
  204–7; book collectors in, 327;
  bookstores in, 283; gazetteers of, 17–18;
  publishing in, 165, 167, 201

Nankang, Jiangxi: gazetteers of, 280, 302; White Deer Grotto Academy in, 279, 280

Nanming Gazetteer, 105

Nanming Zhang Shi zongpu (Genealogy of the Nanming Zhang lineage), 75

Nanxiong, Guangdong, gazetteer, 235

Nanyang, Henan, gazetteers, 277

Nanzhili, 137, 138; costs of gazetteers in, 230–33, 240, 241, 242–43; financing of gazetteers in, 222, 225; gazetteers of, 76, 133, 140, 146, 193, 194, 195, 198, 205, 206, 209, 282, 283, 296, 335; readers in, 252–53, 254, 257. *See also* Jiangning; Nanjing; Xuzhou

National Library of China, 342

Neige cang shu mu lu (Catalog of books held by the Grand Secretariat), 259

Neihuang, Beizhili, 129; gazetteers of, 172, 235

Neiqiu, Beizhili, gazetteers, 304, 305

Neixiang, Henan, gazetteers, 182, 184

Neo-Confucianism, 29, 66

New Policies, 23

Ningbo, Zhejiang (Siming), gazetteers, 31, 134, 334–36

Ningguo, Nanzhili, 205; gazetteers of, 206

Ninghai, Shandong, gazetteer, 25, 151

Ningxia, Shaanxi, 137, 305; gazetteers of, 235, 275

Ningxia Garrison gazetteer, 275

Ningyuan, Huguang, gazetteers, 272

Northern Song dynasty, 23, 117, 164

Novus atlas Sinensis (Martini), 300

Officials: and affordability of books, 247; as book collectors, 326; and compilation, 22, 49–51, 127, 129–30, 154–55, 163; as contributors, 132–33; and costs, 245–46; and craftsmen, 180; and distribution, 282; donations from, 221, 222; and financing, 215–17, 219, 226, 228; in gazetteers, 41, 42, 45, 46, 47; and local elites, 133; and local language, 292, 319; military, 32; and prefaces, 140–41, 290; as readers, 11, 12, 251, 254, 260, 261, 284, 285, 287; reputations of, 299; sojourning, 288–300; status of, 67, 79, 107–8; use of gazetteers by, 33, 289–99; writings by, 301, 334–37; in *Xinchang xian zhi*, 73, 83

Officials, local: and compilation, 8, 24, 58, 66; donations from, 222; and laws, 34; and local lineages, 66; and map guides, 23; native, 57, 58, 59–61; as readers, 25; and *Xinchang xian zhi*, 72; and Yuan gazetteers, 35

Oral culture: and readers, 317, 318; as source, 57, 151–52, 332–33; *vs.* written, 52, 54, 56–57, 63

Ouyang Xiu, 306

Paintings, colophons for, 336

Palace library, 150–51, 260–61, 270, 282, 284

Pan Guangdan, 69

Pan Risheng, 88

Pan Sheng, 72–75, 77, 79–80, 82–83, 86, 98, 99; on genealogies, 87, 89, 90–91; and ritual reform, 92

Pan Tiankuang, 81n75

Pan Xianchen, 81

Paper, 179; costs of, 213, 229–39, 240, 241, 246, 248; sizes of, 233–38

Pei Gaoge, 211

Pei Gaolou, 211

Pei Guocui, 204

Pei Guoming, 204

Pei Jiugai, 204

Pei Jiuqian, 204

Pei Sanyue, 210, 211

Pei Wensui, 211

Pei Yi'e, 204

Pei Yiyuan, 204

Peng Dayi, 334–35

Peng Weiyan, 226

Peng Zuo, 200

People's Republic of China (PRC), gazetteers in, 341–42

Pi Yuan, 220
Piling zhi (Changzhou gazetteer), 186
Pinghu, Zhejiang, gazetteers, 93, 183
Pingliang, Shaanxi, gazetteers, 154
Pingyang, Zhejiang, gazetteers, 142, 219, 246
Poetry, 155–56, 209, 300, 306, 308
Politics, 6, 7; of compilation, 22, 70–75, 107, 310, 317, 324; in *Xinchang xian zhi*, 8–9, 70–75, 93
Population, 36, 40, 44, 114; and regional distribution of gazetteers, 136–38
Postal system, 206
Prefaces, 6, 174; calligraphy in, 191–93; and contributors, 130, 132; and craftsmen, 181, 203, 207; information from, 183, 214, 239, 248, 252, 291; and officials, 140–41, 290; payment for authors of, 140–41
Print culture, 4; Chinese *vs.* European, 5–6; *vs.* manuscript culture, 175–76
Printing: of Chinese Bibles, 237, 239; commercial, 188–89; costs of, 177–78, 240–41; and distribution, 263–69; of gazetteers, 10–11, 168–77, 284; and handwritten copies, 172–73, 175; and legitimacy, 319; locations for, 181–89, 211; with movable type, 5–6, 177–78, 190, 232; regional centers of, 182, 190–91; of single copies, 246–47; staff for, 183–84, 186; and survival, 211; technologies of, 177–79
Printing and Book Culture in Late Imperial China (Brokaw and Chow), 165
Printing for Profit (Chia), 11
Printing Press as an Agent of Change (Eisenstein), 5
Production, 7, 117–248; materials needed for, 215; ongoing, 121–26; rates of, 117–21, 125–26, 164, 232. *See also* Costs; Editorial process; Financing; Publishing
Protestant Reformation, 5
Provincial gazetteers, 1, 127, 273; Henan, 275; Huguang, 22, 274; Jiangxi, 280;

329; *vs.* lower level, 182; Shaanxi, 275; Shandong, 274, 309; Yunnan, 282, 308; Zhejiang, 274, 328, 330, 331
Pu'an, Guizhou, gazetteers, 56–57, 180, 235
Publishing, 3, 165–212; centers of, 11, 165, 167, 177, 201, 211–12, 327; commercial, 189, 190, 204, 209, 214, 233, 258, 334; and communication circuit, 4; costs of, 228–47; economics of, 5, 11; in Europe, 5; and financing, 213, 227; geography of, 165–67; and local government, 166–69, 180, 182, 186–87, 193, 211, 214; in Ming, 211
Publishing, Culture, and Power in Early Modern China (Chow Kai-wing), 228
Pujiang, Zhejiang, 104–5; gazetteer of, 235
Puzhou, Henan, gazetteers, 141–42

Qi, state of, 25
Qi Chengxun, 328
Qi Chengye, 326–33
Qi Ning, 306
Qi sheng (Qi chronicle), 151, 170, 262, 282, 309
Qi Siyuan, 332
Qi Zhengxiang, 200
Qian ji (Record of Qian; Guo Zizhang), 282, 329
Qian xing bian (Compilation of one thousand surnames), 93
Qiantang, Zhejiang, gazetteers, 332
Qin dynasty, 22
Qin Liang, 140
Qinchuan zhi (Changshu, Suzhou gazetteer), 189, 283–84
Qing dynasty: biographies in, 47; book collectors in, 273; and borderlands, 51; and compilation, 62, 63; comprehensive gazetteers in, 48; craftsmen in, 179; distribution in, 280; founding of, 50; gazetteers produced in, 10, 36, 37, 38, 164; gazetteers surviving from, 248; native peoples in, 57–58; official gazetteers of, 127; printing in, 183; publishing in, 165; and Zhejiang, 320

Qingdu, Beizhili, 305
Qinghai, 137
Qingyun, Beizhili, 205; gazetteers of, 193
Qingzhou, Shandong, gazetteers,
    155–56, 274
Qinzhou, Guangdong, gazetteer, 235
Qishan, Shaanxi, gazetteers, 160
Qishui, Huguang, gazetteers, 49, 235
Qizhou, Huguang, gazetteers, 186, 187,
    197, 198, 200, 215, 218, 221, 235, 237;
    costs of, 230–31, 241, 242; paper in, 238
Qu Yong, 283, 284
Quan shan shu (Exhortation to
    goodness), 288
Qufu, Shandong, gazetteers, 193
Quwo, Shanxi, gazetteer, 235
Quzhou, Zhejiang, gazetteers, 154

Rao Yuande, 173
Raozhou, Jiangxi, gazetteers, 261
Readers, 9, 251–85; commoners as, 12, 173,
    247, 254–57, 284, 292; distribution to,
    252, 257, 258–84; emperors as, 260;
    expanding numbers of, 232, 254,
    256–57; and financing, 213; interpretive
    communities of, 12, 286, 339; and
    lawsuits, 310–25; local elites as, 11, 12,
    258, 284, 287; local *vs.* nonlocal, 252,
    257, 286, 287; and manuscripts *vs.*
    imprints, 177; in Ming, 101–9, 232,
    256–57; officials as, 11, 12, 25, 251, 254,
    260, 261, 284, 285, 287; in schools,
    270–71, 273, 287; targeted, 252–57;
    travelers as, 12, 300–309, 340; use of
    gazetteers by, 64, 286–340
*Record of the Shrine to the Worthies of
    Old*, 106
Religious institutions: Daoist, 143, 144,
    293; editing in, 143–44; in gazetteers,
    31, 41, 45, 161, 293; as sources, 160;
    storage of blocks in, 189; use of
    gazetteers by, 299
Ren Guan, 52
Ren Weidiao, 130, 131
Ren Yanfen, 294

Renhe, Zhejiang, gazetteers, 263
Renzong, Emperor, 106
Republican period, 36, 248, 341
Ricci, Matteo, 156, 157, 162–63
Rites of Zhou (*Zhouli*), 77, 106
Ritual reform, 65, 92, 96
Rituals, 34, 155, 293
Rongyin xin jian (Xu Bo), 326
Rugao, Nanzhili, gazetteers, 159–60
Rui'an, Zhejiang, gazetteers, 142
Ruichang, Jiangxi, gazetteers, 236, 296
Ruijin, Jiangxi, gazetteer, 235
Ruizhou, Jiangxi, 198; gazetteers of, 197,
    200, 292
Ruzhou, Henan, gazetteers, 123, 152

Sakugen, 300
Sang Youzhu, 200
Sanshan zhi (Fuzhou, Fujian,
    gazetteer), 189
Schools: booklists of, 269–74, 276–79;
    editing in, 143, 144; and financing, 219,
    244; in gazetteers, 40, 44; gazetteers
    stored in, 172, 173, 258–59, 263, 275–76,
    281, 284; instructors in, 9, 49, 72,
    101–2, 105, 124–25, 129, 131–33, 141, 143,
    184, 219, 287, 292; lands of, 219, 298;
    old editions in, 255; printing in,
    186–87; as sources, 146, 149, 150, 160;
    in Xinchang, 101–3, 105, 107. *See also*
    Academies, private
Script, craftsman, 213
Scripta Sinica, 287
Sedo, Timothy, 135, 136
Shaanxi, 137, 138; lower-level gazetteers
    of, 69, 150, 154, 160, 184, 202, 208, 209,
    277, 305, 306; provincial gazetteer of,
    275. *See also* Hezhou
*Shaanxi, xingdusi ru xue zunjingge zhu
    shu ji* (Record of acquiring books for
    the Shaanxi, Regional Military
    Commission school library; Chen
    Fei), 275
Shaju yezhi (Unofficial gazetteer from a
    mountain abode), 128

Shan Dong lu (Record of Eastern Shan; Yu Rui), 104n146

Shan tang si kao (Peng Dayi), 334–35

Shandong, 137, 138; lower-level gazetteers of, 25, 111, 123, 134, 143, 147, 149, 151, 172, 183, 184, 193, 309; provincial gazetteers of, 274, 309; publishing in, 166. *See also* Dezhou; Qingzhou; Tengxian

Shang dynasty, 304

Shangguan You, 125

Shanghai, 137

Shanglüe quan zhi (Shaanxi), 277

Shangnan, Shaanxi, gazetteers, 277

Shangyu, Zhejiang: gazetteers of, 133, 150, 224, 227, 254, 298, 316n81, 319, 321–25, 339; Lake Zaoli dispute in, 310–20; *vs.* Yuyao, 320–25, 339

Shangyuan, Nanzhili, 17; gazetteers of, 143, 217, 222

Shanxi gazetteers, 137, 138, 144, 206, 272. *See also* Huairen; Lucheng

Shanyin, Shaoxing, 70

Shao Linwu, 283

Shaowu, Fujian, gazetteer, 235

Shaoxing, 109; gazetteers of, 335

Shaoxing, Zhejiang: gazetteers of, 70, 75, 86, 207, 281, 310, 312, 319–20, 333; and lawsuits, 310, 312, 319–20; taxes in, 246–47

Shen Bang, 237, 242

Shen Bin, 203

Shen Chaoxuan, 263

Shen Mei, 203

Shen Ming, 203

Shen Qiu, 263

Shen Wenming, 336

Shen Xingbing, 200

Shen Xuan, 203

Shen Yiguan, 21

Shen Yu, 203

Shendu Book Studio, 189

Sheng Ji, 141

Shi dao zhi (Record of the ten circuits), 294

Shi Huai, 226

Shi Zizhong, 309

Shihu, Suzhou, gazetteer, 94, 95

Shiji (*Grand Scribe's Records*; Sima Qian), 32, 77, 110

Shin, Leo, 57, 60

Shixing, Guangdong, gazetteer, 235

Shou Tianfu, 204

Shouchang xian zhi, 42n75, 281n125

Shouning daizhi (Shouning gazetteer-in-waiting), 128

Shuang jiefu zhuan (Biography of two virtuous women; Pan Sheng), 75

Shuntian, Beizhili, 20, 271

Shuyuan za ji (Miscellaneous records from the bean garden; Lu Rong), 335

Sibao, Fujian, 190, 205, 234

Sichuan: gazetteers of, 58, 137, 138, 139, 144, 335; native succession in, 60; publishing in, 165. *See also* Chengdu; Mahu

Siku quan shu (Complete books of the Four Treasuries), 110

Siku quan shu (database), 287–88

Sima Qian, 32, 77, 110

Siming. *See* Ningbo, Zhejiang

Siming tujing (Siming map guide), 24

Sinan, Guizhou, gazetteers, 186, 235, 291

Singing Earthworm Collected Works, 106

Six Dynasties period, 121, 301

Skinner, William, 167

Social status: in borderlands, 8; and civil service examinations, 65, 79, 83; and compilation, 86; and contributors, 130; and gazetteers, 3, 8, 65, 66, 107–8, 310, 340; and genealogies, 65–66, 83, 92, 107–8; and lineages, 65, 67, 79; and officeholding, 67, 79, 107–8; sources of, 65–66; in *Xinchang xian zhi*, 9, 74, 83, 94, 98, 100, 101, 310, 317

Song, state of, 25

Song dynasty, 33, 214, 253, 335; costs in, 244, 246; decline of centralization in, 4, 29–30, 289, 334; gazetteer categories in, 30–31; gazetteers produced in, 2, 10, 118, 119, 138–39, 171, 289; gazetteers

Song dynasty (*continued*)
surviving from, 2, 139, 261; locations of
printing in, 183, 186; manuscript copies
in, 262; official gazetteers of, 127;
official history of, 35; printing in, 10,
168, 211; regional distribution of
gazetteers in, 138–39; transmission
of gazetteers in, 174–75. *See also*
Northern Song dynasty; Southern
Song dynasty
Song Ji, 29, 259
Song Lian, 144
Song Minqiu, 275
Song Xian, 97
Songjiang, Nanzhili, 19; gazetteers of,
148, 335
Sources: access to, 145–52, 158–61;
commoners as, 145–46; gazetteers as,
13, 86, 214, 287, 326, 328, 331, 334,
336–40; genealogies as, 3, 7, 83, 93,
109–10, 146, 147, 160, 331; hand
copying of, 149–50; manuscripts as,
147, 149, 150, 164; private editions as,
149, 150, 163–64; schools as, 146, 149,
150, 160
Southern Imperial Academy, 220
Southern Song dynasty: gazetteers
produced in, 24, 29, 117, 121, 232;
genealogies in, 67; localist turn in, 29,
63, 135, 164, 289; printing in, 176
Spring and Autumn Annals, 76, 77
Statecraft, 33, 63
Strassberg, Richard, 300, 301, 302
Su Minwang, 218
Su Shi, 297
Su Tianjue, 262
Su You, 140
Suizhou, Huguang, gazetteers, 293
Sun Quan, 40n74
Sun Ribian, 223
Sun Ying'ao, 277
Suqian, Nanzhili, gazetteers, 160
Suzhou, Nanzhili: gazetteers of, 93, 127,
189, 205, 283–84, 287–88, 335, 338;
publishing in, 165; readers in, 257

Taikang, Henan, 198; gazetteers of,
199, 200
Taiping, Guangxi, gazetteers, 57
Taiyuan, Shanxi, 202
Taiyuan shiji ji (Record of the traces of
the matters of Taiyuan), 168
Taizhou, Zhejiang, gazetteers, 142, 144,
171, 255
Tan Xisi, 306
Tang Code, 33–34
Tang dynasty, 23, 325, 335
Tang Qin, 131
Tang Shunzhi, 33, 72, 85, 141
Tang Tianlin, 168
Tangyin, Henan, 202; gazetteers of, 149,
210, 211
Tao Zhi, 174
Taoyuan, Huguang, gazetteers, 188–89
Taxation, 36, 92, 114; cheating on,
218–19; and financing, 217, 218, 219,
223, 246–47; in gazetteers, 40, 44, 291,
298; in Ming, 11; policies on, 295–96
"Technology, Culture, and Economics:
Movable Type *versus* Woodblock
Printing in East Asia" (Heijdra), 228
Temples. *See* Religious institutions
Teng, Emma, 57
Tengxian, Shandong, gazetteers, 132, 140,
147, 151
Thatcher, Melvin, 68
Tian gong kai wu (Devices for the
exploitation of nature), 234
Tian Guan, 64, 65, 70, 72–76, 80, 82, 86,
88, 91, 99, 106
Tian Jiujia, 149
Tian Rucheng, 291
Tianchang, Nanzhili, 205; gazetteers of,
144, 252–53; readers in, 252–53, 254
Tianjin, 137
Tianshun Emperor, 48
Tiantai, Zhejiang, gazetteers, 142
Tianxia junxian zhishu (Gazetteer of the
realm's localities), 43
Tianyige Library (Ningbo), 123, 179,
325–26

Tingzhou, Fujian, 205; gazetteers of, 204, 206, 290
Tong Chengxu, 32, 35
Tong'an, Nanzhili, gazetteer, 172
Tongzhou, Nanzhili, gazetteers, 235, 292
Travel writing, 7, 13, 301–2, 309, 332, 333; of Du Mu, 303, 306, 340
Travelers as readers, 12, 300–309, 340

Ueda Makoto, 67–68, 100

Van der Sprenkel, Otto Berkelbach, 69
Veritable records, 20
Vietnam, 300

Wan Deng, 200
Wan Hao, 132
Wan Peng, 88
Wan Qi, 200
Wan shu za ji (Miscellaneous records of the Wanping yamen; Shen Bang), 237, 241
Wang Bingzhong, 131
Wang Chongxian, 134–35
Wang Duanlai, 118
Wang Gao, 19, 222–23
Wang Guang, 255n7
Wang Guanyinbao, 181
Wang Hengshu (Shixing), 333
Wang Housun, 134
Wang Huyun, 329
Wang Liping, 301, 302
Wang Shangyong, 54, 56
Wang Shenzhong, 134
Wang Shipeng, 104
Wang Shixing, 301
Wang Shizhen, 155–56, 277
Wang Shunmin, 33
Wang Su, 294
Wang Tingchen, 20
Wang Tinggan, 142n74
Wang Tongqian, 313
Wang Yan, 174
Wang Yi, 219
Wang Yuanbin, 132, 140, 147

Wang Zhen, 178, 200, 232
Wang Zongyi, 295
Wanjuantang shumu (Ten-Thousand-Volume Hall catalog; Zhu Mujie), 325
Wanli Emperor, 21
Warring States period, 22
Water control, 297, 298, 310–25
Wei Jun, 49
Wei shan yin zhi (The blessings of doing good secretly), 288
Wei Shu, 325
Weinan, Shaanxi, gazetteers, 208, 209
Weishi, Henan, gazetteer, 25, 114
Weiyang zhi (gazetteer of Yangzhou Prefecture), 128
Weng Jing, 226
Wengyuan, Guangdong, gazetteers, 259
Wenxian tong kao, 151
Wenyuange shumu (Wenyuange book catalog), 119, 126, 259
Wenzhou, Zhejiang, gazetteers, 142
White Deer Grotto Academy (Nankang, Jiangxi), 279, 280
Widow chastity, 65, 74n37, 76, 86
Will, Pierre-Etienne, 2
Wo Pan, 182
Women: biographies of, 9, 31, 32, 47, 75, 253, 337; in *Da Ming yitong zhi*, 281; as readers, 252–54, 284; sources on, 161; in *Xinchang xian zhi*, 74, 87, 97
Woodblock printing: commercial, 188–89; costs of, 228–47; craftsmen for, 179–81; and gazetteer production, 154; *vs.* movable type, 6, 177–78; paper for, 179, 213, 229–39, 240, 241, 246, 248; and print culture, 5–6; problems with, 162; and revisions, 177–78; and survival, 169–71, 172
Woodblocks: costs of, 229–31, 239, 241–45, 247; hardwoods for, 178–79; recutting of, 171, 173; replacement of, 226; reuse of, 242; storage of, 189, 284–85
Wu, Nanzhili, gazetteer, 230–31
Wu kingdom, 40n74, 338

Wu Wendu, 204
Wu Yizheng, 104n144
Wu Zhongwing, 263
Wucheng, Shandong, gazetteer, 235
Wucheng, Zhejiang, gazetteer, 266
Wuding, Shandong, gazetteers, 183
Wujiang, Nanzhili, gazetteers, 144,
    149–50, 227
Wujun tu zhi, 262
Wukang, Zhejiang, 205; gazetteers of, 207
Wuning, Jiangxi, gazetteers, 257
Wuwei, Nanzhili, gazetteers, 242–43
Wuxi, Nanzhili, 205; gazetteers of,
    140, 225
Wuxian, Nanzhili, gazetteers, 152, 242
Wuxing zhi, 246
Wuzhou, Guangxi, 29, 30; gazetteers of,
    180, 221–22

Xia Yuanji, 43
Xiajiang, Jiangxi, 198
Xiajin, Shandong, gazetteers, 134
Xi'an, Shaanxi, 202
Xian xi zhi, 291
Xiang Bian, 194
Xiang Tingji, 299
Xiangfu zhouxian tujing (Prefecture
    and county map guides of the
    Xiangfu era), 23
Xianghe, Beizhili, 198; gazetteers of,
    199, 200
Xiangshan, Zhejiang, gazetteers, 144, 179
Xianyou, Fujian, gazetteers, 149
Xiao Jingao, 328, 331
Xiayi, Henan, 205; gazetteers of, 207
Xiazhou, Henan, 304, 305
Xie Duo, 144
Xie Zan, 131
Xie Zhaozhe, 13, 257, 283
Xie Zhensun, 220
Ximen Bao, 136
Xincai, Henan, gazetteers, 187–88,
    224n47
Xinchang, Zhejiang, 69–114; city wall
    for, 86, 88; Confucian school in, 101–3,

105, 107; politics in, 8–9, 70–75, 93;
    travel writing on, 301
Xinchang, Zhejiang, gazetteer, 64, 141,
    236; accuracy of, 76–77; categories
    in, 73; as community building, 87;
    vs. Da Ming yitong zhi, 281; editions
    of, 66, 69–70, 77–88, 92–98, 101,
    102n142, 104n146, 106; and extended
    families, 114; as family genealogy,
    8–9, 92–98; *fanli* in, 39; financing of,
    78, 217–18, 227–28; graves (*fenmu*)
    section of, 83, 84, 94; illustrations in,
    27–28; influences on, 77–86; and
    local lineages, 78–86, 93–100; and
    local rights, 325; Ming readers of,
    101–9; *vs.* other gazetteers, 135, 136;
    precursors to, 104n146; and Qi
    Chengye, 333; and social status, 9, 74,
    83, 94, 98, 100, 101, 310, 317; travel
    writing in, 309
Xinchang Caiyan Zhao Shi zong pu,
    90–91
*Xinchang dao zhong you Tianmu su
    Guanling ji* (Record of Visiting Tianmu
    and Resting at Gunaling on the Road
    to Xinchang; Qi Chengye), 333
Xincheng, Beizhili, 126n33; gazetteers
    of, 332
Xincheng, Jiangxi, 124–25; gazetteers of,
    242, 260
Xincheng, Zhejiang, 126n33
Xing yuan (Garden of surnames), 93
Xingan, Jiangxi, 198
Xingguo, Huguang, gazetteers, 151
Xinghua, Fujian, gazetteers, 33, 34, 35,
    144, 173
Xinghua, Nanzhili, gazetteer, 209
Xingning, Guangdong, gazetteers, 141,
    145, 155, 188, 217, 236; costs of, 230–31,
    240, 241, 242; paper in, 238
Xinquan Academy (Nanjing)
    gazetteers, 280
Xinyu, Jiangxi, 198
Xiong Neng, 193
Xiong Wenhan, 25

Xiuwu xian zhi, 140n70
Xu Bing, 225
Xu Bo, 110, 326
Xu Lin, 18, 19
Xu Luan, 204
Xu Mu, 152
Xu Shi, 130, 131, 132
Xu shi bi jing (Xu Bo), 326
Xu Taomei, 283
Xu Xiake, 301, 303, 307–8
Xu Xuemo, 274
Xu Zhaoji, 274
Xu Zhidao, 225
Xuanfu Garrison gazetteers, 134–35, 253
Xue Chen, 155–56
Xue Fangshan, 330
Xujiang, Jiangxi, gazetteers, 124, 279
Xundian, Yunnan, gazetteers, 54, 235
Xuzhou, Henan, gazetteers, 110, 180, 191–92
Xuzhou, Nanzhili, 202; gazetteers of, 147, 203, 259, 302

Yan Chaoji, 284
Yan Ruhuan, 304, 306
Yan Xiang, 181
Yan'an prefectural gazetteer, 275
Yancheng, Henan, gazetteers, 193, 236
Yang Family's Guiren Studio, 189
Yang Pei, 157–58
Yang Qian, 223
Yang Sanping, 152
Yang Shengxin, 243–44
Yang Shiqi, 261
Yang Sui, 225, 226
Yang Xinmin, 27
Yangwu, Henan, gazetteers, 183
Yangzhou, Nanzhili, gazetteers, 128, 253, 302–3, 335
Yanling, Henan, 202; gazetteers of, 203
Yanping, Fujian, gazetteer, 133, 235
Yanshi, Henan, gazetteers, 141
Yanting xian zhi, 185
Yanzhou, Shandong, gazetteers, 184
Yanzhou, Zhejiang, gazetteers, 258–59

Yaozhou, Shaanxi, gazetteers, 184
Ye Bingjing, 154
Ye Dehui, 244
Ye Kai, 170
Ye Mengxiong, 314
Ye Mengzhu, 233, 236, 237
Ye Sheng, 325, 337–38
Ye Xiushi, 337
Yi Cunxu, 226
Yi minority, 58, 134
Yi Shizhong, 134
Yi Xi, 226
Yicheng, Shanxi, gazetteers, 206
Yin, Ningbo, gazetteer, 338–39
Yin De, 162
Yin Wenji, 304
Yingshan, Huguang, gazetteers, 235, 293
Yingtian, Nanzhili, 17, 18, 20; gazetteers of, 295, 296
Yingzhou, Nanzhili, gazetteers, 216, 230–33, 240, 241
Yiwu xin zhi (New Yiwu gazetteer), 332
Yixing gazetteer, 18–19
Yizhen, Nanzhili, gazetteer, 236
Yizhou, Beizhili, gazetteers, 261, 293
Yong da ji (He Jingming), 275
Yong lu (Cheng Dachang), 275–76
Yong'an, Fujian, gazetteers, 218, 230–31, 239–40
Yongfeng, Jiangxi, gazetteers, 183, 219
Yongfu, Fujian, gazetteer, 13, 257
Yongfu zheng qi lu (Record of the true essence of Yongfu), 128
Yŏngga chi (gazetteer of Andong Prefecture), 300
Yongjia, Wenzhou, Zhejiang, 142
Yongle dadian (Great encyclopedia of the Yongle Era), 118, 119, 124, 126, 260
Yongle Emperor, 43, 47
Yongnian, Beizhili, gazetteers, 227
Yongping, Beizhili, gazetteers, 113–14
Yongxin, Jiangxi, 197, 198
Yongzhou, Huguang, 166; gazetteers of, 126, 180, 272
You Hu, 162

You mingshan ji (Records of travels to famous mountains; Du Mu), 303, 306, 340

You Shen, 162

Youxi, Fujian, gazetteer, 235

Yu Banghu, 81n75, 82

Yu Bangshao, 82

Yu Bangshi, 80, 81, 82, 92

Yu Binghu, 82, 100

Yu Bingzhong, 82

Yu Chaotuo, 79

Yu Jie, 200

Yu Jing, 200

Yu Jinxiu, 207

Yu Jishan, 224

Yu Qian, 170, 262

Yu Qin, 81n75, 82, 262

Yu Rui, 104n146

Yu Ruqin, 131

Yu Seng, 99

Yu Sheng, 226

Yu Yingshan, 81n75, 82

Yu Yingsu, 82, 99, 100

Yu Zequan, 79, 88, 99

Yu Zhencai, 107n151

Yu Zhengming, 81n72

Yu Zhenqiang, 79, 81, 92

Yu Zhenying, 107n151

Yu Zhi, 81n75

Yu Zifen, 282

Yuan dynasty, 10, 214, 253; and borderlands, 51; costs in, 244, 245; craftsmen in, 179; founding of, 35, 337; gazetteers produced in, 2, 7, 38, 62, 117, 118, 119, 164, 168–69, 171, 232, 261, 289; genealogies in, 67; laws of, 33; locations of printing in, 183; manuscript copies in, 262; official gazetteers of, 127; transmission of gazetteers in, 174–75

Yuan Fang, 184

Yuan Hua, 133, 224

Yuan Liang, 131

Yuan Tangwei, 96n125

Yuan Xuan, 133, 224

Yuanhe junxian tuzhi (Commandery and county map guides of the Yuanhe reign), 23

Yuanshi, Beizhili, 202; gazetteers of, 210, 211

Yuanzhou, Jiangxi, gazetteers, 197, 198, 200, 235

Yudi san qi (Land of the Three Qi), 309

Yueqing, Zhejiang, gazetteers, 168

Yufeng zhi (Kunshan gazetteer), 37, 38

Yugong (Tribute of Yu; *Shangshu*), 22, 32, 38, 40, 43

Yunnan, 137, 138, 283; lower-level gazetteers of, 48, 51, 54, 130–31, 134, 307; native succession in, 60; provincial gazetteers of, 282, 308

Yunnan zhi (Record of Yunnan; Fan Chuo), 308

Yunyang, Huguang, 275, 276–77; gazetteer of, 235

Yuyao, Zhejiang, 205; *vs.* Shangyu, 320–25, 339

"Yuzhang Liu Xijue you Zuiyuan Banmutang ji" (Record of visiting the Drunken Garden's half-acre pond; Liu Xijue), 309

Yuzhang Luo xiansheng wenji (Collected works of Mr. Luo of Yuzhang; Luo Congyan), 229

Zeng Keshan, 336

Zeng Shengwu, 234, 237

Zengcheng, Guangdong, gazetteers, 280

Zhai Xian, 200

Zhai Yi, 200

Zhai Zhi, 200

Zhan Ruoshui, 302–3

Zhang Bangqi, 170

Zhang Bao, 85

Zhang Chuanshi, 174

Zhang Guifang, 206

Zhang Guogan, 117

Zhang Hao, 209

Zhang Jingchuang, 82n83

Zhang Jingfu, 200

Zhang Jun, 315
Zhang Juzheng, 279
Zhang Kui, 200
Zhang Lie, 291
Zhang Long, 204
Zhang Mingfeng, 282
Zhang Mu, 83
Zhang Qianxian, 183
Zhang Quan, 218
Zhang Sanyi, 315–17
Zhang Sheng, 9–10, 118–21, 125, 164
Zhang Taiheng, 131
Zhang Ti, 225, 226
Zhang Tianfu, 70
Zhang Wei, 306
Zhang Xianzhong, 119
Zhang Xiumin, 165, 167, 181, 182, 203
Zhang Xuecheng, 68
Zhang Yanxiang, 173
Zhang Yao, 83
Zhang Yingpin, 47, 133
Zhang Yuanbian, 70, 86
Zhang Yuanyi, 72, 73–74, 75, 77, 80,
    82, 141
Zhang Yue, 130
Zhang Ze, 130, 132
Zhang Zhe, 142, 220
Zhang Zhu, 308
Zhang Zuo, 183
Zhangjiang Book Room, 189
Zhangping, Fujian, gazetteers, 209,
    217, 290
Zhangzhou, Fujian, 166; gazetteers
    of, 271
Zhangzi, Shanxi, 203
Zhao Jing, 85, 98
Zhao Qimei, 326
Zhao shi tie wang shan hu (Zhao
    Qimei), 326
Zhao Tang, 183
Zhao Tianyu, 85, 98
Zhaokuangge (publisher), 283
Zhaozhou, Beizhili, gazetteers, 210
Zhejiang, 6, 137, 138, 205, 207, 326; costs
    of gazetteers in, 230–31, 243, 246;

financing of gazetteers in, 219, 223,
    224; lower-level gazetteers of, 142, 145,
    154, 168, 178, 183, 187, 263; provincial
    gazetteers of, 227, 236, 274, 328, 330,
    331; in Qing dynasty, 320; tourism in,
    301. *See also* Hangzhou; Jiaxing;
    Jinhua; Longyou; Ningbo; Shangyu;
    Shaoxing; Taizhou; Xinchang;
    Yanzhou; Yuyao; Zhuji
Zheng Dongbi, 217
Zheng Qiao, 315–16
Zheng Qingyun, 133
Zheng Tianzuo, 188
Zheng Xingyi, 24
Zheng Yongjiu, 313–15, 318, 319
Zheng Zhongyuan, 193
Zhengde Emperor, 17–18, 19, 20, 260
Zhenjiang, Nanzhili, 205; gazetteers of,
    186, 335
Zhizhai shulu jeiti (Catalog of books with
    explanatory notes of the Zhi studio;
    Chen Zhensun), 176
Zhong Gengqi, 145–46
Zhongdu zhi (Fengyang, Nanzhili,
    gazetteer), 200
Zhongguo difangzhi (Chinese gazetteer;
    journal), 341
Zhongguo difangzhi lianhe mulu (Union
    catalog of Chinese gazetteers), 136
Zhongguo yinshua shi (History of Chinese
    printing; Zhang Xiumin), 165
Zhou Bangjie, 140
Zhou dynasty, 1, 22, 38, 43
Zhou Hongzu, 166–67, 211
Zhou Jin, 180
Zhou Mei, 200
Zhou Wanjin, 129
Zhou Ying, 33
Zhou Yinghe, 121
Zhu Changwen, 262
Zhu Ding, 125
Zhu Gao, 193, 195
Zhu Huakui (Prince of Chu), 21
Zhu Hui, 124–25, 260
Zhu Kui, 130

Zhu Mujie, 325, 326
Zhu Qin, 313, 314
Zhu Shixiang, 162
Zhu Weifan, 312
Zhu Xi, 29, 279, 290, 309
Zhu Xianrong, 21
Zhu Yingtai, 336
Zhu Yingxian, 21
Zhu Yingyao, 21
Zhu Zhen, 207
Zhuang minority, 134

Zhuge Liang, 40, 44, 309
Zhuji, Zhejiang, 67–68; gazetteers of, 113, 224
Zhuzuo kao gai (Outline of the studies on writings; Qi Chengye), 331
Zichuan, Shandong, gazetteers, 184
Zou Tingji, 128
Zou Wu, 209
Zou Xian, 225
Zuo Commentary, 77
Zurndorfer, Harriet, 67

Harvard East Asian Monographs
(titles in print)

100. James Reeve Pusey, *China and Charles Darwin*
101. Hoyt Cleveland Tillman, *Utilitarian Confucianism: Chen Liang's Challenge to Chu Hsi*
102. Thomas A. Stanley, *Ōsugi Sakae, Anarchist in Taishō Japan: The Creativity of the Ego*
103. Jonathan K. Ocko, *Bureaucratic Reform in Provincial China: Ting Jih-ch'ang in Restoration Kiangsu, 1867–1870*
104. James Reed, *The Missionary Mind and American East Asia Policy, 1911–1915*
105. Neil L. Waters, *Japan's Local Pragmatists: The Transition from Bakumatsu to Meiji in the Kawasaki Region*
106. David C. Cole and Yung Chul Park, *Financial Development in Korea, 1945–1978*
107. Roy Bahl, Chuk Kyo Kim, and Chong Kee Park, *Public Finances during the Korean Modernization Process*
108. William D. Wray, *Mitsubishi and the N.Y.K., 1870–1914: Business Strategy in the Japanese Shipping Industry*
109. Ralph William Huenemann, *The Dragon and the Iron Horse: The Economics of Railroads in China, 1876–1937*
111. Jane Kate Leonard, *Wei Yüan and China's Rediscovery of the Maritime World*
117. Andrew Gordon, *The Evolution of Labor Relations in Japan: Heavy Industry, 1853–1955*
119. Christine Guth Kanda, *Shinzō: Hachiman Imagery and Its Development*
121. Chang-tai Hung, *Going to the People: Chinese Intellectual and Folk Literature, 1918–1937*
123. Richard von Glahn, *The Country of Streams and Grottoes: Expansion, Settlement, and the Civilizing of the Sichuan Frontier in Song Times*
124. Steven D. Carter, *The Road to Komatsubara: A Classical Reading of the Renga Hyakuin*
126. Bob Tadashi Wakabayashi, *Anti-Foreignism and Western Learning in Early-Modern Japan: The "New Theses" of 1825*
127. Atsuko Hirai, *Individualism and Socialism: The Life and Thought of Kawai Eijirō (1891–1944)*
129. R. Kent Guy, *The Emperor's Four Treasures: Scholars and the State in the Late Chien-lung Era*

130. Peter C. Perdue, *Exhausting the Earth: State and Peasant in Hunan, 1500–1850*
131. Susan Chan Egan, *A Latterday Confucian: Reminiscences of William Hung (1893–1980)*
132. James T. C. Liu, *China Turning Inward: Intellectual-Political Changes in the Early Twelfth Century*
134. Kate Wildman Nakai, *Shogunal Politics: Arai Hakuseki and the Premises of Tokugawa Rule*
137. Susan Downing Videen, *Tales of Heichū*
138. Heinz Morioka and Miyoko Sasaki, *Rakugo: The Popular Narrative Art of Japan*
139. Joshua A. Fogel, *Nakae Ushikichi in China: The Mourning of Spirit*
140. Alexander Barton Woodside, *Vietnam and the Chinese Model: A Comparative Study of Vietnamese and Chinese Government in the First Half of the Nineteenth Century*
141. George Elison, *Deus Destroyed: The Image of Christianity in Early Modern Japan*
144. Marie Anchordoguy, *Computers, Inc.: Japan's Challenge to IBM*
146. Mary Elizabeth Berry, *Hideyoshi*
147. Laura E. Hein, *Fueling Growth: The Energy Revolution and Economic Policy in Postwar Japan*
148. Wen-hsin Yeh, *The Alienated Academy: Culture and Politics in Republican China, 1919–1937*
149. Dru C. Gladney, *Muslim Chinese: Ethnic Nationalism in the People's Republic*
150. Merle Goldman and Paul A. Cohen, eds., *Ideas Across Cultures: Essays on Chinese Thought in Honor of Benjamin I. Schwartz*
151. James M. Polachek, *The Inner Opium War*
152. Gail Lee Bernstein, *Japanese Marxist: A Portrait of Kawakami Hajime, 1879–1946*
154. Mark Mason, *American Multinationals and Japan: The Political Economy of Japanese Capital Controls, 1899–1980*
155. Richard J. Smith, John K. Fairbank, and Katherine F. Bruner, *Robert Hart and China's Early Modernization: His Journals, 1863–1866*
157. William Wayne Farris, *Heavenly Warriors: The Evolution of Japan's Military, 500–1300*
159. James B. Palais, *Politics and Policy in Traditional Korea*
161. Roger R. Thompson, *China's Local Councils in the Age of Constitutional Reform, 1898–1911*
162. William Johnston, *The Modern Epidemic: History of Tuberculosis in Japan*
163. Constantine Nomikos Vaporis, *Breaking Barriers: Travel and the State in Early Modern Japan*
164. Irmela Hijiya-Kirschnereit, *Rituals of Self-Revelation: Shishōsetsu as Literary Genre and Socio-Cultural Phenomenon*
165. James C. Baxter, *The Meiji Unification through the Lens of Ishikawa Prefecture*
166. Thomas R. H. Havens, *Architects of Affluence: The Tsutsumi Family and the Seibu-Saison Enterprises in Twentieth-Century Japan*
167. Anthony Hood Chambers, *The Secret Window: Ideal Worlds in Tanizaki's Fiction*
168. Steven J. Ericson, *The Sound of the Whistle: Railroads and the State in Meiji Japan*
169. Andrew Edmund Goble, *Kenmu: Go-Daigo's Revolution*

Harvard East Asian Monographs

170. Denise Potrzeba Lett, *In Pursuit of Status: The Making of South Korea's "New" Urban Middle Class*
171. Mimi Hall Yiengpruksawan, *Hiraizumi: Buddhist Art and Regional Politics in Twelfth-Century Japan*
173. Aviad E. Raz, *Riding the Black Ship: Japan and Tokyo Disneyland*
174. Deborah J. Milly, *Poverty, Equality, and Growth: The Politics of Economic Need in Postwar Japan*
175. See Heng Teow, *Japan's Cultural Policy toward China, 1918–1931: A Comparative Perspective*
176. Michael A. Fuller, *An Introduction to Literary Chinese*
177. Frederick R. Dickinson, *War and National Reinvention: Japan in the Great War, 1914–1919*
178. John Solt, *Shredding the Tapestry of Meaning: The Poetry and Poetics of Kitasono Katue (1902–1978)*
179. Edward Pratt, *Japan's Protoindustrial Elite: The Economic Foundations of the Gōnō*
180. Atsuko Sakaki, *Recontextualizing Texts: Narrative Performance in Modern Japanese Fiction*
181. Soon-Won Park, *Colonial Industrialization and Labor in Korea: The Onoda Cement Factory*
182. JaHyun Kim Haboush and Martina Deuchler, *Culture and the State in Late Chosŏn Korea*
183. John W. Chaffee, *Branches of Heaven: A History of the Imperial Clan of Sung China*
184. Gi-Wook Shin and Michael Robinson, eds., *Colonial Modernity in Korea*
185. Nam-lin Hur, *Prayer and Play in Late Tokugawa Japan: Asakusa Sensōji and Edo Society*
186. Kristin Stapleton, *Civilizing Chengdu: Chinese Urban Reform, 1895–1937*
187. Hyung Il Pai, *Constructing "Korean" Origins: A Critical Review of Archaeology, Historiography, and Racial Myth in Korean State-Formation Theories*
188. Brian D. Ruppert, *Jewel in the Ashes: Buddha Relics and Power in Early Medieval Japan*
189. Susan Daruvala, *Zhou Zuoren and an Alternative Chinese Response to Modernity*
191. Kerry Smith, *A Time of Crisis: Japan, the Great Depression, and Rural Revitalization*
192. Michael Lewis, *Becoming Apart: National Power and Local Politics in Toyama, 1868–1945*
193. William C. Kirby, Man-houng Lin, James Chin Shih, and David A. Pietz, eds., *State and Economy in Republican China: A Handbook for Scholars*
194. Timothy S. George, *Minamata: Pollution and the Struggle for Democracy in Postwar Japan*
195. Billy K. L. So, *Prosperity, Region, and Institutions in Maritime China: The South Fukien Pattern, 946–1368*
196. Yoshihisa Tak Matsusaka, *The Making of Japanese Manchuria, 1904–1932*
197. Maram Epstein, *Competing Discourses: Orthodoxy, Authenticity, and Engendered Meanings in Late Imperial Chinese Fiction*
199. Haruo Iguchi, *Unfinished Business: Ayukawa Yoshisuke and U.S.-Japan Relations, 1937–1952*

200. Scott Pearce, Audrey Spiro, and Patricia Ebrey, *Culture and Power in the Reconstitution of the Chinese Realm, 200–600*

201. Terry Kawashima, *Writing Margins: The Textual Construction of Gender in Heian and Kamakura Japan*

202. Martin W. Huang, *Desire and Fictional Narrative in Late Imperial China*

203. Robert S. Ross and Jiang Changbin, eds., *Re-examining the Cold War: U.S.-China Diplomacy, 1954–1973*

204. Guanhua Wang, *In Search of Justice: The 1905–1906 Chinese Anti-American Boycott*

205. David Schaberg, *A Patterned Past: Form and Thought in Early Chinese Historiography*

206. Christine Yano, *Tears of Longing: Nostalgia and the Nation in Japanese Popular Song*

207. Milena Doleželová-Velingerová and Oldřich Král, with Graham Sanders, eds., *The Appropriation of Cultural Capital: China's May Fourth Project*

208. Robert N. Huey, *The Making of 'Shinkokinshū'*

209. Lee Butler, *Emperor and Aristocracy in Japan, 1467–1680: Resilience and Renewal*

210. Suzanne Ogden, *Inklings of Democracy in China*

211. Kenneth J. Ruoff, *The People's Emperor: Democracy and the Japanese Monarchy, 1945–1995*

212. Haun Saussy, *Great Walls of Discourse and Other Adventures in Cultural China*

213. Aviad E. Raz, *Emotions at Work: Normative Control, Organizations, and Culture in Japan and America*

214. Rebecca E. Karl and Peter Zarrow, eds., *Rethinking the 1898 Reform Period: Political and Cultural Change in Late Qing China*

215. Kevin O'Rourke, *The Book of Korean Shijo*

216. Ezra F. Vogel, ed., *The Golden Age of the U.S.-China-Japan Triangle, 1972–1989*

217. Thomas A. Wilson, ed., *On Sacred Grounds: Culture, Society, Politics, and the Formation of the Cult of Confucius*

218. Donald S. Sutton, *Steps of Perfection: Exorcistic Performers and Chinese Religion in Twentieth-Century Taiwan*

219. Daqing Yang, *Technology of Empire: Telecommunications and Japanese Expansionism in Asia, 1883–1945*

220. Qianshen Bai, *Fu Shan's World: The Transformation of Chinese Calligraphy in the Seventeenth Century*

221. Paul Jakov Smith and Richard von Glahn, eds., *The Song-Yuan-Ming Transition in Chinese History*

222. Rania Huntington, *Alien Kind: Foxes and Late Imperial Chinese Narrative*

223. Jordan Sand, *House and Home in Modern Japan: Architecture, Domestic Space, and Bourgeois Culture, 1880–1930*

224. Karl Gerth, *China Made: Consumer Culture and the Creation of the Nation*

225. Xiaoshan Yang, *Metamorphosis of the Private Sphere: Gardens and Objects in Tang-Song Poetry*

226. Barbara Mittler, *A Newspaper for China? Power, Identity, and Change in Shanghai's News Media, 1872–1912*

227. Joyce A. Madancy, *The Troublesome Legacy of Commissioner Lin: The Opium Trade and Opium Suppression in Fujian Province, 1820s to 1920s*

228. John Makeham, *Transmitters and Creators: Chinese Commentators and Commentaries on the Analects*

229. Elisabeth Köll, *From Cotton Mill to Business Empire: The Emergence of Regional Enterprises in Modern China*

230. Emma Teng, *Taiwan's Imagined Geography: Chinese Colonial Travel Writing and Pictures, 1683–1895*

231. Wilt Idema and Beata Grant, *The Red Brush: Writing Women of Imperial China*

232. Eric C. Rath, *The Ethos of Noh: Actors and Their Art*

233. Elizabeth Remick, *Building Local States: China during the Republican and Post-Mao Eras*

234. Lynn Struve, ed., *The Qing Formation in World-Historical Time*

235. D. Max Moerman, *Localizing Paradise: Kumano Pilgrimage and the Religious Landscape of Premodern Japan*

236. Antonia Finnane, *Speaking of Yangzhou: A Chinese City, 1550–1850*

237. Brian Platt, *Burning and Building: Schooling and State Formation in Japan, 1750–1890*

238. Gail Bernstein, Andrew Gordon, and Kate Wildman Nakai, eds., *Public Spheres, Private Lives in Modern Japan, 1600–1950: Essays in Honor of Albert Craig*

239. Wu Hung and Katherine R. Tsiang, *Body and Face in Chinese Visual Culture*

240. Stephen Dodd, *Writing Home: Representations of the Native Place in Modern Japanese Literature*

241. David Anthony Bello, *Opium and the Limits of Empire: Drug Prohibition in the Chinese Interior, 1729–1850*

242. Hosea Hirata, *Discourses of Seduction: History, Evil, Desire, and Modern Japanese Literature*

243. Kyung Moon Hwang, *Beyond Birth: Social Status in the Emergence of Modern Korea*

244. Brian R. Dott, *Identity Reflections: Pilgrimages to Mount Tai in Late Imperial China*

245. Mark McNally, *Proving the Way: Conflict and Practice in the History of Japanese Nativism*

246. Yongping Wu, *A Political Explanation of Economic Growth: State Survival, Bureaucratic Politics, and Private Enterprises in the Making of Taiwan's Economy, 1950–1985*

247. Kyu Hyun Kim, *The Age of Visions and Arguments: Parliamentarianism and the National Public Sphere in Early Meiji Japan*

248. Zvi Ben-Dor Benite, *The Dao of Muhammad: A Cultural History of Muslims in Late Imperial China*

249. David Der-wei Wang and Shang Wei, eds., *Dynastic Crisis and Cultural Innovation: From the Late Ming to the Late Qing and Beyond*

250. Wilt L. Idema, Wai-yee Li, and Ellen Widmer, eds., *Trauma and Transcendence in Early Qing Literature*

251. Barbara Molony and Kathleen Uno, eds., *Gendering Modern Japanese History*

252. Hiroshi Aoyagi, *Islands of Eight Million Smiles: Idol Performance and Symbolic Production in Contemporary Japan*

254. William C. Kirby, Robert S. Ross, and Gong Li, eds., *Normalization of U.S.-China Relations: An International History*

255. Ellen Gardner Nakamura, *Practical Pursuits: Takano Chōei, Takahashi Keisaku, and Western Medicine in Nineteenth-Century Japan*

256. Jonathan W. Best, *A History of the Early Korean Kingdom of Paekche, together with an annotated translation of* The Paekche Annals *of the* Samguk sagi

257. Liang Pan, *The United Nations in Japan's Foreign and Security Policymaking, 1945–1992: National Security, Party Politics, and International Status*

258. Richard Belsky, *Localities at the Center: Native Place, Space, and Power in Late Imperial Beijing*

259. Zwia Lipkin, *"Useless to the State": "Social Problems" and Social Engineering in Nationalist Nanjing, 1927–1937*

260. William O. Gardner, *Advertising Tower: Japanese Modernism and Modernity in the 1920s*

261. Stephen Owen, *The Making of Early Chinese Classical Poetry*

262. Martin J. Powers, *Pattern and Person: Ornament, Society, and Self in Classical China*

263. Anna M. Shields, *Crafting a Collection: The Cultural Contexts and Poetic Practice of the Huajian ji* 花間集 *(Collection from among the Flowers)*

264. Stephen Owen, *The Late Tang: Chinese Poetry of the Mid-Ninth Century (827–860)*

265. Sara L. Friedman, *Intimate Politics: Marriage, the Market, and State Power in Southeastern China*

266. Patricia Buckley Ebrey and Maggie Bickford, *Emperor Huizong and Late Northern Song China: The Politics of Culture and the Culture of Politics*

267. Sophie Volpp, *Worldly Stage: Theatricality in Seventeenth-Century China*

268. Ellen Widmer, *The Beauty and the Book: Women and Fiction in Nineteenth-Century China*

269. Steven B. Miles, *The Sea of Learning: Mobility and Identity in Nineteenth-Century Guangzhou*

270. Man-houng Lin, *China Upside Down: Currency, Society, and Ideologies, 1808–1856*

271. Ronald Egan, *The Problem of Beauty: Aesthetic Thought and Pursuits in Northern Song Dynasty China*

272. Mark Halperin, *Out of the Cloister: Literati Perspectives on Buddhism in Sung China, 960–1279*

273. Helen Dunstan, *State or Merchant? Political Economy and Political Process in 1740s China*

274. Sabina Knight, *The Heart of Time: Moral Agency in Twentieth-Century Chinese Fiction*

275. Timothy J. Van Compernolle, *The Uses of Memory: The Critique of Modernity in the Fiction of Higuchi Ichiyō*

276. Paul Rouzer, *A New Practical Primer of Literary Chinese*

277. Jonathan Zwicker, *Practices of the Sentimental Imagination: Melodrama, the Novel, and the Social Imaginary in Nineteenth-Century Japan*

278. Franziska Seraphim, *War Memory and Social Politics in Japan, 1945–2005*

280. Cynthia J. Brokaw, *Commerce in Culture: The Sibao Book Trade in the Qing and Republican Periods*

281. Eugene Y. Park, *Between Dreams and Reality: The Military Examination in Late Chosŏn Korea, 1600–1894*

282. Nam-lin Hur, *Death and Social Order in Tokugawa Japan: Buddhism, Anti-Christianity, and the* Danka *System*

283. Patricia M. Thornton, *Disciplining the State: Virtue, Violence, and State-Making in Modern China*

284. Vincent Goossaert, *The Taoists of Peking, 1800–1949: A Social History of Urban Clerics*

286. Charo B. D'Etcheverry, *Love after* The Tale of Genji: *Rewriting the World of the Shining Prince*

287. Michael G. Chang, *A Court on Horseback: Imperial Touring & the Construction of Qing Rule, 1680–1785*

288. Carol Richmond Tsang, *War and Faith:* Ikkō Ikki *in Late Muromachi Japan*

289. Hilde De Weerdt, *Competition over Content: Negotiating Standards for the Civil Service Examinations in Imperial China (1127–1279)*

290. Eve Zimmerman, *Out of the Alleyway: Nakagami Kenji and the Poetics of Outcaste Fiction*

291. Robert Culp, *Articulating Citizenship: Civic Education and Student Politics in Southeastern China, 1912–1940*

292. Richard J. Smethurst, *From Foot Soldier to Finance Minister: Takahashi Korekiyo, Japan's Keynes*

293. John E. Herman, *Amid the Clouds and Mist: China's Colonization of Guizhou, 1200–1700*

294. Tomoko Shiroyama, *China during the Great Depression: Market, State, and the World Economy, 1929–1937*

295. Kirk W. Larsen, *Tradition, Treaties and Trade: Qing Imperialism and Chosŏn Korea, 1850–1910*

296. Gregory Golley, *When Our Eyes No Longer See: Realism, Science, and Ecology in Japanese Literary Modernism*

297. Barbara Ambros, *Emplacing a Pilgrimage: The Ōyama Cult and Regional Religion in Early Modern Japan*

298. Rebecca Suter, *The Japanization of Modernity: Murakami Haruki between Japan and the United States*

299. Yuma Totani, *The Tokyo War Crimes Trial: The Pursuit of Justice in the Wake of World War II*

301. David M. Robinson, ed., *Culture, Courtiers, and Competition: The Ming Court (1368–1644)*

302. Calvin Chen, *Some Assembly Required: Work, Community, and Politics in China's Rural Enterprises*

303. Sem Vermeersch, *The Power of the Buddhas: The Politics of Buddhism During the Koryŏ Dynasty (918–1392)*

304. Tina Lu, *Accidental Incest, Filial Cannibalism, and Other Peculiar Encounters in Late Imperial Chinese Literature*

Harvard East Asian Monographs

305. Chang Woei Ong, *Men of Letters Within the Passes: Guanzhong Literati in Chinese History, 907–1911*

306. Wendy Swartz, *Reading Tao Yuanming: Shifting Paradigms of Historical Reception (427–1900)*

307. Peter K. Bol, *Neo-Confucianism in History*

308. Carlos Rojas, *The Naked Gaze: Reflections on Chinese Modernity*

309. Kelly H. Chong, *Deliverance and Submission: Evangelical Women and the Negotiation of Patriarchy in South Korea*

310. Rachel DiNitto, *Uchida Hyakken: A Critique of Modernity and Militarism in Prewar Japan*

311. Jeffrey Snyder-Reinke, *Dry Spells: State Rainmaking and Local Governance in Late Imperial China*

312. Jay Dautcher, *Down a Narrow Road: Identity and Masculinity in a Uyghur Community in Xinjiang China*

313. Xun Liu, *Daoist Modern: Innovation, Lay Practice, and the Community of Inner Alchemy in Republican Shanghai*

314. Jacob Eyferth, *Eating Rice from Bamboo Roots: The Social History of a Community of Handicraft Papermakers in Rural Sichuan, 1920–2000*

315. David Johnson, *Spectacle and Sacrifice: The Ritual Foundations of Village Life in North China*

316. James Robson, *Power of Place: The Religious Landscape of the Southern Sacred Peak (Nanyue 南嶽) in Medieval China*

317. Lori Watt, *When Empire Comes Home: Repatriation and Reintegration in Postwar Japan*

318. James Dorsey, *Critical Aesthetics: Kobayashi Hideo, Modernity, and Wartime Japan*

319. Christopher Bolton, *Sublime Voices: The Fictional Science and Scientific Fiction of Abe Kōbō*

320. Si-yen Fei, *Negotiating Urban Space: Urbanization and Late Ming Nanjing*

321. Christopher Gerteis, *Gender Struggles: Wage-Earning Women and Male-Dominated Unions in Postwar Japan*

322. Rebecca Nedostup, *Superstitious Regimes: Religion and the Politics of Chinese Modernity*

323. Lucien Bianco, *Wretched Rebels: Rural Disturbances on the Eve of the Chinese Revolution*

324. Cathryn H. Clayton, *Sovereignty at the Edge: Macau and the Question of Chineseness*

325. Micah S. Muscolino, *Fishing Wars and Environmental Change in Late Imperial and Modern China*

326. Robert I. Hellyer, *Defining Engagement: Japan and Global Contexts, 1750–1868*

327. Robert Ashmore, *The Transport of Reading: Text and Understanding in the World of Tao Qian (365–427)*

328. Mark A. Jones, *Children as Treasures: Childhood and the Middle Class in Early Twentieth Century Japan*

329. Miryam Sas, *Experimental Arts in Postwar Japan: Moments of Encounter, Engagement, and Imagined Return*

330. H. Mack Horton, *Traversing the Frontier: The Man'yōshū Account of a Japanese Mission to Silla in 736–737*

Harvard East Asian Monographs

331. Dennis J. Frost, *Seeing Stars: Sports Celebrity, Identity, and Body Culture in Modern Japan*
332. Marnie S. Anderson, *A Place in Public: Women's Rights in Meiji Japan*
333. Peter Mauch, *Sailor Diplomat: Nomura Kichisaburō and the Japanese-American War*
334. Ethan Isaac Segal, *Coins, Trade, and the State: Economic Growth in Early Medieval Japan*
335. David B. Lurie, *Realms of Literacy: Early Japan and the History of Writing*
336. Lillian Lan-ying Tseng, *Picturing Heaven in Early China*
337. Jun Uchida, *Brokers of Empire: Japanese Settler Colonialism in Korea, 1876–1945*
338. Patricia L. Maclachlan, *The People's Post Office: The History and Politics of the Japanese Postal System, 1871–2010*
339. Michael Schiltz, *The Money Doctors from Japan: Finance, Imperialism, and the Building of the Yen Bloc, 1895–1937*
340. Daqing Yang, Jie Liu, Hiroshi Mitani, and Andrew Gordon, eds., *Toward a History beyond Borders: Contentious Issues in Sino-Japanese Relations*
341. Sonia Ryang, *Reading North Korea: An Ethnological Inquiry*
342. Susan Huang, *Picturing the True Form: Daoist Visual Culture in Traditional China*
343. Barbara Mittler, *A Continuous Revolution: Making Sense of Cultural Revolution Culture*
344. Hwansoo Ilmee Kim, *Empire of the Dharma: Korean and Japanese Buddhism, 1877–1912*
345. Satoru Saito, *Detective Fiction and the Rise of the Japanese Novel, 1880–1930*
346. Jung-Sun N. Han, *An Imperial Path to Modernity: Yoshino Sakuzō and a New Liberal Order in East Asia, 1905–1937*
347. Atsuko Hirai, *Government by Mourning: Death and Political Integration in Japan, 1603–1912*
348. Darryl E. Flaherty, *Public Law, Private Practice: Politics, Profit, and the Legal Profession in Nineteenth-Century Japan*
349. Jeffrey Paul Bayliss, *On the Margins of Empire: Buraku and Korean Identity in Prewar and Wartime Japan*
350. Barry Eichengreen, Dwight H. Perkins, and Kwanho Shin, *From Miracle to Maturity: The Growth of the Korean Economy*
351. Michel Mohr, *Buddhism, Unitarianism, and the Meiji Competition for Universality*
352. J. Keith Vincent, *Two-Timing Modernity: Homosocial Narrative in Modern Japanese Fiction*
354. Chong-Bum An and Barry Bosworth, *Income Inequality in Korea: An Analysis of Trends, Causes, and Answers*
355. Jamie L. Newhard, *Knowing the Amorous Man: A History of Scholarship on Tales of Ise*
356. Sho Konishi, *Anarchist Modernity: Cooperatism and Japanese-Russian Intellectual Relations in Modern Japan*
357. Christopher P. Hanscom, *The Real Modern: Literary Modernism and the Crisis of Representation in Colonial Korea*
358. Michael Wert, *Meiji Restoration Losers: Memory and Tokugawa Supporters in Modern Japan*

Harvard East Asian Monographs

359. Garret P. S. Olberding, ed., *Facing the Monarch: Modes of Advice in the Early Chinese Court*
360. Xiaojue Wang, *Modernity with a Cold War Face: Reimagining the Nation in Chinese Literature Across the 1949 Divide*
361. David Spafford, *A Sense of Place: The Political Landscape in Late Medieval Japan*
362. Jongryn Mo and Barry Weingast, *Korean Political and Economic Development: Crisis, Security, and Economic Rebalancing*
363. Melek Ortabasi, *The Undiscovered Country: Text, Translation, and Modernity in the Work of Yanagita Kunio*
364. Hiraku Shimoda, *Lost and Found: Recovering Regional Identity in Imperial Japan*
365. Trent E. Maxey, *The "Greatest Problem": Religion and State Formation in Meiji Japan*
366. Gina Cogan, *The Princess Nun: Bunchi, Buddhist Reform, and Gender in Early Edo Japan*
367. Eric C. Han, *Rise of a Japanese Chinatown: Yokohama, 1894–1972*
368. Natasha Heller, *Illusory Abiding: The Cultural Construction of the Chan Monk Zhongfeng Mingben*
369. Paize Keulemans, *Sound Rising from the Paper: Nineteenth-Century Martial Arts Fiction and the Chinese Acoustic Imagination*
370. Simon James Bytheway, *Investing Japan: Foreign Capital, Monetary Standards, and Economic Development, 1859–2011*
371. Sukhee Lee, *Negotiated Power: The State, Elites, and Local Governance in Twelfth-Fourteenth China*
372. Ping Foong, *The Efficacious Landscape: On the Authorities of Painting at the Northern Song Court*
373. Catherine L. Phipps, *Empires on the Waterfront: Japan's Ports and Power, 1858–1899*
374. Sunyoung Park, *The Proletarian Wave: Literature and Leftist Culture in Colonial Korea, 1910–1945*
375. Barry Eichengreen, Wonhyuk Lim, Yung Chul Park, and Dwight H. Perkins, *The Korean Economy: From a Miraculous Past to a Sustainable Future*
376. Heather Blair, *Real and Imagined: The Peak of Gold in Heian Japan*
377. Emer O'Dwyer, *Significant Soil: Settler Colonialism and Japan's Urban Empire in Manchuria*
378. Martina Deuchler, *Under the Ancestors' Eyes: Kinship, Status, and Locality in Premodern Korea*
379. Joseph R. Dennis, *Writing, Publishing, and Reading Local Gazetteers in Imperial China, 1100–1700*
380. Cathy Yeh, *The Chinese Political Novel: Migration of a World Genre*
381. Noell Wilson, *Defensive Positions: The Politics of Maritime Security in Tokugawa Japan*
382. Miri Nakamura, *Monstrous Bodies: The Rise of the Uncanny in Modern Japan*
383. Nara Dillon, *Radical Inequalities: China's Revolutionary Welfare State in Comparative Perspective*